Digital Literacy:
Tools and Methodologies for Information Society

Pier Cesare Rivoltella
Università Cattolica del Sacro Cuore, Italy

T0325045

IGI PUBLISHING
Hershey • New York

Acquisition Editor:	Kristin Klinger
Senior Managing Editor:	Jennifer Neidig
Managing Editor:	Sara Reed
Development Editor:	Kristin Roth
Copy Editor:	Jeannie Porter
Typesetter:	Michael Brehm
Cover Design:	Lisa Tosheff
Printed at:	Yurchak Printing Inc.

Published in the United States of America by
    IGI Publishing (an imprint of IGI Global)
    701 E. Chocolate Avenue
    Hershey PA 17033
    Tel: 717-533-8845
    Fax: 717-533-8661
    E-mail: cust@igi-global.com
    Web site: http://www.igi-global.com

and in the United Kingdom by
    IGI Publishing (an imprint of IGI Global)
    3 Henrietta Street
    Covent Garden
    London WC2E 8LU
    Tel: 44 20 7240 0856
    Fax: 44 20 7379 0609
    Web site: http://www.eurospanonline.com

Library of Congress Cataloging-in-Publication Data

Rivoltella, P. C. (Pier Cesare)
  Digital literacy : tools and methodologies for information society / by Pier Cesare Rivoltella.
    p. cm.
  Summary: "This book defines a conceptual framework for understanding social changes produced by digital media and creates a framework within which digital literacy acts as a tool to assist younger generations to inter-act critically with digital media and their culture, providing scholars, educators, researchers, and practitioners a technological and sociological approach to this cutting-edge topic from an educational perspective"--Provided by publisher.
  ISBN-13: 978-1-59904-798-0 (hardcover)
  ISBN-13: 978-1-59904-800-0 (e-book)
  1. Information society. 2. Digital media--Social aspects. I. Title.
  HM851.R58 2008
  303.48'33--dc22
                    2007047722

British Cataloguing in Publication Data
A Cataloguing in Publication record for this book is available from the British Library.

Digital Literacy:
Tools and Methodologies for Information Society

Table of Contents

Preface

Such as Plato in his *Phaedrus,* we are nowadays witnesses of a cultural transition. This transition is from a literary society to a digital one. In this society the organization and circulation of knowledge and culture is made possible by new technologies like the Internet, PDAs, and mobiles that are changing our social life and more specifically the function and the modalities of education.

Plato sustained that most people, because of writing, would have ended up "believing to know many things, while actually *they do not know them.*" Writing emancipates the subject from the necessity to remember making easier the storage and transmission of the cultural patrimony and at the same time expanding the limits of what can be transmitted to posterity. So, the age of great syntheses, when the poets' formulas still succeed in epitomizing an entire culture has been progressively replaced by a new cultural reality marked by a growing gap between what can be potentially known and what is actually known, a gap which is effectively illustrated by the metaphor of the library.

In the digital age, such gap is getting deeper. The new techniques for storing data (through CD-rom, DVDs, online repositories) and circulating them (through networking) expand the potential for knowledge up to the utopian limits of total availability: a completely transparent and interconnected society whose every single part contains information about all the other ones. The metaphor which best illustrates this new society is that of the hologram:

Not only every part of the world, but the world as a whole is more and more present in all its single parts. And that occurs at the level of nations and peoples as well as individuals. Just like every point of an hologram contains information about the whole it belongs to, similarly every individual receives or consumes the information and substances coming from the whole universe. (Morin, 1993, pp. 22-23)

But digital media also abolish the identity between physical and social space which used to characterize communication before their advent: a mobile call, a network interaction, a teleconference link are all possible ways of communication even if the two interlocutors are not physically present in the same place. In each of these cases, digital media create another place which is the social place of the communication contact they make possible.

A similar situation already existed in the literary age. The simple act of writing a letter, for example, does abolish physical distance by creating a kind of communication which goes beyond the presence of sender and receiver in the same place; yet it cannot render the hot and personal character of face-to-face interaction, although it gives the sender a higher control over the written document than the sender of messages via electronic media. In a literary culture, adults exercise full control over the creation and transmission of knowledge, writing being their instrument, first because to have access to knowledge it is necessary to acquire some specific alphabetical competences, and second because it is the adults who regulate younger generations' reading of certain books rather than others. This power is increasingly being put into question in the contemporary society of images where television and the other electronic media, abolishing all sense of place (Meyrowitz, 1995), addressing the adult and young generations without being able (nor willing) to select what can or cannot be shown; literally, images are unrolling in front of everybody's eyes making no distinction among their audience!

Finally, a third important characteristic regarding digital media is the subject's cognitive re-orienting occurring at least at three levels.

Whereas in the West, language has been evolving in terms of a progressive loss of its global, synesthetic, multisensory relationship with reality in favor of a symbolical-conceptual type of thinking, digital communication seems to be leading back to an old sensory relationship with objects, promoting a sort of *resensualization of language*. We can think, for example, about the interface function in word processing: mouse and tactile/vocal interfaces are definitely extending knowledge from the abstract level of categorization to the practical one of sensory contact.

This sensory recovery implies two more aspects. On the one hand, if alphabetical writing, by virtue of its double articulation, had been progressively emancipating the code from reality, the different forms of digital communication seem to be recovering it, although it is a kind of reality which might be no longer "real." As a matter of fact, the electronic image, given its high degree of likelihood, credibility, and manipulability, can dispense with the reality it is representing and indeed propose itself as a new form of reality. The consequence is *the jeopardization of the relation reality-truth* on which the whole Western gnoseological tradition has been based for centuries. In the pre-electronic age what manifests itself as real is also actually real, but in the electronic age the real, although being absolutely as such, may also turn out to be false. As a result it may be only said that in the new cultural horizon the whole categories of "real" and "false" should undergo a deep critical revision.

On the other hand, it seems that with electronic communication the conceptualizing and abstracting tendency of literary thinking is now being inverted in favor of a new form of culture characterized by immediacy, interactivity, and intimacy. *Thinking is more and more deconceptualizing itself*, gaining back its original relationship with things as well as the capacity to proceed by associations and analogies rather than strict formal implications.

These observations ultimately converge to stress the extraordinary impact of digital media on the educative processes which are, in fact, undergoing a paradigmatic change in their management and organization. This change makes possible we talk about a new form of literacy, with its specific competencies. According with culture and media with which this literacy is working we can define it as digital literacy. This book discusses its characteristics particularly from an educational point of view.

The book is made of four sections. The contributions of the First Section (The Information Society: A Conceptual Framework) give a theoretical framework of the main transformations produced by ICT in our society. This framework is built from different points of view investigating the modalities according to which knowledge is socially built, the tools supporting this social construction, social and epistemological implications of these facts.

In the Second Section (The Information Society: Educative Researches), the idea is to present some recent researches about new media consumption. These researches were selected according to the age of the subjects involved in them (children, adolescents, young, parents) and so that they can give a wide international map, from Europe to North and South America. The aim of the section is to point out that ICT not only transformed social practices, but also represent a real educative challenge for our early future.

The Third Section (Media Literacy: Definition and Perspectives), starting from the acceptance of this challenge, the authors try to define the role and the perspectives of what we can call a New Media Education. In almost two senses, the first is that New Media, thanks to their specific characters (mobility, personality, user generated contents), need new educative strategies and methodologies; the second may be that this upgrade of the traditional methods of Media Education is not sufficient and so what it should be done is a real change of paradigm outlining a new Media Education.

Finally, in the Fourth Section (Media Literacy: Educational Outlines), the book provides some case histories for understanding what does it mean, on the field, developing Digital Literacy strategies in the schools and in informal education environments.

Chapter I. Knowledge, Culture and Society in the Information Age

In this chapter, Rivoltella describes the transformations of the media role in our society. The transition here is from a society into which media were only one of its elements among others, to a society whose structure is made by and of the media. It is the same "skin of the culture," according to de Kerkhove's (1995) definition, that is changed. This means that the mediation of the media becomes our normal way of relationship with the world. As Thompson (1995) says, the media are mediating our knowledge, our experience of the history, and our interactions with other people. In this kind of society, Media Education is not yet one of the focuses of education, but it must be thought such as the main educative goal. The only condition is that Media Education could be able to understand the new aspects of Information Society and prepare a change in its own methodologies and tools, as it will possible to see in the last two sections of the book.

Chapter II. Communicating in the Information Society: New Tools for New Practices

Cantoni and Tardini reflect on the changes that new digital communication tools are rapidly spreading worldwide on the ways we interact and communicate, both in everyday life and in our professional activities. This is done providing a conceptual framework for these tools, introducing them both in their sociological and historical context, and in the main political, economical, legal, and ethical issues they raise. This framework prepares, in the second part of the chapter, the description of a map of the different tools and devices that allow digital communication will be drawn, and the characteristics of the settings and of the language they rely on will be presented (Crystal, 2001). The features of the communications taking place by means of ICTs are strongly dependent on the tools and devices employed: different tools and different devices impose different constraints and offer different options to interlocutors (Clark, 1996; Clark & Brennan, 1991). Special attention will be devoted to so-called "social software," that is, those tools designed to support distance group collaboration, such as blogs and wikis, and to the challenges they're producing on several social practices.

Chapter III. Digital Media and Socialization

Morcellini argues that communication among individuals and society is deeply changed in relation with the post-modern "crisis" we can well define with the metaphor of liquidity (Bauman, 2004). The challenge of the chapter is to try to describe this transition not necessarily in terms of instabilities and insecurity, fear, and distrust: from the point of view of communication, the change isn't a shock, but a chance. The reason why is that digital media become expression of new social and cultural conditions, inducing three dimensions of change. They help people to build a new world vision and new life styles. They prepare the social system to react to the changes metabolizing them. They find in the social dimension a new original way to define concepts, share values, and build up networks.

Chapter IV. New Episthemologies in a Changing Media Environment

Ardrizzo reflects on the changes in the epistemology we can argue passing from Modernity to Information Society. The idea of having "a few and simple laws" ruling man and nature is replaced by the image of a complex universe, the causal thinking by a new epistemology of technology, seen as a necessary element for understanding meanings and making sense of those complex and dynamical universes in their process of construction. In this cultural framework it seems that schools and universities are not able to accept this challenge: they are continuing to provide linear methodologies, while on the contrary students need abilities for building cognitive maps and for selecting information. They don't put mind to the fact that the new media-sphere is really producing a new noosphere with its cultural codes and its languages. They don't have effective tools for interpreting youngsters behaviours that are dependent from these new codes and languages; so the new media challenge in education is precisely an epistemological challenge: Digital Literacy, finally, is a Knowledge Literacy.

Chapter V. Integrating Technology Literacy and Information Literacy

Sharkey and Brandt start on the analysis from the traditional difference between Technology and Information Literacy. The first one seems to be wider, referring to general skills in acting with and through technology; the second one, on the contrary, is more focused on computer, Internet, and the other digital devices. According to the authors, in the so called Information Age, it is necessary to develop both of these literacies. In fact, most of the technological skills are involved with information (as we show in Chapter 11 and 12 of this book) and, on the contrary, it seems really impossible to develop informational skills without technological competencies. The result of the mediation between them is an integrated solution of Technology and Information Literacy; this could be considered as the condition starting from which to imagine the space and the role of what in this book is named: *Digital Literacy*.

Chapter VI. Growing Up Wireless: Peer Culture and Family Education Models in the Age of Mobile Communication

Caronia elaborates her analysis starting from a phenomenological approach to culture and everyday life. According to this perspective, individuals are constantly engaged in constructing the meaningful dimensions of the world they live in. Every day life needs thus to be conceived as a never-ending cultural work through which social actors produce meanings, structures, and social organization of the world they live in, as well as the identities of themselves and the people they interact with. Technologies participate in such a process: as cultural artefacts, they both are domesticated into already existing patterns of meaning and create new ones. This is even more so with information and communication technologies. Their progressive introduction into people's everyday life, the multiplication of possible new courses of action, ways of communicating and getting information, hypothetically expand the range of tools through which individuals construct culture and identities. Overcoming the "subject-object" duality, we need to rethink the relationship between humans and technologies in term of reflexivity that is a mutual construction of meaning and a reciprocal sense making. With this kind of approach, the author focusing on the role of mobile communication in the construction of family and peer social organization and culture. Drawing upon data from recent research, she analyses the role of mobile phone in the rise of new cultural models of parenting and its domestication by teenagers as a tool for group membership and peer culture construction.

Chapter VII. Children and Computers: What They Know, What They Do

Ferri and Mantovani refer in their chapter to the first findings of an ongoing research project aimed at studying how children and adults explore the potentiality of the new technologies in family and in preschool (Tobin, Wu, & Davidson, 1989). Moving from a review of the researches about children and computer, the author discuss the ways in which three to six children use and explore the new digital technologies and interpret their meanings and functions, studying the ideas and representations of teachers and educators in regard to it. Too often computers and digital technologies are introduced in early childhood settings without a greater understanding of their cultural meanings, their cognitive and social potentialities or limits and this is particularly true when the children are in preschool. On the contrary, only creating dialogue opportunities we will promote on one hand a higher awareness and a deeper understanding of the role of the new technologies in the early years, while helping on the other to provide bases to the design of a way *"to mediate"* the introduction of technologies in early childhood. The way in which children explore and use computers (individually, with other children or with the adults) is strictly linked to the adults' ideas and beliefs and to their educational models and representations. New digital technologies may become a catalyst for exchange and sharing among adults who care for young children and a starting point for promoting a new way to overcome the "digital generational gap" (Papert, 1996) between children, teachers, and parents to promote a new digital literacy and fluency in schools

Chapter VIII. Adolescents and the Internet: Media Appropriation and Perspectives on Education

Bevort and Breda refer to the results of the International Research *Mediappro* developed in several European countries about the appropriation of electronic media by youngsters and the problems of safety connected with it. The main hypothesis underpinning the research is that young people's safety on the Internet and in their use of other digital media depends largely on their own actions. Consequently, it is essential to help young people to be as competent as possible when they use network communication devices. In order to do this, the research identifies how young people appropriate digital media and how their practices differ within different contexts of use (at school and at home, for example). The landscape depicted is undeniably more reassuring than the landscape depicted by many media discourses based on exceptional, idealistic, or dramatic events: youngsters are more critic and conscious than we might expect. On the contrary, educational institutions, that is, essentially the school, but also associative educational spaces and media (subject to a more in-depth study) do not seem to have measured the importance that the new media have acquired in the daily lives of young people remaining unable to act so that educational challenges coming from these media could be accepted finding their answers.

Chapter IX. Learning with New Media at the University: From Representations to Utilization

Mamede and Ribeiro present in this chapter the results of a research made at the Catholic University of Rio de Janeiro, in Brazil. The focus of the research were the uses and appropriations of the Internet by young university students; the methodological approach adopts the concept of "social representation" of Farr and Moscovici (1984) for investigating the relationship between youngsters' values and behaviours and those that are developed in the social cultures. The results are quite interesting: it is sure that the social origin of the students influences their access to technology, but otherwise it is also true that is no possible to observe the same gap from the point of view of the practices, practically the same within all the subjects who took part to the research.

Chapter X. Rethinking Cognition, Representations and Processes in 3D Online Social Learning Environments

Jones and Bornack reflect in their chapter on the application of 3D environments in non-game settings, a topic really actual if we put mind to the recent social affirmation of *Second Life* and to the interest of education for its teaching and learning opportunities. In more general terms, it easy to consider how nowadays the Web 2.0 applications are quickly developing, becoming a normal space of social relationship for youngsters. In these environments, they share images and videos, build up their social networks, find out learning opportunities. So it is easy to understand why formal education is so interested to import the same practices to traditional teaching and learning spaces. But this transfer could not happen without a specific instructional design. The chapter provides ideas and samples in this direction.

Chapter XI. Investigating Information in the Multiscreen Society: An Ecologic Perspective

Pinto investigates in his chapter the new challenges that education meets in a society where we are assisting to a proliferation of the screen. This means that individuals more and more are invited to integrate these screens in their lives with important effects on the modalities according to which they interact among themselves. So it seems urgent to develop media education so it could lead this process, providing new forms of cognitive scaffolding for the youngsters. Acting so, media education assumes an ecologic character, thinking of the media as a real new environment.

Chapter XII. From Media Education to Digital Literacy: A Paradigm Change

Rivoltella argues in this chapter that the specificity of digital media (Internet, Mobiles, palms, i-pods) challenges the traditional media education approach to the media. Digital media are no one-way media, but really interactive media; therefore, the problem with them is not only the risk of a passive consumption and a lack of critical thinking, but the necessity to control the modalities with which (young) people interact with them and with other people thanks to their mediation. On the other hand, digital media make easy not only to receive messages (this happened also with traditional media), but mainly to create and to build them, forcing us to reconceptualize receivers also as producers. For these reasons, it is necessary to imagine a new paradigm for media education whose focus is the idea of citizenship. The aim of digital literacy is to help people to become active and conscious citizens of the Information Society (Rivoltella, 2006). In school, this does not mean to make place for a new discipline, but to develop a cross-curricular attention so that students have the chance to learn in a digital environment and teachers to adopt media and communication as a teaching style. Interactivity and user content generation could be the new methodological perspectives of this new paradigm.

Chapter XIII. Creative Remixing and Digital Learning: Developing an Online Media Literacy Tool for Girls

Hobbs and Rowe review in this chapter the theoretical framework, development, and implementation, and assessment of an online creative play environment designed to promote media literacy skills for girls ages 9 to 14. The road-map of the contribution is the search for a new concept of media literacy in a social environment like our where digital media are added to the complex mix of media texts and technologies becoming pervasive in the lives of young people. This concept passes through the idea that highly interactive creative play activities guide users through the process of deconstructing, analyzing, and creating media. Among the practices that pupils can play in this context, remixing is one of the most interesting. In remixing, media texts get reinterpreted by other creative people through techniques of collage, editing, and juxtaposition. Remixing is type of creative expression. Through remixing, people can generate new ideas. It can be a vehicle for people to comment upon the role of media and technology in society. Finally it could be used to promote critical thinking about the media, popular culture, and digital technologies.

Chapter XIV. Dream Schools: The Architecture of New Literacies

In this chapter Tyner investigates digital literacy as a driver for designing contemporary learning environments, where a new generation of students and teachers is demanding "every day" literacy tools both inside and outside the traditional classroom. Existing and emerging research related to digital authorship and reception is beginning to shape a vision for literacy practices of the future. These include theory and practice around digital poetics, remix genre, vast archives of open source materials, and the restructuring of information through database applications. New literacies present immediate challenges, as well as opportunities, for educational institutions with both predictable and unpredictable outcomes in the design of both physical architecture and cognitive design processes. Although it is widely acknowledged that literacy is important for individuals to strategically access a wider range of social benefits, the integration of new literacies into learning environments calls into question the mission, values, benefits, and liabilities of schooling for individuals and societies in the 21st Century.

Chapter XV. Digital Production and Media Education: What do Teachers Need to Know?

Burn starts in his chapter from the 3C Model of Media Education developed by Cary Bazalgette at the British Film Institute and largely shared all over the world. This means to think of Media Education as including a cultural element, a critical element, and a creative element. Since this last involves complex forms of digital production in a range of moving image media, the problem is to understand what teachers need to know in order to manage learning in today's media education classrooms and in those of the future. Burn explores how teachers learn about the design processes involved in digital video and computer games and how they relate these to contemporary theories of the moving image and games, as well as to their own classroom practice. Doing that, the chapter draws on recent research in this field and on the work of teachers undertaking Masters' courses in media education at the London Institute of Education.

Chapter XVI. Globalisation and New Technology: The Challenge for Teachers to Become "Translators" and Children, Knowledge Seekers

The contribution of Caron starts from a question. The question is whether we can consider new technologies as the magic bullet of education. It is clear here the provocation the question contains: to imagine new technologies like a magic bullet means to think that it is enough to introduce it in the schools for producing changing and innovation. The research already showed the error of this deterministic vision. On the contrary, it seems important to consider that the introduction of new technologies in education requires an examination of the actors' role, mainly of the teachers, in facilitating innovation, conveying culture, and acting as a conceptual translator. By modeling and teaching students critical and social skills, teachers can help tomorrow's citizens to use the new flow of information to meet the challenges of globalisation. The chapter demonstrates that.

Chapter XVII. The Future of Digital Society and the New Values of Media

Perez Tornero in his chapter starts from the idea that Information Society is basically a mythological structure. This means three things. First of all he reflects about the role that this myth plays within the most extensive discourse on social change. On the second hand, he points out that this myth is activating an anthropological transformation in our society and in humanity: some aspects of this transformation are clearly presented in the chapters of Caron and Caronia, speaking about a new media anthropology. Finally, the possibility of defending the autonomy of consciousness and the promotion of human dignity through Media Education. This is the creation of a kind of counter-myth that would create an up-to-date and renewed Media Education. About this new idea of media Education, most of the authors of the book reflected in depth.

Chapter XVIII. Digital Literacy and Cultural Mediations to the Digital Divide

Girardello and Fantin discuss this problem of the distance between those who have and those who do not have complete access to the archives of culture made available by the media and the possibilities of recreating them critically. The focus of the contribution is on the new configurations that the problem takes with the intensification of the presence of digital technologies in education and culture, seeking to identify possible contributions to the dilemmas of media education and of digital literacy emerging from the Brazilian scene—a country of continental dimensions, where the pulsation of globalized media culture co-exists with a strong preliterate popular culture, often in the same city and just a few blocks away.

The approach of the authors is based on the pedagogy of dialogue of Paulo Freire. Its aim is to point out some indications to establish a digital inclusion that transcends utilitarian limits and a merely operational access to machines and programs. That is, an inclusion that is also social, cultural, and political. For doing so, it is necessary to develop an educational approach able to include: *culture*—understood as the expansion and possibility for various cultural repertoires; *criticism*—understood as the capacity for analysis, reflection, and evaluation; *creation*—understood as the creative capacity for expression, communication, and construction of knowledge; and *citizenship*—that probably is the synthesis of the three previous concepts.

References

Bauman, Z. (2004). *Liquid Modernity.*

Clark, H.H. (1996). *Using language.* Cambridge: Cambridge University Press.

Clark, H.H., & Brennan, S.E. (1991). Grounding in communication. In L.B. Resnick, J.M. Levine & S.D. Teasley (Eds.), *Perspectives on socially shared cognition* (pp. 27-49). Washington, DC: APA Books.

de Kerkhove, D. (1995). *The skin of culture.* Toronto, Canada: Sommerville House Books Limited.

Crystal, D. (2001). *Language and the Internet.* Cambridge: Cambridge University Press.

Farr, R.M., & Moscovici, S. (Eds.). (1984). *Social representations.* Cambridge, MA: Cambridge University Press.

Papert, S. (1996). *Connected family.* Marietta, GA: Longstreet Press.

Rivoltella, P.C. (2006). *Screen generation.* Milan: Vita e Pensiero.

Thompson, J.B. (1995). *The media and the modernity. A social theory of the media.* Cambridge, MA: Polity Press.

Tobin, J. J., Wu, D.Y.H., & Davidson, D.H. (1989). *Preschool in three cultures.* New Haven, CT: Yale University Press.

Acknowledgment

The editor would like to acknowledge the help of all involved in the collation and review process of the book, without whose support the project could not have been satisfactorily completed. Deep appreciation and gratitude is due to my collaborators in the Centre of Research on Education about Media, Information and Technology (CREMIT). Their presence, their intelligent work, and most of the reflections we normally share in our seminars and meetings are part of the ground from which this book grew.

Most of the authors of chapters included in this book also served as referees for chapters written by other authors. Thanks go to all those who provided constructive and comprehensive reviews. However, some of the reviewers must be mentioned as their reviews set the benchmark. Reviewers who provided the most comprehensive, critical, and constructive comments include: Paolo Ardizzone, Alessandra Carenzio, and Chiara Friso of the Catholic University of Milan, and Andrea Garavaglia of the State University of Bicocca in Milan. Support of the Department of Education at Catholic University of Milan is acknowledged for the availabilty of its spaces and structures to facilitate the review process.

Special thanks also go to the publishing team at IGI Global, whose contributions throughout the whole process from inception of the initial idea to final publication have been invaluable. In particular to Ross Miller, my original personal editorial assistant, to Jessica Thompson, who continuously prodded via e-mail for keeping the project on schedule, and to Michelle Potter, whose enthusiasm motivated me to initially accept her invitation for taking on this project.

Special thanks go to Ignacio Aguaded for his unselfish permission to use excerpts from the conference materials of the Hispano-luso Congress held in Huelva (Spain) in October 2005. I would also like to thank Alessandra Carenzio, Chiara Rizzi, and Elena Tassalini for their factive help in book editing, and Simona Ferrari, who has worked with me since 1995 and read a semi-final draft of the manuscript providing helpful suggestions for enhancing its content. And last but not least, my wife Alessandra and my sons David and Francesco: the happy confusion they create in our home is a form of support and encouragement for my work.

In closing, I wish to thank all of the authors—dear friends and respected colleagues—for their insights and excellent contributions to this book.

Pier Cesare Rivoltella, PhD
Hershey, Pennsylvania, USA
November 2007

Section I

The Information Society:
A Conceptual Framework

Chapter I

Knowledge, Culture, and Society in the Information Age

Pier Cesare Rivoltella, Università Cattolica del Sacro Cuore, Italy

Abstract

Informational society, mainly after the development of online and mobile devices, is changing the forms with which we build our image of the reality. Speed, virtuality, and networking are three of the factors of this change. Speed means that information is circulating faster and faster, but also that it becomes aged very soon, with the necessity of being updated. Virtuality, after its first conceptualizations like a parallel dimension in the 1990s, is nowadays an integral part of our system of relations. Networking, finally, is becoming the main category for interpreting our culture, made of multiple dimensions of sociability, inside and outside the net. Knowledge, in this context, is not yet a truth authenticated; it is, on the contrary, a social activity, a process quite similar to a conversation where each of the discussants is negotiating a point of view. This is the scenario into which modern teachers, parents, and youngsters are acting.

Introduction

Since a few years ago, the research in the field of social and communication sciences has described our time as a transition phase from the industrial age to the information age. This passage is usually seen as a substitution of machines and productive routines with information technologies, but we need to deepen our analysis. Castells (1996) accurately suggests moving the discourse from technology protagonist to the ways in which knowledge is produced and relationships between individuals and systems are constructed within the society. According to this perspective, the industrial age ceases to be identified with Ely Whitney's cotton-gin, Stephenson's locomotive, or the mechanization of labour processes; it rather indicates a particular sort of social organization—based on Taylorism—regarding every single aspect of human activity, from school to family. If Castells' approach is worthwhile, a similar discourse can be promoted in relation to the information age. It cannot be identified with the introduction of information and communication technologies (ICT); better it could be bended with the systematic reorganization that these technologies promote on social level. Rather than talking about information society, the Spanish sociologist prefers to refer to the concept of informational society. In the first case, information is the content of society, while in the second one it defines the nature of society itself. Informational society is a society "made out of information." In the next paragraph, we will better understand how.

The process of rearrangement leading to this society might be interpreted according to at least three meaningful factors:

1. The **speed** of knowledge exchanges and knowledge aging. In fact, the transactions, thanks to network implementation, are not based on goods anymore, but on information. This makes the exchange almost instantaneous (i.e., in the case of tickets release or of home banking). The same speed hits the possibility of individual knowledge, capitalized in initial training through the educational system, to answer properly to the needs of a society adopting an innovative rhythm that is at least double with respect to knowledge updating.

2. **Virtuality**, which means the clearer disconnection between space and time, to which we can refer macrophenomena such as the globalization of industries and markets and micropractices such as teleworking or video conferencing. The separation between space and time means to emancipate information sender and receiver from the need of sharing the same place at the same time. This also means a great flexibility of places and time in information access.

3. **Networking**, which means that the net metaphor becomes a paradigm explaining most of our social practices. Our society is characterized by the need for a collective dimension, even if with evident contradictions: intelligence is collective, work is done in staff, and cooperation and collaboration seem stra-

tegic scenarios in different fields, from economy to didactics. The connectivity becomes a cultural macroindicator; the diffusion of the net is participating to a progressive move from the local to the planetary dimension: besides, in the economy development and in political and social macrophenomena (disappearance of the idea of nation, migratory movements, cultural melting pot), *globalization* mainly consists in aiding the circulation of symbolic meanings and this depends on the telematic-based connectivity.

The consequence of this set of so decisive changes, under the perspective of cultural sociology, has been a new importance of knowledge. Its creation, elaboration, and diffusion are nowadays the main source of productivity and power. This means a new protagonist of symbolic goods. Following Baudrillard (1976), in traditional societies goods had a specific value; today the value is represented by the good itself. It is possible to verify that thinking about commercial "objects" as television formats, Internet services, or about other activities such as financial intermediations or advertisement. This emphasis on symbolic goods produces the growth of a new category of "symbolic workers" (Neveu, 1994) who build their professional identity on the production-diffusion of symbolic good (i.e., trainers, PRs, consulting projectionists, marketing experts, etc.). Finally, this means a new need for a new know-how. This is the actual field of education. A field into which the new media competences become the very important thing. digital literacy is the response to this need.

The Informational Society as a Social Construction

In one of his works, Mattelart (2001, p. 4) states the main coordinates to understand the real meaning of what today is commonly indicated as "Information society." Mattelart's (2001) point of view is clear. He connects the space conquest with Internet diffusion, grasping their common connecting aspect. They are "conquests," using a category proposed by the American sociologists Dayan and Katz (1992), both are accompanied (as always happens with conquests) by a story of emancipation. The main indicators that mark a conquest refer to some elements linked to the exceptionality of the event the conquest represents and to the heroism expressed by men engaged to make it happen. More precisely, a conquest:

- Refers to a situation that appears unsolvable and to the need for an important action to overcome it
- Finds in some men's charisma (according to the weberian declination) the instrument to realize this change

- Thanks to this transition, allows and defines the access of humanity into a new symbolic order

This last definition makes sense of the fact that usually great conquests are accompanied by a story of emancipation. This story, from a social point of view, works as a tool for understanding the event itself, increasing its symbolic value; it is a role that in traditional societies was played by poets and that today is strongly supported through media, particularly through television (Fiske & Hartley, 1978). Just consider Armstrong's and Aldrin's walk on the moon on July 20, 1969, and the meaning it assumed in that specific historical period. Mass media represent and construct it as a story of emancipation in relation to the Cold War and to the need to make humanity free from self destruction and lack of resources.

A close mechanism can be found in relation to the informational society. Similarly we are in front of a conquest and we can effortlessly find out its own structural aspects:

- The idea of the informational society was climbed in the past decade in a context of great transformations and problems. On a geopolitical level, the fall of ideologies and the overcoming of the logic of opposite blocks produced as a main consequence the multiplication of regional conflicts and the dissemination of nuclear potential even within countries considered politically unstable. Economically speaking, the need to affirm a "human capitalism" becomes even more urgent in order to reduce the lack of balances in riches distribution (this lack can easily turn into new conflicts). Finally, on a demographic level, the inverse growth rhythm between Western and Third World countries, and the following enormous migratory mobility between them, put in evidence the problem of an adequate cohabitation of differences on a social and cultural level. We can affirm that we are now facing a complex and uneasy situation that can only be modified by a great action.
- The informational society has its own heroes. There are forerunners such as Charles Babbage and Norbert Wiener, material builders such as Bill Gates, gurus providing a legitimation with their provisions such as Nick Negroponte and Kevin Warwick. The possibility of finding a good answer to the problems mentioned above passes through these men's' work, a work of implementation and reflection.
- Finally, the informational society represents a new symbolic order able to balance conflicts regionalization with the predisposition of a new arena for dialogue, providing the peaceful cohabitation between market and equality through the promises of new economy, fixing new rules for the democratic game. The Internet in this perspective really becomes a new space of mediation where the reduction of social conflicts could be possible.

From these general lines, it looks evident that the informational society should be considered, more than a fact, as the result of a careful and patient work of social construction (Mattelart, 2000). This work is based on three main "emancipation discourses."

The first discourse is represented by the words of science. Mattelart (2000) very well underlines how the idea of an informational society was theoretically diffused since the first part of the 1960s, linked to the theme of the collapse of ideologies. What was described is the origin of a new model of society marked by the organization (*management society*) and the labour dematerialization, by the substitution of the *labor theory of value* with the *knowledge theory of value*, by the getting over of the central position of companies and business men towards a new centrality of universities and research centres. To define this society we introduced the adjective "postindustrial," then substituted with the category of "information society" in the 1970s. The "fathers" of this society have been found in the main representatives of the organizational theory: Saint-Simon's technocratic utopia and Taylor's organizational paradigm connote the functional society as the fortunate result of development and progress. The net metaphor has been soon indicated as the necessary base for the representation of a decentralized and complex organizational model.

The idea of the net, of a network society, is the focus also of the second category of discourses, the provisional discourses promoted by the futurologists. The last 20 years have seen the origin of the figure and role of the *think tanks*, specialists who transform the ability to foresee the evolutionary future scenarios into a real professional competency (*professional prognosticators*). Among them, besides Herman Kahn, Alvin Toffler, and the already mentioned Nicholas Negroponte, we quote also Zbigniew Brzezinski, councilor for international affairs during the presidency of Jimmy Carter. It is due to Brzezinski that the first intuition of a "net diplomacy" should have gradually replaced the traditional force diplomacy.

We arrive now to the hearth of the third discourse level on informational society, related to the geopolitical situation of the planet, marked by a slow dissolution of the role of the nation, by the multiplication of centers, and by the globalization of processes.

While Brzezinski imagined a world architecture aimed to dominate scientific reason—a real obstacle to technological innovation—the new protagonists of the geo-economy undermined in the name of market reasons the traditional foundations of geopolitics. And the idea of the one world supported by multinational companies was based on the growth of industries and information nets, able to free production managers, consumers, and products from the ties of the borders and to let them interact within one self-regulated market, ordaining in this way the unsustainability of the nation-state and, consequently, the frailness of public policies (Mattelart, 2000, pp. 87-88).

The result of specialists' analysis, of marketing provisions, of international scenarios shared within television imaginary, is represented by the perception of the fact that informational society represents something "indisputable," that thanks to it we entered a new period for economy and history, that nothing can be as before. If the NASDAQ grows, to which extent it depends on the strength of informatics companies or on the faith bouncing from specific reviews and the ideas of opinion makers? The dependence on market mood is an old stock market law, but referring to information society and new economy it gains a new interesting meaning: it becomes the specular image of a society that is exactly made out of information. Here lies the meaning of what we underlined at the beginning of the paragraph.

During our analysis this aspect will be underlined applying the category of the symbolic.

Speed, Virtuality, Networking

At least according to the perspective proposed, it seems undeniable that the affirmation of the network society is based on a mythological disposal in which it is hard to discern what is the result of a construction process and what is real; but, on the other hand, the main changes in market and production influenced by telematics and its organizational consequences, with the growth of new professions and new social relationships, are undoubtedly real facts. Failing these conditions, we could not talk about the informational society, even in the presence of the construction of a mythology linked to this form of society created and fed up by the media. As suggested in the introduction, we will focus on three main aspects: speed, virtuality, and networking in their substaining effects towards globalization.

Speed

Speed marks the growth of telematic nets and their impact on social organization with three main attentions. First, it produces time compression and distances erosion. Under this point of view, telematic nets represents both a resolute leap and an inversion in the history of communication technologies. As a matter of fact, until now, the pulling down of distances has always passed through the progressing rise of speed: a horse is faster than a walking man, a car is faster than a horse, a plane is faster than vehicles running on the ground. Concretely, pulling down distances meant in these cases to increase speed or to power the conveyance. According to this logic, the Internet affirms itself as the fastest medium since the transfer of speed is almost close to the instant, but this incredible speed only depends on the fact that what is traveling is information. So the maximum speed lies in the absence of movement:

everything starts from and goes to where we are. This idea gets a perfect explanation in the image of the "sitted journalism" introduced by media sociology to depict the current model of journalism: a journalism far from the facts and dependent on a few sources of information generally searched through a computer standing on his own desk (Neveu, 2002). Agency dispatches allow the journalist to "deliver" news with no need to move and search them (even if this attitude evidently includes strong repercussions on news construction process, as agrees to the mediation of agencies without verifying facts, as usually occurs in classical inquiry journalism).

Information exchange speed brings about some consequences. The most evident, which will be discussed in the next paragraph, is the virtualization of communication. This means its emancipation from space and time sharing. It is not yet necessary to share the same room to communicate, with all its advantages and drawbacks. The other two consequences, on the contrary, shape as two different ways to decline speed within information society.

First of all, in a social system where information is required to be moved in very strict time thanks to information technology, speed itself becomes a new fundamental factor referred to as individual cognitive profile. Knowledge elaboration depends not only on the ability to read facts and produce concepts, but also on specific skills necessary for their expression. When we participate to a brainstorming via chat, discussing a project launching, the fact that we are not able to use a computer keyboard appropriately or that we do not manage the environment we are using (icons, buttons, processes) produces the same effect as if we do not exactly understand the language spoken in a foreign country. I can have great ideas but I will not manage to impose my opinion, because my slowness will turn into a reduced visibility on the screen and this slow rhythm will be interpreted as a lack of personal meaningful contributions. Besides this aspect—the ability to interact with interfaces—a specific quickness in feed-back suggestion will be asked. If information runs fast, what is needed is not only a deep rapidity to process it, but also to produce the required answers, because a subsiding in our feed-back implies a general fall in the system speed and this can create serious organization effects (if I do not immediately answer an e-mail that is fundamental to come to a decision, I deeply stop the resolute process) and an economical loss. Anthropologically speaking, this is an important change, as the syncopated rhythm of electronic communication, which proposes to examine quickly really big amounts of information and to react in an even shorter time, are taking over the long term rhythm linked to retrospective analysis (Godman, 1968) typical of the civilization of literacy (before answering I read accurately, then I read again, I think, I can write a draft, rewrite, and correct, then I can send it). The results are indicated in the substitution of pondered reading with rapid reading practices, the ripening of a synthetic and superficial understanding of reality as to the deep and analytical mode, the information overload. This is one of the most diffused shapes of the impossibility to totalize knowledge, typical of the informational society as observed by Levy (1997). Concerning this topic, Virilio (1998) states that we are facing a real pathology, close to the uneasiness manifested by traditional travelers who suffer car or plane.

The third and last meaning of speed (second effect of the growing of information sharing) refers to knowledge obsolescence. There are two main factors influencing this phenomenon.

On one hand, the speed of technological change imposes a frequent knowledge upgrading. It is a condition well experienced by people working in e-learning market, a case in which it is difficult to exit the experimental phase of a process because when we are about to abandon it in favour of a steady condition, technological innovation radically changes things and imposes to start a new experimental phase, with the common result of a condemnation for the ones who try to interpret innovation, a condemnation that implies the impossibility of reasoning in term of productive routines and vice versa: to be updated means to risk to exit the labour market, always running to innovation; but run to innovation means otherwise to renounce to obtain those productive standards that only allow to recover investments and start to gain profits.

This changing speed, finally, affects knowledge updating also in relation to rapidity in the information exchange processes. We move from a "heavy" knowledge, typical of the pre-electronic age, in which knowledge share and appropriation represented a long term task, to a "light" knowledge that is used in a very short lapse of time. "New knowledges" grow and erase; they are the result of intersections that are often temporary. Speed creates them quickly and soon sweeps them away.

Virtuality

The abundant literature on the term virtuality allows a critical reflection on it, far enough from the futurological (science fictional?) enthusiasms created around it in the first part of the 1990s. Concerning the term virtual, we can distinguish at least three aspects: a punctual meaning (etymological level), the perceptive experience linked to it (technological level), and the significance of its effects (social level).

Concerning the definition of the term, Pierre Levy (1995) is credited with putting order in the debate. On this subject the French philosopher has accurately shown that the term virtual (if we look at its Latin etymology and at the use of the medieval scholastic philosophy) is not opposite to the term "real," but to the term "actual."

The term virtual comes from the medieval Latin virtualis, *which derives from* virtus, *strength, power. For the scholastic philosophy, virtual is what can potentially exist, something which is not in progress. What is virtual tends to come true, nevertheless without being passed through a formal and effective concreteness. A tree is virtually present in the seed. Remaining in the rigorous frame of philosophy, the virtual is not opposed to the real, but to the actual: virtuality and actuality are only two different states of being.* (Levy, 1995, p.5)

In this way we can easily get over the ordinary meaning we usually use to refer to virtual, figuring it out as something that does not exist, that is only an illusion. Virtual reality is not "another" world as regards to reality (reality exists, virtual reality does not), but a different manifestation of reality. Which are, then, the characteristics that inertly define the virtual? Simplifying Levy's (1995) analysis, there are two defining aspects:

- The **problematic nature**, that is the fact of representing a system of forces which is differently realizable. For example, when we talk about a virtual company, its virtuality consists in the fact that the labour distribution and the localization of its main areas do not refer to something finally and totally solved, but that has to be permanently redefined according to the actual needs (management can be moved from London to New York, while production can slide from Taiwan to Brasil, etc.);
- The **delocalization**, which refers to the loss of power owned by localization aspects in defining situations. A virtual company is not yet precisely localizable: its elements are nomadic and dispersed, their geographic position has no more value (Levy, 1995). Virilio grasps the meaning of this concept when he says that nowadays we are spectators of the end of geography more than of the end of the history (Virilio, 1998, p. 9).

The explanation of the terms allows us to gain great advantages also on the second level of our analysis, the technological one. For a long time, in fact, virtual has been identified with a specific technology granting immersion and manipulation of and within a synthetic space. Also, from the point of view of social imaginary, virtual reality has been traditionally associated to all those devices—from head mounted displays to data-gloves, created to support user's interaction with a computer-generated space as if it was real (and here lies again the contraposition between real and virtual that, thanks to Levy (1995), we have already defined as theoretically passed).

For example, the fact that wearing eye-phone, *slipping on a* data-glove, *and a* data-suit *we are able to* access *an illusionary reality and* live *it as if it was real (or almost real), represents a concrete step in favour of what is explained. Now we are ready to reconnoiter from the inside a reality that appears as the counterfigure of our reality.* (Maldonado, 1992, pp. 51-52)

This "strong" meaning of the concept of virtual has fallen into a fast disuse, both because the kind of technology it referred to was too encumbering and because the initial utopia of making virtual reality available for everyone, directly from personal computers, sensationally failed. Actually, technologically, the costs implied to obtain adequate immersion and navigation effects are so high that they allow RV devices purchased only in case of research laboratories. At the same time, with the crisis of the "strong" declination of the virtual, a "weak" meaning of the term has developed and was diffused for its wide social implications, a meaning that joins what is today defined as "culture of virtuality." This culture, which probably finds its origin in the cyber-culture (Benedikt, 1991; Gibson, 1984), is nowadays present in the different forms of virtual communities, form IRCs to Second Life. It confirms the idea according to which the main forms of network existence would be the ones to prefer: more freedom, more possibilities to meet people, more opportunities to create doubles of the self through simulation. A perspective that some authors compared to the different experiences of body escaping promoted by shamanism (Zolla, 1992) or by the platonic tradition.

For instance, the idea of a virtual reality conceived as an escape from reality towards virtuality can be interpreted as an ascendant escape, liberating to the absolute. Above all, when this idea is seen as something happening through a disembodied human sensorial*, through a sensorial made autonomous as regards to the body, thanks to advanced digital technologies. This clearly reminds us that the plotinian ecstasy, the escape from the sensible to the intelligible.* (Maldonado, 1992, p. 56)

Also under this cultural meaning of the term virtual, the contraposition to the real still appears implicit: virtual life is a "life on the screen," to quote the title of the renowned work of Turkle (1995), that has to be seen in antithesis to the "real" life; a perspective that vanishes, on the contrary, if we reflect on what virtuality represents today on a social level. It has to do with all those forms of interaction surrogating physical presence through the mediation of electronic devices. In this way, when we talk about "virtual classroom" within the e-learning field we refer to learning/teaching activities as they are made possible among individuals who do not share the same physical place, thanks to the mediation of a telematic environment such as the current Learning Management Systems. The adjective virtual, in this sense, does not refer to a different dimension where it is possible to experience perceptive simulated situations, nor a world made of fictional interactions supporting masking free play. On the contrary, the term refers to a situation where physical presence resolves into telepresence. So, rather than an alternative place where it is possible to enter, virtual has to be considered as an action scenario conceptualized besides other scenarios: going further with the example of e-learning, it means to consider that, besides personal reading of texts and materials and face to face discussion with colleagues, we can open new scenarios such as forum discussions or chatting with a professor who lives several kilometers away. Both these forms of activity are consistent with the aim of learning, and the only difference is represented by the fact that the first forms require a physical presence, while the others replace it through telepresence (Rivoltella, 2003).

From Networking to Globalization

A society that conceptualizes itself according to the two metaphors of speed and virtuality cannot be anything except a network society. Speed, for instance, comprises always greater possibilities to circulate ideas and knowledges that, on the contrary, would remain local, while virtuality supports the possibility of making a mediate experience of things with no need to move. The main consequence is represented by the origin of new connections point-to-point within the world-system, as properly explained by Mattelart (1996, p. 9):

Progressively extending circulation possibilities, linked both to people and material and symbolic goods, mass media has increased the inclusion of specific societies within wider groups, continuously moving physical, intellectual, and mental borders.

This remark is very interesting and allows us to understand some ideas.

First of all, being connected, or the need to be connected, is not only a fact or a strategic choice within companies, but an effect of technological development. Many years before the advent of the Internet, in fact, the development of rail transport or the diffusion of radio-television frequencies required (imposed) the adoption of common strategies, standards, that progressively supported the growth of an international network among societies and nations.

This fact—the link between media and connection—has become, starting from the Illuminist 18th Century, a guiding topic of those currents that double-locked the possibility of people cohabiting with the realization of a factual network. The configuration of a network society, then, besides being a consequence of technology development, can be read as the founding myth of a certain conceptualization of relationships among individuals and nations.

Finally, network society, technological development, and ideological formulation seem to cross another central category of the current cultural debate, represented by globalization, supporting a new interpretation less focused on economical factors (certainly decisive) and more sensible to cultural logics.

Let us grasp all these suggestions following a unitary path and clarifying in which direction the meaning of networking, as a structural dimension of informational

Table 1. Aspects linked to globalization/networking (Source: personal elaboration)

Items	Globalization outcomes	Networking outcomes
Concentration	Monopoly	Co-ordination
Use practices	Omologation	Circulation of meanings
Access to technologies	Digital divide	Access for everyone
Socio-cultural effects	Occidentalization	Situational appropriation

society, makes it a globalization society as well. Our hypothesis is that what the term globalization tends to evoke negatively (the erosion of cultural specific characters, the growth of planetary poverty, market expansion to the prejudice of the environment, the increase of social differences, Rossi, 2002, pp. 19) finds its positive version in the "mythological" image of the net that Mattelart (2000) precisely described: networking and globalization could then refer to the same phenomenon, declining its opposite implications on the market level and on the second level of individual and social practices.

Two of the main definitions of the term globalization that help explain the current debate on the concept:

The increasing connection among different regions of the world, a process generating complex forms of interaction and interconnection (Thompson, 1995, p. 221)

The process of economical unification of the world and, for extension, of al that refers to the planet. (Mattelart, 1996, p. 95)

Reading attentively these definitions, we can understand that, besides the common "connective" matrix ("interconnection" and "unification" imply a relational process referring to the category of the net), the phenomenon of globalization occupies the same semantic area of other terms with which it is often confused:

- The **transnationalization** (better than multinationalization), considered as the process of polycentric reorganization of the business
- The **internationalization**, that is the progressive reduction—after the Modern Age—of the role of the Nation (the European unification process, but also the new role played by the ONU are a synthomatic example of this aspect)

- The **mondialization**, that is, the final effect of internationalization, or the opening of symbolic negotiation tables among individuals and society to the entire planet (Morin & Kern, 1993), refer to the concept of "planetary age"

- The **homogenization**, conceived as a planetary standardization of tastes and culture (a process that would happen according to the main parameters of the western culture in obedience to the classical thesis of the cultural imperialism, advanced by Herbert Schiller (1969) in his work *Mass Communications and American Empire*)

- The **interculturality**, "good" version of the idea of homogenization, where cultural colonization is replaced by the free integration of different cultures in societies that nowadays are always more multiethnic

Following Thompson's (1995) analysis, every single dimension is part of the phenomenon of globalization without disappearing in it. Concretely, the single ideas we have quickly described can differently refer to the three structural aspects of globalization:

- The placement in a planetary arena (internationalization, mondialization)
- The organization on a global scale (transnationalization)
- The reciprocity and interdependence (interculturality)

These dimensions, as easily evident, are perfectly recognizable in the processes relating to new economy: the planetary market configuration, the partnership logic, and the virtuality of the systems of services production/distribution, the systemic quality of relation forms (something that implies the reversibility of every connection and the co-implication of every element of the system within the transformation processes concerning all the other elements).

Where is the origin of this sociocultural reality? Where do we find the logics identifying its advent and affirmation?

According to Morin and Kern (1993) and Mattelart (2000), referring to globalization, we can find out (1) a remote genesis, (2) two close cultural matrices, and (3) a recent evolution.

The remote genesis of globalization can be found in the discovery of America that, in 1492, interrupts the Eurocentric orientation of history introducing its first evident globalistic acceleration. The cultivation of potatoes or tomatoes, formerly unknown in the West (as syphilis), are symptomatic of the incipient creolezation of cultures and behaviours, right as measles, previously unknown within the New World, that beat more indios than the Conquerors did.

Figure 1. Knowledge level implied in business (Source: Eppler, 2002)

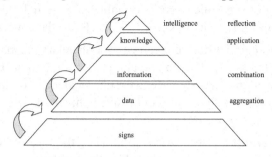

The close cultural matrices in the 18th Century are represented by the universalistic theories of Illuminism and Liberalism. Both of them developed their own ideology on the creative power of the exchange, intending it obviously under two different points of view. The Illuminists underline its capability to circulate ideas guaranteeing democracy. Under this perspective we can read the revolutionary politics aimed to unify the French language against the outliving of regional idiomatic languages as an answer to the logic of the Ancienne Régime that on the contrary intended to block the circulation of ideas and to separate people. Concerning Liberalism, its logic could be identified with J.S.Mill's maxim: Producing means moving. It aimed to build a universal mercantile republic, an extended wide economical community of consumers whose free initiatives replace mighty institutions as the one represented by the State.

In relation to the recent evolution of the phenomenon, finally, it tends to coincide with the development of communication technologies starting from the half of the 19th Century and with their political and cultural implications, as already anticipated at the beginning of the paragraph.

On a *technology level*, just think about the birth of the telegraph and about its function to reduce distances, evidently shown in 1851 with the laying of the first telegraphic cable between Calais and Dover and, in 1902, with the completion of the first transpacific line. A tendency progressively sharpened by the advent of radio and television until the current topics of information highways and the World Wide Web.

But this technological tendency primes a similar process also on a *political level*. In 1865 the International Telegraphic Union arose, with the aim of fixing standards, prices, and principles common to all the countries. It is followed in 1874 by the General Postal Union and in 1906 by the International Radio-telegraphic Union. So, technology not only "narrows" the planet, but it causes the dialogue among States, supporting the international coagulum of relations.

This inevitably affects the *cultural level*. Europe, sunk in the crisis followed by the French Revolution and painfully committed to guarantee a political balance among States, finds in communication the salvation utopia able to point out a future of peace for the world.

Universalism, with Saint-Simon above all, becomes a real redeeming ideology that finds in the industry and in Positivism its basic supports and in the huge universal expositions an effective moment for mythological elaboration as Mattelart (1996) suggests.

Temporarily faded at the end of the century with the fall of the Commune of Paris and the collapse of the States system after the French-Prussian conflict, this utopia had a rebirth during the 20th Century finding in Wiener's cybernetic program its refoundation: the current topics of communication society and the planetary village, as pointed out by Breton (1992), largely depends on it.

On the base of this historical landscape, which is today the image of globalization in relation to telematic communication, adapting Thompson's (1995) analysis, we can underline at least four relevant topics about it:

First of all the concentration of sector industries in very few groups. Just reflect on emblematic examples such as Microsoft or AOL-Warner. In the first case, we are in front of a producer who imposes a real monopoly on the software area, dictating the terms even in the hardware market (machines obsolescence is, in fact, largely defined by the technical characteristics required by the running of new releases of Windows or Office—see for example the case of Vista). In the second, we refer to the joint-venture between the biggest provider in the world and the biggest communication holding. On a market level, these tendencies create a general unbalance in the distribution of economical power and, above all, of symbolic power within a wide collective arena. But if we gain the view of networking rather than about monopolistic instances, we prefer to talk about the logic of partnership that does not comprise a nonlibertarian omologation of markets, but the coordination of productive industries with evident advantages both for the producer and for the consumer.

A second relevant aspect related to the globalization of telematic markets is represented by their own impact in use practices. Network technologies, in fact, clearly dephase national frames in respect to the space of potential global markets they allow to reach. Also in this case, the view seems different according to the perspective of globalization or of networking: the first view underlines the themes of omologation and the loss of cultural identities; the second puts in evidence the topics of free circulation of meaning and the creation of collaborative international networks (the genesis of collective intelligence and of cooperative work lies here).

A third topic particularly useful is the problem of access to technologies. The launch of global context for services distribution and for goods circulation, on one hand, does not appear to cause a balanced access to technologies, that, on the contrary, is based on preference flow on a planetary level (from the leading countries to the rest of the world) or transregional (it is exactly what is happening in Latin America for Mexico and Brasil in relation to the other countries of the subcontinent), but on the other hand it feeds the utopia that connects the constant increase of links with the diffusion of further development possibilities.

The last question concerns the effects of globalization on a socio-cultural level that allows defining in details what we have already forwarded on the impact of globalization on use practices. The thesis dominating the topic for a long time (probably resisting until today) is represented by the idea of cultural imperialism that suggests a progressive cultural colonization of the world, from the Marshall plan on, guided by the American model because the United States always was the main controller of media and communication industry. Following this thesis, then, globalization should be read in terms of an Americanization (more in general, of an occidentalization) of other cultures. Without deepening the analytical critic of this hypothesis, we can anyway put in evidence its main theoretical weakness that consists of an ingenuous explanation of the appropriation process through which an individual assimilates cultural models promoted by the media. This process cannot be seen as a simple mechanic assumption (as the cultural imperialism presumes: I learn consumerism through consumerist programs), but needs to be interpreted as an ermeneuthic model related to the idea that the meaning that people makes to the media messages and the uses they do of them are depending from the contexts of reception and from resources they use in interpretation process.

Knowledge Society

The changes described above support a final reflection on the new meaning of knowledge within a market where information represents the priority value. Synthetically we can describe this change referring to a shift from "transmissive" models, where knowledge is owned and moved from someone to someone else, to "sharing" models, where it is basically coconstructed and available for other people who can freely use it.

Towards a New Image of Knowledge

Weinberger (2002) suggests that the evolution of the idea of knowledge can be articulated in four big phases identified by philosophy, science, computer, and the Web. Passing through them lets us understand the single qualities of each phase and, above all, the definition of knowledge nowadays, as now telematic networks have such vivid effects on the social system that they also contribute to its definition.

Regarding knowledge, the problem of philosophy has always been represented by the issue of certainty, expressed with the search of the forms to be used to fix criteria of knowledge validity. These forms, from Hellenism to Modern Age, have been connoted each time in a different way, even if sharing, generally, the superiority of the rational moment to the sensible one. This aspect is evident in the platonic tradition: according to it the theoretical sight of the reason is the only one able to grasp the idea, understood as an ontological paradigm of reality. It is also confirmed by Aristotle, even in its medieval revisions, for which the real knowledge is the one that goes back to the grounds of reality (*scire est per essentias scire*). This is also connoted by Descartes (and his perspective will be actualized by modern philosophy until Kant and even further on) when he identifies the horizon of reasoning as the only element that can be rescued from the corrosive effects of doubt. The consequence of this formulation has been the progressive contraposition of thought and reality until the extreme limit of their separation. The terms of the problem are already clear with Parmenides. When the Goddess who dictates him the verses of his poem *On nature* appears to Parmenides, he vividly distinguish the indication of the "path of truth" and the indication of the "path of the error." The first is the path of rational reflection; the second is the path of the senses. The error path (according to Parmenides) is the one passed by Heraclitus who suggests that according to the experience everything changes in the world: seasons alternate, night and day follow one another, man grows old and dies. These experiences, passed through the lens of reasoning, are contradictory. In fact, if something exists, it cannot "not exist" at the same time, as recommended by the glimpse of those whom, trusting senses, see that everything unceasingly transforms. Therefore, becoming is a false movement, an illusion of our senses. Reason clearly shows that what we can have is existence or nonexistence, without transitions (as provokingly proposed by the Italian philosopher Emanuele Severino).

Science, right in the same period when Descartes fixes the coordinates of the *cogito*, shifts the terms of the problem. The philosophy-based rational foundation steps aside in favour of the experimental method that, from Francis Bacon to Galileo and Newton, primarily made two victims: prejudice, which means every subjective thing altering the knowledge of facts as they are, and what is not verified, that is everything that did not pass the prove of experiment (Newton emblematically synthesizes it in his rules of method with the well-known "hypoteses non fingo").

Theorically, science works easily. Scientists collect facts, often through experiments, to isolate causes; then they formulate hypothesis on eventual explanations to these facts and try to prove them. Hypotheses are further elaborated into theories that are defined as solid and certified because their essential components—facts—are adequately proved. In this way, science describes a world based on proofs and immune from personal views (value-free) (Weinberger, 2002, p. 164).

Popper (1963) and the epistemology influenced by his thought (Kuhn, 1970, Lakatos, 1980, and Feyerabend, 1975) will intervene on this model, underlining that the fact on its own does not exist and that for scientific work it acquires a meaning only within a plan founded on theory. But this aspect does not shift the problem, typical of scientific knowledge, of the need to deal with the validity of theories to read facts (and in recent debates we note a clear reassertion of the perspective of Realism—Boghossian, 2006).

ICT revolution and computer advent introduce, besides this two "classical" connotations of knowledge, a third perspective. It is a "mechanical" and computational conception of knowledge well represented by the famous principle of informatics: "Garbage in, garbage out." This means that the quality of computer processes on information depends on information itself, on the correctness of their codification. This knowledge view finds its theoretical legitimation in Shannon and Weaver's (1948) mathematical model. It provided for many years to artificial intelligence scholars the basic model to analyze the analogy between human and artificial mind: the calculation ability, the mechanical elaboration of information.

With the Internet (and particularly with the new tools of Social Network), we face a different connotation of knowledge. To know does not mean to reach rational certainty about a problem (as for philosophy), to check a theory comparing it to facts (as for science), or processing pertinent information (as for information technology), but it means to share our point of view. Again, as Weinberger (2002, p. 176) accurately noted, Knowledge is not a truth authenticated: it is on the contrary a social activity, a process quite similar to a conversation where each of the discussants is negotiating his point of view. The social dimension of this form of knowledge, besides confirming the thesis advanced by recent social and organizational theories, implies some interesting consequences.

First of all, the idea of authority tends to change. In the Web, authority is not determined by official criteria (academic title, position in publishing trade market), but by the visibility and the recognition among a professional community. From this perspective, discussion lists or Bloggers' communities represent a knowledge source that is extraordinarily more effective than the enormous amount of pages recorded on planetary servers. These pages, in fact, are just the online version of paper materials, often already available (even if not easily accessible, this is the origin of Web usefulness); regarding online communities, on the contrary, we refer to experts who are consultable and whose capability in conceptual elaboration is continuously in progress in relation to the issues analyzed through the discussion list.

From this first underlining, we obtain a second fundamental predictor. If accessible knowledge in the Internet strictly depends on social interaction online, this means that the more people are connected, the more we have the possibility to build knowledge. This issue has been developed by Bob Metcalfe, founder of 3Com, one of the most important companies in the field of Net hardware. Following Metcalfe, the Vr value of a net increases with the square of the number of people connected to that net. This mathematical connection is known as *Metcalfe's Law* and it is expressed in the formula: $Vr = n (n - 1)$, where n is the number of connected users and $(n - 1)$ stays for the fact that when I connect to myself I obtain the engage tone. Therefore the real knowledge value of the Internet does not lie in documents, but in contacts.

David Reed, professor at MIT and later director of Lotus's research lab, turned back to Metcalfe's Law to correct it (or better to integrate it). In fact, this law appears empirically rejectable only if we note that the exponential growth of connected people does not necessarily imply the exponential growth of contacts. In other words, it is not obvious that if users' numbers increase, also the number of my contacts is going to increase exponentially (banally, the fact that more new users get a telephone line does not mean that my personal telephone use is going to increase exponentially). Reed, reasoning on this problem that apparently seems to question Metcalfe's Law, took this remark as a starting point to rearticulate it. The real value of the Internet is not associated with the number of single contacts, but with the fact that these single contacts contemporarily enter in a multiplicity of groups. *Reed's Law* translate this issue in this formula: $2^n - (n-1)$. Besides numbers, Reed's Law furnishes a theoretical justification to the fact that knowledge in the Internet is shared. The knowledge management and the fact that the capital of a business consists in it is based on this fundamental topic.

Intelligence as Business Capital

While affirming that intelligence is the real capital of a business, we connote it as the capability to use knowledge in a proper way according to different contexts.

This implies, first of all, to define the difference between terms such as "intelligence" and "knowledge" and others that are usually considered as synonymous referring to the question of knowledge within the business context, such as "information," or "data."

Technically we can define a datum as a sequence of numeric values that is a set of signs. When we combine two or more data we get information. When this information is interpreted, that means framed in a context and connected to a system of already existing concepts, we have knowledge. Intelligence implies the reflection on this knowledge, its comparison to others' knowledges, the operative and strategic evaluation of what we can presume or plan from it.

So, in organizations, the value is not made of raw or information, but of the possibility to develop knowledges from those data and, finally, to promote its intelligent exploitation.

The fulfillment of this need depends on the control of two levels of factors:

- First, the possibility to make *explicit knowledge* (processes, encoded practices, information) and to support the socialization of *implicit knowledge* (the know-how belonging to experts which is not easily codified into transferable information).
- Second, the capability to fight against the so called "corporate amnesia," the collective autism and the groups resistance to innovation, "groupthink effects," (Eppler, 2002, p. 3; the structure of the entire paragraph refers to this work).

Both conditions find in the ICT an opportunity for development and applicative field.

Concerning explicit knowledge, a system that is oriented to its management—usually an Intranet—needs to include four functions (Eppler, 2002, p. 5):

- **Collaboration:** This function is assured by technologies for *Computer Supported Collaborative Work* (CSCW), through which, for example, different members of the same organization can co-edit a document, and for *Computer Supported Collaborative Learning* (CSCL), the great part of online courses through which it is possible to provide in-service training. These functions can be integrated in more complex learning management systems thanks to which collaborative work is supported through asynchronous communication tools (as discussion boards) and synchronous communication tools (different systems of chat and virtual classroom);

- **Content management:** This function is usually sustained by personal and group agendas of the single user and the access to shared folders. The significance of this service lies in the possibility of solving eventual issues related to different versions of the same document and to obtain a patrimony of materials that can be a common benefit on different levels (personal, of a small group, of the entire company);

- **Visualization and aggregation:** This function is supported by the so-called *knowledge visualizers* that are the real internal portals of the organization generally planned in order to furnish a structured access to resources (through taxonomies related to processes, projects, etc.) and a conceptual shared lexicon (usually with the implementation of an internal glossary or—better—of a web ontology);

- **Search and intelligent extraction:** Through this faction, it is possible to obtain a facilitation for single users in order to access information that can likely be of interest, a result that is usually achieved through the definition of personal users' profiles to help the automatic delivery of information within electronic mail (*push*) or through a profile-guided search process (*pull*).

The socialization of implicit knowledge can also find a strategic support in Intranet technology. In particular, we have again four possible actions:

- **Knowledge creation:** It is specific to communities of practice, groups belonging to the same organization dealing with the same problems. Inside these communities, generally supported by chat or discussion boards, the creation of knowledge can be pursued through different actions: workshops aimed at problem-solving and pushing innovation (*Team Syntegrity*, see Beer, 1993), work spaces designing future scenarios through simulation (*Future Labs*), discussion and reflective activity voted to the development of new ideas and concepts (*Think Tanks*);

- **Knowledge transfer:** It can be obtained in different ways, such as "telematic market-places" where different project groups can introduce the main themes they are dealing with and interact with other groups in relation to these themes, and the varied forms of tutoring thanks to which new human resources can be guided by senior experts during the learning phase of their own tasks;

- **Knowledge Application:** Also in this situation, simulation systems are usually employed both to socialize actions and steps generally implied in projects realization (*Project Labs*) and to provide *team training*;

- **Evaluation:** During the implementation of a project, people involved bring along their own tacit knowledges to face problems as they occur. The evaluation phase, in the shape of case study, can help the explicitation of this knowledge capturing them in a specific Intranet area where every member of the organization can find, for every single project, the synthesis of "plus" and "minus."

Evidently in both cases (explicit and implicit knowledge), the support of technological infrastructure is fundamental, but it would be of no help without the facilitation of real relationships. This fact decisively shifts the attention from technology to human resources.

Conclusion and Future Trends:
The Learning Economy

The comments related to intelligence management can clear that an organization (a company like a school), to be recognized as a *knowledge organization*, does not necessarily have to belong to the IT or to new economy business. The decisive factor is the level of formalization according to which this organization defines the intellectual component as an integrative part of its patrimony, recognizes the central role of the informative system and of knowledge technologies, and evolves as the critical node of management culture and praxis. In particular, this form of organization reveals itself as deeply connected to the capability to learn, in general and from its own performances.

The concept of *learning economy* starts here and connotes, as the term suggests, the fact that the markets of education and learning represent in the information society one of the most relevant expenditure item for organizations. Evidently times and methods of education had to accept the needs of organizations, planning its own actions according to "light" models, consistent with work time and tasks. So in these last years, the boom in education consisted of the boom in online and mobile education, almost following the logic of identification. The data related to 2007 referred to an increase equivalent to 15-30% in the market of e-learning, with more than $17.5 billion of investments only in the United States: learning economy is actually an e-learning economy and probably it could become a m-learning economy thanks to the diffusion of broad band wireless systems, connected palms, forth generation smart phones.

We have to mark that this is an anomalous economy where knowledge is a particular good, and anomalous is also the market in which it is moved. One reason for this depends on the fact that the benefits deriving from the "purchase" of education are hardly measurable and anyway, even when possible, time passing from the attendance of an online course to the moment when the evaluation of its usefulness to productive capabilities and income is generally very extended. Two examples can explain the topic. The purchase of an online course, designed to help an entrepreneur launch a new innovative production line, could be considered as an unnecessary expense in case that the entrepreneur realized that this choice would involve an unsustainable expense rise. On the same time, a professionist interested in improving his mastery of English could join a collaborative learning community on English, but then the period of time between the conclusion of the course and the experimentation of acquired competencies in English could be too long, risking that when starting to talk he could have lost all the benefits of the online English course previously attended.

A second reason for this anomaly is that, in the case of e-learning, knowledge transfer does not impoverish the one who delivers it: the expertise remains even if shared. The problem is basically different and it can be recognized in the fact that the more knowledges are shared, the more their value tends to decrease. That is why one of the crucial problems in the e-learning market is represented, for the deliverers of education services, by the possibility to sell education without sharing the expertise that allows them to sell. This explains the deep caution shown by corporations in defending their know-how and the relevance assumed within the current debate by the intellectual property and copyright related to processes and good practices.

This new market, with all its anomalies, is at the same time a product and a relevant segment of a new economy. It is a product, as in a new economy, where the need of education, even for senior workers, is definitely higher than in other productive areas, and to fulfill this education the need for *new training* (based on Internet and mobile devices) appears to be as an obliged step. Further, digital learning provides new economy workers those conditions—motivation, performances, collaboration, and innovation—that are an integral part of their profession. The result is represented by the fact that the new economy is an important development factor supporting digital learning, so that it becomes one of its most promising subsegments, even more promising than e-commerce and e-business.

This reciprocity between digital economy and online/mobile education market remarks on and confirms some thesis previously developed.

First of all, digital learning verifies the mythological aspect of information society and its leading factors.

Myth, under the anthropological and functional perspective we have assumed as reference to this chapter, represents a demarcation of reality extensions that is a horizon where men place think to approach and know them. This ordering logic expresses itself through an accompanying narration (*mithologoumenon*) aimed to articulate and radicate it on a social and personal level.

Read under this perspective, digital learning works mythologically because it corresponds to the idea of an information and technology-based society, demonstrating to interpret properly its main characteristics. As a matter of fact, digital learning is an education model that accepts the challenge of speed (connoted both as speed of transference and speed of knowledge updating), it is structurally virtual (emancipating teaching/learning from space and time), it turns the network structure and the global open up into its natural dimensions. Besides this, digital learning also provides an accompanying narration to the myth of the information society. It is a narration about competencies rapidly aging, about information that needs to be at our disposal "everywhere, anytime for everyone," about the collaborative dimension that appears to be effectively possible only in a telematic network.

If we go back to the reciprocity of new economy and e-learning (new economy "pushes" e-learning that, when supported, feeds new economy, promoting it) we easily understand the economical and social origins of the myth and of its accompanying narration: myth feeds economy, through the issue of the need for incessant update it creates a market—the Longlife Education market—destined to extend infinitely, helps the employment of new professional figures.

When knowledge is transformed into a good to share, digital learning confirms also the idea previously advanced, through Baudrillard's (1976) analysis: the fact that information society is connoted by the supremacy of symbolic goods. From this point of view, online education perfectly embodies the third-level of simulacral activities: it plays on secondary needs contemporarily supported; it does not produce goods, but learning, that is something extremely difficult to measure, so that it is not possible to blame only educational actions, when not obtained; it sells competencies to the user, something so immaterial and extremely subjective that can be only embodied by hyperspecialized experts.

So, the learning economy is connoted as a mythological device creating a market on a symbolic good of knowledge and socially legitimating professional figures even more competent in topics that are progressively less decisive. As Panikkar (1990) would say, it is necessary to understand if it is a new starting point, a transitory phase, or only the fulfillment of a destiny. We are in front of a new humanism, or of the despair of finiteness?

References

Baudrillard, J. (1976). *L'echange symbolyque et la mort.* Paris: Gallimard.

Beer, S. (1993). *Origins of team syntegrity.* Retrieved October 2, 2007, from http://www.staffordbeer.com/papers/Origins%20Team%20Syntegrity.pdf

Benedikt, M. (1991). *Cyberspace: First steps.* Cambridge, MA: The MIT Press.

Benjamin, W. (1955). *Das kunstwerk in zeitalter seiner technischen reproduzierbarkeit in schriften.* Frankfurt am Main: Suhrkamp Verlag.

Boghossian, P. (2006). *Fear of knowledge: Against relativism and constructivism.* Oxford: Oxford University Press.

Breton, P. (1993). *L'utopie de la communication.* Paris: La Découverte.

Castells, M. (1996). *The rise of the network society.* Malden, MA: Blackwell.

Dayan, D., & Katz, E. (1992). *Media Events: The live broadcasting of history.* Cambridge, MA: Harvard University Press.

Eppler, M.J. (2002). Le savoir dans le contexte de l'entreprise. Individus, systémes et socialisation. *Quaderni dell'Istituto Comunicazione e Formazione,* 5. Retrieved October 2, 2007, from http://www.icief.com.unisi.ch/quaderno5.pdf

Feyerabend, P. (1975). *Against method.* London: Verso.

Fiske, J., & Hartley, J. (1978). *Reading television.* London: Methuen.

Gibson, W. (1984). *Neuromancer.* New York: Ace Books.

Goddman, N. (1968). *Languages of art: An approach to a theory of symbols.* Indianapolis, IN: Bobbs-Merrill.

Kotler, P., Jain, D.C., & Maesincee, S. (2000). *Marketing moves. A new approach to profits, growth and renewal.* Boston: Harvard Business School Press.

Kuhn, T. (1970). The structure of scientific revolutions (2nd ed). Chicago: U Chicago .

Lakatos, I. (1980). The methodology of scientific research programmes. Cambridge, MA: Cambridge University Press.

Levy, P. (1995a). *Qu'est-ce que le virtuel?* Paris: La Découverte.

Levy, P. (1997). *Cyberculture. Raport au conseil de l'Europe.* Paris: Odile Jacob.

Maldonado, T. (1992). *Reale e virtuale.* Milano: Feltrinelli.

Mattelart, A. (1996). *La mondialisation de la communication.* Paris: PUF.

Mattelart, A. (2000). *Histoire de la société de l'information.* Paris: La Découverte.

Morin, E., & Kern, A.B. (1993). *Terre-patrie.* Paris: Editions de Seuil.

Neveu, E. (1994). *Une société de la communication?* Paris: Montchrestien.

Neveu, E. (2002). Profession : Journaliste. *Sciences Humaines*, *129*(7), 22-25.

Panikkar, R. (1979). The myth of pluralism: The Tower of Babel. A meditation on non-violence. *Cross Currents, 29,* 197-230.

Popper, K.R. (1963). *Conjectures and confutations: The growth of scientific knowledge*. London: Routledge and Kegan Paul.

Rivoltella, P.C. (2003). *Costruttivismo e pragmatica della comunicazione on line. Socialità e didattica in Internet*. Trento: Erickson.

Rossi, A. (2002). *Il mito del mercato*. Troina: Città aperta.

Schiller, H. I. (1969). *Mass communications and American empire*. New York: M. Kelley.

Shannon, C., Weaver, W. (1948). *The Mathematical theory of communication*. Urbana: University of Illinois Press.

Thompson, J.B. (1995). *The media and the modernity. A social theory of the media*. Cambrdige: Polity Press.

Turkle, S. (1995). *Life on the screen. Identity in the age of Internet*. New York: Simon & Schuster.

Virilio, P. (1998). *La bombe informatique*. Paris: Galilée.

Weinberger, D. (2002). *Small pieces looseley joined*. New York: Perseus Books.

Zolla, E. (1992). *Uscite dal mondo*. Milano: Adelphi.

Chapter II

Communicating in the Information Society:
New Tools for New Practices

Lorenzo Cantoni, University of Lugano, Switzerland

Stefano Tardini, University of Lugano, Switzerland

Abstract

The present chapter provides a conceptual framework for the newest digital com-munication tools and for the practices they encourage, stressing the communication opportunities they offer and the limitations they impose. In this chapter, Internet-based communication technologies are regarded as the most recent step in the development of communication technologies. This approach helps have a broad perspective on the changes information and communication technologies (ICT) are bringing along in the social practices of so called knowledge society. As a matter of fact, these changes need to be considered within an "ecological" approach, that is, an approach that provides a very wide overview on the whole context (both in synchronic terms and in diachronic ones) where ICT are spreading. In the second part of the chapter, the authors present two examples of relevant social practices that are challenged by the most recent ICT, namely journalism (news market) and Internet search engines.

Introduction

New digital communication tools (information and communication technologies, or ICT) rapidly spreading worldwide have a deep impact on the way we interact and communicate, both in everyday life and in our professional activities; they are changing our social life and our social practices. For instance, the way we can access, edit and share documents (movies, songs, pictures, images, texts or any other kind of documents) has changed, as well as the way we relate to government, access health, banking, and other public services, the way we work, play, learn, buy and sell, search information, meet (un)known people, and so on (Cantoni & Tardini, 2006).

The rapid growth of these new technologies has raised the issue of *digital literacy*, creating a divide between those who can (are able/have access to) manage them and those who cannot (are not able/do not have access to), as well as between those who are *digital natives* and those who have "migrated" into digital technologies (*digital immigrants*). The term *digital divide* refers to "the inequalities that exist in Internet access based on income, age, education, race/ethnicity, and ... between rural and metropolitan areas, through such factors as pricing and infrastructure" (Hill, 2004, p. 27).

However, a first important clarification is needed here: it is not the first time new communication technologies have arisen and caused changes in a society, nor will it be the last. Suffice it to think of the enormous changes brought along by the invention of writing and the alphabet, which made it possible also for people who are both spatially and temporally separated to communicate (Danesi, 2006); again, the invention and the diffusion of letterpress print gave rise to the first assembly line, embedding "the word itself deeply in the manufacturing process and [making] it into a kind of commodity" (Ong, 2002, p. 118).

Generally speaking, every "technology of the word" has always brought along larger or smaller, positive or negative changes in the contexts where it was adopted (McLuhan, 2001), always raising the issues of literacy and access to information.

In a sense, every new communication technology spreading in a given society has always configured social class of "scribes," that is, of those people who are able to use that given technology within that society. After being managed only by social elite of the scribes, some technologies are then "socialized," that is, they get to be mastered by most of the society. It is the case, for instance, of reading and writing, which remained a long while after it was invented only a matter for scribes: those who needed a written text had necessarily to turn to them. For instance, Charlemagne (747-814) could be the emperor of the Holy Roman Empire even though he was hardly able to write (hence the legend that he could not write at all) and learned to read only in his adulthood; nowadays illiterate people are in fact almost excluded from social life. Not all communication technologies reach the stage of socialized literacy: for example, the use of the telegraph has always remained in the hands of some operators who had the knowledge of how to send and receive telegrams. Furthermore, some technologies get to be socialized only with regard to the fruition of the message, while its production remains a matter for experts. In the Western society, for instance, TV and radio are nowadays completely socialized in the sense that everybody is able to use TV sets and radios in order to receive the programs they broadcast; but when it comes to the production of TV and radio messages, only skilled operators can do that (although this state of affairs is being challenged by digital audio and video editing).

Something similar is happening to digital information and communication technologies (ICT), which are becoming more and more a necessary tool in order to be fully introduced into the information society ("a society in which low-cost information and ICT are in general use") or "knowledge society"—where "knowledge" stresses "the fact that the most valuable asset is investment in intangible, human, and social capital and that the key factors are knowledge and creativity" (europa. eu.int/comm/employment_social/knowledge_society/index_en.htm). In other terms, digital literacy is more and more a requirement in the knowledge society, at least in terms of digital fruition: being able to access digital information is something that cannot be anymore referred to "digital scribes," but is becoming more and more a personal requirement.

The comparison with the model of linguistic change can help explain how a technology is accepted or rejected by a given community/society. The introduction of a new element into a language system follows three steps: the new element is created/invented by someone who first coins it and uses it (or a new sense is given to an existing element: *innovation*), the new element is then adopted and used by the hearer (*adoption*), and finally, the new element spreads in the system: a new word becomes part of the lexicon of a language, is inserted in the language dictionaries, and so on (*change*). "Linguistic change is the diffusion or the generalization of an innovation, that is, necessarily, a series of subsequent adoptions" (Coseriu, 1981, p. 56). Similarly, a technological innovation needs different steps and—often—a long-term process (Rogers, 1995) in order to be accepted and to spread in a society, where it must partly overlap with other existing technologies, partly overcome old ones (Cantoni & Tardini, 2006, pp. 7-18).

As a matter of fact, the media market is like an ecological system where the introduction of a new element (e.g., a new animal species) affects the whole system, entering in competition with the other existing elements and causing a re-organization of the whole system. With respect to this process, Roger Fidler coined the term of *mediamorphosis*, stressing the fact that new communication media do not arise from nothing, as through spontaneous generation, but emerge step by step from the metamorphoses of earlier media, in a context where other communication technologies pre-existed, which had their own role in supporting specific social practices. Furthermore, pre-existing media are usually not completely displaced, but they go on evolving and adapting themselves to the new context, usually by carving out a niche for themselves (Fidler, 1997).

Thus, it is crucial to understand the context where new ICT are spreading. Generally speaking, the emerging of digital technologies is driving the media market towards globalization thanks to the opportunities offered by digitization.

The present chapter aims at providing a conceptual framework for understanding the newest digital communication tools and the practices they encourage, stressing the communication opportunities these technologies offer and the limitations they impose. The first paragraph will outline the framework, presenting the main tools and devices that allow digital communication and the characteristics of the settings they rely on, and providing a four-layer taxonomy for the understanding of new digital communication tools. The second paragraph will present two examples of relevant social practices where ICT play a seminal role, namely journalism (news market) and Internet search engines. It will then explore how they are changing as a consequence of the diffusion of new ICT.

Background

Before presenting some new practices that new communication technologies support, and in order to better understand them, it is important to have an overview of the devices and the tools that make these practices possible.

Devices and Tools

The most common device that supports communication in the knowledge society is no doubt the *computer*: it is no accident that the kind of communication that takes place by means of new ICT has been often referred to as *computer mediated communication* (CMC), usually intended as the interpersonal communication through a computer. However, this term, referring to this particular device, does not take into account the interactions that ICT allow by means of other devices, such as mobile phones, PDAs, iPods, and other mp3 players, TV sets, videogames consoles, and others. As a matter of fact, nowadays the same kind of interaction that is made possible by a computer is made possible also (at least partially, in some cases) by these devices. The basic technology that underlies communication mediated by new ICT is the *Internet*, the "global network connecting millions of computers" (http://www. Webopedia.com/TERM/I/Internet.html). Through the Internet almost every kind of communication is allowed: it is possible to have spoken conversations as well as written interactions; one-to-one communications as well as one-to-many or even many-to-many ones; it is possible to publish written texts with images and audio and video as well; it is possible to communicate in real time or to send messages that will be read later; it is possible to send and share documents of all kinds; and so on. The features of the communications taking place over the Internet are strongly dependent on the tools employed: different tools impose different constraints and offer different options to interlocutors. (Cantoni & Tardini, 2006, p. 43)

The Internet offers indeed a variety of communication tools. The most common and most diffused one is *e-mail*. Through e-mail it is possible to send a text message to one or more addressees simultaneously. E-mail is a low-bandwidth, text-based technology, but since it is possible to attach all kinds of files to an e-mail message, it allows also the exchange of multimedia documents between interlocutors. E-mail is mostly used as an asynchronous tool, somehow like normal mail. Two other tools, based on the technology of e-mail, are to be mentioned here: *mailing lists* and *newsgroups*, which allow for an easy delivery of a text message to a group of addressees.

Over the Internet it is possible to have also interpersonal synchronous communications, either spoken or written. *Chat* or *messenger systems*, for instance, allow for a synchronous exchange of written text messages, while *desktop (audio/video) conference systems* and *VoIP systems* allow for spoken interactions over the Internet, where interlocutors can either hear each other (as in VoIP systems and in audioconferences) or even (partially) see each other, as in videoconferences. A more complex interaction environment is that of *3D multi-user virtual environments*, where subscribed participants are represented in a 3D virtual world (also called *metaverse*) by an *avatar*, that is, a virtual character users can move in the virtual space in order to get closer to other participants, chat with them, perform actions allowed by the virtual world, and so on. One of the most known and diffused of such environments is *Second Life* (http://secondlife.com), a 3D online digital world imagined, created, and owned by its residents. In June 2007 Second Life had more than 7,500,000 residents; its virtual environment has been exploited by companies, businesses, universities, and other institutions to expand and support their commercial, educational, and institutional activities (see, for instance, Kemp & Livingstone, 2006).

Of course, the Internet-based communication tool that, together with e-mail, is the most known and used is the *World Wide Web* (WWW), a system of Internet servers that support specially formatted documents. The documents are formatted in a markup language called HTML (*HyperText Markup Language*) that supports links to other documents, as well as graphics, audio, and video files. This means you can jump from one document to another simply by clicking on hot spots. (http://www.Webopedia.com/TERM/W/World_Wide_Web.html)

The most important "space" of the WWW are the well-known *Web sites*; however, we will focus here on the main tools and services of so-called *Web 2.0*, that is, the second generation of the World Wide Web that is focused on the ability for people to collaborate and share information online. Web 2.0 basically refers to the transition from static HTML Web pages to a more dynamic Web. (http://www.Webopedia. com/TERM/W/Web_2_point_0.html)

In other terms, rather than aiming at providing users with information, Web 2.0 tools "enable user participation on the Web and manage to recruit a large number of users as authors of new content," thus obliterating "the clear distinction between information providers and consumers" (Kolbitsch & Maurer, 2006, p. 187). Thus, we can claim that Web 2.0 tools have the potential of moving further the process of socialization of Internet-based communication technologies, by socializing also the activity of publishing on the Web.

The main tools we are referring to here are blogs and wikis. *Blogs* (short for *Web logs*) are Web pages that serve as a publicly accessible personal journal for an individual or a group, a sort of Web-based electronic diaries that reflect the person-alities of their authors. Blogs are very useful tools for micropublishing, since they "enable the process of quickly and easily committing thoughts to the Web, offer limited discussion/talkbacks, and syndicate new items to make it easier to keep up without constant checking back" (Hall, 2002). Blogs "are not open to the public for authoring, and there is no well-defined publishing process as in newspapers" (Kolbitsch & Maurer, 2006, p. 190). The rapid spread of blogs has given rise to the creation of a real network of more or less loosely interconnected Weblogs (so-called *blogosphere*), where the author of one blog can easily comment on the articles of other blogs.

Strictly connected to blogs is RSS (Rich Site Summary or RDF Site Syndication), an XML format developed to syndicate Web content, thus helping people receive new information items as soon as they are published. Users can subscribe to RSS content, and automatically receive new info, such as news feeds, updates, blog's items, and the like. Similar in nature is *podcasting*, the possibility of automatic download of audio files onto an iPod (or other mp3 players) from Web services one has subscribed to.

Wikis (from the Hawaiian word "wiki wiki," which means "quick") are collaborative Web sites comprised of the perpetual collective work of many authors. Similar to a blog in structure and logic, a wiki allows anyone to edit, delete or modify content that has been placed on the Web site using a browser interface, including the work of previous authors. (http://www.Webopedia.com/TERM/w/wiki.html)

In a sense, wikis seem to have materialized the dreams of the pioneers of hypertext, such as Vannevar Bush, Ted Nelson, and Douglas Engelbart, and of the early hyper-text theorists, that of having a shared environment where anybody could produce, edit, and store any kind of information, thus blurring the distinction between authors and readers. The most famous wiki-based Web site is no doubt the Wikipedia, the "free encyclopedia that anyone can edit" (http://en.wikipedia.org/wiki/Main_Page). As observed by Kolbitsch and Maurer (2006), "the success of Wikipedia builds on the tight involvement of the users, the sense of the community, and a dedication to developing a knowledge repository of unprecedented breadth and depth" (p. 195). Started in 2001, in December 2007 the English version of Wikipedia had more than 2,100,000 articles, the German and French Wikipedias more than 500,000, and also the Polish, Dutch, Japanese, Spanish, Italian, Portuguese, Russian, Swedish, and Chinese versions had more than 150,000 articles; in December 2007, 250 different Wikipedias were online (the complete list can be found at: http://meta.wikimedia.org/wiki/List_of_Wikipedias).

Finally, the diffusion of *community-based networking services* has to be mentioned. These are Web-based services that rely on the community of their users in order to let them store, organize, and share different kind of documents, such as photos (e.g., Flickr—www.flickr.com) and bookmarked Webpages (e.g., del.icio.us—http://del.icio.us). Users of such services can add their documents to their online space in the service, tag them, comment on them, and share them with other users; the key element of the system is the tagging activity, since the tags added by a user to his/her documents are used for describing and categorizing the documents, thus making them available for other users' searches. Such services can be seen as a Web-based evolution of file sharing systems (such as Napster and Kazaa), which allow users to share (sometimes illegally) their files by means of a peer-to-peer architecture.

Conceptually similar to community-based networking systems are some features of Web services like eBay, Amazon, and similar ones; in these services the behaviors and the opinions of users (in the form of a rating given to a seller, of a comment on a book, and so on) are used to create "social" (in a broad sense) networks, such as clusters of users with similar interests, which are in some way connected with each other, but cannot communicate. Community-based networking services are often used as an alternative to "traditional" search engines; however, as we will see in the next section, also Internet search engines are undergoing a pragmatic/social turn, in the sense that they are trying to take more and more into account the actual behaviors of their users (Cantoni, Faré, & Tardini, 2006).

Features of Electronic Communication

All these tools allow for different kinds of communications, since they provide different communication settings. Generally speaking, Internet-based communication has peculiar features that differentiate it from both oral and written communication; at the same time, it shares many features with both oral and written communication. Some authors coined the word Netspeak (Crystal, 2001, p. 17), which emphasizes the double face of CMC: "The heart of the matter seems to be its relationship to spoken and written language" (Crystal, 2001, p. 24). We will not focus here on the different settings allowed by the different tools; we will just outline the main features of electronic texts, which depend both on their support and on the communication setting in which they are produced (Cantoni & Tardini, 2006, pp. 54-57).

Electronic texts are *directly inaccessible to human senses.* Whereas books can be directly accessed by human senses (sight in particular), texts coded in computer files need the mediation of other tools (hardware and software) in order to be seen and read. Electronic documents share this feature with other supports for information, such as, for instance, vinyl records, or audio and video cassettes. Furthermore, electronic texts are inaccessible as a whole, since it is possible to access only a part of an electronic text at a time, namely the part that appears on the monitor.

Electronic texts are *immaterial*, since they are physically just a sequence of bits. The immateriality of digital documents makes them very easy to transport, reproduce, and access.

Electronic texts are perfectly *reproducible*. Of course, technical reproduction is not a novelty of electronic texts (Benjamin, 1973). However, digitization brought this process to an end. In electronic texts, not only it is impossible to distinguish the master from the copies, as, for instance, in printed books and in cinematographic films, but often it is not even possible to locate them in the space, due to their immateriality.

Electronic texts may be made—thanks to computer networking—*always accessible* without any limit of space. A document published on the Internet is always "close" and available to its readers, wherever they are, provided that they have an Internet access.

An electronic text *can be modified* as much as one wants. In digital documents, parts of a text can be added, deleted, or edited at a user's will. Unlike printed texts, which cannot be modified anymore once they have been concluded and printed, electronic texts remain always at the author's (and reader's) disposal and can be altered whenever required; in this sense, electronic texts may be said to be "never over," as wikis clearly show. With regard to this feature, digital writing is similar to hand writing, which allows as many text modifications as one wants; however, in hand written texts, modifications leave tracks and remain visible always, while electronic ones can be altered without leaving any trace.

Electronic texts are potentially *multimedia* documents. As a matter of fact, thanks to their digital nature, in electronic documents elements belonging to different semiotic codes can be integrated, such as pictures, images, audios, videos, and animations.

Electronic texts are *persistent*: persistency is a basic feature of CMC, because of the very nature of the medium used. Digital documents leave a persistent trace in the electronic world, which can be recorded and read many times.

Electronic texts are often the result of *interactive communications*: as a matter of fact, computer mediated communication is always interactive, since it makes it easy and fast for senders and receivers to interact. In this way, Internet communication is really (potentially) dialogic and interactive, thus differentiating itself from the mass-media model where the message is unilaterally broadcast. Furthermore, Internet communication allows a higher degree of *customization* than mass-media communication: electronic messages may be designed in order to meet more closely the needs of single users or of specific groups.

A Four-Layer Taxonomy

The different technologies of the word mankind has invented can be organized according to different perspectives, taking into account their peculiarities as well as their common features. We thus propose the following taxonomy, organized along four relevant layers to be considered in relation to the Internet, and underline what is the place of the Internet (Cantoni & Tardini, 2006, pp. 23-25).

The first layer considers *which aspects of communication a technology is able to fix* outside the evanescent live act of communication. In fact, every technology can represent only some aspects of the world communicative acts refer to, such as their verbal content, still images (black and white or colored), moving images, sounds, and so forth, while omitting many others: intonation, physical setting, flavors, smells, and so on. From this point of view electronic media allow for a great convergence of previous media. Written digital texts can be combined with digital images, sounds, movies, graphics, and so forth.

The second layer considers *the activities and processes required for fixing and objectifying* parts of reality into a communicative act, the resources and costs needed. What are the processes required to produce, modify, replicate, and preserve a communication object belonging to a given technology of the word? If we think of handwriting, we know that it requires a big effort to reproduce a book but we know also that manuscripts can last many centuries without being corrupted or damaged. With the printing press, reproducing a text has become much more efficient (both from the point of view of time and resources and from the point of view of accuracy). In handwriting, cancellations and modifications are easy to carry out, while in print they are not at all easy, and require the set-up of a new "original" document. Electronic texts, on the other hand, partake of both modes, since they can be modified and reproduced very easily. Yet, the electronic world seems very fragile in terms of preservation, and we do not know whether an electronic document will be preserved for centuries. What we do know is that physical supports are not strong, and hardware and software standards change at a very fast pace, requiring a continuous upgrading of every digital collection.

Connected with the physical supports of communication is also *the possibility of moving them in space*, which constitutes the third layer of taxonomy. While in the period of orality, knowledge moved along with the knowing persons, distribution of written and printed documents made this movement much easier. If books are physical objects to be moved in space, the telegraph and the telephone required only a physical connection (the wire) and allowed for almost immediate transmissions. Wireless telegraph, radio, television, and mobile phones are all technologies which dispensed with the need for any physical link (besides the obvious hardware for sending and receiving signals). The Internet, from this point of view, allows for almost instant bidirectional and multidirectional communications, at a global level, being able to convey elements belonging to all sorts of semiotic codes.

Communication artifacts need also to *be accessed and interpreted*. Every technology of the word imposes a number of conditions for its fruition: speaking requires the air (the simplest condition to be met); writing requires light, whether natural or artificial; the telegraph, radio, and TV require electricity and suitable apparatuses. Electronic documents require hardware and software to be accessed. This raises the very delicate issue of *obsolescence*. Today we can read cuneiform documents because they require just eyes and light to be accessed, but we are unable to access a CD-ROM or a file on a hard-disk or the Internet without having suitable hardware and an appropriate piece of software. Obsolescence here is so fast that some supports used only a few years ago are no longer available (think, for example, of many data cassettes' or floppy-disks' formats), and files codified in "old" operating systems and software cannot communicate anything anymore. In the electronic world changes are the only stable rule.

Two Examples: The Practices of Providing and Searching Information in the Knowledge Society

In this section two examples of practices that in the last years have been seriously challenged by the spread of new technologies will be presented: journalism (and the news market) and Internet search engines. As it is clear, these practices are strictly related to one another, since both of them have to do with information. The news market deals with providing specific kinds of information, while Internet search engines deal with making any kind of information easily available to Internet users.

The News Market

Since the 1980s, the news market has been challenged by the diffusion of digital technologies: the computer first, the Internet and the latest tools, such as blogs. The changes these technologies are bringing in the sector are thorough:

The development of communications technologies in the news sector is transforming workplace relations and encouraging labour mobility. ... It is also enabling new media organizations to emerge with new types of work and new workplace activities. ... Opportunities to develop new types of content, use new forms of delivery and to develop new workplace practices are consequently challenging traditional practices within established news media organizations. (Harrison, 2006, p. 72)

Generally speaking, the situation digital technologies are configuring in the news market is a convergence of new technologies with existing ones: on the one side,

The Internet is being incorporated into other mass-media, in particular acting as a new and very important information source for them; on the other side, the Internet tends to include the existing media as an extra channel for the information they broadcast. (Cantoni & Tardini, 2006, p. 152)

As concerns the Internet as an information source for journalists, several studies show that the number of journalists using online sources is increasing more and more over time: for instance, the Eleventh Annual Survey of the Media, conducted by Euro RSCG Magnet together with the Columbia University, which in 2005 for the first time involved not only U.S. journalists, but also international ones, claims that:

Online news sites grew dramatically in importance, with 64% of journalists reporting that they often or sometimes use Web news in their day-to-day reporting, up from 34% in 2003... Reporters are increasingly taking advantage of the wealth of up-to-the-minute information at their fingertips ... This increasing reliance on online sources suggests that journalists, pressured by deadlines and other factors, may be forced by the challenges of their profession to sacrifice accuracy in their stories for immediacy of information. (Euro RSCG Magnet, 2005, pp. 16-17)

Among the online sources which journalists rely upon, blogs are gaining more and more consideration. Blogs are growing on the whole. According to a research conducted by comScore Networks, in the first quarter of 2005 50 million U.S. Internet users (i.e., about 30% of all U.S. Internet users) visited a blog, up from 34 million in the first quarter of 2004 (comScore Networks, 2005). In the particular case of journalists, according to Euro RSCG Magnet, 51% of them use Weblogs, a percentage that is significantly higher than that of blog visitors as a whole. Of those journalists who use blogs, 70% do so for work-related purposes, and in particular for finding story ideas, 53% for research and reference, 42%, and 36% for finding sources for their stories (Euro RSCG Magnet, 2005, p. 2). However, the reverse of the medal must be considered as well: the widespread use of blogs—and of online sources in general—by journalists has raised some critical issues. We dwell here upon two of them: the issue of trust and that of the role of journalists itself.

The issue of the credibility of Web information sources is one of the main concerns when dealing with the relationship between the Internet and other mass media. In a sense, the Internet has reproposed a situation similar to that which occurred when radio emerged (see Gackenbach & Ellerman, 1998, pp. 9-15):

Since the same receiving set and the same procedure allowed access to the pro-grams of broadcasting stations that were very different with regard to the quality of their contents and to the target public they addressed, how, then, was it possible to distinguish high-quality stations from low-quality ones? The hierarchy of sources the press had established suddenly appeared to be disrupted, in an undifferentiated jumble of words, sounds and programs. Analogously, in the Internet everything can be accessed by means of the same software (the browser), in a seemingly flat and indistinct network. (Cantoni & Tardini, 2006, p. 133)

Of course, this point becomes even more relevant in journalism. The same survey by Euro RSCG Magnet, points out also that journalists admit that they do not trust blogs: they see blogs as just another advertising outlet for corporations. Only 1% of them consider blogs as very credible sources, and only 22% foresee that blogs will become valuable journalistic tools (Euro RSCG Magnet, 2005). The big chal-lenge brought along by online sources in terms of trust is proved also by the fact that in 2005, 93% of journalists agreed "that they are excruciatingly careful about fact-checking their stories" (Euro RSCG Magnet, 2005, p. 21), while in 2003 only 59% of them agreed with this statement.

The widespread diffusion of blogs has challenged journalists' perception of their role and their work (and bloggers' perception as well). On one side, often journalists have a blog of their own, where they can express their opinions more freely than in traditional mass-media. On the other side, bloggers are "struggling to define their role as it relates to the media" (Euro RSCG Magnet, 2005, p. 27). What is their role within the mainstream media? Are they to be considered as journalists? Do they want to be considered as journalists? As a matter of fact, many bloggers do consider themselves as journalists, while others prefer to stress their outsider status, thus es-chewing the name of journalist and making of blogging a real profession (*professional blogger*). Furthermore, blogs are strongly fostering the diffusion of so-called *citizen journalism* (or *grassroots journalism*), that is, a kind of journalism where citizens have an active role in gathering, analyzing, and spreading news and information; the power of this kind of journalism consists in the quickness and easiness with which a citizen can tell the world what s/he has seen and experienced. For instance, in the case of a sudden and disastrous event, citizen journalists and bloggers are quicker than any other journalist, because they happen to be on the scene. This occurred, among other events, with the tsunami—when the lists of the survivors in the hospitals that were published on the blogs were more updated than those published by governments and institutions—and with the terrorist attack in London, when blogs could publish almost in real time news, comments, photos, and so on (Faré, 2006). In this context, of course, the issue of trust and credibility is—once again—pivotal, as some recent scandals concerning unfounded and unverified information published and spread by bloggers confirm. Blogs, however, have proved also to be useful in unmasking unfair journalistic practices, thus playing a role of control towards the media system, as well as the political and economical ones.

When it comes to the Internet as a channel for broadcasting news, the situation seems to be—at least in the U.S.—that of a deeper and deeper integration of online capabilities into "traditional" practices.

Still, Ross and Middleberg (1999, p. 3) noticed that broadcast stations have been slow to establish Web sites, and to showcase news over promotional material. Of the Web sites affiliated with local broadcast television stations, only a small fraction take full advantage of the capabilities of the Internet by offering "real news."

Only 3 years later the situation looked very different, and the integration of online and off-line information was accelerating: Middleberg and Ross (2002) found that "Web readership now often rivals or surpasses print readership. The Web is not an incremental add-on to readership, viewership or profitability. Increasingly, it is the soul of a publication" (p. 4). Moreover, original content on Web sites increased as well, in particular for newspapers, thus showing that more journalism jobs were becoming online-only. With the advent of Web 2.0, new challenges have arisen for newspapers: a survey conducted in 2006 with the most 100 circulated newspapers in the U.S. showed that "newspapers are taking advantages of online capabilities, and have expanded upon their traditional strategies to launch aggressive online programs that include many sophisticated elements" (The Bivings Group, 2006, p. 2). According to this survey, 76 of these newspapers offer RSS feeds on their Web sites, 31 offer podcasts, 80 offer at least one reporter blog, 33 offer a sort of "most popular" function, only 7 a bookmarking function. It is interesting to note that only 23 Web sites of these newspapers require registration to view articles online (significantly, 7 of the 10 most circulated, and only 2 of the bottom 10), and in most of them registration is free of charge. From this research it might be concluded that "newspaper publishers are responding to decreasing print circulation and audiences by developing more aggressive and extensive Web strategies" (The Bivings Group, 2006, p. 22).

However, the situation in other countries is not the same as in the U.S. An analogous research conducted in Italy on the 50 most diffused newspapers, for instance, shows a different situation, where the adoption of the most recent Web capabilities is still very low, as if the Internet were still considered as a competitor to newspapers rather than a complementary opportunity: 19 of the 50 most diffused Italian newspapers require registration, very often with a charge, to access the newspaper's archive; 13 of these newspapers offer RSS feeds, 8 offer a blog, only 8 offer videos and only 3 offer podcasts; furthermore, a large gap emerges between the 10 top newspapers and the 10 bottom ones (Conti, 2006).

To sum up the issue, we can single out five areas where online information presents a clear added value: (1) *multimedia*, online information sources can offer information coded through different media: texts, audio, pictures, photos, animations, movies; (2) *interaction*, information Web sites can offer a higher level of interactivity than any other mass medium, allowing users to interact both with the Web site's system and with other people through the Web site; as we have seen, the interaction possibilities offered by Web 2.0 tools are currently the major challenge for the online presence of newspapers; (3) *persistence*, online information can be easily archived, re-used, and left continuously at readers' disposal; (4) *in-depth studies*, the easiness of online publishing makes it possible also to provide in-depth analyses and studies of given information, and to make them always available to readers; (5) *immediateness*, nowadays online information can be published almost just-in-time, updated very easily, and used just-in-time, as the case of blog clearly shows (Cantoni & Tardini, 2006, pp. 155-157).

Internet Search Engines

As it has been already mentioned before, one of the advantages of ICT, information availability at levels never possible or even thinkable before, is at the same time one of its most relevant issues and challenges, the so called *information overload*. Users can access so many resources and so many documents on the Internet that they are flooded with information and are not able to understand which ones are really relevant and useful to them and to select them among the others (Cantoni et al., 2006).

Over the Internet, search engines are the tools specifically developed to address this issue, helping users finding relevant sources, which can answer their informative needs.

In this section, a brief presentation of search engines is done, stressing how they have integrated and are integrating users themselves to better their own answering strategies.

First of all, search engines can be divided into two different families: that of directories and that of proper (full text) search engines.

The first ones (e.g., Yahoo! Directories, About, and Dmoz) have a tree-shaped structure, list Web sites as a whole, and are managed by human editors. In fact, a human editor has to decide whether a Web site is of enough quality to be included in the directory, and—in case the answer is yes—on which branch.

Proper search engines (e.g., Google, Yahoo! Search, MSN, AOL, Ask, etc.) are, on the contrary, pieces of software, which crawl the Internet (an activity usually referred to as "spidering"), copy single Web pages in their databases and index them following given rules, according to which pages are assigned to given keywords in a given order/rank. While strategies to analyze Web pages in order to identify their relevant keywords have been bettered over the last years, due to great improvements in natural language processing (computational linguistics), search engines had to incorporate in their ranking algorithms also "extrinsic" elements, that is, elements that are not deducible from the code and the address (URL) of the Web page itself.

In fact, in order to provide relevant answers, search engines started to consider (of course, we are using the verb as a metaphor, being applied to a piece of software) not only the single pages, but also the Web as an ecological system, and the way users behave when accessing it.

The most used extrinsic element is the so called "link popularity," which plays a relevant role, for instance, in Google. According to it, pages are given a page rank depending on the number of back-links they have (the links referring to the page from other Web sites), and on the page rank of the Web sites from which the back-links come. In other words, link popularity reinterprets a link as being a citation. The more a document is cited, the more it is considered important, or, like votes, the more a page is voted, the higher it goes. Links are furthermore also an indirect measure of accesses: the more back-links a Web site has, the more it is likely that visitors will access it (in ancient times, there was the motto: *all roads bring to Rome...*, that is, the capital of the empire).

If link popularity takes into consideration *directly* the actual citations/votes by Web publishers, and *inferentially,* the actual paths of Web surfers, click popularity measures them directly. It takes into consideration the actual clicks of users on the search engine's result page, reorganizing the presented elements depending on how users react to them, clicking or not.

Another extrinsic element being integrated into search engines' ranking algorithms is money: Web publishers can buy given keywords, getting then a better positioning for them. Of course, it is a quite extra-content element, but it can be useful to measure the commitment of the publisher, which "puts its money where its mouth is," to quote a popular saying, and goes perfectly in line with the search engine business (unfortunately this sometimes makes them accept political censorship in order to be allowed in given countries, as it happens, for instance, in China; see Deibert & Villeneuve, 2005).

Other extrinsic elements take into consideration how much frequently the Web site is updated, on the publisher's side, or the position of the users, on their side (for instance, if one is looking for a laundry, no point in answering the "better laundry" in itself as it is much better to provide a list of laundries in close proximity).

A few words are to be spent to present the Alexa service, which is quite similar to that of a search engine. It relies onto the actual navigations of its users, who have to install a dedicated plug-in in their browser: once its users visit a Web site, Alexa tells them which other Web sites are shared by those who visited that same Web site, offering a service similar to that of Amazon, which tells "Customers who bought this item also bought..."

For a certain period, search engines used in their indexing activities dedicated meta-tags, namely the keywords meta-tag, a tag listing the keywords relevant for a Web page, added by its own editor in the source code itself. After a while, however, due to a massive search engine spamming (i.e., an unfair use of that meta-tag, for instance listing, for the Website of a little B&B in Tuscany keywords like: "tourism in Italy," "Florence," etc.) its use in ranking algorithm has dramatically declined. To provide the same kind of information, in the Web 2.0, folksonomies were born (see, for instance, del.icio.us at http://del.icio.us). A folksonomy, or social tagging, is a list of tags collaboratively attached to a resource by its users (and publishers). While a single publisher can lie declaring a document's meta tags, many independent readers will not, at least if numbers are high enough, this is the folksonomy's claim, a claim similar to the one supporting the Wikipedia.

In this section, a brief presentation of search engines has shown how they have to take into consideration not only the content of Web sites, as it can be understood through its Web pages' source code, but also their context, be it the ecological system of the Web itself, or the actual navigation practices of Web surfers.

Conclusion and Future Trends

In this chapter, Internet-based communication technologies (and Web 2.0 tools, in particular) have been regarded as the last step in the development of communication technologies. This approach is particularly useful in order to have a broad perspective on the changes ICT are bringing along in the social practices of so called knowledge society. As a matter of fact, new ICT emerged in a media market already covered by other technologies, where they had to "negotiate" their space. The new configuration of the media market has brought along new communication practices, and these, in turn, made new social practices emerge, since communication permeates any other social practice.

Two specific practices have been presented in the chapter, both dealing directly with information management, namely journalism and Internet search engines.

Journalism and the news market have been seriously challenged by the spread of Internet-based technologies and of Web 2.0 in particular. As has been shown, the information sources of journalists are changing, thus reraising the issue of their trust and credibility; the process of delivering news is changing, since the Internet is gaining more and more space in comparison to newspapers; the role itself of journalists is challenged, since bloggers are entering the market; and so on.

Analogously, even a very recent and ICT-based practice, such as that of searching information over the Internet, is undergoing some radical changes, due mainly to the diffusion of Web 2.0 tools. Internet search engines, "are trying more and more to rely upon pragmatic features of Web sites, that is, they are taking into account the behaviors of people who publish a Web site and people who visit it. This turn can be traced back to the growing awareness that Web sites—and, broadly speaking, electronic communication—are used by real communities of persons in order to fulfill real communicative needs." (Cantoni et al., 2006, p. 61)

Both examples show the importance of digital literacy in the knowledge society: in the specific fields of journalism and Internet search engines, being able to publish online information and/or to retrieve it guarantees inclusion in the society, while those who are not able to deal with online information will be more and more excluded from social life. As has been shown, Web 2.0 tools and services are increasing the possibility for Internet users to publish information on the Web, thus lowering the digital divide not only in terms of access to digital information or services, but also in terms of the publication of digital content.

These changes concern not only the field of information management, but also many other social practices, as is shown by the changes in the way we teach and learn (e-learning), work, buy, and sell (e-business and e-commerce), relate to government and other public services (e-government), access health (e-health), use banking services (e-banking), and so on.

References

Benjamin, W. (1973). The work of art in the age of mechanical reproduction. In H. Arendt (Ed.), *Illuminations* (pp. 211-44). London: Fontana Press.

Bivings Group. (2006, August 1). *The use of the Internet by America's newspapers.* Retrieved October 3, 2007, from http://www.bivingsreport.com/campaign/newspapers06_tz-fgb.pdf

Cantoni, L., Faré, M., & Tardini, S. (2006). A communicative approach to Web communication: The pragmatic behavior of Internet search engines. *QWERTY. Rivista italiana di tecnologia cultura e formazione*, 1(1), 49-62.

Cantoni, L., & Tardini, S. (2006). *Internet (Routledge introductions to media and communications)*. London, New York, NY: Routledge.

comScore Networks. (2005, August). *Behaviors of the blogosphere: Understanding the scale, composition and activities of Weblog audiences.* Retrieved October 3, 2007, from http://www.comscore.com

Conti, L. (2006, August 7). *I quotidiani italiani e internet*. Retrieved October 3, 2007, from http://www.pandemia.info/studio%20giornali%20online.pdf

Coseriu, E. (1981). *Sincronia, diacronia e storia. Il problema del cambio linguistico*. Torino: Boringhieri.

Crystal, D. (2001). *Language and the Internet*. Cambridge: Cambridge University Press.

Danesi, M. (2006). Alphabets and the principle of least effort. *Studies in Communication Sciences*, 6(1), 47-62.

Deibert, R.J., & Villeneuve, N. (2005). Firewalls and power: An overview of global state censorship of the Internet. In M. Klang & A. Murray (Eds.), *Human rights in the digital age* (pp. 111-24). London, Sydney, Portland: GlassHouse Press.

Euro RSCG Magnet. (2005). *Rebuilding trust: Rebuilding credibility in the newsroom and the boardroom. Eleventh annual survey of the media with Columbia University Graduate School of Journalism*. New York, NY: Euro RSCG Magnet.

Faré, M. (2006). *Blog e giornalismo, l'era della complementarietà*. Lugano, Switzerland: University of Lugano, European Journalism Observatory. Retrieved October 3, 2007, from http://www.ejo.ch/analysis/newmedia/blog.pdf

Fidler, R. (1997). *Mediamorphosis. Understanding new media*. Thousand Oaks, CA: Pine Forge Press.

Gackenbach, J., & Ellerman, E. (1998). Introduction to psychological aspects of Internet use. In J. Gackenbach (Ed.), *Psychology and the Internet: Intrapersonal, interpersonal, and transpersonal implications* (pp. 1-26). London, San Diego, CA: Academic Press.

Hall, M. (2002, December 16). Give your users the power of the press with Weblogs and wikis. *Intranet Journal*. Retrieved October 3, 2007, from http://www.intranetjournal.com/articles/200212/ij_12_16_02a.html

Harrison, J. (2006). *News (Routledge introductions to media and communications)*. London, New York, NY: Routledge.

Hill, E. (2004). Some thoughts on e-democracy as an evolving concept. *Journal of E-Government*, 1(1), 23-39.

Kemp, J., & Livingstone, D. (2006, August 26). Putting a Second Life metaverse skin on learning management systems. In D. Livingstone & J. Kemp (Eds.), *Proceedings of the Second Life Education Workshop at the Second Life Community Convention* (pp.13-18), San Francisco, Paisley, UK: The University of Paisley. Retrieved October 3, 2007, from http://www.sloodle.com/whitepaper.pdf

Kolbitsch, J., & Maurer, H. (2006). The transformation of the Web: How emerging communities shape the information we consume. *Journal of Universal Computer Science*, 12(2), 187-213.

McLuhan, M. (2001). *Understanding media. The extensions of man*. London, New York, NY: Routledge.

Middleberg, D., & Ross, S.S. (2002). *The Middleberg/Ross media survey. Change and its impact on communications, 8th annual national survey*. Middleberg and Associates.

Ong, W.J. (2002). *Orality and literacy. The technologizing of the word*. London, New York, NY: Routledge.

Rogers, E.M. (1995). *Diffusion of innovations*. New York, NY: The Free Press.

Ross, S.S., & Middleberg, D. (1999, October). *The first annual Middleberg/Ross broadcast media in cyberspace study*. Middleberg and Associates.

Chapter III

Digital Media and Socialization

Mario Morcellini, University "La Sapienza," Rome, Italy

Abstract

The chapter reflects about the idea of crisis making evident that, in the case of communication, it doesn't mean a reduction of importance, but on the contrary increasing and growth. The actual communication fortune is in fact built on what seems a lack in our societies that is the vaporization and loss of social capital. In front of the modern individualism, the social system moves people to search other functions able to balance it: communication is certainly one of the functions. It doesn't help only individuals to get through the crisis, but it also promotes the increase of relations in the social system. The communication covers up the decline of traditional institutions (school, family, and religion) configuring a chance. Digital media, more than any other medium, becomes an expression of new social and cultural conditions.

Introduction

In order to understand the action of communication on individuals and on society, both as an industrial force and as a narrative and poetic force, it is important to look beyond the syntax of communication and to start from a reflection on the sociocultural framework of the passage to "late-modernity," which is often identified as a "crisis" from which to interpret the new meaning of communication with regard to the process of the construction of the self.

In the modern condition, the passage to modernity hinges on three elements of modification: the social actors, the institutions, and the liquid substitute of the media.

With regard to the first, the change solicited by communication relates to three dimensions:

1. **To the sphere of the self** and to the construction and redefinition, therefore, of the subjective identity of the social actors by means of the stimulation of an *interior revolution*: self-reflection. It is as though communication helps the individual to prepare for new visions of the world and for different styles of life which, in the long term, reflect on social relations and on the narration of the scenarios of life.

2. **To relationships,** whereby with a double key of interpretation communication is both a *symbolic gesture* to measure and improve oneself with regard to others, and also *passion*, in that modern man, overwhelmed by contextual crises, looks for a sense to life and for orientation in dealings with others.

3. **To action,** since communication helps both to multiply the exchanges between individuals and to react to states of crisis.

As far as the institutions are concerned, we intend to emphasize the semantic and sociocultural transformations undergone by the school, the family, and at work in the passage to the modern; that is to say, everything which in the past was defined as a source of stability, equilibrium, and social and personal certainty.

Many sociologists use the term *crisis* to describe this transformation, a term which is today a part of the history of any society (starting from the premodern world). However, the present state of sociocultural transition presents different characteristics in that rather than a crisis of sector or of a social subsystem, it regards all those institutions which, in past societies, organised time in society (religion, school, the family, work). In this scenario the crisis regards socialization in particular; that is, those processes which allow for the reproduction of values, of collective orientation and, therefore, of that cultural orientation which is the basis of subjective action.

A world in search of itself could be a suitable metaphor to describe the image of a time which is characterized by the triumph of uncertainties, the great accumulation of sources of insecurity, of fear, and of lack of trust, counterpoised to the idea of a society founded principally on certainty, on trust, and on the possibility of recognition (Bauman, 2000; Beck, 2000; Giddens, 1991).

It is as though there had been a change in the relationship between rights and obligations compared with the past, and the unravelling of the sense of obligation corresponded to an exponential increase in the expectations of the individual (the rights) with regard to social organization.

This liquid dimension (Bauman, 1998) of modern society gives substance to the subject and to the individualistic matrix of communication, removing sense from social prescriptions. In this respect, communication, and digital communication in particular, becomes the liquid substitute of the late-modern crisis.

From here we arrive at the third key concept: the media. The fortunes of communication are constructed literally on the vaporization and the loss of the weight of society on the individual. The scant involvement and sense of orientation of the social system often causes the subject to look for other repairing functions. One of these is certainly communication, which is viewed as a low cost resource with which to react to the crisis of the emptying of social relationships (the liquid substitute of the media). Communication reacts powerfully to change, reacting to the weakening of the system, to the devaluation of the values, to the growth of disvalues, that is, those individual values which are not recognized by others.

Communication, in fact, does not only help to get through the crisis, to fill the "black holes" in our interactions (Morcellini, 1997, 2004), but it also fills these gaps with relationships with the social system. That is to say, it literally carries out a function of substitution for socialization. This means that communication, in fact, covers the decline in all the institutions which in the past organized and prescribed individual behaviour (the school, the family, and religion).

Starting from this viewpoint, the "crisis" takes on another meaning: in connection with the sense of change in communication, it is no longer seen as "diminishing in importance," but rather as "multiplication and growth." *The theatre of communication* is useful not only to stimulate exchanges and interrelations between individuals, but also to stimulate the individuals themselves to change. Communication does not simply gratify the need for relationships, it multiplies them.

Specifically, the media stimulate the three dimensions of the social actors:

that of the self, filtered and explored in the dream dimension of the media and of the interaction mediated by technology, which induces the individual to prepare a new vision of the world and new styles of life; that of behaviour and of action, that is to say, that transformation which it is possible to meet in the symbolic scenarios of representation, identification and information in social interaction. There has been enough research to maintain that the good fortune of communication lies in its capacity to educate people to interiorize knowledge in a mitridatic way, that is, with a daily homeopathic dose of communication. In this way the organism prepares to react to the virus of change, which we perceive as a risk, or a threat, as a result of the effort associated with the idea itself of change; that which exalts the group as a privileged situation of change: people change in groups.

The Self in the Era of the New Media

Evolution or metamorphosis are terms which conjure up a process which is too linear to relate the complex and reticular nature of modern change. To emphasize the upheaval and the transformation of the social contest, in which unpredictable or uncontrollable forms emerge in the area of cultural and value models, in attitudes and behaviour, in customs and lifestyle, as well as in the transformation of the social order, it is therefore far more appropriate to use the term *revolution* (Morcellini, 2004, 2005).

The progressive weakening of memory and of inherited values, the consequent loss of points which anchor us to tradition, the exaltation of dynamism, of flexibility, of the capacity of subjective adaptation to the multiplicity of situations of the present, have favoured this "passage" to the late-modern.

The impact and the development of communication have contributed to the acceleration of these processes of social change, in some cases determining the phenomenon of *transitionality* (Grasso,1989), often used by sociologists to narrate the youth culture and the sense of discomfort which has developed from the revolutionary unpredictability of the modern condition.

On the basis of this first reflection, the media is far more than simply an environment for the transmission of knowledge. The media appears as places for exchanging and sharing values, ideas, and symbols which condition the processes of individual and collective identification (Morcellini, 1997) creating what is almost a semantic environment of socialization in which the young satisfy their need for individualization, on the one hand, and on the other reconstruct symbolic and linguistic membership within a sociocultural framework which is now empty of points of reference and of anchors of values (Bessotti, 2006). From this angle, communication takes on a new significance: it no longer carries out a *function of substitution* (Morcellini, 1997, 2004) to the modern crisis, but it produces a multiplication of opportunities for dialogue and for interaction, thanks above all to the continual updating offered by technology. The universe of the media and in particular of the new media has become for the individual a space of *capitalistic accumulation* (almost flexible) of symbols, of signs which increase the chances of identification, of recognition, of discovery and exploration of the self, and of the surrounding sociocultural dimension.

The process of modernization and of technological and scientific development, which have also taken place in the field of communications, have certainly favoured the exercising of citizenship and of democratic practices. Possession of the media, in fact, legitimizes the processes of participation of the individual in the dynamics of our times, above all with regard to access strategies to territories of knowledge and the symbolic sphere. This first interpretation is an integral part of a widely accepted point of view, of a lifestyle and expectations about communications which are referable to a vision of a *society of knowledge* founded on the search for and the promise of a social well-being, in which education (Ranieri, 2006) and communications are the emerging infrastructures.

"Only those who know more than they can do will avoid being swept away by change" (Ranieri, 2006, p. 52) because they can move more freely in society and can face the flexibility and sociocultural heterogeneity. Today knowledge has, in fact, become the means of constructing a sense of identity and belonging; that is to say, the way in which individuals continually redefine themselves in relation to their surrounding reality. Investment in permanent further education, in knowledge, and in culture represent, therefore, one of the actions which will guarantee more competitiveness in the job market and will help cope with social and cultural complexity and lack of homogeneity (Ranieri, 2006; Rullani, 2004).

In this context, communication represents, to an even greater extent than in the past, the most immediate and all-involving of forms with which to know the social world. By nature it is not impositional, or it does not at least present itself as such, and it is handy, available, immediately consumable, friendly, and low-cost. All of this means that the type of socialization which derives from it is not authoritarian, where the competencies of the adult meet the supposed incompetence of the pupil, but in tendency egalitarian. This key-aspect is still waiting to be explored, but if we consider with greater attention the sphere of those needs which are satisfied by communication and the modality by means of which this particular type of relationship unfolds (for example, through media education), it will certainly be possible to improve the structure of the media narration and the mechanisms of production and distribution of information which conquer the imagination and meet the imaginary and the need of the modern individual to dream.

This new investiture of communication is easily seen in the relationship of young people to cultural consumption; young people prove to be capable of independence and self-orientation when placed in front of a multimedial keyboard, and they form a relationship which is almost symbiotic with the media, with a natural organization and control of the language and of the codes (Meyrowitz, 1985).

Yet if on the one hand innovation and the technological "race" promote a cultural democratization, on the other they signal new differences because of the increase in the opportunities of access to communicative "competencies." The chance to participate in democratic life, in fact, does not resolve the problem of the new forms of inequality which communication consigns to the *society of change*, marking further the loss of social reference points and the radical sense of loss of traditional cultural mediations (Morcellini, 2004). Thus, from the more traditional gap relating to the different technological availability of the media, which does not consent the construction of personal experiences to all, we pass to the intergenerational gap, determined by the embarrassment and discomfort of adults in comparison with the experience and media competence shown by the young.

A further gap regards the capital of the individual with regard to culture and knowledge, or, rather, the disparity of competence in the field of communication, which is useful to handle and interpret the sociocultural changes of the media and to develop a mature and independent orientation regarding both decision and action. In synthesis, behind the appearance of an isomorphic distribution of communication and of its instruments, are hidden forms of different properties, different title, and different capital.

As far as this gap is concerned, there is a close connection with the issue of the "crisis of cultural mediation." The Italian education system has always been behind when it comes to progress in communication. It is sufficient to remember that Italy was the only European country in which the spread of the media, and in particular of television, came before mass literacy. In this process, which was all but linear, television fulfilled a wide-scale educational function which the school itself was not able to develop, contributing therewith to the spread not only of a common language, but also of a shared culture (Farnè, 2003; Morcellini, 2005).

Family, School, Work:
An Album of Semantic Changes

Modern times have certainly contributed towards the erosion of the mediation function of the school and of the family, in order to celebrate the value of direct experience, of subjective self-searching, and of the active exploration of the individual (Maffesoli, 1988).

The first critical problem regards *the family*: young people today are faced with a dimension which in the past was always a guarantee of stability but which today has been fragmented.

The weakening of this social institution dates back to the years of youth protest, when the bourgeois model with its functionalist nature, was condemned. According to this scheme, the task of the family was to contribute to the emancipation of the individual so as to guarantee an efficient social integration, the function of which was the maintenance of structural and cultural equilibrium. This model was thrown into crisis in the 1970s at the same time as the affirmation of educational and cultural polycentrism and following a series of social transformations. It has lost the typical connotations of the institution, transforming itself into a social group, or indeed into a space wherein to construct projects of personal life, relationships, and affective and educative relations (Besozzi, 2006). We come, thus, to delineate a framework which it is difficult to circumscribe in a standard model. This is because the quality of the interaction between parents and children comes under scrutiny, which determines its educative efficacy in the process of construction of the self.

In spite of the heterogeneity and the complexity of the picture which has just been outlined, today the sense of the family still seems to be present in the universe of values of the individual. According to the findings of a recent national survey by ISTAT (2005), confirmed by more localised and restricted research, the family is to be found in first place among the values recognized by the young in the hierarchy of the "most important things," in spite of the fact that relations within the domestic walls are in fact often conflictual, contradictory, and, therefore, difficult to reconcile with quality relationships. Besozzi (2006) describes this trend through a game of expectations and desires for the future, typical of the young, and closely connected to the sense of precariousness and of social uncertainty; in other words, for young people the family represents the symbol of security, of stability, and of protection compared with a reality which is fragmented and fragile. The value of this agency of socialization increases above all in the dimension of the imaginary, representing for young people the desire for stability as opposed to the state which is eternally transitory. However, if the family represents a *value-refuge*, it does not constitute a future projection around which to construct a project for living, probably because of the sense of individual responsibility and of subjective effort that the construction of a family nucleus involves (Besozzi, 2006).

The second critical problem regards the *work crisis*. In the past this represented an economic resource which led to a stable positioning in society, but it was above all a dimension which resulted in identity and socialization. The job determined a significant form of individual emancipation, functioning as an instrument of access and legitimization within social categories and classes, as well as a motor of mobility and of meritocratic reward. The choice of flexibility, apparently comprehensible within the prospective of an enlarging of the job market, has resulted in a fundamental error: that of considering the question as merely economic, overlooking its function of socialization, of preparation for roles, and of the attaining of objectives, but above all of the construction of identity (Bauman, 1998). The modern society no longer provides a safety net for individual behaviour and the weakening of prescriptions regarding action and socialization, and the weakening of values and of behavioural norms has put the burden on the individual, who has become the protagonist not only of his or her choices, but also of defeats. Placing this weight and focusing attention on the individual, however, involves an assumption of responsibility for the sociocultural orientation towards action, causing the subject an increase in discomfort and difficulty in front of the many choices society presents.

An indicator of excessive individualism is given by the concentration of attention on the corporal, which is ever more the territory of recapitulation of the need for happiness and of subjective realization, and it is not chance that in these modern times, compared with the past, human beings have more consumer goods, through which they seek to satisfy the sense of satisfaction of the individual identity (Code-luppi, 2003). But the desired expectations, however, do not seem commensurate to the possibility of restitution: the increase in wealth and material goods corresponds paradoxically to a sharpening of the sense of discomfort. Society today seems to be less and less a dispenser of well-being and of participation, and has become a territory in which individual expectations take precedence by force, overriding the mediations upheld by society.

The third critical problem regards the *educational improbability of the school system.* This more than other areas has suffered from the weakening of society's capacity to transfer culture and knowledge which are not negotiable to the new generations. In the past, values and knowledge were transmitted to young people, but what they assimilated was in reality the architecture of the adult age and the relative learning of that role. Today it is the school itself which is feeling the effects of the weakening of society and is in a state of crisis because it is still founded on traditional pedagogi-cal prescriptions which are ill adapted to the requirements and the characteristics of modern society. It is in the scenario of *educational improbability* that we see that the idea of school as a "parking lot" has become to an ever greater extent incorporated into the institution. It is here that we see the sense of an absence of values and a lack of communication particularly between the generations, except in those cases where the teacher, with significant effort, manages to regain the role of mediation. Evidence of this is the increasing lack of interest of the young in the education, which is visible in the evident arrogance and vulgarity present to an ever greater extent in their attitudes and, on the other hand, in a decrease in the willingness of teachers to involve themselves more in the educational process. One of the triggering factors of this crisis, therefore, is the loss of confidence and of "faith" of the teachers; the school runs the risk of becoming *a void-producing mechanism,* because it produces architecture and schemes, but not culture.

To this we must add the rapid penetration of communication technologies in the social and cultural experience of the individual, which has intensified this perception of an emptying of sense. The media, in fact, by its technological nature, often gives priority to direct experiences of the use of the medium and stimulate processes of symbolic construction of individual and subjective realities, which therefore lack cultural filters. For this reason, those intellectual spaces through which the learning processes of the individual were often *mediated* in the past (such as, for example, the school and the family), are today in decline in comparison with the development of communication.

In the face of this transformation, the school has always had to confront the dilemma of its social function: should it uphold the conservation of a cultural heritage by the transmission of what has been legitimated by tradition as "knowledge," or should it risk adapting to innovation and to the changes which surround it, taking on the responsibility for filtering cultural forms and knowledge that are too new?

Since the 1960s a number of researchers have observed that over the course of time the school seems to have been over-concerned to affirm traditional values, giving priority to an abstract dimension, which was often coldly ultracognitive, to the detriment of those more concrete aspects which are connected to the development of the individual's personality emotions (Alfassio Grimaldi & Bertoni, 1964, p. 63). This attitude was without a doubt consistent with the social characteristics and the dominant cultural model of those years, but it is a resistance which we have not yet left behind us. The scholastic institution still today, in fact, maintains forms of influence on the sociocultural condition which are present in the language and in the instruments of the media. Inevitably this conditions the position of teachers with regard to communication and risks compromising their passion for education, increasing the difficulty of adapting the content of the programmes to the expressive forms and dynamics of the media. The same condition reflects, moreover, on the students and removes value from the educational context, which is perceived and experienced as a place of socialization but not of learning and education.

Through communication, this institution can find again its cultural impetus and represent itself as the intellectual terrain in which and through which to interpret modern change. Technological progress is not enough to guarantee cultural sense and quality to the contents of the media; the channel and its signifier, which are present in the codes of the means of communication, are not enough to convey meaningful messages. As Luciano Galliani affirmed in the title of a thought-provoking book in 1979, *The Process is the Message*, certainly not the technology.

Intellectual space and critical comparison are also the basis of the cultural *humus* of media products. Investment in a communicative policy and ethic would, on the one hand, serve to rejuvenate, or rather reinvigorate, the expressive language and the contents of the media, balancing the processes of the handling of the communicative apparatus. On the other hand it would serve to re-establish, particularly in the action of consumption, situations of dialogue and symbolic comparison from which to stimulate a process of semantic construction of the experiences.

Through communication, the school could carry out its task of accompanying the young in this modern sociocultural evolution, observing and investigating in what way the changes affect and condition the need for identification, and modifying the dynamics of socialization in a project of intervention and qualification of the requests for participation, relationships, and comprehension of the modern world. In fact, if it is true that the young develop a harmonious relationship with the media from early infancy (Buckingham, 2004), it is also true that this *naturalism* is not always a guarantee of an equally natural acquisition of awareness of the mechanisms of the process, which are hidden in the construction of a message. For this reason, a progressive education in communication and in its languages (media education) could contribute to the development of an awareness of the sociocultural function and of the power to condition the media with regard to everyone's symbolic universe. Only on this condition can the school become the preferred environment of the culture of change, taking back that role of mediation which will enable it, and also serve mass culture, to reclaim its function as guarantor of equal opportunities.

The Digital Media as Expression of the Late-Modern

The digital media, more than any other, can be considered emblematic of the new late-modern sociocultural condition in that they inaugurate forms of interaction and of action, both individual and collective, which reflect the relations of the subject to a complex and "multimedial" reality.

The first common factor regards the reticular articulation of the digital world and its extension free from space-time limits which grants the subject an open explorative navigation, directed only by individual interests and motivations and guided by the sense of responsibility and by the level of independence and subjective critical sense which condition the choices. The process of individualization of the modern condition (Beck, 2000), in the digital media translates, thus, into the capacity of orientation, of independence of choice and of subjective action in front of the many cultural proposals of the virtual Web, and in the construction of a personalized path of consumption, starting from those needs and desires which need constantly to be satisfied and from the capacity to construct new media diets according to the social circumstances in which each of us acts.

Individualism can be found, therefore, in the capacity of choice and of selection of virtual and real information on the Web, in the ability to combine and hybridize it in a creative and selective way, without letting it enter into contradiction. In this way there is the development of the so-called *subjective activism* (Morcellini & Cortoni, 2007) or *consumeristic attitude* (Codeluppi, 2003), according to which the critical character of a cultural and medial behaviour derive from the capacity of the individual to release, during the moment of decodification, the dominant ideological interpretations, connected to the productive act, in order to reconstruct subjective interpretative pathways, which are often hybridized with personal life experiences. This renewed behaviour has been defined *networked individualism* (Marinelli, 2004), in that it allows for the satisfying of new forms of subjective identification, for the appeasement of the need for protagonism, and for explorativity, leading to new processes of interpretation of the self, of the others, and of reality. The young are the principle protagonists of these technologies, often activating processes of auto-socialization in that they succeed in declining with flexibility the characteristics of the different technologies to different uses, contexts, and opportunities to such an extent that they can be defined the *networked generation* (Tirocchi, Andò, & Antenore, 2002). In this space all are transformed at the same time into producers and consumers, transmitters, and receivers. In other words, the spectator becomes actor, expressing his or her willingness to enter the text and actualize it, taking as a starting point the personal prospective of interpretation.

If this form of virtual individualism can appear as an expression of liberty and of subjective emancipation, it risks, however, transforming itself into a condition of excess, and of scant cultural mediation, resulting in fragmentation and a loss of direction. The capacity for self-orientation, in fact, depends on the level of independence, responsibility, and personality which each individual matures, starting from daily experience and educational experience; that is, depending on the individual background of culture and experience. Also in this case, the cultural, affective, and informative patrimony of the family and of the school have a strong effect on socialization in the age of digital media, on the level of self-respect and assuredness, and, as a result, on the sociocultural attitudes of the individual which are expressed when surfing the Internet. In other words, a solid cultural mediation from the family and from the school in the process of socialization helps to guarantee all the basic instruments the individual needs to orientate him or herself in the digital world in an independent and creative manner, and when this is lacking the subject has difficulty in the media network.

Moreover, a strong instability and fluidity of knowledge and of values often corresponds to the immateriality of place in the late-modern era, so much so that the same process of socialization takes on a symbolic value. Thus, if the identity fragments and becomes fragile due to a lack of solid and concrete points of reference, the processes of identification become multiple and parallel, in that the subject seeks elsewhere for that which the traditional agencies of socialization are not able to guarantee. This allows for the appeasing of heterogeneous needs and the satisfying of aspects of the personality which are equally divergent through their immersion in virtual worlds.

The objective is always the same: the realization of the self and the attainment of an internal well-being by constantly involving oneself in the experiences of daily life, although the contexts and the times of the socialization change.

Through digital technology, therefore, new forms of interaction and immediate communication, without filters, are realized. They are independent of spatial distances and make it possible to satisfy the need to relate in a way which is coherent with the characteristics of a late-modern condition and of a digitalized society (Maffesoli, 2004).

According to some researchers, in fact, one of the peculiarities of the post condition in today's society regards the rediscovery of the social, of the sharing and collective participation which lead to a new form of interaction and intersubjective comparison. This is a form of reaction to the excesses of modern individualism, a "cure" for its side effects of subjective sense of loss, which has developed due to the lack of solid reference points to which the individual can anchor him or herself in the process of definition of identity. This leads the subject to seek new forms of participation, giving origin to the so-called phenomenon of de-individualization (Bauman, 2000; Maffesoli, 2004).

This reclaiming of the relational dimension in the digital world can be interpreted starting from two aspects of interpretation: that which is carried out within the virtual space and that which is closely connected to real experience.

In the first case, we are speaking of those relationships of virtual interaction which are played out in the semantic sharing of ideas, myths, rites, and interpretations of reality in the new spatial dimensions which are generated by technological convergence. Far from being impersonal, these new environments make it possible to appease the need for identification and the search for the self through comparison and exchange with those who choose to share the same semantic community, exploring different worlds according to the presuppositions of the classic sociology of Alfred Schutz. It thus becomes possible to satisfy the need for a "common understanding" through contact with the other and the re-appropriation of the relational dimension, developing a sense of belonging and sharing, often semantic or symbolic, which affects the process of the search for and the construction of the self, social network (Marinelli, 2004).

On the other hand, the increase in relationships in the virtual environment does not necessarily mean the weakening of concrete experience and interaction. Paradoxically in the late-modern era we are seeing the rediscovery of certain dimensions of the real connected to traditional experience, such as, for example, aesthetics, physical space as space-symbol of the bond, of celebration, and of rituality and, therefore, as *alchemy of the social*, of contact and comparison with the alter (Maffesoli, 2004, p. 81).

In support of this new dimension of late-modern relationships there have been a number of studies by ISTAT in recent years into the cultural behaviour of young Italians which announce a new tendency: the discovery of and search for collective, shared experiences in which the dimension of relationships is reclaimed, for direct participation, and for plurisensorial involvement through the experience (Morcellini, 2005, 2004a). In the last few years, in fact, there have been cultural modifications in all those areas which in the past were labelled elite or niche markets. So we find in a 10-year period (from 1996 to 2005) that the theatre, classical music, and visits to archaeological sites have increased their appeal, not only among the young, in spite of the explosion that has taken place regarding the means of communication.

In spite, therefore, of the structural instability of the social context, particularly of the economic sector, there has been an increase in cultural activity founded on contact and on social and emotional involvement. There has been an increase in the number of cinema goers of 16.1%, for the theatre of 10.6%, and so on for other activities: museums and exhibitions (+17.3%); classical music concerts (+3.1%); other music (+0.6%); sports events (+4.5%).

It is 2005 specifically in which all the forms of live entertainment reach their maximum historical level in terms of users over a 10-year period. The only form of entertainment which is in decline is the discotheque (-2.53% from 1996 to 2005). This data helps to radicalize the differences between the new generation and that of the 1980s (see Table 1).

If we wish to narrow the research to the year 2005 and focus attention on different cultural behaviour, taking into consideration the different age groups among the young, it is possible to see that the cinema occupies the first place in the classification of entertainment. It is therefore the most popular medium among all age groups, although with different percentages. Discotheques and dance halls, on the other hand, are frequented by the over-15s and their popularity increases with age, reaching second place in the classification of outdoor activities in 2005. As far as

Table 1. New encyclopedia of culture and communication. Spectators between 6 and 19 years of age at different entertainment events between 1996 and 2005

YEAR	The-atre	Cinema	Museums and exhibitions	Classical music concerts	Concerts of other music	Sports events	Disco-theques and danc-ing
1996	19.1	-64	26.1	5.8	23.1	39.3	31.1
1997	13.9	69	39.2	8.3	24.6	43	31
1998	20.6	71.3	38.2	6.3	-22	40.4	28.9
1999	23.2	69.3	38.6	7.5	22.6	40.8	30.2
2000	22.7	66.9	41.3	7.3	23.5	41.7	30.4
2001	25.6	75.8	40.6	7.5	23.6	42.8	30.3
2002	25.1	78.6	42.3	7.6	24.4	42.5	28.6
2003	23.4	74	41.2	7.1	24.8	44.2	28.8
2005*	29,7	80,1	43,4	8,9	23,7	43,8	28,6
Escursione 2000/2005	+7	+13.2	+2.1	+1.6	+0.2	+2.1	-1.8
Escursione 1996/2005	+10.6	+16.1	+17.3	+3.1	+0.6	+4.5	-2.5

Source: elaboration based on ISTAT data

* data not at present available for 2004

the younger members of the group are concerned (from 6 to 10 and from 11 to 14), museums and exhibitions are the most popular activities, in third place after the cinema and sports events. The theatre also shows a significant number of spectators, particularly among children between 6 and 10 (28.4%), followed by pop music and classical music concerts.

A new way of relating to the context of reality and of forming relationships has been established. This is certainly fluctuating and dynamic, consistent with the social flexibility and cultural fragmentation/fragility of the real which is still to be explored. In general the young pass from one space to another to satisfy their need to belong in different contexts, which reinforces the semantic or symbolic sharing of gestures, and expressive and ideological forms. In other words, the post-modern ethos is acted out in shared spaces, in participation and in collective and material events.

If we wish to synthesize the cultural behaviour of young Italians with reference to the stimuli of modern society, it is worth highlighting certain key points:

1. **Multimediality** and **explorativity** as styles of consumption and individual attitudes in front of the range of cultural and media stimuli of modern society; according to ISTAT data, from 2000 to 2005 there was an enormous increase in the cultural activities of the young who have at their disposal different media contemporarily in a productive and creative way to satisfy multiple needs, or rather desires. There is no longer competition between the media, but a synergy of stimuli, instruments, and languages.

2. **Subjective activism and protagonism** as symbols of the centrality of the individual in the choice and personalization of the different media stimuli. The received wisdom in that the subject has been transformed from consumer into producer of symbols, knowledge, and meanings conveyed by the media and recontextualized in everyday experience.

3. **Relationships and participations** which define the cultural behaviour of the young and the processes of socialization in the late-modern context. ISTAT data, for example, shows that between 1998 and 2005 there is a growth in young people's need to spend time with their contemporaries, a characteristic which increases with age in correspondence with the process of socialization. Naturally, there is a progressive abandoning of the domestic environment in favour of the informal world of their peers. Along with friends, we must not underestimate the practice of sport in free time. This increased between 2000 and 2005, particularly among girls and it gains in popularity with age. In conclusion, participation in cultural events represents a form of reaction to modern hyper-technology and is a symbol of the re-appropriation of a traditional dimension, that of face-to-face interaction.

PC and the Internet: Terrain of Desires and Risks

"After twenty years of hypnosis by the television, the new generations are beginning to rub their eyes and the audience is changing from passive to active." In an interview Paolo Ferri, lecturer in Didactic Technology and Theory and Techniques of the New Media at the Bicocca University of Milan used these words to synthesize the metamorphosis in act in the relationship of the young with the new technologies. "The PC beats the TV, Here is the Generation" is the title of an article in a section of *Repubblica*, following the publication of data by Nielson on the new technologies (2005), which recounts the increase of these media in the diet of the young. The PC, in its different forms, is experiencing the same history of penetration that the TV experienced with regard to the cultural habits of the Italians 50 years ago. The risk seems to be the same: the speed of this process is such that it does not allow the social institutions, in particular the family and the school, to keep pace with the times, so that they risk yet again appearing inadequate with regard to the communicative, interactive, and creative characteristics which the new media offer. The question, therefore, is no longer whether or not to use the medium, but how to use it correctly within the different social and educational contexts so as to emphasize the potentials and reduce the possible risks of an undesirable use. The ISTAT data of 2005 confirm that the use of the PC and Internet has literally doubled within the family compared with the year 2000, to the extent that 83.3% of children between 3 and 17 use it. The use of the PC increases with age and is prevalently a male activity, particularly when we consider daily use. Females seem to have a less familiar and less frequent relationship with this technology; indeed, as age increases its use decreases even more until by adulthood it has all but disappeared (see Table 3). Statistics naturally only make it possible to provide a photograph of the extension and the radicalization of a social and cultural phenomenon such as that which regards the new technologies. However it is not possible to provide adequate information to enable us to motivate a certain use or to restrict the use to specific social and cultural contexts. Every analysis, therefore, is only partial when it comes to reconstructing an overview of a generation also with regard to the use of new technologies.

If almost every family possesses this technological artefact, the same situation is not present in the scholastic context where, according to ISTAT data and in spite of the policy of technological investment undertaken by the state, there is still a reduced use of the medium in the classroom compared with the rapidity of the processes of technological advancement and scientific investment abroad. A more consistent investment and attention on the part of the schools and of the ministry to the use of the new media, therefore, could help to reduce the number of children who do not use the PC simply because they do not have one at home. Possession, however, relieves us from the need to ask further questions regarding the new technologies: knowing how to use this media with "awareness of cause," in a way which is focused and not casual is a problem which *in primis* regards adults rather than the young.

According to the ISTAT data of 2005 on the frequency of use of the PC by age and sex, it is possible to affirm that males in particular, and specifically young males, have a better, more natural, and more continuous relationship with the new technologies, and specifically with the PC. This latter group are in fact the most assiduous and frequent users (they use it every day in greater numbers than females), while girls and women seem to congregate at the antipodes of the classification regarding styles of use; that is to say, they use the PC less than males and in a more sporadic manner.

If we analyze the picture presented by ISTAT 2005 (Table 2) vertically and focus our attention on females, we can see that in spite of their scarce familiarity with the new technologies, girls are more open and well disposed towards the digital media compared with women: until the age of 24 they use this medium once or more a week in greater numbers than males, even if this habit weakens as age increases (see Table 2).

Table 2. Towards the Technoeval age. Use of the Internet by sex and age group (2005)

Age group	Every day		Once or more a week		A few times a month		A few times a year		Does not use the PC	
	M	F	M	F	M	F	M	F	M	F
3-5	4.4	1.4	8.6	5.4	5.7	5.5	0.9	1.9	74.9	81.6
6-10	9.1	6.2	33.3	37.1	8.0	9.0	1.5	2.2	46.0	43.9
11-14	27.4	14.9	41.6	44.2	4.8	9.0	1.2	3.9	23.5	27.4
15-19	36.5	21.7	35.5	47.9	4.6	6.5	2.2	1.6	20.1	20.6
20-24	38.3	30.6	24.1	30.2	5.1	5.8	1.4	2.6	27.6	27.4
25-34	38.4	32.7	17.7	14.8	3.2	4.0	1.6	2.8	37.3	42.8
35-44	39.6	26.4	13.1	12.5	3.4	4.8	1.6	2.4	40.3	52.4
45-54	32.6	19.2	11.5	9.2	2.8	3.1	1.2	2.0	50.3	64.3
55-59	19.4	9.3	10.0	4.2	2.6	1.2	1.7	1.5	63.4	81.2
60-64	9.6	3.0	7.5	2.1	2.0	1.1	0.8	1.8	77.5	89.8
65-74	4.5	0.6	3.6	0.9	1.1	0.2	0.6	0.4	87.8	94.3
75 +	1.5	0.1	1.0	0.2	0.3	0.3	-	-	94.1	96.5
Totale	25.6	16.0	15.3	13.4	3.2	3.5	1.2	1.8	52.3	62.8

Source: elaboration of ISTAT data 2005

Key: for each age group the higher percentage value of use between the sexes has been highlighted.

The scenario which is gradually emerging has led many researchers, among paedago-gists, psychologists, sociologists, and mass-mediologists, to question the cognitive, perceptive, behavioural, and relational metamorphoses that this new symbiotic relationship risks determining. It is not a question of assuming apocalyptic and integrated positions towards this new reality, but rather of reflecting and analyzing in a strategic, synergic, and transversal manner the social effects, the psychological consequences, and the strategies with which to use these instruments to the best in everyday life. The objective could be to predispose conditions so that the new me-dia can become a support for the "do-it-yourself" process in children, transforming them from surfers to planners.

It is worth adding a few reflections to the above on the process of familiarization with the new technologies (Silverstone, 1999) or indeed on the new forms of socialization which derive from their modality of use and from social practices constructed around the act of consumption. According to researchers in the field of digital technologies, the virtual and the real dimension are progressively demolishing the confines which previously delimitated them and are constructing forms of parasocial communication in which the virtual dimension is transformed into a cultural humus and stimulus for sharing and participation in a relationship between equals, nourishing, fortifying, and enriching the exchange of emotions and meanings in face to face interaction. It is as though reciprocal forms of influence and conditioning were activated between the real world and the virtual world.

Among the new technologies, the Internet warrants a separate chapter. According to data collated by ISTAT in 2005, the use of the Web is established among minors, and it increases with age. Also in this case the tendency towards "regular" virtual surfing (every day or almost), is prevalently male. If girls do not use the PC, they will not as a rule use Internet. In fact, from the ISTAT data of 2005 on the frequency of use of Internet by age group and sex it again emerges that the highest percentage of those who do not use Internet are predominantly female, regardless of age (see Table 3). Starting from the picture which has just been delineated, if we wish to focus our attention on females and identify a profile of a "Web surfer" among those few who relate to the new technologies, this would be of a girl between 6 and 24 years old who surfs a few times a month more than males, even if the girls lose this habit progressively, again with age.

It is certain that the pragmatism implicit in the use of the new technologies, the protagonism in the processes of construction of knowledge, the perceptive, cogni-tive, and emotional immersion in virtual reality, and the simulation of experiences separated from the physicality of the acts, represent determining characteristics which help to intensify the interaction of the young with these technologies. This union which was already presumed in the 1990s, when the technological explosion was merely an intuition and a wager for the future, has today been transformed into a condition sine qua non which characterizes the experience of the young, "the best teachers of communicative technologies" (Tirocchi et al., 2002). Restricting

Table 3. Towards the Technoeval Age. Use of the Internet by sex and age group(2005)

Classi di età	Tutti i giorni		Una o più volte a settimana		Qualche volta al mese		Qualche volta all'anno		Non usano Internet	
	M	F	M	F	M	F	M	F	M	F
3-5	-	-	-	-	-	-	-	-	-	-
6-10	1.3	0.9	5.4	6.5	4.0	4.1	2.0	1.9	84.0	84.8
11-14	7.1	4.2	22.8	21.1	10.9	11.3	6.2	4.6	52.7	57.9
15-19	18.0	9.4	34.7	38.5	9.4	11.5	3.5	3.6	32.5	32.6
20-24	25.2	15.4	27.8	40.8	8.1	10.0	2.5	4.4	32.9	33.9
25-34	24.6	18.2	21.1	19.5	5.1	7.1	3.0	2.7	43.1	49.4
35-44	22.6	12.6	19.6	14.6	5.0	6.2	2.3	3.5	48.2	61.4
45-54	16.6	8.7	15.9	9.4	5.2	4.5	2.2	2.6	58.1	71.9
55-59	9.8	4.1	11.3	4.6	4.2	2.0	2.0	0.8	69.3	84.4
60-64	5.3	1.4	7.6	2.0	1.7	1.0	1.3	1.6	80.9	91.0
65-74	2.4	0.3	2.9	0.5	1.3	0.3	0.6	0.1	90.0	94.6
75 +	0.6	0.0	1.1	0.0	0.2	0.2	0.2	-	93.8	96.4
Totale	14.5	7.9	15.7	12.1	4.7	4.7	2.2	2.2	60.2	70.2

Source: elaboration of data ISTAT 2005

Key: for each age group the higher percentage value of use between the sexes has been highlighted.

the analysis of the new media to the PC and Internet, as some national institutes of research such as ISTAT still do today, is however reductive because it does not allow for the question of technological convergence, of the hybridization of languages and meanings which satisfy the desire for eclecticism, explorativity, and protagonism of the subject. The terminological choice of "digital media" itself with which to describe the new *new-medial* world lets us understand a reality which is more complex and articulated than the Internet, which also embraces the new frontiers of TV, the mobile phone, the radio, or indeed of those generalist media which, to respond to the activity of exploration and manipulation of the technological contents of the subjects according to the logic of constructivism, develop new forms of interaction and of action.

The dimension of the community, the new prospective of dialogue among equals, the different opportunities for socialization, the perception of an expressive freedom behind the mask of an identity which could be fictitious, as well as the possibility of being open to change without necessarily destabilizing oneself, all the above represent keys of interpretation, perhaps over-optimistic, which help to edify a relationship of reciprocal trust between the young and the new communicative technologies

The experience of reaffirmation of the self and of the construction or search for an identity are at the basis of every educational process, whether real or virtual, for the young and for many behavioural orientations with regard to the technological possibilities of today. In the case of the Internet, the awareness of the virtuality of the real and the perception of a dimension which is parallel to the tangible one, stimulate the individual to expose him or herself to risk, in the awareness that experiences lived through the screen do not constitute real life.

Conclusion

We could compare the technologies to a "no-man's-land" where identities and roles are played out, certainties, equilibriums, and knowledge are both constructed and destabilized, a sense of belonging is established and acquaintances developed, but risks and dangers are also met. It is a place of risk, where everything is mobile and dynamic and the possibility of cognitive growth is proportional to the possibility of encountering environments which are insalubrious and often dangerous for the young, above all on the Internet. Also in this case the responsibility for the journey falls on the explorer, on the safety of the route, on the compass and the map, but also on the destination and the previous experience of *surfing*. In other words, the framework of reality conditions the approach and the experience of the young with respect to the prospects of socialization offered by the new technologies. A cultural and socio-educational humus which is constantly present in the choices and experiences of consumption can facilitate the maturing of a critical sense which is sufficient to conduct the relationship with these technologies harmoniously and independently. In this way the risk of transforming the actors of the virtual into "victims" can be avoided.

When we speak of digital technologies, we are not referring exclusively to the Internet; digital TV, the potential of the mobile phone for digitalization, and the recent arrival of the radio on the Web are symbols of the integration of two realities, the virtual and the real, which influence each other, exchanging symbols, signifiers, and signs, and exerting a strong influence on the development of socialization in the young. Virtual experiences thus echo real ones, particularly in those aspects which do not manage to emerge through concrete everyday experience, while real life provides a key of interpretation to relate to and exploit adequately the experiences and activities connected to the new technologies.

The virtual reality of the Web and that which is perceived, put into practice, constructed, or imagined in the continuous relationship with the digital technologies mirrors the real world, particularly when, through immersion and integration with the languages and characteristics of the new media, it attempts to gratify needs and desires which the individual is not always able to satisfy in everyday life. The hybridization of languages and multimedial convergence, therefore, increase the possibility of contact, of communicative and semantic exchange between individuals, removing the barriers not only of space and time but also of sex, creed, ideology, and so forth, producing a sensation of communication between equals. However, it is also true that they can conceal unexpected situations of violation of privacy, of violence, and particularly psychological violence, which invade personal space. This too, however, is a reflection of what happens in the tangible world, but at an experiential acceleration which is directly proportionate to the prospective of interaction and contact offered by the digital media.

In second place, this interpretation of the relationship of the young with technology in the adult world seems yet again to present a point of view which does not always correspond to the view they put forward of themselves. The young are born and brought up in a technological environment and they learn to handle independently the different media and the multitude of stimuli which come from a reality which is in itself complex. They get used to progressively facing, observing, listening to, and selecting or reorganizing in their experience of life the wide range of inputs offered. The propensity towards the digital media produces with time a modification in the way of observing, thinking, and interpreting the surrounding reality, which becomes eclectic and reticular, in accordance with a precise order which is closely connected to subjective experience. The young, who have grown up immersed in these continual cultural and technological stimuli, develop a *forma mentis* which is able to handle and control these same stimuli and they present themselves to the adult world with this awareness and cultural and experiential maturity.

The story of the numbers recounts a process of cultural appropriation by Italian society which, while certainly not linear, is seductive and interesting. However, the reaching of certain percentages does not solve the problem of the cultural competence of the Italians in the use of the languages and instruments of the media. The numbers recount neither the position of this communication in people's lives, the intensity of the media experiences in everyday life, nor indeed the level of influence they have on life style. They limit themselves to supplying a photograph of the situation from which to investigate in depth into the cultural, symbolic, expressive, and behavioural relationship between the media and the young.

The numbers indicate an encouraging trend. An observation of the data, in fact, indicates that the change is determined principally by the young. It is therefore possible to introduce the concept of *communicative activation* with which to intend not only the activism of the public but also a different attitude of independence in the new generation with regard to the communicative and technological stimulation of which they are protagonists. This communicative analysis should be carried out as part of their education to show that it is enough to have access to the media to find forms of communication and thereby avoid anxiety-provoking incomprehension between the generations. As these processes are taking place with such rapidity, the least we can do is help them along.

References

Alfassio Grimaldi, U., & Bretoni, I. (1964). *I giovani degli anni '60*. Bari: Laterza.

Bauman, Z. (1998). *Work, consumerism, new poor*. London: Open University Press.

Bauman, Z. (2000). *Liquid modernity*. Cambridge, UK: Polity Press.

Beck, U. (2000). *Risk society: Towards a new modernità*. New Deli, India: Sage.

Besozzi, E. (2006). *Società, cultura, educazione*. Roma: Carocci.

Buckingham, D. (2006). *Media education. Literacy, learning and contemporary culture*. Cambridge, UK: Polity Press.

Codeluppi, V. (2003). *Il Potere del consumo*. Torino: Bollati Boringhieri.

Farné, R. (2003). *Buona maestra tv. La rai e l'educazione da Non è mai troppo tardi a Quark*. Roma: Carocci.

Giddens, A. (1991). *Modernity and self-identity: Self and society in the late modern age*. Stanford, CA: Stanford University Press.

Grasso, P. (1974). *Personalità e innovazione: Ricerca psicologico-sociale sulla condizione giovanile di transizionalità culturale*. Roma: Coines.

Grasso, P. (1989). *Parabola giovanile dagli anni '50 agli anni '80*. Roma: Euroma.

Griswold, W. (1994). *Cultures and societies in a changing world*. Thousand Oaks, CA: Pine Forge.

Maffesoli, M. (1988). *Le temps des tribus*. Paris: Le Livre de Poche.

Maffesoli, M. (2004). *Le rythme de vie. Variation sur l'imaginaire post-moderne*. Paris: Editions Table Ronde.

Marinelli, A. (2004). *Connessioni*. Milano: Guerini e associati.

Meyrowitz, J. (1985). *No sense of place*. New York: Oxford University Press.

Morcellini, M. (1997). *Passaggio al futuro. Formazione e socializzazione tra vecchi e nuovi media*. Milano: FrancoAngeli.

Morcellini, M. (1999). *La TV fa bene ai bambini*. Roma: Meltemi.

Morcellini, M. (2004). *La scuola della modernità. Per un manifesto della media education*. Milano: FrancoAngeli.

Morcellini, M. (2005). *Il Mediaevo. TV e industria culturale nell'Italia del XX secolo*. Roma: Carocci.

Morcellini, M., & Cortoni, I. (2007). *Provaci ancora, scuola. Idee e proposte contro la svalutazione della scuola nel Tecnoevo*. Trento: Erickson.

Ranieri, A. (2006). *I luoghi del sapere*. Roma: Il sole 24ore.

Rullani, E. (2004). *Economia della conoscenza*. Roma: Carocci.

Sciolla, L. (2002). *Sociologia dei processi culturali*. Bologna: Il Mulino.

Silverstone, R. (1999). *Why study the media?* London: Sage.

Tirocchi, S., Andò, R., & Antenore, M. (2002). *Giovani a parole. Dalla generazione media alla networked generation*. Roma: Guerini e Associati.

Chapter IV

New Episthemologies in a Changing Media Environment

Giuseppe Ardrizzo, CIES—Università della Calabria, Italy

Abstract

This chapter draws the landscape of the passage from modernity to information society. This is a passage referring to our idea of the universe, the way we're thinking, the modalities with which we make sense of the world. Describing them, it is also possible to understand the main challenges for education: a shift from linear to complex methodologies, the need to provide students with abilities for searching and evaluating information, and the development of a new episthemology with its cultural codes and its languages. If school doesn't individualize new tools for interpreting youngsters' behaviours, it shall not be able to understand its new role in this changing society: to work at digital literacy thinking of it as a knowledge literacy.

Introduction:
New Strategies for Knowledge Building

It is well-known that, even if in a not always conceptually articulated way, our world has become a building yard in these last years, a place of work in progress whose effects are unpredictable from many sides. There is a general feeling that traditional ways of meaning man and nature, organizations and values, lifestyles and history, knowledge and behaviour models, individuality and collectivity are going out of tune.

The concept of space expands until it coincides with the network of communication flows, which wrap the operators of various systems in a thick web and connect them to other near or remote systems.

Conceptualized as a woof and as a net, the present constitutes the very cognitive root from which the *thought of complexity* springs. *Complexity* does not mean complication or difficulty. Complexity—term of great importance in the contemporary reflection—refers back to the Latin *complexus*, from the verb *complecti*, to weave, to intertwine (the whole and together) many times, that is, "co-knotting." It is what happens in any emergency when the plot, the outcome of that intertwining, visibly turns out it is not reducible to the element that has been intertwined, as well as the web is not reducible to the thread of which it is interwoven. This means that we live in a context made of a spread relationship and that a lot of the events happen just because a relationship exists between and among things, as stated by an abundant scientific literature.

Substantially, we are observing a falling of barriers and an acceleration of exchanges among practices and domains for a long time unrelated: the developments of a particular knowledge are often influenced by developments of knowledge for a long time considered distant. And this leads to the emergence of woofs of universes that do not find any space in the presence of isolationist paradigms. The immanent complexity of things can not express itself according to predetermined and unilateral positions. Indeed, it springs from the intertwining between regularity and aleatoriness, laws and chaos, the causal and the casual... In our case, this implies that nothing of what has been elaborated in the past has to be rejected: many of the constructions that had guided acts and behaviours for centuries are still precious; and they are not in the same way of antiques, but in the "economic" dimension of knowledge tools, as vital and irreplaceable.

These are some barely visible features given as a background for the following discourse. Hence the convincement, however not arbitrary, that the current transformative phase entails a revision of cognitive equipments put into action in order to grasp the sense and the possibilities that it offers. It is a question of necessities which can not be detached from the capability to answer by institutions committed with educational task.

Innovation referring to institution almost appears an oxymoron, given the evolution indolence connoting the institutionalization of things. But one of the most important challenges is here issued: How may traditional organizations answer a world that makes acceleration, globalization, and nonlinearity the main terms of the new social and cultural configurations?

In this sense, it is not unlikely that education must orient itself towards the construction of spelling books open to new forms of syllabication, thanks to which it will be possible the construction of the denominative words of a world that makes mobility its own trait.

The following text is divided, more ideally than practically, in three parts: the first aims at identifying quickly some of the fundamental structures on which the modern thought has been constructed and the ties underlying the educational thought, beginning to take shape above all in the XIX century; the second part intends to identify some important critical points, which reveal evident forms of discontinuity and invite to find educational solutions and strategies not recoverable in the application of classic paradigms of causal kind; finally, the third part means to outline a significant epistemological orientation that identifies in the *contingency* the privileged moment in which to measure oneself and from which to derive a "lesson" in order to construct methodological paths, as they result necessary, to reach further cognitive goals that, in accordance with the spirit of the ages, will have by this time the constant feature of temporary landing places.

The Heirs of Modernity

Education activity, as it took form and was conceived in its institutional dimension, is to a great extent heir of a vision of the world that finds its own epistemological "parenthood" in the assumptions of the experimental science inaugurated by Galileo and in those of the cognitive-methodological reflection done by Cartesio. Many, and more or less, explicit consistencies about man's and nature's behaviour exist between these two fathers of modernity, but the strategical object that more deeply correlate them is the methodological dedication of the purging mechanism; that one which sets itself up as a guardian of the fact that the variables seen as disturbers do not have to interfere in the scene of knowledge. And this implies to enter a one-dimensional way, seen as the one able to lead to the *pure* moment—immanent (in) to truth—that necessarily underlies the logical construction of an order as much as possible safe from capricious behaviours of the phenomenal reality. Thus, the regulatory ideal of knowledge relates to the image of a compact world, internally united, uniform, without smudges. In such direction, the moves to make lead to the construction of governing criteria that assign to the domains of disciplines the territories pertaining to them, in order to make them obedient.

Substantially, the birth of "good manners" is not limited to the regulatory activity of social being prescribed by the etiquette. This latter, indeed, may be read as a paradigmatic metaphor of a more profound and (omni)comprehensive activity organizing things, that has the power to legitimize or delegitimize the approach to a phenomenal reality, the knowledge of which is directed to identify regularities, and to confer them legal citizenship.

The purging strategy will shape knowledge and its transmission according to the regulations of modernity. In this sense and except some occasional discordances, not even the Darwinian revolution, with its reintroducing history into natural phenomena, will bring significant changes within the influential thought of the time: the strength of the progressive ideology, of Enlightenment origins, will give credence to a selective operating, on the basis of which nature will be gradually seen intent on sieving itself (to purify itself) in the accomplishment of an ameliorative way according to a trajectory teleologically oriented. The "step by step," by conjugating itself with "the exception that confirms the rule," will form those guiding principles which any cognitive undertaking will have to relate to, above all any educational undertaking (Bocchi & Ceruti, 2004). The condition of ideality peculiar to the experimental laboratory basically expands into a generalized syntax: eliminating the disturbing action produced by any noise to take precautions against dangers of deviances, so as to give life to a limpid and linear concatenation of causes and effects, becomes the first and one move legitimate to make, the only one that allows not to controvert itself, thanks to its own capability to always produce identical responses in space and in time.

To collocate the discoveries of knowledge in the timelessness means to make them safe from whims and mutabilities of history, to give them assured fundaments, only traceable in the antecedence of that nontime situated before the great and frescoed floor on which the narration of the "unordered" human affairs and natural occurrences then will be painted. Above all it falls to science—whose metrics is mainly dictated by classical mathematics—to find out that undefiled background rhythm that dictates times and ways, by resorting to a scope of canonical practices epistemologically oriented towards the oneness of the method (Ceruti, 1986). Correlatively, the educational thought of modernity arranges an apparatus of its own markedly turned to identify a didactic path that has to conform with the conditions connoting scientific practices so as to be able to title itself of scientific reliability. In particular, it has to conform with those more specifically expressed by truth capability that assigns imperiality to the so-called hard sciences. The primary task of education is that of teaching literacy to the observance of a method seen as the one main way, the only one which can guarantee superimposable outcomes, in space and time.

Indeed, the text underlying the narration (and that beats the time) of disciplines sets up as a continuous invitation not to overflow from the linearity of deterministic tracks: the briefest, the most immediately visible, the most calculable, the purest, and the most suitable one to clear out the way from the distracting weirdness of surface, frequently present in phenomenal reality. Related to this, some tools—made transparent by their continuous presence—accompany the educational course so that possible deviances can be brought again within the domain of a container which results to be the only legitimate space of the possible.

Programs, texts, explicative, organizational and executive modalities, added to those of hierarchical ordering, have to be extremely indifferent to space and time: if I have to live the space belonging to the form of the winning knowledge, then I cannot but go into a world different from the specificities of my local and historical context to adhere to spaceless and timeless forms. By letting cultures meet, those forms without time and space reduce knowledge strategies, elaborated over various singular stories, up to suppress them. Indeed, the purging mechanism requires an active, unexhausted work of decontextualization, of rescission of relationships that objects (even mental) maintain among themselves. This in accordance with the necessity to continually redefine themselves in the vital dynamism of relationship and with galaxies of other objects dialoguing in their turn. Obedience and submission to manipulation can be demanded from the isolated object, hardly obtainable by other and less reductionist ways.

Basically, the perspective of the literacy designed by modernity educates to an ideal reachability of a privileged point of view (the same which leads to the Self), thanks to which it is finally possible to reveal that core made of "a few and simple laws" which rule man and nature. Found the linear causalistic method, the attainment of the goal turns out in a gradual accumulation of knowledge on knowledge, according to the well-known normative and epistemological image of "step by step" (Ceruti, 1986).

The passage from a universe that is considered simple to another one seen as a complex universe shows the turning point occurred to oppose not the classic thought, but its presumed exhaustiveness. And that passage was made necessary because of unavoidable questions related to the advancement and the multiplication of those moments seen as exceptional ones, eliminated by the scientific thought over the previous centuries as elements of trouble. As from the second half of the 19th century, some inklings of the necessity to operate changes of direction start to appear. Those inklings become more and more insistent till the radical turning point, datable halfway through the last century, above all with "machines that think," the computers, entering the society. Actually, their appearance marks a sort of methodological revolution. A very influential one: divisions among disciplines fail. On the contrary more disciplines, some of them considered unrelatable by traditional classifications, start to dialogue about a common project, shared by all. And that shall lay the basis for the birth and the evolution of the systemic thought.

Once failed the immune strength of the one method, the finiteness and the alleged exhaustivenesses of definitions, which tended to isolate objects and make them mute, fail as well, with their vocation for circumscribing. What emerges with greater strength in every ambit of inquiry is, in fact, the existence of a complex net of relationships among the various constitutive parts of a construct, read as a system; rather, in most cases, relationship is the condition for the possibility itself of existence of each part (Latour, 1993).

This does not bring to dismiss classical science or not to acknowledge its capability of identifying statistically regularities which exist as well; if anything, it invites classical science to integrate itself in a wider spectrum of knowledge paths, made possible by the paradigmatic necessity to adopt other points of view, as well.

The change, therefore, implies the revision of the strategies of positioning. If now objects show themselves as tentacular and advance beyond the territorialities of the disciplines into which they had been compressed, then garrisoning the confines they cross over becomes necessary so as to identify the branches and the relationships that they set up with objects allocated in different territories and not necessarily concomitant. From a history of universes prevalently unrelated, the internal history of science of the 19th century becomes a history of relationships punctuated by limitative theorems, by distances as regards certain assumed balances, by instabilities, dissipations, orders born of disorders, recursiveness, asymmetries, non-linearities, chaotic realities, temporal courses which, after centuries of phenomena seen through timelessness, enter again the knowledge scene with a primary constructive role (Capra, 1996).

Physics, mathematics, biology, chemistry, science of evolution, science of cognition, science of communication, are only some among the numerous domains which, in a metacognitive direction, think again of the way they had thought (of) themselves; in this way, they open onto new and unknown relationships through the necessity to build bridges, to institute transits among knowledge, to elaborate metaphors so as to overlap places semantically heterogeneous, to organize among the different disciplines those forms of dialogue that can be at the same time cooperative, competitive, antagonist, complementary, causative, impedimental, and so forth.

Even if summary, these are some of the significant traits indicating the dynamism connected to the re-orientation of many and influential knowledge related to the sciences of man and nature. Nevertheless, the panoramic view cannot also ignore the definite presence of those knowledge related to technological domains which, with their pressing rapidity of proceeding and overpassing themselves, oblige to newer and newer ways of organizing observation and relationship, to new organizational reflections about the very organizing ways.

The acceleration that connotes technological innovation speeds up and emphasizes the difference between "before" and "after." It leads the "awkwardness" of the antecedence to a continuous derision and obliges to the obsolescence those practices which do not operate in direction of newer and newer and unpredictable morphologies of acting.

Man has always been creator of technology and has established with technology a relationship of interactive nature; but this relationship has developed for some decades according to a dimension that reveals a growing intimacy, so as to give birth to a manifest crossbreeding of biological and cognitive order. *Bio-* takes shape increasingly as a *technobio-* and *techno* increasingly as a *biotechno-* . This also makes clear the extraordinary colonizer power got by technology. And in virtue of this power it has definitively disproved those images that wanted it (to be) in a subordinate position as for science, that assigned to it the part of impure child, because instrumentally submitted to the interests of the world, the part of something born of immateriality uninterested in theoric reflection. Basically, we are assisting at a sort of "reckoning of accounts" directed to revise the assignation of places, which produces a curious overturning. Today, a large part of the scientific activity devotes itself to interpret what technology produces; and that it is produced, as stated before, with innovative rhythms more and more accelerated and sometimes without the necessity to provide theoric basis to the artefacts it gives birth to (Stengers, 1993).

The technosphere is one of the relevant living and operating contexts to man, but paradoxically, and unlike what happened in the "mechanistic" civilization, the more technology evolves in the micronized and nanofied dimension of electronics, biology, bioelectronics, and so forth, the less users seem to be interested in the knowledge of those conditions of functioning that, in case of need, would allow them to intervene in the processes.

In fact, this disinterest masks a pretence: to ignore that the relationship with technology demands the carrying out of real tasks. Aware of this "unwillingness," technology silently intervenes in making up through the creation of conscientious agents that, with their operation, solve problems and remove obstacles so as to allow users to (inter)act in the unawareness of the "duties" they should face. The birth of the actual interest in the most advanced forms of technology coincides with the birth of the disinterest, as well as actual, in their conditions of functioning. This is due, likely, to the failure of the certainties created by determinist paradigms of classical science.

As though the failure of the gears with their mechanical movement, didactically repetitive, "by the light of the sun," had made current facilities opaque, as though the entry of nonlinearity, of bricolage, of weakness of the scientific "absolutes," of causality, had created a sort of new anthropological territory that does not question the rational curiosity, but it awakes the desire of magic, the desire of that disproportion that elapses between the accomplishment of a minimal gesture and the achievement of a overabundance. The icon on the desktop, with its physicalness, hides the processes that its function presupposes: it is sufficient the mouse button so that it opens a world of "at pleasure" dimensions, but if on the one hand this discloses its friendly availability in introducing into a path devoid of obstacles, on the other hand, it gives value to its presence by dramatizing the existence of a world to which none, if not a priest, can think to enter (Norman, 1988).

All the ongoing events, above all in the domain of technology and technosciences, with particular reference to the universe of digital communication—involve not secondary modifications in the ways of seeing and practising the world. The net, in the light of the new historical conditions which it creates, forces to renew the interpretation of several pivotal elements of knowledge that have contributed noticeably to the construction of civilizations, in particular of the Western civilization. Likely, the quality of the questions whose answers gave birth to the fundamental reflections of classical science has to be rethought; for instance, the quality of the questions about the ways of experiencing time, or the ways of conceptualizing space, causality, relationship, balance, evolution, and so forth.

The awareness of the ongoing changes imposes to review also the map of knowledge. And it is in relation to those knowledge that a new reflection about the ways of knowing has to evolve.

In that direction, what becomes important is to reconsider the territorial acquisitions of traditionally meant knowledge and, in case of necessity, to integrate them (and/or to reformulate them) with the new realities correlated to technology (to technoscience) and to the conditions more or less immediately visible that it poses. This means to assign new and demanding commissions to an epistemology of technology, as a sort of vedette, seen as a necessary element of reflection about nature, meanings and senses of technology itself and about its ways of referring to man. It deals with a moment of knowledge directed towards the elaboration of equipments inter and transdisciplinary, suitable to a first comprehension of the complex properties emerging from those mobile universes that are under construction (Stengers, 1993).

Modernity of the Heirs

Substantially, at the moment we are offered the privilege to be present at historical and radical manoeuvres of adjustment, that, for several aspects, mark some detachments, separations, and decisions, as to practices maintained completely pertinent and exhaustive in an even recent past. In front of this panorama, it is compulsory to look over the situation concerning that crucial moment of social organizations constituted by educational institutions commonly meant. That is, those institutions inspired by a pedagogical project meant for the construction of cognitive maps (through which) to see the world.

By pondering our impressions, it seems that they prove to be disoriented in relation to the great revolution afoot, that they are still affected by isolationist paradigms in a world that makes connection a vital condition, if not a need of life, that they are still tied to the deterministic method and its purging action in a world that finds in mixing (*heteropy*), in bricolage, in contamination, in impurity, the conditions of its own construction (Bateson, 1972).

By observing the map of the cultural agencies, it seems that schools and universities, save some significant and isolated instances, have difficulty in replacing themselves in their historical position of a roundabout, because they are not able to set up new qualities for a dialogue with the nodal points which connote senses of direction often trespassing the settled linearity. The new roundabout junctions, in fact, find their reason in the loss of that immobility which made them work as the Benthamian controller eye; that is as mechanisms prepared to conform a priori the flows and to direct them towards the "right" direction to take. Now and in prospect, they can play again a primary social and cultural role only in acquiring mobility, in knowing how to move within worlds more and more characterized by the tangle of differences, in being able to indicate connections also with other places of nontraditional learning and indifferent to geopolitical frontiers, in knowing how to be bound to the singular cognitive histories, peculiar to the individual, so as to open him/her to a plurality of possibles. And above all, it is for them the difficult task to know how to research the most appropriate connections to create relational plots among individuals bearers of cognitive experiences, the most varied, detached, and dissimilar, whose sources are constitutive of the complexity that characterizes the mediasphere.

Educational institutions are called into question not about their greater or lesser ability to transfer contents, but whether transference of contents may still be part of their primary tasks, competing with other numerous issues, perhaps even more reliable than them in the process of communication and monitoring of the contents themselves (Bocchi & Ceruti, 2004).

If the work of internal revision that educational institutions make is still based on the cadence "step by step," on the check of updating skills, exclusively ruled by the cumulative principle, then a serious misunderstanding is shown. It cannot be seen how the strategic pivot of the educational project may reside in the capability of elaborating a plurality of methodologies and heuristics necessary to avoid the *trans* and *over*historical immobilism of a one method. The same that, by corroborating the timelessness, prevents from constructing, time after time, the most suitable paths, that is the true guidance object of reflection. The construction of the paths is, actually, the domain where most of the didactic virtues, related to the educational processes, come into play.

Until some decades ago, the existence of an inviolable order, of an order that governed definitively the construction of maps (also cognitive maps) according to a pervasive thought which assigned "every thing in its place," could be still taught. But today there is no longer the possibility of reserving places to meet things, since they have become mobile, endowed with a morphological and topological inconstancy that often collocates them into temporary places, exactly because their possibilities of life reside in that relational activity, by its nature always dynamical, that they establish with galaxies of other things. So, a movement that approaches the itinerant process of doing by doing becomes pre-eminent, a process not compressible in the exact execution of an a priori thought project, which shows the possibility of achieving a fruitful path through the ability to play strategically with the bonds that the way will present.

Such a condition singles out a proximity with the artistic doing: when one says "the pen leads the writer," or "the paintbrush leads the painter," it means it becomes necessary to learn to properly consider ("in perceptively listening" and in learning to take that Heideggerian "back step" which makes one safe from arriving at standing too over things) those "suggestions" that, from time to time, come from a movement in the contingency; the same ones that, by often disproving the metrical short cuts of the modern, are able to show the briefest route to reach a goal, as a result of a sensible way and not as a result of a forced one.

The contingency, with its pervasive breaking-in, is traceable not only in the complex, unpredictable, and never totally explainable routes of the artistical doing. A new awareness is increasingly focusing that its presence is necessary to avoid that taking a step is not taking any step; but it deals with a step that, by learning to play with the accidents of the route, produces generative occasions of knowledge. We are moving in the contingency, and—above all for some decades—are being able to construct more and more sensitive artefacts, that make the contingency a condition of their knowing how to self-organize themselves, of their learning to answer appropriately little by little (Morin, 1999a, 1999b).

If the internal reflection has not yet led the educational issues to co-evolve with significant social practises and interests, it is possible that practises and interests, with their intransigent being tentacular, may turn to elsewhere by ignoring traditional educational institutions, or may force them to leave the conditions of isolation where they lie, to the point to draw them to that itinerary they have not yet been able to accomplish all by themselves. Although we have to move in the direction of social interests, we must not omit, however, that the educational itinerary cannot be planned by them, because it would run the risk of finding itself serving particular interests. Thence, school and university may work only by continually negotiating a degree of autonomy that allows them to find a difficult and never definitively reached critical distance; that is, a necessary position to feel safe from attempts of exploitation and to feel authorized to identify the most reliable paths, able to fulfil the tasks the polis refers to them, in view of its knowing how to get in the emerging cognitive dimensions.

In any case, a problematic consideration is necessary since, as already mentioned above, it is not understood that the transmission of contents may still form part of the primary tasks of educational institutions, or that it is what is most expected by them however (Bruner, 1977). By carrying out this activity for historical reasons and for long, they could enjoy a sort of delegation temporally unlimited and exclusive; but today, in front of changed conditions, the knowledge level invites to choose among several and diversified offers originated by several and diversified sources, in the first place by digital media sources. And it is not certain that schools and universities have qualitatively got the best proposals or the most winning channels; not only: it is neither certain that the cognitive experiences planned by institutions are the most fruitful, since they inexhaustibly reconfirm semiotic maps that, in terms of discipline, are functional to views of the world which several beneficiaries hardly recognize.

It is not possible to ignore that the youngest generations are at least partially "emigrating" in an interconnected world, made *of* and *by* a plurality of voices, images, sounds, and writings, *of* and *by* a plurality of voices-images-sounds-writings, able to put into shape not predictable cognitive processes. The debate centres on the greater or lesser pervasiveness and on the greater or lesser transformative capabilities, correlated to technological changes of media and tools that process information (Gardner, 1999). The debate is still open but it seems undeniable that a recursive relationship is being established among the outcomes of the new media and the changes about the ways of knowing, that are deeply connected (Turkle, 1995). By practice, this risks conducting to an actual distance. On the one hand, a miscellaneous panorama of views of the world and of constructions of worlds irreducible to the only unity; on the other hand, the difficulty in understanding and taking part to these new issues by educational institutions, still intent on garrisoning definite territorialities which make them unable to answer qualitatively and adequately the emerging questions.

Once more, the misunderstanding of talking about media literacy and its use is to solve the whole in a function only interested in contents and that concerns the technological use of the machine. Even though endless checking confirms that young people seem to show a surprising familiarity in approaching autonomously technologies of this nature, the didactic activity of training to their use is proving to be certainly important, but scarcely productive of knowledge if it is not tied to questions concerning the incidence of the new media on cognitive processes, on those of symbolization, individual and collective, and on the co-evolutive ones.

Substantially, it is not possible to underestimate the risk of being taken prisoner by idealizations that lead to aphasia, to that real-like, privative condition prophetically narrated by Swift in the geometrized existence led on the island of Laputa. Actually, if the learning of the technique is a necessary condition, the literacy directed to reflect on the technique, in particular, on the ways of expression used by media technologies, lies as an unavoidable condition in order to be *subjects of* practices and not *subjected to* practices.

Anyway, the two moments do not oppose each other, but they are in a dialogic condition: each of them dynamically performs a recursive role of a very influential part, constitutive of the surroundings where the other finds stimuli to live and operate. Their relationship cannot be reduced to the technical moment related to the artefact functioning, but it takes shape in a relational dimension for the technique of producing knowledge.

The ship—great technological product, the most relevant of the ancient world, whose function is today applied with metaphorical pertinence in relation to Web navigation, that is *net surfing*—is of course a container of the navigator (the *netsurfer*), but at the same time it is contained by the latter, in the sense that it is navigated by him; but the self-organizational play requires that the navigator, to be able of navigating (by) the ship, must need in his turn to be contained by the ship itself... Freedom of movement implies awareness of living, at least partially, in a necessary imprisonment. No person can be so unwise as to define himself external with respect to his own language; analogously, none can be so inexperienced as to consider himself external with respect to the technique he resorts to. It is certain that, not to be acted by those practices, it becomes necessary to garrison their confines, to dislocate oneself on those limits which allow to find oneself not confined within them (Longo, 2001).

The situation that is possible to identify, even in its own constitutive but faded contours, may find a first moment of knowledge by looking over the passage afoot from constant and preoriented maps to inconstant ones that, in order to give directions, demand the art to be placed according to cardinal points differently orienting and located if need be. Such a transition entails a continuous work of conceptualization and reconceptualization, of categorization and recategorization, so that it is possible to establish a constant tension between the partiality of a point of observation and the awareness that numerous and otherwise prepared paradigms have to be put close, so as to let their reformulation open.

From a cognitive point of view, talking about telematic nets, about the big nets like Internet, means rightly talking about transits, virtual frontiers to cross, were they even those connected to the less promising link. Actually, the net derides the rigidity of borders pertaining to disciplines or geopolitics, or orders of institutional organizations such as school and university. The static nature of liminal definiteness is less and less credible about its capability to produce and spread knowledge; it tends to close ways by anachronistically hindering those paths which let minds domicile at always new and different territories (Tagliagambe, 1997). The same that impose on those who enter it to have to adapt according to a mimetic gesture, isomorphous to the one impressing the complex activity of translating, that is a gesture radically constructive. In order to be in relationship with the other, I must assume forms not utterly mine; to translate myself, I need somehow to betray myself.[1] This is a transformative betrayal, indispensable to maintain one's own identitary forms, by a dynamics of having to revise oneself, related to the learning of knowing how to revise oneself. To pass confines, physically or virtually, is not compatible with the gesture of indifference: one always "emigrates" when an interest is present, even if generated as a "simple" curiosity, and in the perspective of constructing a nest, though temporary, but endowed with objectivity, so as to be able to rely on it; and not less indispensable is to construct a life of relationship that, as such, derives resources if it develops in diversity.

Specific to digital media dimension is the migratory gesture that, for instance, gets underway from the sedentariness of being in front a computer; it deals with being able of constructing communities disengaged as to metrical bounds of proximity and farness, because interested in distances of cognitive nature, measurable with conceptual metrics that refer to plural views of the world; finally, it deals with being able of constructing one's own nest, that assumes characteristics of objectivity in the cotextual architecture (for example that of MUD). And the fact to be able to enjoy a great mobility that allows the same person to be member of many communities, each constructor of its own peculiar anthropologies, due to a sort of automatism given by *being in net*, involves that the subject has to translate him/herself to construct him/herself and to be constructed in manifold and different ways, so as to acquire those identitary multiple traits, altogether consonant with the needs of a worldwide community of destiny (Lévy, 1995; Turkle, 1995).

If relationship is the base of all, it cannot be forgotten that the space of relational dimension opens to the space of simulation. And it is a simulation that entails first of all the construction of models of worlds, even structured and narrated counter-factually, and that secondarily only entails pretence or deceit. But if the more and more tumultuous "space" of the immaterial city reflects somehow the impulses and the interactions radically constitutive of the real city, it means that the distance from balance becomes condition of life for both of them. In a direction of sense, it becomes legitimate to join both of them in this enlightening cognitive reflection that Ilya Prigogine and Isabelle Stengers propose in the form of rhetorical question, and sounding approximately as follows: "The intensification of social relation-ships that urban life favours [...] has not it been a source of waste, pollution and, at the same time, of intellectual, artistical and practical inventions?" (Prigogine & Stengers, 1988).

Among the tasks of literacy, the primary one consists maybe in teaching to sway on the confines that separate the daily reality from the virtual world, in teaching to live the interface; so as to learn to place oneself between an "inside" and an "outside" in order to trigger the recursiveness that fosters both without gestures discharging the one or the other. A strategic position that, by connecting the constructions operated within the two domains in a relational way, leads to a continual revision of concepts and categories, according to the necessity of a world that can find its own vital paths only in the conditions of a dynamical balance, mentioned above.

The immobility that necessarily hesitates about that always excessive immersion in one universe or in the other, leads to division in order to attribute omnipotence to the one or to the other. And we owe to it a rising commonplace that, by seeing Internet as the oracular space of the totality, of the assured exhaustiveness, of the satisfaction of any question, works for the creation of a fetish that prevents from emancipating.

It is sacrilegious to forget that the one form of totality, visible to man, can come from a donation by a god; by an Efestus that, once forged the shield for Achilles, makes the cosmo*logy* known, that *lógos* which—by establishing nexuses, almost never visible to man, among the constitutive entia of the *kósmos*—allows the world to exist in the complexity of human and natural, human-natural, relationships.

These years the word *reality*, always bearer of problematic semantics, is more and more enriching itself with further meanings, correlatively to the aggressiveness that shows in the attempt at annexing newer and newer territories. And it is just its annexationist pretension to oblige it to open a range of meanings whose manifold richness makes its contours faded. This determines that concepts and categories it makes friends to, often live in a fertile asymmetry. A sheer *chance* of knowledge that finds evidence in the less superimposable drawings the more concerning with different "departments" of a by the way constructed reality.

It is about asymmetries that demand dissonant and somehow interacting interpretative ways: the concept of space and the experience of time change meaning and consistency according to the universes where they are collocated (Cooper &Law, 1995; Meyrowitz, 1995). Analogously, the concept of territory finds in the progressive living density of the city a progressive condition of spatial narrowness to the individuals who reside there; while it finds in living density of the net the main reason of its own real expansion: the more the users who enter the net, the more its "territory" spreads out, according to a principle that does not indicate the existence of an a priori given space and awaiting of being filled, but of a space that is built and widened exactly when someone decides to take sides. The space of the net grows with the use of the net itself, in the presence of its attractive capability. An influential datum, because of the multifaceted implications it involves, comes from the widespread sense of deterritorialization brought by the advance of nonplaces constructed with indifference as to space; and the dispelling of spatial differences entails the dispelling of various textures of sense, constructed in time and in the plot of relationships and experiences, singular and plural.

In front of such a condition, the net plays an ambivalent role: it would aim for constructing recognizable sites, bearers of sense, actual places where to offer every person the possibility of finding oneself and the others; but it is continually restrained by its global vocation that prevents it from making a particular mistake, that happy oxymoron of constructing a *place* in an isotropic space.

The planetary dimension ineluctably exceeds, and if were not it so, the net would take form as a construction unable to perform its own connective task. However, a phenomenon that calls for a sort of dialogic complementarity creeps from within the planetary dimension: the expansion of the net and the advance of the deterritorialization lead to the emersion of a strong desire of *terrenean* forms—to resort to a happy image by Massimo Cacciari—the unalienable need of finding roots and emancipated singularities that give sense to new forms of localization into the global (Cacciari, 2004). It deals with a distinctive necessity very widespread that, by subtracting territory to the homogenization, recovers that diversity which makes everyone interesting to the other also in dialoguing in net, on condition that one learns the art of not falling into the net.

Educational institutions, if they want to recover positions of centrality, have to surpass a sort of paradigmatic fidelity that lead them to validate outdated practices as well as to fall into that misunderstanding which makes the place of education like that of a sought isolation.

It is about a misunderstanding, that of a purging detachment from the stimuli of the present constantly seen as chaotic that, by satisfying the temporariness of its urgencies, tends to devalue the questions maintained as fundamental, of which school and university set themselves up as guardians. In this way of thinking of themselves, educational institutions assume all the time the function of representatives of past images and feel less and less the need of being an active part in interpreting what is happening in the present in order to participate to its construction. The ongoing changes are of such an epistemological significance and extent to decree the organization of new maps that, by putting aside several ways of thinking and of thinking of oneself, decree the end of historical barriers in the split of knowledge domains. For instance, since the active part played by history in the evolution of phenomena was discovered, the historical frontier between sciences of man and sciences of nature has lost its consistency, that very frontier which in its anxiety to assign positions, was ever so alert and zealous in verifying vocations, or in imposing devotions, punishments, and excommunications.

If every epoch innovated—because man is never lazy—the present one has made innovation one of its main distinctive reasons. And to innovate does not entail an updating cumulatively oriented to get hold of the most recent step progressively taken by something already known; but it entails a knowing how to dislocate oneself offshore, there where things were born.

Our epoch, better, the present moment is full of inedited things, of initiatives that, in accord with the heterogenesis of the purposes, put more than a question among the thought results they should have and the actual results they might have. In any case, a planetary society at the height of its educational phase calls for taking sides, for entering constitutively that reticular textile constantly at work in re-giving dynamic shape to the planet, even in its most intimate corners. Knowledge society, information society, risk society, uncertainty society, weak needs society, these are only some of the phrases that try to portray the inclinations which most distinguish the planetary city under construction. Over the last decades, many institutions that contributed for centuries to organize communities have been dispelled, as it is possible to notice, for example, in that more and more definite renouncement to public life that leads to desert the city with its historical capability to self-organize strategies of sociality.

In exchange, the need of individuality and singularity moves forward in the clearing of those universalistic abstractions of ideological nature that have led to the homogenization, to the fidelity to roles and places in relation to which collective identities have been constructed. In other words, the detachment from even recent pasts gets more and more definite, and it is possible to notice how, over the last decades, the heterogeneity has replaced the researched uniformity which a sort of platonic "well-ordered" city had to tend to.

Witnesses to such a sudden detachment are above all the new generations, bearers of a sort of metropolitan intellect that, in their behaviours, expresses hetrogeneous cognitive experiences, largely related with unedited capabilities to access and live a world definitely media*fied* and definitely fragmented by the heterogeneity of sounds, messages, images, ways of being in relationship, aesthetics, technologies, and so forth, that come to give new and manifold faces to the ways of structuring knowledge. Basically, the revolution afoot in the mediasphere is completely consonant and interrelated with the radical changes occurring in the noosphere.

Educational institutions might perform an important task within such a characterized panorama, bearer of very problematic requests and correlated, in particular, to the necessity of finding the "codes" able to tie young people's behaviours to bring them into unity, by safeguarding their singularities (Morin, 1999a). But, as far as it can be seen, institutions are outdated and dissonant as regards a complex world that demands to be visited according to manifold and different scales and perspective angles. If schools and universities suffer from those closures mentioned, they run into a paradoxical situation of aphasia: their difficulty in dialoguing with that temporal piece we call contemporaneity designs them to make also the past less knowable because lacking in that semantic endowment necessary to give again the fore and sense to unavoidable knowledge, elaborated in other historical periods.

Conclusion: Changes of Direction

Not to be practical with "today" entails the impossibility of translating "yesterday." To the alphabets of immobility, of balances, of idealizations, of abstract impressionisms, of mechanisms, of quantitative mathematics, of a priori defined orders, and so forth, new alphabets have come up by their side—with the request of not secondary territorial rights—and that give citizenship to mobility, to distances from balances, to dynamical systems, to dissipative systems, to self-organizational moments, to qualitative mathematics, and to nonlinearity... As regards the routes traced in advance, today the routes are traced throughout the path: it has been learned that very rarely—even if they can be helpful—geometries are able to assure the temporally briefest and surest itineraries. That greater guarantees come from constantly knowing how to face *contingencies* (Gould, 1993), from knowing how to perceive the "voices" of the environment when they advise changes of route not to challenge the impossible in the name of idealizations built on geometric truths.

Schools and universities may do a lot if they learn to reflect on their practices to operate, certainly not easy reconversions, but the ones able to set them in navigation, by subtracting them from consolidated and outdated immobilities. About this, a teaching of Morinian inspiration may be helpful; in order to change the route of a literacy, become largely sterile because too self-confident, it invites to teach literacy to the literacy itself (Morin, 1977).

Acknowledgment

The author thanks Francesca Garenna for the translation of the text.

References

Bateson, G. (1972). *Steps to an ecology of mind.* New York: Ballantine.

Bocchi, G., & Ceruti, M. (2004). *Educazione e globalizzazione.* Milan, Italy: Raffaello Cortina.

Bruner, J. (1996). *The culture of education.* Cambridge, MA: Harvard University Press.

Cacciari, M. (2004). Nomadi in prigione. In A. Bonomi & A. Abruzzese (Eds.), *La città infinita.* Milan, Italy: Paravia Bruno Mondadori.

Capra, F. (1996). *The Web of life.* New York: Random House.

Ceruti, M. (1986). *Il vincolo e la possibilità.* Milan, Italy: Feltrinelli.

Cooper, R., & Law, J. (1995). Visioni distali e prossimali dell'organizzazione. In S.B. Bacharach, P. Gagliardi & B. Mundell (Eds.), *Il pensiero organizzativo europeo* (pp. 285- 323). Milan, Italy: Guerini e Associati.

Gardner, H. (1999). *The disciplined mind. What Alla students should understand.* New York: Simon & Schuster.

Gould, S.J. (1993). *Eight little piggies: Reflections in natural history.* New York: W.W. Norton.

Latour, B. (1993). *Have never been modern.* Cambridge, MA: Harvard University Press.

Lévy, P. (1995). *Qu'est-ce que le virtuel?* Paris, France: La Découverte.

Longo, G.O. (2001). *Homo techonologicus*. Rome, Italy: Meltemi.

Meyrowitz, J. (1985). *No sense of place*. New York: Oxford University Press.

Morin, E. (1977). *La Méthode. 1. La Nature de la Nature*. Paris, France: Edition du Seuil.

Morin, E. (1999a). *Les sept savoirs nècessaires à l'éducation du futur*. Paris, France: UNESCO.

Morin, E. (1999b). *La tête bien faite. Repenser la reforme. Reformer la pensée*. Paris, France: Edition du Seuil.

Norman, D.A. (1988). *The psychology of everyday things*. New York: Basic Books, Inc.

Prigogine, I., & Stengers, I. (1988). *Entre le temps et l'éternité*. Paris, France: Librairie Arthème Fayard.

Stengers, I. (1993). *Le politiche della ragione*. Rome-Bari, Italy: Laterza.

Swift, J. *Gulliver's travels*. New York: Oxford University Press.

Tagliagambe, S. (1997). *Epistemologia del ciberspazio*. Cagliari, Italy: Demos.

Turkle, S. (1996). *Life on the screen: Identity in the age of the Internet*. New York: Simon & Schuster.

Endnote

[1] An implication more linguistically evident in Italian than in English—where the betrayal has just occurred—that is, *tradurre=tradire*, for its linguistic nearness to the Latin paronomasia, *traducere*, to lead *trans*, is *tradere*, to hand over sb., and so, to betray (translator's note).

Chapter V

Integrating Technology Literacy and Information Literacy

Jennifer Sharkey, Purdue University, USA

D. Scott Brandt, Purdue University, USA

Abstract

Information technology literacy can be seen as an integration of what are commonly two separate literacies—technology literacy and information literacy. This chapter defines them, reviews issues related to both, and argues that both must be acquired and functionally utilized for students and workers to achieve success in our heavily technology-oriented society and workplace. The authors address learning outcomes and design components that should be considered in training and instructional settings, and give examples of instructional strategies for achieving them.

Introduction

To succeed in today's higher education and workforce environments, one cannot rely solely on either technological or information literacy skills. The two are complementary, and they must be interlocked to provide a complete inventory of needed skills and knowledge. In some places the phrase "information technology literacy" is used to address both; here they are addressed separately before describing why they are complementary. Integrating and utilizing standards and competencies for both through an instructional systems design (ISD) approach strengthens curriculum and program development in the digital age. Building skills upon skills allows for continued proficiency acquisition and adaptation to changing environments, and infuses the concept of continued lifelong learning.

The need for technology skills and knowledge in schools, the workforce, and society is an obvious extension and consequence of living in the digital environment of what Alvin Toffler coined as "the Information Age." Computers and computing have become a way of life and the primary means for doing work in today's world. Governments, schools, and business have attempted to address issues in acquiring specific technical skills for some time. Often missing from discussions about technology literacy is technology's interdependent relationship with information. There is a reason, after all, why it is not called the Technology Age—technology is tools or the use of tools, but it is the result of using them that is important. Computers have not only made creating, acquiring, tracking, storing, retrieving, and analyzing data and information easier; they have made it more accessible than their original creators could have ever imagined. The skill sets needed at the very center of this vortex where technology interfaces with information are both technology literacy and information literacy.

Background

Traditionally, technology skills have been thought to be the responsibility of employers. Duemestre (1999) argues that while arts and technology should be balanced in education, the latter is more likely best addressed by employers in a work setting. However, the Deputy Director of the National Science Foundation noted in his October 24, 2002, address to participants of the Advanced Technology Education program that this was a challenge—the skills students need for the workplace is an issue that should be reviewed in the context of the traditional college curriculum. Bordogna (2002) avers that technical skills are increasingly the purview of community colleges. Others have suggested that in particular, information technology skills should be incorporated into a minor as part of college programs (Bailey & Stefaniak, 1999).

Early on, information literacy was taught primarily in undergraduate environments, where the need for honing research skills was seen to be the greatest. Information literacy, as it is now known, began in the '70s when computers were first used in publishing, and the amount of information began to grow. In the '80s, computers began to be used as tools to organize and retrieve published information, and accessing information became even more complicated for end users. The '90s, of course, saw the proliferation of both published and unpublished information via ubiquitous networked computers and the World Wide Web (Murray, 2003). A recent review of trends in librarianship noted that information literacy research has progressed from codifying a doctrine for librarians, to proving its effect in supporting both general education and lifelong learning for students, to integration into specific curricula through collaboration (Arp & Woodard, 2002).

The two literacies have taken parallel, if not mutual paths. Each was once considered the responsibility of a specific constituency—employers or librarians. Each became more complex as computers became a driving force in both the workplace and education. And each has begun to be seen as set of skills and knowledges which underlies larger needs and outcomes in both areas. The two paths have, at this point, crossed.

Defining the Literacies

What comprises technology literacy, knowledge, and skills? Often it depends who you ask. People in a higher education setting tend to view technology literacy as either the ability to work with technology within a given discipline, such as biology, or as a generalized set of IT skills necessary to perform perfunctory work in a computer-rich environment (Kock, Aiken, & Sandas, 2002). Educators in K-12 settings view more narrowly the skills of "computer literacy" as being able to use the computer for keyboarding, basic programming, and so forth (Murray, 2003). Government and industry view things in very applied and outcome-oriented terms; technology literacy can be described as mastery over technological tools, usually specific to a company and the products it produces (Bailey & Stefaniak, 1999).

The National Academy of Engineering's (NAE) (2001) Council on Technological Literacy notes that in addition to specific skills (including, for instance, the ability to change a fuse), people who are technically literate also have "a sense of the risks, benefits, and trade-offs" in using technology in various situations. Many technology inventories of competencies are available on the Internet and show a wide range of skill sets. The CPSI Technical Skills Inventory (1999) identifies hundreds of specific industry skills by categories, such as software and hardware engineering, operating systems, data bases, Web/Internet, desktop publishing, and so forth. For schools, the Carl D. Perkins Vocational and Applied Technology Education Act of 1990 has had a major impact. Many schools now address a variety of technology competencies at both K-6 and 7-12 levels, including such specifics as demonstrating "knowledge and use of appropriate connectivity methods, basic networking, and communication hardware and software" (Conroe Independent School District, 1999, Section 1, Paragraph 2).

Information literacy encompasses a different domain of skills and knowledge, those involved in finding, retrieving, and using information. The context has been computer-based information, even as noted in the American Libraries Association (ALA) report of 1989 which predates the World Wide Web. Like the NAE, university librarians believe information literacy must include knowledge and understanding of the context of information in today's society, its composition and organization, as well as its use in lifelong learning (Dupuis, 1997). K-12 educators take a simple, though related view: information literacy includes skills for locating and using information, as well as knowledge for interpreting and evaluating it (Murray, 2003).

Specific information literacy approaches include identifying standards, goals, objectives, or outcomes. For instance, from the ALA, information standards include accessing, using, and evaluating information "critically and competently" (American Association of School Librarians, 2004). Examples of K-12 goals include abilities to define information problems, determine range of possible sources, and extract relevant information from a source (Eisenberg, 2003). University objectives tend to be more specific, such as: "Given an industry-related task, the user can identify and obtain critical information to support the decision-making process" (Purdue University Libraries Faculty, 1995, Goal 1, Paragraph 5).

Increasingly, the skills and knowledge used in information seeking and retrieval require sophistication using computers as tools of access, analysis, and formatting. The Association of College & Research Libraries' (ACRL) (2000) Information Literacy Competency Standards for Higher Education is an updated framework for information literacy in an academic setting. It notes: "Information technology skills enable an individual to use computers, software applications, databases, and other technologies to achieve a wide variety of academic, work-related, and personal goals" (Association of College & Research Libraries, 2000). Basic skills that support information literacy may include using e-mail, managing personal databases, and troubleshooting operating system problems. In many ways, it is impossible for anyone to work and survive in the Information Age without information technology skills (Latham, 2000). And at this point in time, it could go without saying that these skills and knowledge extend to networks, the Internet, and the World Wide Web.

Overall standards for literacies vary. As noted, the nomenclature used to describe them can be expressed as objectives, skills, expectations, competencies, or standards, depending on the context. Generally, standards are the highest conceptual level of expression, and objectives are concrete and detailed expression of outcomes designed for an instructional session, course, or program. A sampling here indicates the variability in scope and specificity of skills.

University Setting (Instructional Technology Committee of the Campus Computing and Communication Policy Board, 1998):

- Handle e-mail attachments (send, find, open, read, and store).
- Open a browser and find various sites.
- Download/save images and files.
- Find help and search university's Web page.

Public School Setting (North Carolina Department of Public Instruction, 2003):

- Select and use technological tools for class assignments, projects, and presentations.
- Practice and refine knowledge and skills in keyboarding/word processing/desktop publishing, spreadsheets, databases, multimedia, and telecommunications in preparing classroom assignments and projects.
- Use word processing and/or desktop publishing for a variety of writing assignments/projects.
- Select and use appropriate technology tools to efficiently collect, analyze, and display data.
- Use electronic resources for research.

Statewide Setting (Linberg, 2000):

- Manage large hierarchical file system, organize tools, re-order scattered files.
- Find, install, and use plug-ins; use secure space, manage advanced browser features.
- Import/export to/from text, tab, or other delimited formats.
- Devise solutions/workarounds when no help is available.

Figure 1. ABCD model applied to an objective

Audience	Students
Behavior	will present to the class
Condition	a critical analysis of fresh-water ecosystems literature
Degree	through an electronic presentation

Designing Literacy Components

A closer look at designing literacy objectives gives further insight into how outcomes and skills can be facilitated. When developing any instructional sessions or courses, basic instructional systems design (ISD) principles can go a long way in helping develop effect activities and solid learning outcomes. One main benefit of using basic ISD principles is that learning outcomes can be tied directly to the types of activities and projects assigned to students. To use these principles, an appropriate model should first be identified to create the effective integration of skills. Gagné, Briggs, and Wager (1988) state that developers of instruction must pay close attention to internal and external influences on the learning environment and how this affects the learning process. A common instructional systems design model used is the ADDIE model. This model focuses on key components of the instructional design process, which can be easily applied by an individual or design group. The ADDIE model is an acronym for Analysis, Design, Development, Implementation, and Evaluation.

The model used isn't as important as keeping in mind what is to be accomplished by the instruction. "All stages in any instructional systems model can be categorized into one of three functions: (1) identifying the outcomes of the instruction, (2) developing the instruction, and (3) evaluating the effectiveness of the instruction" (Gagné et al., 1988, p. 14). Prior to instruction the first three steps of the ADDIE model help with the creation of the instruction. The *Analysis* step determines the need for instruction and what learners should gain overall from the instruction. *Design* and *Development* is the process of creating the structure of the instruction. This includes determining outcomes and objectives, developing assignments and activities, and creating methods of assessment. How the structure is built directly influences the level of success when conducting or implementing your instruction. Morrison, Ross, and Kemp (2001) recommend using the following questions to address the components of designing instruction.

- For whom is the program developed? (characteristics of learners or trainees)
- What do you want the learners or trainees to learn or demonstrate? (objectives)

- How is the subject content or skill best learned? (instructional strategies)
- How do you determine the extent to which learning is achieved? (evaluation procedures) (p. 5)

As with Gagné, Briggs, and Wager's recommendations for instructional design, these points focus on key components of the overall process of developing instruction.

When incorporating technology, it should not overwhelm or supplant content to be taught or substitute class time that is typically spent on content. Just using technology will not bring benefit to the overall outcomes of the instruction or the students. Using an ISD model can help one avoid this trap. A design model, called eTIPS (educational technology integration and implementation principles), was developed specifically to help teachers design instruction with effective incorporation of technology. This model helps anyone using technology to avoid the trap of using technology for technology's sake. Specifically, this model encourages "a teacher-designer to consider what they are teaching, what added value the technology might bring to the learning environment, and how technology can help to assess student learning" (Dexter, 2002, p. 57).

Writing quality objectives will help determine the rest of the instruction's structure. In the context of most classes, creating objectives that just focus on the use of a particular technology can take time away from the content of the class and the overall learning outcome. When writing objectives, focus on the use of a technology as it supports the established learning objectives and desired behavior of the student either in assignments or assessment (Dexter, 2002). Examples of these types of objectives can be as follows: 'Students will conduct a half-hour interview of a local historian using a digital camcorder.' or 'Students will present to the class a critical analysis of fresh-water ecosystems literature through an electronic presentation.' These objectives demonstrate that the focus of the assignment is on the content of the class, but use technology to support the achievement of the objective and therefore the overall learning outcomes.

Developing concrete outcomes can be a challenge if someone is not used to creating curriculum from an ISD standpoint. Using the ABCD model to create solid objectives can make the development of them much easier. The acronym stands for Audience, Behavior, Condition(s), Degree (of success). Each component of the model has a specific function in the creation of an objective. Essentially, this type of objective guides the learner (Audience) to perform (Behavior) in a certain situation (Condition) to a specified level of success (Degree) (Schuman & Ritchie, 1996). See Figure 1 for an example of this model and its application to a learning objective.

Projects or assignments developed for instruction need to be in direct support of the objectives of the course. When developing a project, some basic questions should be asked: How does this project support the overall goal of the course? What main objectives are directly supported by this project? Is the project focused on the course content and not directly on the tool? One pitfall professors and instructors tend to fall into is creating an assignment for using a tool which does not support the curriculum. If it is important for students to know how to develop a Web site, a Web development assignment should not arbitrarily be created; the Web development assignment should be put into the context of the course. Students can create a Web site that demonstrates their knowledge of main concepts of the course or shows their research and critical thinking skills through an examination of the course content.

When integrating technology and information literacy, students can acquire skills in multiple ways. While there are many studies and models discussing how these skills should be gained, more recent discussions show that the point-and-click demos in particular are no longer the best way for skills to be transferred. A report produced by the Panel on Educational Technology (1997) recommends that projects, assignments, and instruction overall should not just focus on the technology or hardware, but use these as a complement to support the instruction. A research project, for instance, contains the traditional aspects of information literacy such as using scholarly journal articles and providing critical analysis. However, the container in which the project is handed in to the professor can vary in format. Some examples of containers can be a Web site, video presentation, documentary short, or e-portfolio. The appropriateness of the container greatly depends on the course content as well as overall learning outcomes.

Another key to the successful use of technology for learning is to encourage the interactivity of learners with curricular material and one another. Multimedia learning materials are well designed if they encourage learners to be active, engaged, and purposeful about their learning. Computer conferencing tools and applications are well designed if they also foster constructive dialogue among learners around critical concepts. (Abrami, 2001, p. 118)

Specific Literacy Outcomes

Information and technology literacy skills can be acquired in several ways, as well as on multiple levels. The basic research paper requires fundamental technology skills such as word processing to write the paper and a Web browser to access online sources. The same research paper may require higher-level information literacy skills such as finding multiple types of sources, evaluating the validity of the sources, and critically analyzing the content of the sources as they support or refute the student's hypothesis or thesis statement. These higher-level information literacy skills don't need to be compromised for the technology component of the project to go to a higher level. If the traditional research paper is just one type of container for the research project, then other, more technology-based containers can be produced.

Some examples have been mentioned above on how to incorporate technology into instruction. Specific examples of instruction that can be used in academic courses are given below. All three examples have been used at Purdue University in association with the Digital Learning Collaboratory. These examples were used in English literature classes, a communications class for PR majors, and a Botany class.

Electronic presentations have become quite standard as a requirement for student projects. Many people use PowerPoint because of easy access and familiarity. However, people typically don't move beyond the basic functionality of PowerPoint, often creating dull and unimpressive presentations (Abram, 2004). PowerPoint's capability to apply custom animations, embed video and audio, and create voice-over narration can allow a student to create a presentation that pushes his or her creative envelope.

Since literature classes often require the critical analysis of text, a group presentation was created as a final project in three English literature courses. Each group of four to five students was to develop a 20- to 25-minute presentation that examined, developed, and expanded an idea, theme, or metaphor in literature, which embodied personal as well as cultural aspects. Students were required to include both personal views and scholarly documentation. Students could use photos (personal or commercial), newspapers, magazines, journals, books, music, DVDs, videos, personal narrative, and so forth to support their views and critical analysis. This assignment was created by Dr. Binnie Martin while a PhD student in the English department.

As students advance through their major, it is not uncommon for higher-level classes to require a semester-long project. The subject area greatly influences the container type of the final project, but it is not unusual for the project to be in the form of a 25-plus-page research paper. As universities focus on alternative learning experiences such as service learning, opportunities are provided to incorporate exploration of scholarly communication, various types of technology, and applied experience into semester-long projects.

Developing campaigns is a standard component of the Public Relations industry. To help students gain practical experience, a service learning assignment was created by Dr. Mohan Dutta-Bergman, Assistant Professor of Communication. Students working in groups of nine to ten were to create an advertising campaign for a local non-profit agency to help promote awareness, address an issue, or solve a problem in the contingency served by that agency. This project required the development of a campaign plan and materials in physical or electronic format. The campaign plan needed to be a strategic document that presented the different elements of communication strategy proposed by the students to help address the agency's need.

The materials could be created using various hardware and software such as digital cameras, scanners, graphic editors, video editors, Web development, and so forth. The development of the plan and materials needed to be supported by scholarly research and published statistical data.

E-portfolios are becoming a more common way for students to showcase their skills, expertise, and accomplishments during their college career. The e-portfolio format provides a way for projects and products to be shown in a way paper cannot. A quality e-portfolio also demonstrates a student's skill and knowledge of technology. An e-portfolio is typically considered a tool for presenting specific work when seeking employment. However, it can be used in the classroom environment to effectively support learning and provide an assessment tool (Cole, Ryan, & Kick, 1995). In the classroom setting, the e-portfolio is often the container in which the final project is enveloped; the content of the final project greatly depends on the assignment and course subject. An effective research project utilizes the components of information literacy, which are then evident in the products included in the e-portfolio. Because the e-portfolio can easily incorporate multimedia, components of the e-portfolio can include audio files, video files, animations, digital images, 3D graphics, and electronic documentation.

In a class focusing on Plants and the Environment, students were required to examine how plants influence and are influenced by the environment. The students' research and findings of this semester-long project were to be encapsulated into an e-portfolio. The project required students to find scholarly research relating to plants and the environment, grow actual plants and capture this growth as digital images, interview a local scholar using a digital camcorder, and develop a field study report tying together their work over the course of the semester. The e-portfolio could be in the form of a Web site, DVD, or CD-ROM, but needed to include effective navigation to the various portions of the project requirements. This project was created by Dr. Carole Lambi, Associate Professor of Plant Pathology.

Conclusion

Technology and information will continue to influence academic, work, and personal environments. To function effectively in these environments, individuals will need to be both technology and information literate. It is no longer a viable option for employers or universities to expect the other to handle the development of these skill sets. It is argued here that a university setting affords a great opportunity to combine and integrate these literacies in a variety of learning situations. Inclusion of technology into curriculum, while it should not be arbitrary, does not have to be an overwhelming or complicated process. Utilization of an instructional systems design model can guide the development of instruction, creation of objectives, and application of technology. To be successful, instruction must be designed to balance the two literacies, and integrate them with course content and goals to create meaningful results for students' immediate outcomes, to prepare them for the workplace, and to position them for lifelong learning.

References

Abram, S. (2004). PowerPoint: Devil in a red dress. *Information Outlook, 8,* 27-28.

Abrami, P.C. (2001). Understanding and promoting complex learning using technology. *Educational Research and Evaluation, 7*(2-3), 113-136.

ALA Presidential Committee on Information Literacy. (1989). *Final report.* Chicago: American Library Association.

American Association of School Librarians. (2004). *Information literacy standards for student learning.* Retrieved February 29, 2004, from www.ala.org/ala/aasl/aaslproftools/informationpower/informationliteracy.htm

Arp, L. & Woodard, B. (2002). Recent trends in information literacy and instruction. *Reference & User Services Quarterly, 42*(2), 124-132.

Association of College & Research Libraries. (2000). *Information literacy competency standards for higher education.* Retrieved February 18, 2004, from www.ala.org/ala/acrl/acrlstandards/informationliteracycompetency.htm

Bailey, J.L. & Stefaniak, G. (1999). Preparing the information technology workforce for the new millennium. *ACM SIGCPR Computer Personnel, 20*(4), 4-15.

Bordogna, J. (2002, October 24). From pipelines to pathways. *Proceedings of Assessing the Impact: ATE National Principal Investigators Conference.*

Cole, D.J., Ryan, C.W., & Kick, F. (1995). *Portfolios across the curriculum and beyond.* Thousand Oaks, CA: Corwin Press.

Conroe Independent School District. (1999). *Texas essential knowledge and skills.* Retrieved January 13, 2004, from www.conroe.isd.tenet.edu/instructional/teks/bench7-12.htm

Currier Professional Services, Inc. (1999). *Skills inventory menu.* Retrieved January 15, 2004, from www.currierprof.com/ts_ol.htm

Dexter, S. (2002). eTIPS—Educational technology integration and implementation principles. In P.L. Rogers (Ed.), *Designing instruction for technology-enhanced learning* (pp. 56-70). Hershey, PA: Idea Group Publishing.

Duemestre, M. (1999). The impact of technology on U.S. higher education: A philosophical approach. *Journal of Information Technology Impact, 1*(2), 63-72.

Dupuis, E. (1997). The information literacy challenge: Addressing the changing needs of our students. *Internet Reference Services Quarterly, 2*(2&3), 93-111.

Eisenberg, M. (2003). *A Big 6 skills overview*. Retrieved February 18, 2004, from www.big6.com/showarticle.php?id=16

Gagné, R.M., Briggs, L.J., & Wager, W.W. (1988). *Principles of instructional design* (3rd edition). New York: Holt, Rinehart and Winston.

Instructional Technology Committee of the Campus Computing and Communication Policy Board. (1998). *Information technology literacy for effective use of instructional technology*. Retrieved March 7, 2004, from ist-socrates.berkeley.edu/~edtech/cccpb-it/itliteracy.html

Kock, N., Aiken, R., & Sandas, C. (2002). Using complex IT in specific domains, developing and assessing a course for nonmajors. *IEEE Transactions on Education, 45*(1), 50-56.

Latham, J. (2000). The world online: IT skills for the practical professional. *American Libraries, 31,* 40-42.

Linberg, S. (2000). *Adult literacy and basic education teacher technology competencies v2.1*. Retrieved March 7, 2004, from www2.wgbh.org/mbcweis/ltc/alri/abecomps.html

Morrison, G.R., Ross, S.M., & Kemp, J.E. (2001). *Designing effective instruction* (3rd ed.). New York: John Wiley & Sons.

Murray, J. (2003). Contemporary literacy: Essential skills for the 21st century. *MultiMedia Schools, 10*(2), 14-18.

National Academy of Engineering. (2001). *Characteristics of a technologically literate person*. Retrieved January 13, 2001, from www.nae.edu/nae/techlithome.nsf/Weblinks/KGRG-55SQ37?OpenDocument

North Carolina Department of Public Instruction. (2003). *Computer/technology skills curriculum: Grades 9-12*. Retrieved March 7, 2004, from www.ncpublicschools.org/curriculum/computer.skills/9_12.html

Panel on Educational Technology. (1997). *Report to the president on the use of technology to strengthen K-12 education in the United States*. Washington, DC: President's Committee of Advisors on Science and Technology.

Purdue University Libraries Faculty. (1995). *Information literacy curriculum (ILC) goals and objectives*. Retrieved January 15, 2004, from www.lib.purdue.edu/rguides/instructionalservices/ilcgoals.html

Schuman, L. & Ritchie, D.C. (1996). *Understanding objectives*. Retrieved March 3, 2004, from edWeb.sdsu.edu/courses/EDTEC540/objectives/ObjectivesHome. html

This work was previously published in Technology Literacy Applications in Learning Environments, edited by D.D. Carbonara, pp. 64-74, copyright 2005 by Information Science Publishing (an imprint of IGI Global).

Section II

The Information Society: Educative Researches

Chapter VI

Growing Up Wireless:
Being a Parent and Being a Child in the Age of Mobile Communication

Letizia Caronia, University of Bologna, Italy

Abstract

This chapter illustrates the role of the mobile phone in the rise of new cultural models of parenting. According to a phenomenological theoretical approach to culture and everyday life, the author argues that the relationship between technologies, culture, and society should be conceived as a mutual construction. As cultural artefacts, mobile communication technologies both are domesticated by people into their cultural ways of living and create new ones. How are mobile phones domesticated by already existing cultural models of parenting? How does the introduction of the mobile phone affect family life and intergenerational relationships? How does mobile contact contribute in the construction of new cultural models of "being a parent" and "being a child"? Analysing new social phenomena such as "hyper-parenting" and the "dialogic use" of mobile phones, the author argues upon the role of mobile communication technologies in articulating the paradoxical nature of the contemporary cultural model of family education.

Beyond the User-Technology Dichotomy:
A Phenomenological Approach to Everyday Life

"Some day we will build up a world telephone system making necessary to all peoples the use a common language, or common understanding of languages, which will join all the people of the earth into one brotherhood" (Dilts, 1941, p. 11, cited in de Sola Pool, 1977, p. 129)

Like an underground current, the same social discourse reappears each time a new technology enters the social world: the technology purportedly produces new unexpected behaviours and causes major changes in the way people live. Whether it is for the worse or for the better is not important. What matters more is the underlying unidirectional causal-deterministic model that putatively accounts for the influence of technologies in people's lives.

The deterministic approach to social phenomena and particularly to technological evolution has had a long and strong tradition that spans the 20th Century. Even if today no one would say "science discovers, industry applies, man conforms,"[1] the deterministic model persists in both scientific and commonsense approaches. At least within commonsense reasoning and theories, information and communication technologies are supposed to determine not only people's behaviours but also their attitudes, relationships, and even identities. Empowered technologies are perceived as overwhelming unskilled people as if they dominate their lives. Such a view of the role of technologies in people's everyday life has the hallmarks of all commonsense theories. It is self evident, taken for granted, and ready made. It shares commonsense's advantages: it provides easy to grasp explanations for a number of social events and allows people to cope with more dramatic circumstances. Like most practical reasoning, the one concerning information and communication technologies is a shortcut. It reduces the complexity of the phenomenon making it simpler and apparently more manageable.

Often echoed by media discourse and sometimes reinforced by references to simplified expert discourse, commonsense reasoning and layman theories constitute a shared cultural system through which we make sense of technologies in our daily life.

Although the deterministic approach to social phenomena has nurtured commonsense theories more than any other approach, it is not the only one. A major philosophical approach has been supporting concurrent views on social phenomena and providing a different paradigm for understanding technologies in everyday life: the phenomenological approach to social life.

Since Edmund Husserl's and Alfred Schutz's philosophical investigations, scholars in both Europe and the United States have emphasized the role of individuals in constructing culture, social organization, and their relation to the material features of everyday life contexts. Against any form of social and cultural determinism, ethnomethodology has demonstrated that people create their social and cultural world through their everyday actions and interactions (Garfinkel, 1967). Everyday practices of ordinary people are the effective tools that make supposedly passive users behave as active subjects. Defying and subverting any determinism of both dominant culture and the systems of production, social actors invent and create, moment by moment, the meaning and functions of things that circulate in their social space (De Certeau, 1984). Far from obeying implicit logics inscribed in goods, consumers develop their own tactics and follow paths in often unforeseen and unpredictable ways. The uses and gratification approach to information and communication technologies (Katz, Blumer, & Gurevitch, 1974) is consistent with this antideterministic paradigm. Proponents of this stream have shed light on the role of users' needs and goals in the adoption or rejection of a technology and its intended uses.

These approaches to social life and phenomena share a crucial theoretical assertion: the strength of human agency (Giddens, 1979, 1984) and subject intentionality in making the meaningful dimensions of the world people inhabit.[2]

Accordingly, everyday life is conceived as a never-ending cultural work through which social actors produce the meaning, structures, and social organization of the world they live in, as well as their own identities and those of the people they interact with. Everyday language and interaction are the primary tools of this culture construction. However, social structures as well as the material features of everyday life contexts are more than an inert background for culture construction. Disregarding any radical subjectivistic drift, the phenomenological approach to culture and everyday life does not underestimate the constraints of the world of things nor does it claim for an omnipotent actor. Rather it conceives the process of culture creation as radically embedded in the cultural frames and the material resources available in the world people inhabit, which in turn makes this creation possible.

As renewed attention to the material aspects of social life indicates (Appadurai, 1986; De Certau, 1984; Gras, Jorges, & Scardigli, 1992; Latour, 1992; Semprini, 1999), the artifactual dimension of daily life is a crucial component that affects and is affected by everyday interactions, social organizations, and cultural frames of reference. Things, whether technological or not, participate in such a process of creating cultural models of living: as cultural artefacts, they are domesticated by users into pre-existing patterns of meaning and create new social scenarios and identities.

As people establish meaningful interactions with objects and artefacts, they make them exist in their social world, making sense of and domesticating them according to their frames of relevance and "moral economy" (Silverstone, Hirsch, & Morley, 1992). Literature on the social uses of media and the cultural ways of coping with a technological environment has shown how these uses, like other social practices, may be considered semiotic actions in the strict sense of the term; that is, ways of communicating and tools for constructing meanings and social realities.

The available technologies, the material features of the objects which support them and the daily routines they create or are integrated in, are all tools for the everyday production of culture and identities. Through media-related practices, individuals construct themselves in specific ways and produce the forms of their social participation (Caronia, 2002). Simply put, through our uses of media, through the way we act out these uses, we define (at least locally) the communities to which we belong and our identities.

We define but we are also defined. If face-to-face interaction and talk may still be considered the basic forms of socialization (Boden & Molotoch, 1994), the ways in which media uses become topics of everyday conversation are powerful tools to construct their meanings and the identities of those who use them. People's ways of using media, whatever real or imagined, enter everyday conversations as parts of the narratives through which people constantly construct who they are and who the people they talk about are (Ochs & Capps, 1996).[3]

If human beings construct the meaning of things and make sense of them according to their goals, the reverse is also true. Things are not neutral nor are they "pure" material objects waiting to be defined. Even though they do not determine people's life, things delineate the conditions of possibility for new behaviours and ways of life. Their features and engineering anticipate paths of action and project new possible identities for the users. By moving the image from the permanence of the analogical universe to the ephemeral digital world, the digital camera demands and proposes a radical nonrealistic ontology for photography. Even the social perception of the photographer's work and identity has changed. The digital camera has definitively legitimized photography as a manipulation of reality through iconic representation. Whereas the assumption of the nonreferential nature of documentary images has always been taken for granted by epistemologists and philosophers, the digital camera has integrated this representation of photography in the layman's culture. Allowing people to make, remake and unmake iconic representations of reality, the digital camera has produced a new everyday culture of photography.

Overcoming the "subject-object" duality, we need to rethink the relationship between humans and technologies in terms of reflexivity, that is, a mutual construction of meaning and reciprocal sense making.

This need is even more pronounced for information and communication technologies. Their progressive introduction into people's everyday life, the multiplication of possible new courses of action, and ways of communicating and getting information, expand the range of tools through which individuals construct culture and identities.

Faced with this changing and growing technological environment (Livingstone & Bovill, 2001), it then becomes relevant to investigate how the work of everyday culture construction may be affected by the new forms of technologically mediated actions, and vice versa.

The process of mutual construction among technologies, culture, and society may be analyzed at the macro level of patterns of diffusion and uses, as well at the micro level of ordinary everyday interactions. Drawing upon data from qualitative and ethnographic research on mobile communication devices in ordinary life,[4] this author of this chapter discusses the role of these technologies in the construction of family relationships and inner culture. Particularly, the chapter focuses on the following aspects: the creation of a cultural model of "parenting" (hyper-parenting), the dialogic use of mobile phones in connecting the different socio-cultural universes to which children belong (i.e., family and peer), and the role of mobile communication technologies in articulating the paradoxical nature of the contemporary cultural model of family education.

Contemporary Studies on Mobile Phone Diffusion and Appropriation

In recent years, considerable research has examined the adoption and diffusion of mobile phone technology. It seems quite evident that, even though important differences exist across different countries (Kats & Aakhus, 2002), adolescents are a major well-established target for the adoption of this technology (Colombo, & Scifo, 2005; Kasesniemi & Rautianen, 2002; Ling, 1999; Lobet-Maris, 2003).

It is not surprising, then, that research has focused on young people's uses of the mobile phone, especially in European countries where the adoption rate among adolescents and young people had been quite high.[5] Investigating adolescents' uses of mobile phone, Ling and Yttry (2002) show how adolescents hypercoordinate their social life and construct social encounters moment-by-moment. Mobiles phones allow for "perpetual contact" (Katz & Aakhus, 2002), a form of social link that seems to fit perfectly with young people's peer culture and developmental tasks. Rather than voice calls, young people have made the Short Message System (SMS) their typical use of mobile phone (Cosenza, 2002; Grinter & Eldgridge, 2001; Grinter & Palen, 2002; Riviére, 2002) Along with the economic advantages, the diffusion of the SMS among teenagers may be explained by social and cultural factors (Taylor & Harper, 2003). The silent dimension of this distant communication is at the core of its domestication in young people's underground life both in the family and in school (Caron & Caronia, 2007). Allowing for silent and hidden communication, the mobile phone perfectly integrates a typical teenagers' cultural pattern: constructing their social world outside of their parents' control and the official rules governing life in school. Young people have also interpreted the technical constraints of SMS according to their specific peer culture. The limit of the numbers of available characters has been transformed into a resource for constructing a new language and new language games. Competence in this language defines the boundaries of a community of users, creates group membership and cohesion, and distances users from adults' culture (idem).

Studying teenagers' discourses on mobile phone, some scholars have noted that this technology is a detonator of social thinking: it provokes reflective thinking on the ethics, politeness, and aesthetic rules of everyday action and social life (Caronia & Caron, 2004). Reflecting upon social uses of the mobile phone, teenagers explore the identity-making processes involved in the presentation of oneself on a public scene. They interpret and make the uses of the mobile phone work as a social gram-mar through which people supposedly define themselves and those around them. In this sense, using a mobile phone in a teenage-appropriate way is not a matter of technical competence; it requires broader communicative skills that include cultural knowledge of when, where, why, and especially how to use this technol-ogy. Similarly, researchers have analyzed the normative aspect of mobile phone use among teenagers' groups. In particular, they focus on the implicit cultural rules governing the sharing of the technology (Caron & Caronia, 2007; Weilenman & Larsson, 2001). According to teenagers' cultural frames of reference, the owner-ship of a communication device is not an individual matter. Rather it is a radically social affair. Alliance and friendship, leadership and membership, require sharing individual property: mobile phones are loaned and borrowed among the members of the group and this performance entails a system of reciprocal obligations. This "gift exchange" (Mauss, 1954 {1924]) reinforces social links and ritually defines who belongs to the group.

These studies shed light on different aspects of what can be conceived as a single process: the domestication and integration of the mobile phone into youth-specific culture. The mobile phone seems to work as a developmental tool that meets the needs of the growing up process. Particularly, young people use it to attain a cer-tain degree of autonomy with respect to family world, to mark their belonging to a community of peers, to create their specific social organization, and to develop the skills and share the knowledge needed to become competent members of their own community.

Less explored than the world of teens are the cultural and social micro-aspects involved in parents' uses of the mobile phone in communication with their chil-dren. Research on this issue mostly describes mobile phones' usefulness in mutual coordination of children and working parents and their perception of mobile phone as a security/safety/control device (Caronia & Caron, 2004; Ling & Yttri, 2002; Rakow & Navaro, 1993). These studies have investigated relevant dimensions of the process through which mobile phones affect and are affected by family culture. However, more detailed knowledge and a deeper understanding of the cultural and interpersonal aspects of such a process is required.

Our hypothesis is that this mobile communication device contributes to the creation of new cultural models of being a parent and being a child.

Cultural Models of Parenting:
A Theoretical Approach

The cognitive approach to culture conceives cultural models as prototypical, language-based scripts of events, actions , and social actors. These shared definitions of situations supposedly work as frames of reference for inference-making and as guides for appropriate, mutually understandable, and accountable actions. Shared by individuals belonging to the same linguistic and cultural community, cultural models are models of reality as they define what counts as an occurrence of what type of event. They are also models for reality insofar as they are used as references to act in accordance with these shared definitions of social events. Cultural models thus constitute a background cultural knowledge providing resources to understand and to perform in culturally appropriate manners (D'Andrade, & Strauss, 1992; Holland & Quinn, 1987). Just as linguistic competence and grammatical knowledge make linguistic performance and language use possible, the shared set of cultural models of reality generates social actions. Conversely, people's actions, discourses, and behaviours are seen as merely reflecting or expressing their mental representations of the social world.

The cognitive approaches to social knowledge and praxis give primacy to knowledge over praxis, to culture over everyday actions and discourses. This top-down theoretical perspective has been strongly criticized and programmatically reversed by radical bottom-up views. Building upon philosophy of language and speech act theory (Austin, 1962; Searle, 1969), ethnomethodology (Garfinkel, 1967; Heritage 1984), social constructionism (Gergen, 1985), conversation analysis (Atkinson & Heritage, 1984), and discursive psychology (Edwards, 1997; Potter & Wetherell, 1987), conceive cultural models that organize everyday life in intersubjectively shared ways, as constructed moment by moment by the ways people participate in social events. Actions and discourses do not merely reflect an existing culture stored as information in people's minds. Rather, they are tools for constructing cultural definitions of reality. From a radical constructivist perspective, knowledge is thus a product of praxis.

In contrast, dialectical perspectives have emphasized the reductionism of both the knowledge oriented and action oriented approaches. Phenomenology (Giorgi, 1990), cultural psychology (Bruner, 1996), critical discursive psychology (Wetherell, Taylor, & Yeats, 2001), and contemporary linguistic anthropology (Duranti, 1997) propose a theoretical perspective that captures the reflexive relationship between culture and action. Individuals are historical beings belonging to an existing life-world. This background of taken-for-granted assumptions, beliefs, and traditions provides established, normalized ways of understanding the world and sets the limits and the opportunities for acting and thinking (Foucault, 1980). However, background cultural knowledge does not determine people's actions and behaviours. Through their everyday actions and discourses, individuals become crucial agents of a creative process of culture making, remaking, and unmaking. In essence, "knowledge and praxis create each other" (Ochs, 1988, p. 15).

Praxis is also technologically mediated actions and communications. How does the use of mobile communication devices shape cultural models of "being a parent" and "being a child" and vice versa?

Hyper-Parenting:
A Technologically Mediated Achievement

As the mobile phone became a tool for parent-child communication, it has been shaped by a pre-established culture of parenting. Pagers and mobile phones have been interpreted by parents as means to exert control over and fulfil their responsibilities toward their children. They have thus been completely domesticated in the family's moral economy and transformed into tools for family socialization. By analyzing parents' and children discourses on their use of mobile phones, we can reconstruct the repertoire of official reasons family members invoke to make sense of the adoption of this technology.[6] Some patterns of meaning are recurrent, namely being in touch and responding to emergencies.

In the following example, Guy, a father in his mid-fifties, sees the mobile phone and pager as a kind of "umbilical cord," since they allow him greater contact with his children:

Guy: *But we also used it, now less, it used to be a lot like an umbilical cord with the kids. The kids could call us... Now it's less important... they're 19 and 20 now. They both have pagers. Bruno who didn't want one, we twisted his arm to get him to have one, so we could get in touch with him.*

Parents may also insist on their children calling them, as we can see in the following discussion between Louis (age 10) and his parents, Gerry and Madeleine (in their 40s) that lend him their cell phone to reach them:

Researcher: *Do you call your parents often?*

Louis: *Well, yes. Even when I'm going to school.*

Gerry: *Let's say you don't call, it's because we tell you to call...*

Researcher: *Why do you call them, for example?*

Louis: *Well! Sometimes when it's important or something that uh...*

Madeleine: *But he doesn't call us. We have to insist on him calling us.*

Gerry: *In fact, it's because we are starting to leave him at home alone a little. So we tell him, "before you go, you call."*

Children also can perceive the mobile communication device more as a kind of "electronic leash" that allows their parents to contact them at any time:

Barry (19 years old): *It is a pager heu.. (...) and then afterwards there, it happened, what we call.. it becomes a bit like an electronic leash for my mother...*

Researcher: *An electronic leash?*

Barry: *For my mother and then so... It lets her call me all the time and then uh... any time.*

Andrée (mother, age 50): *Well, it's true, I appreciate it.*

Barry: *Yeah, she finds it very useful.*

Andrée: *I can reach him everywhere because he has it and it's reliable, you always have it?*

Barry: *I alw... I almost have it all the time on me. Sometimes I forget but otherwise it is always on, always, always.*

The image of the cellular phone as a piece of emergency equipment is another recurrent pattern of meaning in parents' accounts of the reasons they introduced cell phones. Parents and children often construct narratives of hypothetical dangers and imagined scenarios in which having a mobile phone helps the owner resolve a problematic situation. The emergency discourse is actually one of the most recurrent themes in explanations of why the mobile phone came into informants' family and how they were supposed to use it:

Researcher: *You told me you'd have a cellular?*

Louis (son, age 10): *Yes.*

Madeleine (mother age 40): *When did we talk to you about having a cellular?*

Louis: *When we were in the car.*

Gerry (father, age 45): *That's right.*

Louis: *To call each other in emergencies.*

Gerry: *That is we will lend him one of our cell phones so that when he is on the mountain, if ever something happens, that he would get lost, like when he went to blue mountain and he got lost, well he would have his cellular and it is going to be programmed, because, you know, you can program the cell phone, so he will have to program the number.*

Louis: *At Green Mountain I had it.*

Gerry: *Had you lent it to him?*

Madeleine: *Yes I remember.*

As these examples show, the use and the functions of mobile phones are shaped by typical features of cultural model of parenting characteristic of contemporary western society. Exerting control over children, ensuring that they are safe, handling emergencies, managing time to create family moments, assuming responsibility toward children, supervising children's life out of the home, and mutual coordination to be in touch are all behaviours consistent with the cultural definition of being a parent. From this point of view, remote parenting (Caronia & Caron, 2004; Rakow & Navaro, 1993) seems to be nothing more than a new way to perform old functions and to act according to established models of fulfilling parental roles.

Our hypothesis is that mobile communication devices are not only an expression of an existing family culture and social organization, they are also ways to create them. By tracking their children's movements, finding out who they are spending time with, claiming to know that their children are safe, reminding their children when they have to be back or scolding them if they are late, parents realize the rights and duties involved in "being a parent."[7] By participating in these remote parenting interactions, children are socialized in the commitments and responsibilities of being members of the family. Mobile communication devices' practical uses are thus meaningful actions: they establish and confirm family boundaries, they state "who makes family with whom" and what behaviours belong to family members. They make the link between relatives permanent and work as teaching-learning strategies on the rights and duties governing family community life. Through the courses of action implicit in mobile phone use, parents do more than exert their role: they construct culture by legitimizing the definitions of what counts as "being a parent," "being a child," or "being a family" inscribed in their mobile phone mediated actions.

The following example from our ethnographic fieldwork on mobile use in the family sheds light on the cultural and social consequences hidden behind the most visible functions of remote parenting.

Scene: *It is Saturday afternoon in Bologna. Silvia, a divorced mother in her 40s, is talking on the land phone to her friend, participant researcher Laura. Mafalda, Silvia's oldest daughter, age 13, is in Milan at her father's house. Silvia's mobile phone rings:*

1. **Silvia to Laura:** *Wait, just a minute, it's "Serafini-Milano." (reading on the display)*

2. **Laura:** *Okay.*

3. **Silvia to Mafalda:** *Yes, sweetheart, I'm on the phone, talking with Laura.*

4. **Silvia:** *"Wear?" (English in original), W-E-A-R? (spelling the word) It means to bear on the person.*

5. **Silvia:** *"Back?" (English in original), it means "at the rear" or "been returned," It depends. You have to consider the sentence.*

6. **Silvia:** *"Appear?" (English in the original), I don't know, wait, I'll ask Laura...*

7. **Silvia to Laura on the land phone:** *Laura, what does it mean, "appear?" A-P-P-E-A-R?*

8. **Laura:** *"To have an outward aspect."*

9. **Silvia to Mafalda:** *"To have an outward aspect." Laura said that it means to have an outward aspect.*

10. **Silvia:** *"Fail" (English in original), I don't know, I'll ask Laura.*

11. **Silvia to Laura:** *And "fail?" (English in original), F-A-I-L?*

12. **Laura:** *To deceive, fail, to not succeed in doing something.*

13. **Silvia to Mafalda:** *To not succeed, okay sweetheart? Is it correct? I love you.*

14. **Silvia to Laura:** *Hey, many thanks, many thanks from Mafalda, too. It's fantastic, I never do that, helping Mafalda with her homework in this way. She's in Milano and I'm in Bologna and you, you're at home, it's great!*

Remote parenting is more than an easy way to attain practical purposes or carry out typical functions related to the parental role. Through this mobile phone mediated interaction, Silvia is not only helping her daughter do her English homework. The sequence of her "mobile" actions is a meaning making devices.

Consider first the opening sequence of this multiparty telephone conversation. Silvia interrupts her conversation with Laura to give priority to her daughter's call (turn 1.). "It is Serafini-Milano": reading aloud the identity of the caller appeared on the display, she tells Laura whose needs come first. In this family culture "Serafini-Milano" is a shortcut for "daughters when they are at their father's house." Sharing this background local knowledge, Laura accepts Silvia's shift to her daughter's call (turn 2.). Acceptance is an action: through this action Laura legitimizes her being put in standby position. Then, Silvia does more than merely shift her attention to her daughter. After addressing Mafalda with some instances of intimate talk, she formulates this move with words (turn 3). Describing in words what one is doing is one of the linguistic moves though which participants negotiate the meaning of what is going on (Garfinkel & Sacks, 1970) and construct a shared definition of the event and its implications. This can be summarized as: "if children call, their mother is available and their needs come first."

The second part of the conversation is a typical mother-child scaffolding interaction: the mobile phone guarantees a direct, always open access to the caregiver and makes it possible to carry out this kind of joint action despite physical distance.

In the closing sequence, Silvia formulates what happened as a new, original way to perform as a parent (turns 13 and 14).

The actions performed in and through this technologically mediated conversation are culture building activities and socialization devices. By doing "being a parent" in certain ways, the mother locally constructs and proposes dimensions defining her cultural model of parenting: being always available, giving priority to children's needs over adults' needs, interrupting the ongoing course of action to open up a parallel one, using intimate talk to address one's own children, and giving children a scaffolding to overcome their difficulties.

At the same time, the mother's actions convey a cultural model of the child: a child is a demanding individual whose needs come first. He or she has the right to expect his or her parent to divert attention from an ongoing adult-adult interaction to take care of the children.

What about the other participants? By participating in such an interaction, Mafalda is learning more than the meaning of some foreign words: she is being socialised in the cultural models of "being a mother" and "being a child" that are at stake in this family. Accepting her role as a collateral participant, Laura legitimizes the definition, under construction, of "what is going on and why."

The participants officially involved in this interaction, are jointly constructing and ratifying, at least locally, a shared definition of "being a parent" and "being a child." That is, they are constructing a cultural model of parenting as a technologically mediated achievement.

If "reciprocal availability" can be considered a trait of an existing culture of parenting, how does mobile phone shape this trait?

Mobile communication devices are distinctive because they allow anytime and anywhere reciprocal availability. This is nothing more than a suggested way of acting, a "possible world" inscribed in the technology. It is through everyday and ordinary ways of using the mobile phone that this cultural model becomes a (technologically mediated) accomplishment.

A pre-existing cultural definition of being a parent has clearly shaped parents' and children's use of the mobile phone far beyond the management of urgency, safety, and control. In very reflexive ways, the use of this technology has created a new original way to be a parent. The possibility of remote parenting has been turned into hyper-parenting.

Through their everyday mobile interactions, parents and children have transformed physical distance into relational proximity; they have overcome the spatial and temporal constraints of face-to-face or traditional telephone interactions, and transformed almost every moment into an opportunity for coconstructing joint actions and care-giving. Family relationships seem to perfectly mirror the contemporary paradox of a wireless world producing hyperlinked people.

Linking Macro and Micro: Socio-Cultural Changes in Family Education

One of the most relevant contributions to the construction of the contemporary cultural model of parenting has been the historical change in the notion of parental authority. Since the end of the 17th Century, western societies have progressively moved from a political model of authority based on the concept of natural inequality and on the related notions of power and obedience to a definition of authority legitimized by a social consensus among equals. According to the political model, the pater familias' supreme authority over his children was analogous to that exerted by a sovereign over his subjects. Power and submission were the expected behaviours defining parents' and children's reciprocal and naturally unequal status. This notion of authority was profoundly questioned by Locke and Rousseau according to the principle of the natural equality of all human beings. Obedience to the authority does not stem from the presumed inferior status of some individuals. Rather, it derives from the social contract. Individuals have to obey the law because it expresses the will of all the people concerned.

Since Toqueville, and throughout the 19th Century, this model of authority has strongly affected western societies' macrohistory, politics, and laws. While in a slow often inconsistent way, it has also brought major changes to microhistory: it has affected the cultural models of all social relationships including those typical of the private family universe. The patria potesta no longer has a natural foundation, and negotiation is presumed to be at the core of family members' distribution of authority. The translation of this consensus-based model into actions and interaction is less obvious with respect to the parent-child relationship. Here, a "natural inequality" (now referred to as "asymmetry") is at stake: it defines the psycho-physical dependency of children on their caregivers. The gap in competences, skills, and knowledge is precisely what defines the reciprocal status of parents and children. Parents' authority—whatever that means—is a tool to overcome this gap, a necessary condition for children's development. Yet this necessity is no longer an argument for a power-based definition of parental authority.

At the end of the 20th Century, the inner logic defining parental authority was completely reversed. Until at least a century ago, parents had almost absolute power over their children, who were not considered to have rights. Now it is parents that have duties toward children. Most western societies have substituted the notion of patria potesta with those of parental cares and responsibilities, protection and supervision. The United Nations Convention on the Rights of the Child, introduced in 1989, emphasized that children have their own rights; adults' "authority" is clearly defined in terms of duties, obligations, and responsibilities that parents have over their children. The notion of power as the probability of obtaining obedience no longer defines the contemporary model of parenting.

How can this new image of a child as a subject that is no longer expected to obey be reconciled with the notion of parental authority and governance? How can authority be invoked without power? How does one cope with a child that is considered both a vulnerable and dependent individual and an autonomy-oriented person with rights?

Traditionally, parents had the right to exert power over children who had the obligation to obey. Aside from any other consideration, this model was inherently consistent. It offered a clear distribution of complementary rights and duties and traced a path for mutually coordinated actions.

The change in the definition of parental authority has broken the inner consistency of the traditional model. Now, children's rights and parents' duties often appear incompatible, and family education practices need to be conceived as ways to cope with the inherent paradoxes defining contemporary democratic education.

It may sound hazardous to relate these macro cultural, historical, and political changes to everyday life and social practices. Yet it is in the micro-order of ordinary life that cultural changes are both reflected and accomplished. The cultural changes in the status of children and in the notion of parental authority have directly and indirectly affected family education practices.

Aside from tragic exceptions, mainstream parents and children in contemporary western societies interact according to the social consensus framework. While recognizing the difficulties of creating such a consensus, sometimes shifting to or mythically evoking the simplicity of the authoritarian traditional model, contemporary parents have assumed the basic principles of democratic education.

Negotiation more than obedience, competence more than power, trust more than authority are the basic principles underlying parents' and children's reciprocal interactions. Mobile communication devices have been shaped by such a cultural framework. They have been appropriated as unexpected and efficient tools to negotiate parents' and children's often conflicting perspectives on children's developmental needs, and as ways to articulate their often incompatible rights and obligations.

In other words, mobile communication devices play a role in coping with the slightly paradoxical nature of the contemporary model of family education.

Parents' and Children's Incompatible Rights: Mobile Phones as a Negotiation Tool

One of the domains where the paradoxical nature of parents' and children's reciprocal status emerges the most is children's gradual shift towards the peer universe.

As they grow up, children multiply their universes of references and have to negotiate their progressive belonging to multiple socio-cultural worlds. Family and peer community are different, often conflicting, demanding worlds.

It is mostly at this point in their developmental trajectory that pre-adolescents start demanding autonomy, freedom, and the right to make their own decisions, choices, and even mistakes. Moreover, it is then that they construct social links beyond their parents' filter. Not surprisingly, it is at this moment that parents officially enforce their responsibility, their obligation, or even their right to exert control and supervision. Less than 10 years ago, these conflicting perspectives were managed in two ways: talking with children about the where, when, what, and with whom of their extra-family life and negotiating the limits of time spent outside the home. These educational practices are rarely mutually exclusive. Depending on the family's pedagogical model and on children's behaviours and attitudes, the transition to the peer universe may be more dialogic-oriented or more control-oriented. In either case, borders are clearly identified and the transition becomes a field where parents' and children's differing perspectives often conflict.

As mobile phones became part of the family's technological equipment, they are interpreted as a means of coping with children's belonging to multiple socio-cultural worlds. They have opened a new arena to manage the transition from family universe to that of peers. Crossing the boundaries of these two worlds, mobile phones become tools to negotiate children's right to develop autonomy and parents' right to control a still dependent child.

Consider first the arrival of a mobile phone in children's life. Often, parents offer their children a mobile phone at some ritual milestone of their development. This gift-giving is a meaningful symbolic practice: parents recognize that their children have attained a stage of relative autonomy and allow them to privatize their social contacts. In contemporary societies, mobile phone gifts are rites of passage marking the (culturally perceived) beginning of adolescence. Like other goods provided by parents that symbolically mark the beginning of children's autonomy, the mobile phone marks also children's dependence on their parents for a wide set of needs and activities. Children's dependence on their parents for mobile phone use seems even more obvious when we look at management of the related costs. As some adolescents, age 15, explain[8]:

Researcher: *Generally, among your friends who have mobile phones, who pays?*

All: *Our parents!*

Mishan: *Well, I think it is half and half because teenagers want to have a little independence so they pay half. But they can't pay for the whole cost so their parents pay half.*

Since children or even adolescents do not have the means to cover the costs, parents pay the fees. As soon as they are able, adolescents want to express their independence and give themselves some freedom by taking responsibility for part of the cost. Yet when parents are paying all or most of the related costs, they acquire the right to set rules on mobile phone use. This economic leash defines the boundaries of children's autonomy. If the mobile phone is a bridge connecting children with the outside family universe, the bridge is built by parents who partially control access to this universe. Allowing for an economically controlled independency, mobile phones are used as cultural objects to mediate and gradually modulate children's construction of a life outside of family boundaries and constraints.

Besides the strategic use of costs, the role of the mobile phone as a mediating device emerges from the way it is used both by parents and children.

As a 15-year-old girl told us, parents often take advantage of the fact that their children have mobile phones to keep an eye on them, watch over them from a distance, and even control where they go:

Karine (age 15): *Well, it's because my parents, it's become like they really want to know where I am, so my parents always want to contact me, they're always afraid when I'm outside. When I'm out they can't contact me because there's no phone, when I'm at someone's it's okay but if I go somewhere and I don't call when I'm going, well they start freaking out, so... I need one.*

Anxiety when children go out is an emotional experience strictly related to parenting. Mobile phones allow parents to cope with such a common experience in a totally original way: they do not need to choose between either allowing children be out of supervision and enduring their own anxiety, or radically limiting children's social life to avoid painful apprehension. The mobile phone thus opens an alternative course of action:

Pénélope (age 15): *Often there are, well I know some where it's the parents who want to know where their kids are...*

Researcher: *Ah?*

Pénélope: *It's a form of security for them, like, you know, parents buy it for their kids to give them, to give the kids some freedom, but at the same time the parents can know where the kids are any time.*

For parents, the function at stake is not only to reduce their own apprehension. By tracking their children's movements and finding out with whom they are spending time, they fulfil the duties and rights related to their parental role while respecting the children's right to live an autonomous life. As we have seen in the extract above, adolescents seem to be quite aware of the dual nature of mobile phone contact. It is exactly this feature that allows them to use the technology in very strategic ways to negotiate their right to autonomy.

Adolescents usually accept that parents use cell phones to exert parental control. The duty to inform parents is generally well integrated in young people's specific culture: this ritual practice is commonly assumed to be a way to gain more permission:

Sophie (age 15): *It's safer, not just for us, but for our parents too… Sometimes there are families that are separated; in ours, we're all together, but even so my mother likes to be able to call me…*

Antoine (age 17): *In that sense, it's sure that it's another advantage, maybe to be able to get more permission to go out because you tell them something like "hey, you can call me any time, there won't be any problems."*

Sophie: *"If there's anything, I'll call you, Mom, Dad…"*

Karine (age 15): *Because some people go out a lot, they have a really big social life and for their parents, it would help them a little.*

Researcher: *To be able to contact them?*

Karine: *To contact them, yeah, so the parents won't freak out, so they won't be there going "Aaaack!"*

As this discussion among adolescents shows, mobile phone has opened a totally new arena for negotiating children's belonging to both family and peer worlds. Allowing users to reach and be reachable all time, the phone creates a symbolic space where parents and children can take into account the rights of the counterpart. When provided with a mobile phone, children are willing to accept the parents' right to know where their children are, and they are willing to attend to and cope with their parents' anxiety (It's a form of security for them; It's safer not just for us, but for our parents too.). Conversely, helping them manage their own right to apprehension, mobile phones help parents cope with their children's right to go out and have a "really big social life:"

Layla (age 15): *Why did you get a mobile phone?*

Jean (age 15): *Well, one, to communicate, like to have more independence. You know, when your parents tell you, like in a mall, you have something, a means of communicating, to contact you. Like with your friends, let's say we say, "okay, let's meet like at the movie theatre."*

Layla (age 15): *Okay.*

Carl (age 15): *Me, it's about the same too. It's like the parent-child relationship. It's sure that you know if, if you're going to be late, you're on your way, so then you just have to call your parents on your mobile and then you tell them, "I'm coming, I'm about 15 minutes late, uh, I'm just in front of such-and-such a place, I'm coming." Then they say, "oh, okay, that's fine."*

Children consider autonomy, freedom, and peer life coordination the fundamental reasons for owning a mobile. However it is not surprising that they strategically focus on safety reasons when impressing on parents the need to get one. Grasping the unique opportunities they offer, adolescents use mobile phones as a means to act in ways that are consistent both with their needs and rights and with those of their parents.

Camera phones have amplified the repertoire of parents' and children's mediating tools. They provide parents and children with a more sophisticated strategy to negotiate their incompatible rights and to construct a bridge that connects the worlds of family and peers:

Layla (age 15): *Then you say, "yes, Mom, see my friends," then you take a picture with your phone. It's so your mom can see that you're really with your friends.*

Researcher: *Could you repeat what you just said?*

Layla: *It's because I say to myself, okay, let's say I call my mother, then my mother really wants to know if I'm somewhere or if I'm really with my friends, you take a picture, then you say, "yes, Mom, I'm with my friends, look."*

Researcher: *So you've got proof.*

Layla: *Yeah, I've got proof.*

Aside from their impressive role in creating a community of peer where instant pictures circulate and are shared by members, camera phones fit perfectly into parents' and children's typical interactions. It would be easy to invoke the image of Bentham's panoptikon and wonder if this kind of visual remote parenting is nothing more than a contemporary version of power and control dynamics. Rather, we propose a different interpretation that focuses on the strategic use of this otherwise controlling device: the dialogic use of mobile phones. By letting their parents enter their peer world, by giving them visual proof of what they probably have stated in words, adolescents establish a contract of trust with their parents. Gaining in trust implies gaining in freedom and autonomy. Adolescents have turned the constraints of remote parenting to their advantages as in peer culture gaining more freedom is an advantage. Less hidden then it once used to be, adolescents' underground life with respect to family can be strategically and at least partially shared with parents. The new sharable quality makes peer community experience a negotiable affair.

Sending photos via camera phone to parents may thus be seen as a paradox-resolving practice. In and through this process, parents and children articulate their symmetric and opposite rights, while creating much more room for negotiation and for consensus construction.

Mobile phones are also used to transgress this dialogic model. Transgressing family norms, pushing the boundaries of what has been consensually established as legitimate, and eventually breaking the terms of the trust contract, are all typical dimensions of adolescents' growing up process. Mobile phones can be strategically turned off (i.e., when children do not want to be reached by their parents) or simply ignored if the caller ID device signals that parents are calling:

Tania (age 15): *It's like, I don't really like that. You're with your friends and then your mother calls you.*

Researcher: *So, you'd rather not have one? It's your mother who insists?*

Tania: *Yeah, but it's really like, uh, to know where I am, if I'm going to be late or something.*

Researcher: *So how do you deal with it?*

Tania: *I turn it off.* [Laughs]

Researcher: *You take it but you turn it off...*

Tania: *Well, I turn it off, yeah, or else I say I was in the subway.*

The following is another example of the strategies used by adolescents to filter parental control calls. In this case an additional function of the technology enables Sandrine to transgress the rule:

Delphine (15 years old): *On top of that, I don't have call display, so I have no choice but to answer.*

Sandrine (15 years old): *I have call display, you know, when it's someone, let's say I'm somewhere and it's my parents and I don't want to talk to them, I don't want them to bug me, so I don't answer.*

Turning off the mobile phone and not answering if parents are calling are behaviours that have to be justified or accounted for: no signal and low battery are the arguments commonly used by children to justify their being unreachable. The need for explanations defines these behaviours as exceptional transgressions. Invariably, transgression reveals and confirms the rule at stake. In this case, the rule is dialogic use of the mobile phone, a pattern of interaction legitimizing both parents' right and duty to supervise their children and children's right to be autonomous.

Parents' and Children's Dialogical Use of Mobile Phones: Conclusions

Although they are incorporated in existing cultures of parenting and strongly dependent on each family moral economy, mobile communication devices nurture these worlds of meaning. Culture and praxis create each other. Everyday uses of mobile phone are no exception: they participate in the process whereby people constantly create and recreate their cultural ways of living their lives.

Entering the family's and teens' everyday life and allowing new forms of interaction (such as remote parenting), this device works as a culture making object. It plays a major role in the rise of new cultural models of "being a parent" and "being a child." Hyper-parenting is one such model.

Beside allowing coordination of children and working parents, besides facilitating single parents' multitasking or connecting divorced parents to their children living away from their home, mobile phones are used to create and constantly confirm social and affective links among parents and children. Building upon traits of a shared, pre-existing model of parenting and seizing the opportunities of mobile phone, parents in contemporary western societies go beyond its practical functions. They have transformed the "reaching children and being reachable" dimension into anytime and everywhere reciprocal availability. Wireless parents and children perform as hyperlinked members of a family. Beyond any practical purposes or topic of mobile conversations, it is the contexts of mobile phone use and the ways in which it is used that give their interactions meaning. Their mobile verbal exchanges are meaningful actions that define their social and affective ties as relevant and prior to almost any other course of action. Simply put, mobile phones have magnified and overstated a totally cultural and unnatural parental model: children come first. It may sound obvious, yet it is not.

Mobile phones uses confirm, naturalize, and literally objectivize what is nothing more than a socially constructed definition of "being a parent." These technologies participate in the silent and almost invisible process in and through which individuals create their cultural world as a quasi natural one.

The same process underlies the use of the mobile phone as a bridge connecting family and peer worlds. As we have seen, contemporary parents must contend with a definition of parental authority and children's rights that make family education almost paradoxical. Mobile phone use has been totally integrated in a dialogical model of exerting parenthood. Thanks to its engineering, it leaves room for negotiating the symmetric and opposite rights defining the status of contemporary children and parents.

The mobile phone has opened a symbolic space to manage the transition from family universe to that of peers and to cope with paradoxes of the developmental process such as the typical autonomy-dependency dimension. Parents and children use the technology to blur the boundaries of the different socio-cultural universes to which children belong, and to make a smooth supported transition from family culture to the peer world. In particular, the mobile phone is used by family members to negotiate the often conflicting perspectives of parents and children with respect to the developmental needs and to articulate an often incompatible system of reciprocal rights and duties.

In a social and historical context where parental governance is no longer legitimized by power and obedience, mobile communication devices are used as an educational tool consistent with a consensus-based notion of parental authority. Performing according to such a cultural and even normative model of being a parent is a way to constantly recreate it. Through a dialogic use of mobile phones, parents and children participate in the process of defining a contemporary model of family education as a democratic social practice.

References

Appadurai, A. (Ed.). (1986). The social live of things. Cambridge, MA: Cambridge University Press.

Atkinson, J.M., & Heritage, J. (Eds.). (1984). *Structures of social action: Studies in conversational analysis.* Cambridge, MA: Cambridge University Press

Austin, J.L. (1962). *How to do things with words.* Oxford: Clarendon Press.

Boden, D., & Molotoch, H.L. (1994). The compulsion of proximity. In R. Friedland & D. Boden (Eds.), *Now/here. Space, time and modernity* (pp. 257-286). Berkeley, CA: University of California Press.

Bruner, J. (1996). *The culture of education.* Cambridge, MA: Harvard University Press.

Caron, A.H., & Caronia, L. (2001). Active users and active objects. The mutual construction of families and communication technologies. *Convergence. The Journal of Research into New Media Technologies, 7*(3), 39-61.

Caron, A.H., & Caronia, L. (2007). *Moving cultures. Mobile communication in everyday life.* Montreal, Canada: McGill-Queens University Press.

Caronia, L. (2002). La socializzazione ai media. Contesti, interazioni e pratiche educative, Milano: Guerini.

Caronia, L. (2005). Mobile culture: An ethnography of cellular phone use in teenagers' everyday life. *Convergence. The Journal of Research into New Media Technologies, 11*(5), 96-103.

Caronia, L., & Caron, A.H. (2004). Constructing a specific culture: Young people's use of the mobile phone as a social performance. *Convergence. The Journal of Research into New Media Technologies, 10*(2), 28-61.

Colombo, F., & Scifo, B. (2005). Social shaping of the new mobile devices. Representations and uses among Italian youth. In L. Haddon, E. Mante, B. Sapio, K-H. Kommonen, L. Fortunati & A. Kant (Eds.), *Everyday innovators, researching the role of users in shaping ICTs* (pp. 86-103). London: Springer.

Cosenza, G. (2002). I messaggi SMS. In C. Bazzanella (Ed.), *Sul dialogo.* Milano: Guerini.

D'Andrade, R., & Strauus, C. (Eds.). (1992). Human motives and cultural models. Cambridge, MA: Cambridge University Press.

De Certeau, M. (1984). *The practice of everyday life.* Berkeley, CA: University of California Press.

De Sola Pool, I. (Ed.). (1977). *The social impact of telephone.* Cambridge, MA: MIT University Press.

Dilts, M.M. (1941). *The telephone in a changing world.* New York: Longman's Green.

Doxa Junior. (2005). Indagine sui ragazzi tra i 5 e i 13 anni. Retrieved October 3, 2007, from http://www.doxa.it/italiano/nuoveindagini/junior_2005.pdf

Dunfield, A. (2004, November 12). Students like their cellphones. *Globe and Mail.* Retrieved October 3, 2007, from http://m1.cust.educ.ubc.ca:8200/news/studentslikecellphones

Duranti, A. (1997). *Linguistic anthropology.* Cambridge, MA: Cambridge University Press.

Edwards, D. (1997). *Discourse and cognition*. London: Sage.

Foucault, M. (1980). *Power/knowledge*. New York: Pantheon.

Garfinkel, H. (1967). *Studies in ethnomethodology*. Englewood Cliff, NJ: Prentice Hall.

Garfinkel, H., & Sacks, E. (1970). On formal structures of practical action. In J. McKinney & E. Tiryakian (Eds.), *Theoretical sociology: Perspectives and developments* (pp. 337-366). New York: Appleton.

Gergen, K.J. (1985). The social constructionist movement in modern psychology. *American Psychologist, 40,* 266-275.

Giddens, A. (1979). *Central problems in social theory: Actions, structures and contradiction in social analysis.* Berkeley, CA: University of California Press.

Giddens, A. (1984). *The constitution of society: Outline of the theory of structuration*. Cambridge: Polity Press.

Giorgi, A. (1990). Phenomenology, psychological science and common sense. In G.R. Semin & K.J. Gergen (Eds.), *Everyday understanding: Social and scientific implications* (pp. 64-82). London: Sage.

Gras, A., Jorges, B., & Scardigli, V. (Eds.). (1992). *Sociologie des techniques de la vie quotidienne*. Paris: L'Harmattan.

Grinter, R.E., & Eldridge, M.A. (2001).Y do tngrs luv 2 txt msg? In W. Prinz, M. Jarke, Y. Rogers, K. Schmidt & V. Wulf (Eds.), *Proceedings of the Seventh European Conference on Computer Supported Cooperative Work* (pp. 219-238). Dordrecht: Kluwer Academic Publishers.

Grinter R., & Palen, L. (2002). Instant messaging in teen life. In *Proceedings of the ACM Conference on Computer Supported Cooperative Work.* New Orleans, LA: ACM Press.

Heritage, J. (1984). *Garfinkel and ethnomethodology*. Cambridge: Polity.

Holland, D., & Quinn, N. (Eds.). (1987). *Cultural models in language and thought.* Cambridge, MA: Cambridge University Press.

Kasesniemi, E., & Rautiainen, P. (2002). Mobile culture of children and teenagers in Finland. In J.E. Katz & M.A. Aakhus (Eds.), *Perpetual contact. Mobile communication, private talk, public performance* (pp. 170-192). Cambridge, MA: Cambridge University Press.

Katz, J.E., & Aakhus, M.A. (Eds.). (2002). *Perpetual contact: Mobile communication, private talk, public performance.* Cambridge, MA: Cambridge University Press.

Katz, E., Blumler, J., & Gurevitch, M. (1974). *The use of mass communication*. Beverly Hills, CA: Sage.

Latour, B. (1992). *Aramis, ou l'amour de techniques*. Paris: la Découverte.

Ling, R. (1999). C'est bien d'être joignable: l'usage du téléphone cellulaire et mobile chez les jeunes norvegiens. *Réseaux, 92-93*, 261-291.

Ling, R. (2006). The role of mediated ritual communication. *Telenor.* Retrieved October 3, 2007, from httpp://intermedia.uib.no/public_files/_2006_06_mediated_ritual_communication.ppt

Ling, R., & Yttri, B. (2002). Hyper-coordination via mobile phones in Norway. In J.E. Katz & M.A. Aakhus (Eds.), *Perpetual contact. Mobile communication, private talk, public performance* (pp. 139-169). Cambridge, MA: Cambridge University Press.

Livingstone, S., & Bovill, M. (Eds.). (2001). *Children and their changing media environment. A European comparative study.* London: Lawrence Erlbaum.

Lobet-Maris, C. (2003). Mobile phone tribes. Youth and social identity. In L. Fortunati, J. Katz & R. Riccini (Eds.), *Mediating the human body: Technology, communication and fashion* (pp. 87-92). Mahwah, NJ: Lawrence Erlbaum Associates.

Mauss, M. (1954 {1924]). *The gift; forms and functions of exchange in archaic societies.* Glencoe, IL: Free Press.

Ochs, E. (1988). *Culture and language development: Language acquisition and language socialization in a Samoan village.* Cambridge: Cambridge University Press.

Ochs, E., & Capps, L. (1996). Narrating the self. *Annual Review of Anthropology, 25,* 19-43.

Potter, J., & Wetherell, M. (1987). *Discourse and social psychology. Beyond attitudes and behaviour.* London: Sage.

Rakow, L., & Navaro, P. (1993). Remote mothering and the parallel shift: Women meet the cellular phone. *Critical Studies in Mass Communication, 10*(2),144-157.

Rivière, C. (2002). La pratique du mini-message. Une double stratégie d'extériorisation et de retrait de l'intimité dans les interactions quotidiennes. *Réseaux, 20*(112-113), 139-168.

Searle, J. (1969). *Speech acts.* Cambridge: Cambridge University Press.

Semprini, A. (Ed.). (1999). Il senso delle cose. I significati sociali e culturali degli oggetti quotidiani. Milano: Franco Angeli.

Silverstone, R., Hirsch, E., & Morley, D. (1992). Information and communication technologies and the moral economy of the household. In R. Silverstone & E. Hirsch (Eds.), *Consuming technologies. Media and information in domestic spaces* (pp.15-31). London: Routledge.

Taylor, A.S., & Harper, R. (2003). The gift of the gab? A design oriented sociology of young people's use of mobiles. *Computer Supported Cooperative Work, 12*(3), 267-296.

Weilenmann, A., & Larsson, C. (2001). Local use and sharing of mobile phones. In B. Brown, N. Green & R. Harper (Eds.), *Wireless world: Social and interactional aspects of the mobile age* (pp.99-115). Godalming and Hiedleburg: Springer Verlag.

Wetherell, M., Taylor, S., & Yates, S.J. (2001). *Discourse theory and practce. A reader.* London: Sage.

Withers, K. (2006). *Mobile have key role for young.* Institute of Public Policy Research. Retrieved October 3, 2007, from http://news.bbc.co.uk/go/pr/fr/-/2/hi/technology/6070378.stm

Endnotes

[1]   This is the famous slogan of Chicago World's Fair in 1933.

[2]   The notion of intentionality as the human competence in making sense of reality and in creating the crucial dimensions of people's *life-world* was introduced by Brentano and Husserl at the beginning of the 20th Century. It is perhaps one the more heuristic notions of XX century philosophy.

[3]   Aside from any theoretical consideration, the relevance of talk-in-interaction in meaning making and culture construction has strong methodological consequences. Notably, it legitimizes the analysis of discourse as a social practice per se (Wetherell, et al., 2001). According to this framework, we conceive and analyze the uses of mobile communication devices as well as the discourses on such devices, as ways to make sense of them.

[4]   This chapter draws on data from a 7-year multiple research project on the appropriation of communication and information technologies in families' and adolescents' worlds (Caron & Caronia, 2001, 2007; Caronia, 2005; Caronia & Caron, 2004). We used different yet complementary methodological and recording devices: family interviews and participant observation, log books on everyday practices, focus groups with adolescents, ethnographic case studies among natural groups of adolescents, analysis of naturally occurring mobile conversations and SMS exchanges. These studies have been conducted jointly with André H. Caron (Department of Communication, University of Montreal, Montreal), with financial support from CITÉ (Center for Interdisciplinary Research on Emerging Technologies, University of Montreal). I wish to thank my colleague André H. Caron for the support and the suggestions he gave me.

Most of the ideas and interpretation proposed in this chapter have emerged from the joint analysis of data.

[5] In some countries the diffusion and appropriation of mobile phone by young people is an important social phenomenon. In Europe, 23% of children ages 8 to 10 have a mobile phone. In Italy, one in three children between ages 5 and 12 has and uses a personal mobile phone. At age 9, 28% own a mobile phone. Among 14 and 18-year-olds, the percentage of mobile use and ownership is around 100% (Doxa Junior, 2005). In Norway, nearly 80% of children ages 9 to 12 have and use a mobile phone. The percentage rises at 13 (around 96%) to reach 100% at 16 (Ling, 2006). In Britain, 49% of children ages 8-11 and 82% of 12-15 year-olds own a mobile phone (Withers, 2006). The phenomenon is less apparent in Canada but is still growing. According to Statistics Canada, 17.5% of children in primary school have a cell phone and 42.8% of high school students have one (Dunfield, 2004).

[6] The following verbatim come from family interviews made during a larger ethnographic research on the integration of new communication technologies in family everyday life (Caron & Caronia, 2001).

[7] From an empirical point of view, we have strong evidences of remote parenting as a new way to perform the parental role. Whether it is considered as a way to dissimulate adults' escape from their responsibility or as a way to manage the contemporary parents' multitask life, strictly depends on the actors' points of view and cultural models of "what counts as good parenting." I advance the hypothesis that the common sense shared cultural model of "good parenting" is strictly anchored on notions as "face-to-face interaction" and "physical contact." On the basis of such a cultural model, remote parenting may be considered as not consistent with the ideal-typical behaviour of a "good parent." This is the point: are not these new communication technologies participating in the change of the cultural models we live by?

[8] All the following transcripts come from conversational focus groups with adolescents on their uses of mobile phones (Caron &Caronia, 2004).

Chapter VII

Children and Computers:
What They Know, What They Do

Paolo Maria Ferri, State University Milan—Bicocca, Italy

Susanna Mantovani, State University Milan—Bicocca, Italy

Abstract

This chapter describes the design, the methodology, and the preliminary results of the research Children and Computer. Experience and Conceptual Frameworks (3-6). The research, started in 2004, is supported by IBM Foundation Italy and University of Milan-Bicocca—Dipartimento di Scienze Umane per la Formazione "Riccardo Massa." The research team, led by Professor Susanna Mantovani, includes: Chiara Bove, Paolo Ferri, Valentina Garzia, Susanna Mantovani, Anna Poli, Donata Ripamonti, and Angelo Failla (IBM Foundation Italy), Morgana Stell (IBM Foundation Italy).

Introduction

Engagement, effort, pleasure, concentration, happiness in exploring, trying and producing ideas, experience and performance, and cooperative action, all these aspects are very conspicuous when we observe young children using computers in educational settings. They seem to love technology, computers, and digital networks. How can we observe the way they approach, explore, discover, and use these very special cultural artifacts (computers and digital networks)? How can we investigate the ways in which they interact with them? We probably need a "phenomenology of motivation" (Lumbelli, 2000, 2001; Lumbelli & Zidari, 2001) aimed to develop educational eyes capable of seeing children, who are experimenting and learning with ICT. This would provide a basis to develop and organize learning paths and tools which may make the most of children's energy while avoiding wasting their happiness to connect. Today, observing and studying the way children gain interest, explore, and use computers, whether individually, with other children, or with an adult, is a key issue in early childhood education, as it is connected with adults' educational ideas, and their influence on relations and teaching practices, as well as with the roles children can play as mediators of shared experiences (Bove, 2004; Ferri, 2004, 2005; Ferri & Mantovani, 2006; Mantovani, 1998, 1996). The research project presented in this chapter studies how children and adults explore the potential of new technologies in family and preschool settings. We took as our starting point some shots videotaped and discussed through focus groups with teachers and parents, following the approach outlined by Joseph Tobin in the study "Preschool in Three Cultures: Japan, China, United States" (Mantovani, 1998; Mantovani & Musatti, 1996; Tobin, Wu, & Davidson, 1989).

What We Mean: The Key Words of Our Chapter

Child

An active, curious, and competent person who constructs his/her knowledge by interacting with peers and close adults. This conception challenges the idea that children are passive receptors of notions, empty boxes to be filled, "tabula rasa" on which adults imprint their knowledge.

Interobservation

When we find something, we instinctively feel the need for interobservation (…) because looking together with people who know enough and are used to observing and discussing with them enables us at the same time to observe the fact in a richer and more reliable way, and to view the problem from several different perspectives. (Bozzi, 1978)

Interobservation as a methodology consists in "looking together" and "discussing," mutually exchanging views.

Visual Etnography

Visual etnography is a research methodology that draws on anthropological findings, combining descriptive data collected through observations and reflective interpretations. By putting together both textual and visual dimensions, visual ethnography generates a multivocal exchange which elicits reflective dialogical processes, rich in training implications. Such a methodology can be used to observe, describe, and record what happens in educational contexts: these video materials are then employed to elicit a process of discussion and interpretation which may help highlight the cultural representations of the people involved.

Observation

Observation is a specific behavior showing attention to a given phenomenon; it differs from simply looking at something, as it implies aiming one's attention specifically at something, focusing on what the observer considers meaningful and relevant to the observer's own interests and motives. It proves to be a key tool in educational contexts (we refer primarily to ethological observation, based on principles of analytical description, and nonevaluative, noninterfering attitude on the part of the observer).

Educational Relationship

Hinde (1981) defines the relationship as "a series of interactions between two individuals who are known to each other" (where interaction means "one or more exchanges like: A does X to B and B does Y in response"). He further emphasizes that there is a mutual influence between the participants' individual characteristics and the social situation in which they are engaged (1986). The educational relationship is therefore determined not only by the specific interactions that take place between the subjects involved, but also by the characteristics of the social context in which it takes place.

Social Constructivism

According and other scholars, children's learning is the result of active efforts to understand the world, rather than of passive processes. Such efforts prove more successful if children act in cooperation with other people. Accordingly, sociocultural factors are viewed as active determinants in gaining experience and understanding.

Research Goals and Theoretical Background

The aims of the research are:

- Discussing the ways in which three to six children use and explore new digital technologies and interpret their meanings and functions at home and in preschool settings;

- Exploring teachers' and parents' ideas and representations with regard to the use of computers, at home and in preschools, and to their educational roles;

- Working out a methodological approach for the study of these issues in early childhood settings and for eliciting and making explicit the educational models;

- Stimulating opportunities for dialogue and interpretation on issues like education and technologies, learning tools in the early years, collaborative learning, and so forth;

- Developing training materials based on this approach. with computers in the early years;

- Outlining some patterns for the development of "new" media education for teachers and schools.

The basic assumption of our research is that in order for teachers and parents to promote a "good" use of new technologies in the early years (especially in preschools) they need to gain a deeper understanding of the way in which children *spontaneously* approach these technologies together with an improved awareness of adults' representations and ideas (Ferri & Mantovani, 2006). Too often computers and digital technologies are introduced in early childhood contexts without adequate understanding of their cultural meanings, cognitive and social potentials, or constraints, which is particularly true in preschool settings as shown by in a constructivist perspective by Varisco (2002) and Albanense, Migliorini, and Piertrocola (2000).

On these grounds, our research focuses on exploring the way in which young children approach computers, how they relate to theses tools (both at an individual level and at a social level), what they do with them, and what they think about them. Along with observing children, we aimed at understanding the way in which teachers and parents interpret the role of technologies in early childhood education and their educational responsibilities.

Having among its goals a broadening of our theoretical understanding and the development of training materials, our research is based on the assumption that creating dialogue opportunities (focus groups) may promote higher awareness and deeper understanding of the role played by new technologies in the early years. Creating this kind of dialogue may also help provide a sound basis to the design of a way "to mediate" the introduction of technologies in early childhood (Rogoff, 2003; Rogoff, Goodman Turkanis, & Bartlett, 2001; Siraj-Blatchford, 2004).

Observing the first natural approaches to computer and Web technologies, the changes in systematic use of tools, the cognitive strategies, and the relational patterns involved is a way to clean up our minds from adults' prejudices on children's use of technologies. For example, videotaping and observing young children in front of computers helps us understand how the solipsistic concerns and the social exclusion concerns associated with the use of computers are only teachers', parents', and scholars' fears: young children always approach computers and networks in a cooperative way and get bored with them very fast. Obviously, we are talking about educational software and not about videogames (Ferri & Mantovani, 2006, pp.75-121).

As early as the 80's, Robert Taylor (1980), in his book *The Computer in the School: Tutor, Tool, Tutee*, put forward the idea that, at school, digital technologies could play three different roles: tutor, tool, and tutee. It's clear that each of these roles depends on the kind of dialogue established between the computer, intended as a teacher, and the student. Some software thought to teach stimulates a real dialogue between children and computers. In the same way, on-line communication software mediates symmetrical and unsymmetrical communication between teacher and student through specific interfaces. In spite of that, nobody has yet defined the best way to establish a dialogue between children and computers and a way to understand educational and communicational patterns. This is a fruitful field of research, if related to the role digital technologies may play in different learning phases, even though deep cultural changes have meaningfully influenced learning processes in the last few years. Therefore, it will be very important to study the way children gain interest, explore, and use computers and get bored with technologies. And it will be very important to do so, observing children on their own, with other children, or with adults, because this melds with adults' educational ideas, with related consequences in educational relations and in didactics, and with the behaviours of children as mediators of shared experiences in on-line environments of cooperative construction of knowledge.

To achieve these goals it will be necessary to consider critically and investigate video ethnographic field material also in order to understand some specific educational aspects:

1   The meaning of the expression "projects for digital education," both in CMC and hyper textual environments, with special attention to the design of hardware and software interfaces. Some software propose an institutional, repetitive use of technology, but is there an "effective" way for introducing computers in preschool settings and for promoting user-friendly patterns of interaction with these tools in the early years?

2   The way digital tools (hardware and software) can be approached by children of different ages. It is important to analyse the role of some tools (keyboard, mouse, and screen) and it is also important to study the best way to design these output and input peripherals according to children's needs;

3   Analysing the best way to introduce children to usage of cooperative tools for on-line communication (LCMS for e-learning), in order to avoid communicative autism that some e-learning methodologies imply.

4   The definition of concrete learning paths with the aim to help teachers and families to be able to overcome the "digital divide" with their children.

Methodology

The core method of this study follows the approach taken by Tobin et al. (1989) in the seminal study "Preschool in Three Cultures" and combines the use of video as a "stimuli" to provoke discussions and sharing among adults with some qualitative research tools, such as narrative interviews and focus groups. We have done videotapes with three to six children and computers (at home and in preschool) and we have used them not "primarily" as data, but as tools to stimulate a multivocal dialogue (Bove, 2004). Three municipal preschools have been involved in our research and others will be involved in the future (*Scuola Comunale Clericetti, Milan; Scuola Andersen, Vimercate, Scuola Costa, Milan. These schools are also part of the "Bambino autore project," www.bambinioautore.org*). So far, videotapes have been discussed with teachers and the discussion will be extended to parents in the second phase of our research (Bers, New, & Boudreau, 2004).

We assume, from a constructivist point of view, that the way in which children explore and use computers (individually, and with other children or with adults) is strictly linked to the adults' ideas and beliefs and to their educational models and representations. In our study, the voices of parents and teachers will therefore enrich our interpretations and extend the repertoire of possible educational practice with technologies. We also assume that by studying the way in which children approach computers we will promote higher awareness of how children can be considered as "mediator" of a broader collaborative experience of learning based on the use of digital technologies.

We will also conduct some micro-experiments using our previous findings as the starting point for creating settings of "semi-experimental observations," which will help us create educational settings for cooperative learning and e-learning with children.

Description of the Research Program

Our research program includes the following phases (most of them already accomplished):

1. Observation of children-computers interaction based on an "etnographic-visual dialogical" approach that considers learning situations as social contexts, with the purpose of generating a qualitative field of research. This phase combines qualitative research tools (observations and interviews) with anthropological research tools, usage of video materials as reactor, and focus groups (Tobin et al., 1989). Direct observation will be one of the tools used during the research on the field. Paths of observation will be created, using narrative and descriptive modalities, together with "almost experimental" methods. Videos will be taken both in family and school settings. Based on this, it will be easier to formulate the hypothesis that will lead the "almost experimental" observation, which can be modified or improved by the observer.

2. "Micro experiments," which will help encourage or control some explorative behaviours with ICT on the part of children. Field observations on the use of some tools and cooperative environments of e-learning were conducted in several schools:
    *   Scuola Comunale Clericetti, Milan;
    *   Scuola Andersen, Vimercate;
    *   Scuola Costa, Milan;
    *   the group of Scools that participate in the project Bambino Autore (www. bambinioautore.it).

3. Discussion of videos and observation highlights in focus groups with teachers and parents to build and validate the first data collected through observation based on a dialogic and narrative approach, this with the aim of creating exchange and sharing of the hypothesis formulated on the collected material by the research group with teachers and parents. The video made during the first phase will be used to stimulate exchange among participants according to the method of visual and vocal ethnography already experimented (Tobin et al., 1989).

4. This phase provides for discussion of first findings based on field observation and research hypothesis, through interviews, research meetings, and focus groups organized by researchers, national and international public, and private research and teaching Institution.

5. Design and development of supporting tools (Virtual Classroom, KM tools) for children and teachers communities, with the aim to create, share and manage knowledge according to the co-constructed method of introduction of ICT in school. This technological part of the project has been developed as a part of the LCMS open source Docebo. This LCMS system has been designed by the software house Docebo srl, in cooperation with the University of Milan-Bicocca e-learning team (Paolo Ferri, Andrea Garavaglia, Livia Petti, Francesca Bossi). The LCMS has been customized to be used directly by young children and teachers for discussing and sharing knowledge in a constructivist way with other schools and with parents.

7. On the basis of the results of previous phases, new operative and blended" educational paths for teachers will be built and implemented.

Research Results

We outlined here some of the findings that emerge from our video ethnodialogcal observation. The use of "video-ethnography," Tobin et al. (1989) method, have permitted to create a "semi-objective video material" In order to better understand the way young child interact in the very first years with computers, and in order to make more affective the results of focus group with teachers and parents. In our view, the emergent phenomena, we observed, in the approach of young children (K3/6) to computer are:

- New paths and new for cooperative learning, in the peer to peer relationship using computers and ICT.

- The adoption by the children of a "cognitive multitasking style" in using computer and an intense use of video and musical code (Veen, 2003; Veen & Vrakking, 2006)

- Multiple intelligence at work (Gardner, 1993) through multimedia device: emphasis on video and graphical and musical intelligence. Exit from "only alphabetic" paradigm in learning and teaching (Bolter & Grusin, 1999).

- New peer to peer interaction, more written and multimedia communication, less deep personal communication, as results from the observation of the children working in the Bambino Autore Project www.bambinoautore.it

- A tricky use "grasshopper mind" (Papert, 1994): Bite and run—distractatten-tion.

- A new mediated way to "construct" and share individually and socially the word through media (user generated content, mobile phone video, sms, vsm (Goodmann, 1978).

We can now better understand how the use of ICT changes the cognitive skills of children and young people in many ways:

- Stressing a multitasking use of media. Our research parents and teachers focus group results testify they strongly agree with this idea. Their children use a multitasking approach in gaming, playing, and learning. Sometimes they feel this difference with fear that they are not able to act in this way.

- Promoting cooperative learning. This is the way children adopt also when they are very young, 2 to 6 years, in approaching computers and ICT. As our observation testifies, they very rarely stay alone when they are using a computer al school.

- Learning by doing the ICT and with the ICT is strongly preferred by the children we observed. Emphasizing the need of meta-reflexion on practical experience lead by teachers.

- Online communication, especially instant messaging, messaging, and so forth, are very spread pattern of use ICT (mobile phone Instant messaging) also in the 6-10 year old range of age. In Italy, particularly the use of mobile phone is a tool used by nearly all children both to communicate with peers (mostly in a written way, SMS) and with parents (voice communication). In Italy, parents use mobile phone with children not only to communicate but also as a control/care tool. Mobile phone use, in Italy, has became a mediated tool for parental care. In school, the mobile phone is forbidden and teachers are very concerned about the use of such a technological tool by children in the same way they are very concerned about video game and video user generated content.

- The children at home, as testified from our observation, learn from parents using a modelling style; at school this style is very rarely adopted by the teacher.

- In Italy, children from extra-European countries are particularly found on ICT because ICT (Skype at the Internet café, e-mail, and so forth) is useful for them to keep in touch with parents. It can help their integration in school because they have an excellence skill to share with peers and teachers.

- In our view, children often dislike educational software because the software is far more poorly designed and low budget than video game and commercial

Web sites on the Internet. Other hints that come up from our qualitative research are the following:

- In Italy, the digital native (Prensky, 2001) is not clear as to whether this concept is exactly similar to NML) phenomenon begins relatively late. It starts with children born after 1993, not earlier. This is probably because of the gap with U.S. and Northern Europe in the spread of computers at home and in the schools. The first serious government plan of new media introduction in school was built in 1996 PSTD (Italian plan for the development of instructional technology).

- In Italy, the use of ICT is a domestic phenomenon, the use in school is rare and only a few days per month. There is, in fact, a big divide between the family and social appropriation of ICT and the primary and secondary schools use.

- In Italy, there is no specific formal teacher training on technology of education and new media education, except for Indire PuntoEdu project. Unfortunately the technological culture is not an issue for the Italian scholastic system. The children and young girls and boys use very rarely technology as a creative and free tool for education.

- In Italy, gender issues are fundamental, particularly in the early childhood years. Teachers in primary school are mostly 1950s born female (the "baby boomers" generation). They, as our focus group pointed out, learn technology mostly from the romantic partners. In the same way, they perceive technology as male, mechanical, and alien. That is why they are very resistant to introduce ICT to kids and female world.

- Gender issues interact also with the way female "baby boomers" teachers (90%) use technology with kids. They are mostly scared that computers can transform kids into machines.

- From the point of view of educational innovation, we point out that it is not a tech issues but a cultural issue. In training teachers to new tech is far more important investigate which kind of prejudices they have on technology than train them about technological issues. Understanding and share the meaning of resistances and prejudice is very important for over come them.

Conclusions and Further Development

We believe that new digital technologies may become a catalyst for exchange and sharing among adults who care for young children and a starting point for promoting a new way to overcome the "digital generational gap" (Papert, 2006) between children, teachers, and parents is to promote a new digital literacy and fluency in schools. Our research has already reached a number of its "medium term" goals, among which include:

1. Supporting young children in exploring the multiple functions of these technologies and helping them to "protect" themselves from the "isolation" and the "communicational autism" that some e-learning methodologies, especially "instructionism," imply. To achieve this goal we outlined and projected a specific methodology of the coconstructive method of blended learning (in the classroom and on the LCMS). This method main guideline is creating situated, active, and child-centred, techno-learning paths.

2. Gaining a better understanding, through video analysis and focus groups of teachers' and parents' "fears or concerns" about the cultural impact new digital technologies may have.

3. Developing a methodological approach which combines the sound theoretical grounding of the reflection on education and on "digital education and learning" with the importance of being aware of the ways in which children and adults approach these tools and react to their stimulation

The next steps of our research will involve:

1. Longitudinally examining and mapping the evolution of the real and virtual learning communities we have promoted (beginners and advanced groups).

2. Disseminating these method in other contexts, in early childhood settings and primary schools;

3. Creating, with children and teachers of early childhood and primary schools, specific learning objects coherent with the approach of a situated and cocostructed use of technology. These learning objects are open-source, strongly contextualized, and enriched by personal experiences.

4. Mapping the tacit and unstructured knowledge that is now at work in our project. For the time being, virtual communities do not have user-friendly tools for "knowledge management."

These tools should manage the problems of informative-documental management, providing virtual communities with the tools required to build clear and shared conceptual frameworks.

Acknowledgment

This chapter was written with the collaboration of Chiara Bove, Valentina Garzia, Anna Poli, and Donata Ripamonti.

References

Albanese, O., Migliori, P., & Pietrocola, G. (Eds.). (2000). *Apprendimento e nuove strategie educative. Le tecnologie informatiche tra teoria e pratica didattica.* Milano: Unicopli.

Bers, M., New, B., & Boudreau, L. (2004). Teaching and learning when no one is expert: Children and parents explore technology. *Journal of Early Childhood Research and Practice, 6*(2).

Bolter, J.D., & Grusin, R. (1999). *Remediation. Understanding new media.* Cambridge, MA: Mit Press.

Bove, C. (2004). *Le idee degli adulti sui piccoli. Riflessioni e ricerche per una pedagogia culturale.* Bergamo: Junior.

Demetrio, D. (2003). *Ricordare a scuola. Fare memoria e didattica autobiografica.* Roma-Bari: Laterza.

Fabbri, L., & Grassilli, B. (2003). *Didattica e metodologie qualitative. Verso una didattica narrativa.* Brescia: La Scuola.

Ferri, P. (2004). *Fine dei Mass Media. Le nuove tecnologie della comunicazione e le trasformazioni dell'industria culturale.* Milano: Guerini & Associati.

Ferri, P. (2005). *E-Learning. Didattica e comunicazione e tecnolgie digitali.* Milano: Le Monnier.

Ferri, P., & Mantovani, S. (Eds.). (2006). *Bambini e computer. Alla scoperta delle nuove tecnologie a scuola e in famiglia.* Milano: ETAS.

Garavaglia, A. (2006). *Ambienti per l'apprendimento in rete:gli spazi dell'e-learning.* Bergamo: Junior.

Gardner, H. (1993). *Multiple intelligences: The theory in practice.* New York: Basic Books.

Geertz, C. (1973).*The interpretation of culture.* New York: Basic Books.

Goodman, N. (1978). *Ways of worldmaking.* Indianapolis, IN: Hackett Publishing Co.

Griswold, W. (1994). *Cultures and societies in a changing world.* Thousand Oaks, CA: Pine Forge Press.

Healy, J.M. (1998). *Failure to connect. How computers affect our children's minds.* New York: Simon & Schuster.

Lumbelli, L. (2000). La televisione tra ludico e ludiforme. *CADMO. Giornale italiano di pedagogia sperimentale, 22,* 7-18.

Lumbelli, L.(2001). La comprensione di testi come farsi e disfarsi del problema. In M. Bagassi, L. Macchi & M.G. Serafini (Eds.), *Discorsi e pensieri.* Bologna: Il Mulino.

Lumbelli, L., & Zidari, C. (2001). Televisione e multimedia: Quale comprensione? *Ikon, 43/44,* 7-20.

Mantovani, S. (Ed.). (1998). *La ricerca sul campo in educazione: i metodi qualitativi.* Milano: Bruno Mondadori.

Mantovani, S., & Musatti, T. (1996). New educational provision for young children in Italy. *European Journal of Psychology of Education, 11,* 2.

Merlo, S. (Ed.). (2006). *Il Bambino Autore. Comunicare e cooperare in Internet.* Bergamo: Junior.

Papert, S. (1993). *The children's machine: Rethinking school in the age of the computer.* New York: Basic Books.

Papert, S. (1996). *The connected family: Bridging the digital generation gap.* Atlanta, GA: Longstreet Press.

Papert, S. (1998, June). Does easy do it? Children, games, and learning. *Game Developer, Soapbox.*

Papert, S. (1999). *Logo philosophy and implementation. Logo Computer System Inc.* Retrieved October 5, 2007, from http://www.microworlds.com/company/philosophy.pdf

Prensky, M. (2001). *Digital game-based learning.* New York: McGraw-Hill.

Rogoff, B. (2003). *The cultural nature of human development.* New York: Oxford University Press.

Rogoff, B., Goodman Turkanis, C., & Bartlett, L. (Eds.). (2001). *Learning together: Children and adults in a school community.* New York: Oxford University Press.

Siraj-Blatchford, J. (2004). *Developing new technologies for young children.* NewYork: Trentham Books.

Tapscott, D. (1998). *Growing up digital, the rise of the net generation.* New York: McGraw-Hill.

Tapscott, D., & Williams, D.A. (2006). *Wikinomics: How mass collaboration changes everything.* London: Penguin.

Taylor, R.P. (Ed.). (1980). *The computer in school: Tutor, tool, tutee.* New York: Teachers College Press.

Tobin, J.J., Wu, D.Y.H., & Davidson, D.H. (1989). *Preschool in three cultures*. New Haven, CT: Yale University Press.

Varisco, B.M. (2002). *Costruttivismo socioculturale*. Roma: Carocci.

Veen, W. (2003). A new force for change: Homo zappiens. *The Learning Citizen, 7,* 5-7.

Veen, W., & Vrakking, B. (2006). *Homo zappiens, growing up in a digital age*. London: Network Continuum Ed.

Chapter VIII

Adolescents and the Internet:
Media Appropriation and Perspectives on Education

Evelyne Bevort, CLEMI, Paris, France

Isabelle Bréda, CLEMI, Paris, France

Abstract

This chapter deals with young people's digital media appropriation in an education perspective throughout Europe and Quebec. The comparative study, Mediappro, shows that 12 to 18-year-olds develop numerous and shared uses in fundamental domains such as ethics or social issues of IT, but their appropriation remains incomplete, mostly in information and creative activities. The study also highlights such a significant gap between home and school appropriation in all the countries that for the adolescents Internet activities in school are not part of "their Internet." The benefits of this research study lay on a more precise knowledge of adolescents' attitudes and skills and therefore the possibility to elaborate recommendations towards the main participants in education issues, parents as well as school systems.

Introduction

To better understand the impact of digital media in the context of its social and cultural environment, it is essential to study the use and the modes of its appropriation. At the same time, to foresee or even modify its evolution in the future, it is imperative to analyse the habits of youth with regards to digital media.

Mediappro (Media Appropriation) is an applied research project focusing on the appropriation of new media (the Internet, mobile phones, and video games) by 12 to 18-year-olds. Between January 2005 and June 2006, a number of associations and foundations, universities and government ministries from nine European countries (Belgium, Denmark, Estonia, France, Greece, Italy, Poland, Portugal, and the UK) collaborated on this project, coordinated by Thierry De Smedt from the University of Louvain-la-Neuve in Belgium, in the framework of the European Commission's Safer Internet Action Plan.

These various institutions (1), specialising in media education, aimed at proposing different recommendations. A similar survey was also carried out during the same period in Quebec, Canada. This complementary approach allows for comparison and a better understanding of the situation in Europe and North America.

The study of the appropriation of new information technology is central to the thought processes involved in how to advance and put in place learning techniques. Information technology is not simply an "object" of knowledge. Familiarity and a certain level of skill are required. Moreover, the education of these media, as either a project or a process, inevitably demands the observation of how they are appropriated by youth, taking into account their specificities as well as their unknown factors.

Using a straight-forward approach and a combination of methodology, the Mediappro study draws on the statements of young Europeans to elucidate and propose recommendations in the learning of these media, coherent with the modes of appropriation observed. The results of the Mediappro study serve as a strong reminder of the educator's role. For the first time, in light of the statements of the youth who participated in the study within nine European countries as well as in Quebec, it has been possible to establish the use of the Internet within schools. Indeed, the project dramatically underlines the fact that neither the views of the educational institute, those of the educator, nor of the student superimpose. The differences are further accentuated with regards to the Internet.

Research Axes and Questions

We proceeded with a preliminary survey and general overview of all previous work and research conducted in the field, so as to avoid duplicating existing studies. This allowed us to accurately develop the bases of our investigation, but also to establish the most pertinent and adequate method in achieving this end.

Current State of Affairs in the Selected Nine European Countries

The joint survey of common research questions was determined through a background analysis based on three key elements. First, we carried out an assessment of all previous research conducted in the sector. Second, we collated data on the equipment and material available throughout the selected countries, and finally, we conducted an initial overview of educational strategies that have been put in place (Mediappro, 2005).

In fact, very little research has been undertaken in the field and it seems not to solicit much fact-finding. This is rather surprising, given the social importance of the subject. This could reflect the temporal gap between a societal phenomenon and its application to research.

Research projects and studies are often attributed to official institutions or authorities in the field, including operators such as France Télécom (France), or regulators as the Office of Communications (UK), not to mention specialised institutes (the National Statistics Institute), or national ministries (Education, Family, Science and Technology), as well as various foundations (in the UK, Estonia). Academic research is generally quite limited in field and in scope, with the exception of an in-depth study that looks at the experiences of children with regards to the Internet in the UK (Livingstone & Bober, 2004). Generally, these studies are initiated by different university departments: Science of Education (France, Estonia), Sociology (Denmark, Sweden), Philosophy (Greece), and Cognitive Psychology (Greece).

Youth over the age of 18 are rarely the subject of research as opposed to other categories of the population.

By analysing the emerging trends of this particular landscape, we can identify elements that are common to all European countries selected for the study:

- An increasingly high amount of available material (laptops, mobile phones, ADSL, and so forth) with a few varying differences.
- Households with children aged 12 to 18 were the most equipped, compared with the average home in each of the countries.

- More questions came up regarding the use of these media.

- The school seems to play an auxiliary role in the use of digital media, oriented towards establishing functional skills rather than essential ones. Rarely do schools focus on the fun aspect of new media and its potential role as an educational tool.

The study incorporates different approaches in view of cultural contexts:

- The relation between young people and technologies of communication diverge depending on the educational steps involved, either prompting autonomy or, on the contrary, protection. Whether youth hold a positive or negative vision suggests that expectations towards these technologies are either cultural or technical.

- Data on equipment is difficult to compare between the different countries.

- Research conducted derives from varied disciplines of study. This inevitably led to the development of an original European research project, based on an identical line of questioning and a comparable sample groups.

Research Questions

The principle axes of research cover four central areas of study:

- The multi-media environment (access to media, context of use)

- Knowledge and cognitive processes (knowledge of the Internet, the perception, or not, of learning via the Internet)

- The psycho-social dynamic (manner in which these methods of communication affect sociability, group belonging)

- Capacity to imagine the future within a technical and democratic context.

The questions asked:

- On representation: Spontaneously, what words do the youth associate with the Internet? In what register do the youth situate it?

- On the use of these different media and within their different context (family, school, in pairs) in order to ascertain where and how the Internet, mobile phones, or video games are situated and to explore the relation with other media (press, television or radio) and spare time activities.

- On their knowledge of the Internet through the Internet: What do they really know about the Internet, how it works and functions? Where do they obtain such information? Do they consider themselves technically competent in terms of accessing content?

- On how they consider the school's role and what they would like to see: Do they feel they need training? If so, on what aspect and by whom (the school, family, others)?

- In terms of their sociability, how do these techniques work? Do they consider they should always be available to communicate with others? "Stay connected"? What exactly does this mean to them? In this optic, do they have the impression to be a part of an open world or a restricted one? What respective roles do they attribute to blogs, SMS's, MSN, and so forth.

- How do they situate these new tools in the future? How do they imagine them to be? What changes do they foresee? What is the place for these new modes of communication in a democratic society?

Questions to better apprehend the relationship young people have with these varying tools of communication.

Methodology

About 9000 young people aged between 12 and 18 participated in the study (7400 in Europe and 1350 in Quebec).

For practical reasons, each national team selected participants from their schools with the consent of the school principal and parents. In order to construct a relevant sample at the international level, schools were selected according to their geographical location and their social, economic, and cultural setting.

Three school grades, representing three age groups, were defined: 12 to 14 (beginning of secondary school), 15 to 16 (middle of secondary school), and 17 to 18 (end of secondary school).

In using this method, we were able to obtain a diversified sample, representing the differences in young people's life contexts, reflecting national differences that exist across Europe.

Basing the interviews at schools represented a certain element of risk to the study. Answers obtained could be biased, where young people might attempt to respond in a manner expected of their school. Group tests demonstrated that the relationship between these youth and new media is such that young people have maintained complete freedom of expression on their habits and opinions. In addition to the responses obtained, we were able to understand that for the youth concerned, the Internet and, a fortiori, the mobile phone had a very minimal role to play in the world of education and that any interference between the two was weak.

In order to provide the most updated and pertinent information for this research project, two complementary approaches were used: a printed questionnaire to be filled out anonymously, with closed-ended questions, coupled with individual interviews with a select number of participants, chosen for the different ways in which they appropriated media.

The Mediappro research team elaborated a common questionnaire that included 63 items. This was distributed to the entire sample during class time, between September and October 2005. Based on the results obtained during this quantitative phase, 240 young people (24 in each country) were selected according to their different levels of Internet usage, ages, and gender, for individual interviews. Each interview took place at school and lasted about 40-60 minutes. The interview was based on a grid co-elaborated by the research teams and in coherence with the questionnaire each young person had filled out.

Aside from the statistical analysis of the questionnaires, Mediappro teams conducted each phase of the survey themselves in order to guarantee a coherent process and to assure high quality analysis.

Main Tendencies from the Survey

Mediappro results highlight an increasing development of Internet and mobile phone usage by youth, in Europe as well as in Quebec.

It is clear that Internet use is almost universal across these countries for youth aged 12 to 18, though small numbers of nonusers remain and these vary across the countries.

Nine young people in 10 say that they use the Internet. The highest number of users is in Quebec where almost all the respondents say they know and use the Internet. The lowest is Italy where 78% say they use it, plus 7% who declare no longer using it.

The majority of young Europeans have used the Internet for a period spanning between 1 and 3 years (35%) or for 4 years or more (31%).

The situation is quite the same in Quebec, but for a more prolonged period of time (three fourths have used the Internet for more than 4 years). In several countries, the

Table 1. Declare to have used the Internet

Quebec	100%
Estonia	99%
Denmark	98%
UK	98%
France	96%
Poland	96%
Portugal	96%
Belgium	93%
Greece	89%
Italy	85%

© Mediappro, 2006

extent of Internet use correlates with levels of print literacy, suggesting that these two "literacies" might be usefully treated as connected in educational practices.

Major Uses

Uses are concentrated around the following activities: personal communication, search for information, and leisure.

Information

Looking up information is by far the most common activity in all the countries: more than 9 young Europeans in 10 say they use search engines sometimes, often or very often (highest: United Kingdom and Quebec: 98%; lowest: Greece 81%). The French study (Bevort & Bréda, 2006) demonstrates that youth do not systematically use search engines for finding information, but go to sites they are already familiar with. The Danish study (Tufte, Rasmussen, & Christensen, 2006) underlines the fact that the youth in the sample group consider Google and search engines to be synonymous. This fact is established in all the countries.

Communication

Online communication continues to be popular. Seven out of ten European youth use Instant messaging (MSN) and electronic mail. Messenger is what they use most frequently: 42% use it very regularly as opposed to 23% for e-mail.

Table 2. Activities on the Internet (sometimes + often + very often)

	Search Engines	E-Mail	Instant Messenger	Chat Rooms	Downloading
Belgium	95%	74%	81%	28%	58%
Denmark	92%	66%	87%	26%	50%
Estonia	90%	69%	88%	33%	73%
France	94%	67%	69%	32%	49%
Greece	81%	46%	39%	41%	65%
Italy	86%	59%	49%	33%	59%
Poland	91%	62%	75%	34%	67%
Portugal	95%	69%	77%	38%	60%
Quebec	99%	94%	93%	58%	79%
UK	98%	81%	78%	20%	60%
Average	91%	66%	71%	32%	60%

© Mediappro, 2006

The study also reveals sensitive differences between countries. Instant messaging (very closely linked to the availability of equipment, particularly the presence of a high speed Internet connection in the home) is used by 63% of Estonians, as opposed to only 12% of Greeks; 20% of Estonian households were equipped with high speed Internet in 2004, vs. no homes in Greece (Eurostat 2004). "Greek students ignore or are not interested in basic Internet functions, such as MSN, e-mail, personal pages, blogs" (Aslanidou & Ikonomou, 2006). In Quebec, youth used electronic mail and instant messaging much more than in Europe: 80% and 90% respectively either often or very often. More than half the participants stated they wrote SMS messages often or very often (36% very often) and young Quebecers most of all (73%).

Instant messaging is used, above all, to stay in touch with friends (62% of the European youth, 89% in Quebec) rather than one's family (14% claim to use this method of communication with their parents). Instant messaging has supplanted chat rooms in all the countries: two thirds of youth claimed to have never or very rarely visited chat rooms, in that they prefer to communicate with their friends rather than with strangers. Instant messaging enables them to contact people of their choosing and their address books can contain more than 50 names (30% of youth). According to the Quebec study (Piette, Pons, & Giroux, 2007),

The core contact group is always composed of a restricted number of people: close friends or family. However, the circle expands by integrating other relations that are more or less close. Even if one is not communicating with a lot of people, contacts are kept on file as a permanent link to the different relations established over time. This network also reflects the young person's ability to reach out to others and helps to define their personality. The names appearing on their MSN Messenger list takes on great significance, as it represents marks of their own identity and lays out the crucial steps of their socialisation.

Table 3. Declare to have their own mobile phone

Denmark	98%
Italy	98%
Estonia	97%
Portugal	97%
UK	96%
Belgium	95%
Greece	94%
Poland	90%
France	88%
Quebec	41%

© Mediappro, 2006

Instant messaging is an important vector of socialisation. For a significant number of young people, it represents the contentment of feeling connected to their network of friends, even from home. The French study observes that electronic media often contributes to appeasing relationships within the family. It can enable some young people to reconcile their double family life if they live in re-composed families, or for those who have left their community or country of origin. These methods of communication can equally attenuate internal struggles that young people experience, by allowing them to take on childhood or teen-age activities, with these same tools.

Of young people, 95%, have their own mobile phone (highest: Italy 98%; lowest: France 87%). It is very clear that they see these as vitally important to their lives, something they would find it difficult to live without. A majority of them consider it important to be connected with their friends all the time. The situation is completely different in Quebec, where only 4 young people in 10 have their own mobile phone, and very few of them send text messages (22%).

Mobile phones were mainly used in Europe to communicate with friends, including planning events, telling someone they are thinking of them, or gossiping. With the exception of Estonia, where calling is more popular than texting, they are more likely to send text messages (79%) than to call (65%). One reason for this is financial: sending a text message is clearly cheaper than a phone call (72% of the young people agree with this affirmation). They also use text messages for planning activities and informing their parents, and to tell someone that they are thinking about them. There is some evidence (as noted in the UK and Portuguese interviews, for instance) that they value the distance provided by texting, which makes difficult communication easier. The Danish interviews suggested that the

Table 4. Consequences on cultural practices

	Less TV	Less reading	More music
Belgium	43%	20%	38%
Denmark	31%	23%	45%
Estonia	49%	40%	62%
France	40%	17%	40%
Greece	24%	16%	40%
Italy	17%	11%	44%
Poland	50%	20%	45%
Portugal	34%	29%	45%
UK	39%	29%	44%
Average	36%	23%	45%

© Mediappro, 2006

older age group use phones for flirting, and also appreciate the distance afforded by texting to reduce embarrassment.

There is minimal use of other functions of mobile phones such as photography, image-sending of mobile gaming. There is almost no interaction between the cell phone and other media, for instance, for transferring pictures onto a computer or for participating in contests or television, radio, or Internet games.

Other Activities

If communication holds an important place in the habits of youth aged 12 to 18, they also frequently devote themselves to the Internet for a host of other accompanying activities:

- Downloading material from the Internet is widely-practised: 61% say that they download a range of material from the Internet sometimes (17%), often (18%), or very often (26%). Strikingly, 44% of the young people said that they download music even when it is forbidden. Awareness and regulation concerning downloading, strongly differs from one country to the next. When such rules exist, the youth take different positions, but generally believe that pirating is acceptable for personal use.

- Music or online radio programmes are very popular: 67% of young people listen sometimes (21%), often (20%), or very often (26%).

- The number playing online or network games seems small: only 18% of them say that they play frequently or very frequently, though again this varied

Table 5. Use every day + several times a week

	At home	At school
Belgium	69%	9%
Denmark	89%	33%
Estonia	83%	30%
France	57%	10%
Greece	38%	25%
Italy	56%	7%
Poland	68%	45%
Portugal	62%	22%
Quebec	86%	18%
UK	79%	56%
Average	67%	26%

© Mediappro, 2006

considerably between countries. For instance, 30% in Denmark, 26% in the UK, but only 11% in Poland. In Quebec, more than one of two declare to be an online gamer. However, this may represent a considerable rise in use over the last few years.

- Creating their own content is much less widely-practised than forms of communication. For instance, 18% of young people say that they have a personal site and 18% a blog. A blog is quite popular in Belgium (38%), Quebec (35%), and France (25%), while in some cases, young people seemed uncertain what a blog was (one-third of the Danish sample, for instance). The Belgian study (De Smedt, Geeroms, Verniers, & De Theux, 2006) observes that the life-span of young people's blogs is typically very short, while the French and Quebec studies note that a large proportion of blogs owned by young people are dormant.

The Gap Between Internet at Home and at School

Across all countries, including Quebec, it is clear that the Internet is used far more at home than at school. Eighty-one percent of the young people say they use it at home (95% in Denmark and Quebec vs. 64% in Greece). Thirty-eight percent go on it every day—with huge differences between countries, from Estonia (65%) to Greece (8%)—and 30% multiple times a week. Sixty-seven percent of the students say that they have a high-speed connection at home (highest: Estonia 90%; lowest: Greece 31%). The Estonian report (Ugur & Ollivry, 2006) notes that "the private character of their activities may explain why respondents clearly prefer to use the Internet at home and use public access points as little as possible."

It is within the home that the young people seem to have the most freedom to do what they want on the Internet. Their preferred activities are communicating with friends (via instant messaging), visiting Web sites, listening to music, playing games, and downloading material. The use of search engines is also highlighted as a popular activity in some countries, especially United Kingdom, Belgium, Poland, and France.

Generally, uses of the Internet seem to increase with age. Older teenagers use the Internet more, leading us to conclude that using the Internet increases with maturity. Also, unsurprisingly, use of the Internet at home for school-related purposes increases: the Danish study, for instance, notes this use by 16 to 18-year-olds, and the availability of online notes to assist homework.

The home is where many young people feel they learn about the Internet, either through self-teaching or from siblings. Learning from parents also occurs, though from young people's point of view, parents do not seem to be great users of the Internet : 25% use it sometimes, 25% often, and 15% very often.

Use of the Internet does not seem to have reduced the use of other media, with the exception of television (40% of the young people say that they watch it less than before) and books (32% of them read books less often than before). The Polish report (Wenglorz, 2006) mentions that "the Internet changes the behaviours at home and young people usually notice that fact. The Internet takes advantage over TV." The last finding is more complex and ambivalent when broken down, however: the French study pointed out that "almost 3 young people in 10 declare they read less than before, mostly the 17 to 19-year-old girls, but 1 in 10 say they read more than before."

While home use of the Internet is extensive, it is equally clear that school use is severely limited and constrained in Europe and in Quebec as well. Although young people have physical access to the Internet at school in theory, in practice it is used much less than at home. Indeed, 22% (highest: Belgium 42%; lowest: Denmark 6%) of young people say that they never use the Internet at school during class and 30 % rarely.

Students mostly say they use the Internet for their schoolwork through retrieving information. The most likely context for use cited in the interviews (in the UK, Portugal, and Poland) was for ICT lessons. The UK qualitative study (Burn & Cranmer, 2006) notes that "school uses were often talked of without enthusiasm compared with the zeal with which young people spoke about MSN, games, music and other home uses."

The interaction between the school or college and the young people does not seem developed in relation to the Internet. Explicit teaching about the Internet in schools seems to be seriously under-developed: 82% (90% in Quebec) of the young people never or rarely talk about the Internet with their teachers or educators (highest: Estonia 94%; lowest: Italy 68%). A small majority (56%) are aware of rules regulating the use of the Internet in their school (highest: Portugal 72.4%; lowest: Italy 26.5%). Children in several countries say that they have learned more from friends and parents than anyone else about Internet use: in Greece, for example, they are most likely to learn from friends, then from family (mostly siblings), and only then from school. However, at least in France, half of young people consider their teachers are competent on this matter, and one-third express no opinion.

Physical restrictions also play a part. In some countries, computers are simply not available freely to children. In Poland, for instance, computer suites are closed during breaks; in Italy, some schools are still not connected; while in Portugal, the computer-student ratio is low. In other countries, however, physical access is not the problem (Belgium, Estonia, Denmark). More importantly, use is restricted by school policy. In Greece, the Internet is only used in ICT lessons, for instance, while the prohibition of Internet use for communication (chatting, e-mail, instant messaging), and leisure uses such as games and music, is widespread in schools across all the countries in the project.

The international case for urgent improvements to use of the Internet in schools, and the need to teach about it effectively, is dramatically underlined by the views of the young people themselves. While their experiences of the Internet in school are largely disappointing and constrained, they consider that the school should be an important resource, and one that they need. The majority of the young people think it is important or very important that the school teach them how to find useful sites (52%), and to help them evaluate the information they find on Web sites (42% of them think it is important, 20% think it is very important). The school should also provide better access to the Internet (39% important, 29% very important) and teach the young people how to quickly find information on the Internet. Finally, although the widely-reported experience of young people in this study is that teachers do not talk to them about the Internet, they clearly believe that their teachers have the necessary skills: 45% of young people think that their teachers are familiar with the Internet (highest: Poland 60%; lowest: Estonia 31%).

Safety Issues

There is a high degree of awareness of safety issues among the young people surveyed and interviewed. They do not seem to be naïve or ignorant of the dangers they could be confronted with. They say that they never (47%) or rarely (22%) talk to people they do not know face to face. They seem to be aware of certain rules they have to respect on the Internet: for example, 68% believe they should not show images of people on Web sites without their permission. However, it seems likely that they over-estimate their competence: 79% consider they know well how the Internet works; but only 52% of them are able to evaluate the information they retrieve.

In certain countries such as France or Quebec, awareness of the limits and dangers of the Internet has greatly progressed within the last 6 years. Some Europeans are quite critical regarding the information available on the Internet: more than two-thirds of French youth compared to 60% of Quebecers, claim they do not blindly accept what is conveyed on the Internet. This critical view increases with age, particularly amongst girls. Since 2000 (Bevort & Bréda, 2001), there has been a complete reversal in France in the trend that information acquired on the Internet is reliable. Then only 16% were sceptical of the information obtained through the Internet; today that figure has increased to 68%. The Quebec study reports the same conclusion, though its authors point out that the Google, Wikipedia tandem, do not induce distrust, but on the contrary, evoke a sense of definite trust (Piette et al., 2007).

The need to control what is accessible on the Internet has also increased from 67% of young Quebecers in 2000 to more than 80% today (90% of girls).

The survey data suggest that for young people the Internet is mostly a means of keeping in touch with friends and the people close to them. It appears that young people appropriate the Internet as a tool to enhance their established relationships and activities. The emphasis on communication with friends and people they know, and of the decline of use of chat rooms and interest in meeting strangers, is a positive feature of the study. However, there is an increase in online gaming, another context for communicating with strangers; though there was no evidence that this was experienced as dangerous. Where harmful situations were referred to in the interviews, they were most commonly cited as experiences heard about from friends rather than experienced directly.

While there are debates in some countries about the dangers of bullying with mobile phones, through voice, text or, most recently, image, this is not reflected as a serious problem in this study. The Danish report indicates a very small number who have had problems, but conclude that the problem is not widespread. Similarly, the UK study contains very little reporting of negative experiences; and of those reported, most had had been heard about rather than directly experienced. The Italian report (Rivoltella & Zoffi, 2006) underlines:

The strong connection between risk perception declared by students (pornography, hackers, dangerous relationships, inconvenient images) and media representation of risks and bad experiences on the Internet, especially on television. Generally students never had bad experiences on line, but they saw them on TV.

The survey data suggests that parents across all the countries, including Quebec, hold fairly liberal views and do not restrict young people's Internet use to a large extent. For instance, young people engage in the following activities: instant messaging (86%), chat (75%), e-mail (89%), games (81%), visits on sites (69%), and downloading (77%). In Quebec, 9 in 10 young people say their parents control what they do on the Internet only rarely or never. Parents do not seem to be included in their children's "Internet universe." The young people say that they talk to their parents about this medium rarely (32%), sometimes (31%), often or very often (15%). Twenty-one percent never talk about it. However, this varied across countries: in France, for instance, 37% talk to their parents about the Internet sometimes, and 25% often or very often.

It appears that parents do not restrict their children's cell phone uses. Eighty-four percent of the young people say that their parents give them permission to call whoever they want. Moreover, they consider it acceptable that their parents use this tool to know where their children are (84% clearly accept this affirmation). By contrast, mobile phones are strictly regulated or even forbidden in schools in all countries. Parents tend to moderately control game activity: they pay most attention to the time their children spend on playing (48%), than on the people their children play with (44%), and finally on the type of games their children play (28%). Examples of parental regulation seemed mostly to do with safety issues, with prohibitions applied to chat rooms and certain types of Web site. However, also common were restrictions on time of use, suggesting more general concerns about health or spread of activities. The Greek study indicated little intervention by parents except to limit costs.

There is also, importantly, wide evidence of self-regulation by young people. This includes awareness of violent and pornographic sites, sometimes in relation to concern about younger siblings, as in the Danish study; it may be that young people here replicate adult anxiety, adopting adult roles towards younger children. It also includes anxiety about chat rooms and concern about viruses, spam, expense (buying ring tones, for instance), and hackers. However, awareness of risk and ability to deal with it varies considerably from country to country. In France, the young people were aware of a wide range of risks, and expressed sensible, cautious attitudes, which the French study attributed to extensive and successful public information campaigns and teacher training. Similarly, in Estonia, respondents were well aware if a wide variety of risks, from communicating with strangers to the dangers of Internet shopping. By contrast, the Polish study found evidence that young people were sometimes too trusting of Web sites and in need of education to evaluate risk, while the Greek study found generally low awareness of risk.

Questions Related to Media Education

Appropriation

What does the Mediappro study reveal about how and to what extent the Internet is integrated in the daily habits of young people? The study aims not only to evaluate the impact and influence of these new practices in the daily activities of youth, but also, aims to identify how young people adopt technology to meet their needs. For instance, to what degree does access to the Internet modify, enhance, or even alter social behaviour, learning techniques, habits in media, and cultural consumption? What is their level of awareness on these issues?

The appropriation of new media rests on two phenomena. Media is accessible to young people, who in turn modify its usage. Youth integrate these media in their own way and for their own purpose, to do what they can and/or what they want, in relation to other users.

The interaction between media and youth is continual and a highly dynamic process. Questioning the appropriation of new media leads to the identification of the uses and methods in terms of one's own chronology, practicalities, oversights, and difficulties.

Studies demonstrate how youth movements are deployed almost instantaneously and spread extremely rapidly and contagiously. This necessarily leads to foreseeing what actually impacts youth: the influence of family background (attitudes towards education, kinship, household organisation) and of friendship, shared values, representation, access to these media through both technical and educational training.

By closely observing the "true" appropriation of these new media by youth, one must ask, what elements are missing and how can youth have a better grasp on its usage? While young people aged between 12 and 18 are strongly interested in the Internet and use it frequently, many of these youth are not actually as competent as they think or say. Often they lack the terminology and the notions to explicitly describe and detail their habits, and by consequence, are unable to develop their own opinions on these media. Their knowledge remains superficial, while in-depth savoir faire and insight is clearly needed. This also extends to the need for documented research despite the fact that schools have already taken this into consideration.

As school, work is often delimited by the imperative of acquiring knowledge rather than acquiring skills, adolescents do not learn how to effectively use these new means of communication, particularly as it relates to legal or ethical issues, aspects of online communication and publication of media. As a result, for instance, youth are not entirely clear on the notion of Internet anonymity. French youth are as numerous in believing that one can be identified even if they use a pseudonym, as believing the opposite, and only 44% of youth realise that anyone can access their personal blog.

On the other hand, many of these young people are quite aware of the laws and regulations regarding civic rights on the Internet, such as a person's rights to their image and royalties linked to downloading, as compared to other Europeans, who often have no clue on these issues. In France, the protection of one's private life and rights to one's image are sensitive subjects on which much information is diffused, notably in school. But once again, young people's knowledge is often vague and does not prevent them from overlooking rules, of which they have a very faint idea.

As already mentioned, the emergence of scepticism in front of information obtained through the Internet is a proof of a more critical appropriation by the adolescents, even if Google and Wikipedia are considered in certain countries, especially Quebec, as trusty sources.

Finally, the majority of young people perceive electronic media as technologies in constant movement and rapidly adopt new tendencies. The Portuguese team (Reia Baptista, Balthazar, & Mendes, 2006) however, points out that "Even though students are usually interested in new activities and new "fashions," they tend to always do the same thing on the Internet, they follow a pattern." This undoubtedly results from the inadequate and insufficient appropriation of the Internet. In this case, we could apply the metaphor of a young person who doesn't know his neighbourhood very well, though he goes there several times a day, but never thinks to take short cuts or new streets. Even at the age of 17, youth do not have a very clear idea on the societal impact of these media and rarely have an educational outlet that would allow them to reflect conceptually on the matter.

The Study's Conclusions

Perhaps the most striking conclusion of the whole study is the marked gap between home and school use of the Internet. This gap, across all the countries including Quebec, was evident in terms of frequency of use, access, regulation, learning and skill development, and type of activity. The data indicates a great gulf opening up, in which all the functions important to young people exist outside school, as well as most of the learning (albeit self-teaching or peer learning), while schools restrict access, unnecessarily forbid certain practices, fail to understand the communicative function of the Internet, and, worst of all, fail to teach the skills of information retrieval, search, site evaluation and creative production that are presumably most important to them. Consequently they most often learn about the Internet without the help of adults, in either pairs, or individually by the process of trial and error.

It is equally clear that young people cannot adequately gain the necessary skills. While in some countries, they are sophisticated users of the Internet, with well-developed understandings of moral and cultural issues, notably France, there are areas where they are much weaker, particularly in understanding any kind of legal question in relation to the Internet. Furthermore, there is evidence in all the countries that they over-estimate their own ability to evaluate. These are areas of knowledge and critical skills that only schools can teach.

While the creative potential of new media is much discussed in academic literature, the evidence here was that creative work was limited, with a minority of young people developing their own Web sites or blogs, and some evidence that these products could easily become inert. Again, there is an obvious role for schools in developing these less easily acquired skills.

Except in Quebec, phones emerge as vitally important to young people's lives: they are used to develop and cement relationships, to attain independence (though also to retain safe contact with parents), and to finely discriminate between different degrees and levels of social proximity. Again, it seems that schools have not properly considered the educational potential of phone uses, or indeed how to explicitly teach about them; but rather revert, again, to prohibition and regulation.

Games seem to be rather less important to these young people than popular wisdom often suggests, but they are still an important leisure and cultural medium, and it may be that online gaming, while still a minority, is growing. Schools, again, are clearly not responding by considering the educational potential of computer games (a well-developed domain of educational research), but tend to prohibit.

Finally, with respect to questions of safety, the study shows young people report being in dangerous, or even uncomfortable, situations extremely rarely. They are mostly aware of the possible dangers and the shift from chat room use to instant messaging alone considerably reduces practices which expose them to meeting with strangers or even unwelcome people they know. While the debate about new forms of risk in relation to phones and online games is clearly alive in many of the participant countries, it is equally clear that, again, there is very little evidence of reported danger. However, all of these issues would benefit from further research, particularly longitudinal study.

Recommendations

With varying reports on information technology and media, it is quite normal to have different points of view—between Mediappro, which focuses on the perceptions of young people, or the studies conducted for teachers, educational systems or parents, not to mention reports from international organizations (UNESCO, the European Commission), public institutions (interministerial structures, territorial units), industrial operators, or groups of educators.

If institutions are to manage political unity with its blended facts and data and its financial mass, if the teacher is wrapped up in his subject of study, the school where he teaches, or the choice of his teachings, if industry looks to develop its market and seeks to innovate, then the lives of students revolve around their private life of friends and family and their life at school. Yet, all these actors can not operate in separate or independent worlds, since the ultimate goal is that political and economic choices combined with the activities of teachers, coincide to meet the real needs of youth and society.

These facts result in the recommendations aimed at the key actors in the field, namely, the family, the educational system, and politics.

In Relation to Parents

There exists a huge gap between home and school regarding the 12 to 18-year-olds' use of media. Where school is the place for learning and mainly goal-oriented searching in relation to school work, then the use of media at home is characterized by fun, entertainment, and learning through peer-to-peer communication. And much more time is spent on media at home compared to use in schools:

- It is a common trend in the recommendations by the different countries participating in Mediappro study that parents today have to consider their children as "experts" regarding Internet and mobile phones due to their heavy use of these media and competence in relation to media technology.

- Parents and children have different opinions regarding the risks related to Internet use. Where parents seem to focus very much on the risks related to chat rooms, violence, pornography, and so forth, then the children consider the most serious risk to be viruses on the Internet.

- In general it is recommended that parents talk with their children about their use of the Internet. Although it is a problem that parents in general know less about the Internet than the children, they can contribute skills that are not necessarily technical from which their children could also benefit. To cope with this fact, it is suggested that training sessions be organised which focus on new media usage in schools as well as in parent associations—and also to try to create discussion groups where parents can interact and exchange experiences about the use of new media—for parents as for their children. Both teachers and parents should be guided and encouraged to talk to children and young people about how they manage their online and off-line relationships. Furthermore, emphasis is put on the need for critical literacy skills and competences rather than prohibitory practices, filters, and blocking software.

There are differences among the countries regarding the recommendations to the parents. For instance, in countries where children already seem to have a critical approach to chat rooms and general use of the Internet, and where the parents have a rather relaxed and permissive attitude to the children's use of the new media, there seem to be less focus on recommendations to parents than in countries with a more restrictive approach.

In Relation to Schools and Teachers

There is consensus among all nine countries that media literacy, especially with focus on the new media, is needed in schools. The children's use of the Internet and mobile phones is a challenge to the traditional school culture and way of teaching. This means that there is a need for a broad concept of media teaching in the schools. Schools and colleges need to adopt a positive and inclusive attitude towards uses of new media in schools in order to capitalise on the innovative potential of these technologies. However, there are—in all the countries—barriers to this, consisting mainly of two things: lack of equipment in the schools and lack of teachers' competences regarding new media.

It is a fact, however, that these two problems are closely related to each other, due to the fact that as long as the teachers are not competent and do not see the need for media literacy, including the Internet, mobile phones, and other new media, they will not insist on more media technology in the schools and will probably not require further purchase of media equipment for the schools.

It is suggested that, as initiated by the Council of Europe at the beginning of year 2000 (Richardson et al., 2006), an educator's/teacher's guide about the new media uses, focusing on its potential risks and challenges—and proposing some related activities for media teaching—is created.

There are also proposals that the emphasis often placed on regulation and prohibition on online media within the schools is substituted by pedagogical interventions aimed at developing children's and young people's critical literacy skills and competences.

Peer-to-peer teaching and development of teachers' in-learning practices are central themes, just as emphasis is put on the general need for promotion of a holistic approach to media literacy and promotion of teacher training and lifelong learning regarding new technologies. Training sessions for educators/teachers are suggested as well as a stronger focus on cooperation between teachers, parents, and students regarding new media.

Altogether all the countries have agreed, on the basis of the results of the Mediappro survey, pointing at the fact that new media are used much more at home than in school and that there is a lack of critical approach to the media, that there is an urgent need for media literacy in the schools, across the curriculum, and on all levels. However, as is emphasized by all the parties, this is only possible if the teachers get a deeper insight in and further training in media literacy.

In Relation to Politicians

There is general consensus among the countries that the politicians have a respon-sibility regarding the introduction of media literacy into the schools. Efforts have been made throughout Europe to develop access to Internet in schools, but there is still much progress to be made: political leaders ought to promote media literacy into educative programmes including the pedagogy of the Internet into a broader concept of pedagogy. The politicians ought to develop a policy that focuses on the ethical as well as the educational aspects of the new media technologies and sup-port integration of media education and media literacy contents and subjects into the teachers' curricula and into the pupils' curricula.

Furthermore it is suggested that politicians support the creation of campaigns that not only are focused on the dangers of the media but are focused on all dimensions of the media.

It is also suggested that the politicians support the promotion of an easier Internet access in public places like library, public administration, young people's houses, cultural centres, and so forth.

The politicians ought to understand and accept the shift of paradigm from traditional culture to media culture, especially as far as young people are concerned. They have to support, ideologically as well as economically, the introduction of media literacy into all levels of education, in relation to children as well as to grown ups.

There is an overriding need that the decision makers on the political level realize the necessity of teaching every single citizen a deep insight into the role and func-tion of media. This may, hopefully, be developed through qualified and competent media literacy, an important cornerstone in the process of developing democratic citizenship in the globalized digital society.

Future Trends

- The Mediappro research shows that new communication paradigms are ris-ing. We can notice at the same time a burst of the private sphere, linked to the development of instant communication devices and an easier access to them on the one hand, and absorption of intimate topics as new mediatic contents by the traditional media on the other hand. In the emerging multimedia culture society, the boundary between private and public spheres is changing.

  Do the European young people understand the difference between what should be public sphere and private sphere, namely when they arrive home from school and continue communicating with friends, when they watch TV reality shows, when they publish personal information online, when they communicate through a Web cam, and so forth? Do they feel the need for a private sphere and do they think it is important to maintain some privacy? Are they aware of the role the electronic and traditional media play in this evolution?

- We pointed out some big differences in the way young people consider their parents' and their teachers' educational attitude toward them. Concerning parents, our recommendations refer to attitudes to set up as one of the main dimensions allowing young people's media appropriation. For teachers, it seems that they do not integrate the electronic media in their teaching even when they are extremely skilled in ICT's, like in Denmark. So how do technological and cultural changes impact relationship between young people and teachers, young people and parents, and within the family?

Teachers have to be considered as persons and as professionals as well, having their own usage of the electronic media. Is there a gap between their personal and their professional uses? How do they consider the main stakes of the development of new information and communication practices for themselves, for their pupils? What do they expect from school system and policy? Which are the brakes upon a wider use of the electronic media in classrooms?

These questions should lead to further research on the following items:

- It appears very important to focus on the very beginning of the practices. Our research allowed us to verify that at 11 years old, real and autonomous uses are already settled. A research on the ages of 7 to 11 should highlight how they enter the electronic media world, their very first appropriation paths. A specific research protocol should be adapted to young children.

- The learning process has to rely on specific competencies and not on subjects only. Which competencies do young people build up spontaneously vs. through an educational process, how do they develop them, to which extent are they innovators in the use of new electronic media? This topic should be observed through a complex protocol including both questionnaires, interviews of young people and teachers/parents, and observations of students' practices.

- Concerning young people playing online or network games, even if their number seems small, we need further study to clarify some implications: clearly cost implications, where online games require subscription, and implications for meeting people online, in role.

- Is media education making a difference? How do we cope with the broad, fragmented, and mosaic formed media pedagogy? There is a need to define new guidelines for multimedia cultural literacy (MCL) within these cognitive contexts, with a specific stress on new ways for an evaluation process and the role of the nonformal educational setting as one of the partners of a relevant and fruitful media education, aiming to a higher degree of literacy and less alienated assimilation processes of the media pedagogical dimensions in general.

Conclusion

The findings that result from the Mediappro study should not be intrepreted as pessimistic. On the contrary, there is much building to do. The study demands an evaluation of the field data and of the decisions concerning the habits and expectations of youth. Moreover, considering the actual "true" skills of youth, as opposed to their perceived skills, demonstrates the neccessity of providing a structured framework, of redefining certain terms, of conceptualising certain fields, and an initiation of the thought process on the current socio-economic evolution as well as its impact on society.

Schools are where young people could have the opportunity to shed their tentative approach and effectively learn how to master their use of the Internet and future new media. Indeed they could potentially acquire a true digital culture. As cited by Serge Proulx (Proulx, 2002) in the manifesto for the development of technical culture (CRCT, 1981):

It is seemingly evident that those without technical culture, live in ignorance of their own environment. This presents a double form of alienation: On the one hand, not having understood one's own proper surroundings, and on the other hand, unawareness leads to a permanent dependance on organisations and individuals who have the skills that are missing.

With regards to appropriation by youth, it is not simply a question of indifference nor a complete lack of knowledge, but rather a dependance on those who do not master the theories on usage and are themselves dependant on the structures and organisations that govern the Internet. They know how to use the Internet through intermediaries and the way they use it has been imposed by the Internet itself. Digital culture is an indispensable factor of societies of knowledge and, in turn, demands that its appropriation be reflexive, creative, and supported by true critical thinking.

References

Aslanidou, S., & Ikonomou, A. (2006). The appropriation of new media by youth. Mediappro final report. Retrieved October 5, 2007, from http://www.mediappro.org/publications/finalreport.pdf

Bevort, E., & Bréda, I. (2001). Les jeunes et Internet: Représentations, utilisations, appropriation. Retrieved October 5, 2007, from http://www.clemi.org/jeunes_internet.html

Bevort, E., & Bréda, I. (2006). Mediappro, appropriation des nouveaux médias par les jeunes: Une enquête européenne en éducation aux médias. Retrieved October 5, 2007, from http://www.clemi.org/international.html

Burn, A., & Cranmer, S. (2006). The appropriation of new media by youth. Mediappro report. Retrieved October 5, 2007, from http://www.mediappro.org/publications/finalreport.pdf

De Smedt, T., Geeroms, C., Verniers, P., & De Theux, P. (2006). The appropriation of new media by youth. Mediappro report. Retrieved October 5, 2007, from http://www.mediappro.org/publications/finalreport.pdf

European Commission. (2006). Benchmarking access and use of ICT in European schools. Retrieved October 5, 2007, from http://ec.europa.eu/information_society/eeurope/i2010/benchmarking/index_en.htm

European Commission. Eurostat (in Population and Social Conditions). Retrieved October 5, 2007, from http://epp.eurostat.cec.eu.int

Livingstone, S., & Bober, M. (2004). UK children go online: Surveying the experiences of young people and their parents. London School of Economics and Political Science, Department of Media and Communications.

Mediappro. (2005). Analysis and synthesis of existing data. Retrieved October 5, 2007, from 2007 from http://www.mediappro.org/stat_3_1.htm

Piette, J., Pons, C.M., & Giroux, L. (2007, March). Les Jeunes et Internet: 2006 - Appropriation des nouvelles technologies. Final report to the Ministry of Culture and Communication, Quebec Governement.

Proulx, S. (2002). Trajectoires d'usages des technologies de communication: Les formes d'appropriation d'une culture numérique comme enjeu d'une société du savoir. Annales des Télécommunications, 57(3-4), 180-189.

Reia Baptista, V., Balthazar, N., & Mendes, S. (2006). The appropriation of new media by youth. Mediappro report. Retrieved October 5, 2007, from http://www.mediappro.org/publications/finalreport.pdf

Richardson, J., Milwood Hargrave, A., Moratille, B., Vahtivouri, S., Venter, D., & de Vries, R. (2006). The Internet literacy handbook. Strasbourg, France: Council of Europe.

Rivoltella, P.-C., & Zoffi, E. (2006). The appropriation of new media by youth. Mediappro report. Retrieved October 5, 2007, from http://www.mediappro. org/publications/finalreport.pdf

Tufte, B., Rasmussen, J., & Christensen, O. (2006). The appropriation of new media by youth. Mediappro final report. Retrieved October 5, 2007, from http://www. mediappro.org/publications/finalreport.pdf

Ugur, K., & Ollivry, J.-P. (2006). The appropriation of new media by youth. Mediappro report. Retrieved October 5, 2007, from http://www.mediappro. org/publications/finalreport.pdf

Wenglorz, J. (2006). The appropriation of new media by youth. Mediappro report. Retrieved October 5, 2007, from http://www.mediappro.org/publications/finalreport.pdf

Endnotes

[1] **Mediappro member teams**

Coordinator: Catholic University of Louvain, Research group in learning's mediation (Belgium); Professsor Thierry De Smedt, Catherine Geeroms

- Center for Higher Education, Copenhagen and North Zealand (Denmark): Birgitte Tufte, Jeanette Rasmussen, Ole Christensen

- Catholic University of Milano, Department of pedagogy (Italy): Pier Cesare Rivoltella, Elsa Zoffi

- Clemi, Ministry of Education (France): Evelyne Bevort, Isabelle Bréda

- Foundation for Economic Education (Poland): Justyna Wenglorz

- London Institute of Education, Center for the Study of Children, Youth and Media (United Kingdom): Andrew Burn, Sue Cranmer

  - o Media Animation a.s.b.l. (Belgium): Patrick Verniers, Paul De Theux

  - o School of Pedagogical and Technological Education (Greece): Sofia Aslanidou, Andreas Ikonomou

- University of Algarve, School of Education (Portugal): Vitor Reia Baptista, Neusa Baltazar, Samantha Mendes

- University of Tartu (Estonia): Epp Lauk, Veronika Kalmus, Jean-Pascal Ollivry, Margit Keller, Pille Runnel, Anneken Metsoja, Kadri Ugur, Reelika Raamat

In collaboration with the Province of Quebec, Canada:

- University of Montreal, Luc Giroux
- University of Sherbrooke, Jacques Piette and Christian-Marie Pons

Chapter IX

Learning with New Media at the University:
From Representations to Utilization

Maria Apparecida Mamede-Neves, The Catholic University of Rio de Janeiro, Brazil

Flavia Nizia Da Fonseca Ribeiro, The Catholic University of Rio de Janeiro, Brazil

Abstract

The following chapter aims at discussing the possible uses of new media for teacher work at universities based on an analysis of data collected from research carried out at the Catholic University of Rio de Janeiro's Department of Education in Brazil. Such research looks at the level of insertion of university students into the computer society and at the representations they make of the new medium. In the first section, responses from students are analyzed, mainly from young scholarship holders from less favored communities in Rio de Janeiro in contrast with other students' responses. A second section comparatively analyzes the social representations of the book, television, and the Internet made by the students as means to gain information and knowledge. This chapter concludes that one must acknowledge both how youths value new media and the importance of relating presential culture to cyberculture in teaching, as well as the need for a change in mentality on the part of teachers and for their effective training to adopt new media in their pedagogical practice.

Introduction

Currently, Brazilian university life is increasingly providing teachers with the use of new pedagogical strategies which make students more interested in the contents of subjects; this reality is becoming commonplace in institutions of higher education. However, the social representation of the university remains as a place where knowledge is sacred, the greatest part of lessons are anchored on teachers' talk and predominantly based on the textbook, perpetuating a devaluation of students' autonomous thinking and emphasizing the mastery of the syllabus. These represent a hierarchy as well as rites centered mainly around the teacher's figure, failing to take into consideration other elements which constitute this scenario, and, most of all, to open up to what is new.

In this sense, new media, among other elements, are overlooked, many times based on the premise that they present superficial knowledge which is inadequate to the "seriousness" demanded by academic life. Another very common argument in university halls holds that access to these new media is a privilege of the higher classes and, therefore, inaccessible to poorer students.

We believe it is opportune to point out that we are referring to the reality in South America, Brazil, more specifically the state of Rio de Janeiro, which, among Brazilian states, has well-defined social classes. Such a reality does indeed account for some differences which are mostly significant. However, we believe there is a universal essence which we shall focus on henceforth, having as a background research on youths and the Internet in which the study of social representations was the highlight.

We took this path because we consider that investigating social representations means bringing to the surface contributions by the individuals in a certain group without minimizing reciprocal and dynamic influences. Thus, specific knowledge of the modes of appropriation and production of meanings engendered by the researched community, along with its social practices and representations, widens the possibilities of understanding in which way "gestures change according to time and place, to the objects read and to the reasons for reading" (Chartier, 1999, p. 77; 2001a, 2001b).

New Media: Instruments of Cohesion or Separation?

Based on the premises stated above, the research *Youths Online*, carried out at the Catholic University of Rio de Janeiro (PUC-Rio),[1] Brazil, had as its main objective the identification, among youths recently entering university, of the Internet's fields of representation and their meaning to this group in contrast with the representations of the book and television. This research was a social inquiry, using, as the main tool, an extensive questionnaire about the relationship between young people and the use of computer and Internet. The group studied had 973 students, representing 75% of all youths recently entering university, registering in February, 2006.[2] This group statistically represents youths coming from middle to higher classes and those coming from lower income classes who have access to university through the ProUni[3] program. The group's profile was totally balanced as regards gender. In terms of age, the higher percentages were between 17 and 19-year-olds, with 18-year-olds being the largest (42%), followed closely by 17-year-olds (31%) and 19-year-olds (12%), which is understandable, since this is the expected university entrance age in Brazil.

We verified that the selected youths can use the computer, with 97% of students owning a computer and 13% accessing computers either at friends' houses, at school, or at community centers. The variation between middle to higher income students and lower income students can be explained by the fact that the former have more than one computer at home, as well as personal laptops, while the latter have no more than one computer per household and predominantly have a dial-up connection to the Internet, rather than broadband.

This difference, however, does not produce significant differences in the opinions of both groups as regards the value of computers and of the Internet and their social representation.

In relation to the activities young university students engage in in their free time, most in both groups highly enjoy computer activities, whether to play games or to communicate, in this case through the Internet. However, lower income students watch television more than they use the computer in their free time, which is certainly due to the widespread use of television, all over Brazil, by all social classes, mainly the lower ones.[4]

The same situation happened when the students were asked which medium they mostly use to stay informed. Most pointed to the Internet and to television, with less favored students once again showing a higher percentage as regards the use of television.

When asked which representations they made of the computer even at a time when they still could not use one, between 54% and 75% affirmed that they were *curious about* and *attracted to* this technology, *highly expectant of it,* mainly because *they believe in the efficiency of the computer,* and *that its use can solve most problems*!![5] We can notice here the myth of the "philosopher's stone," which, for Wolfram von Eschenbach, in his novel Parzival, was considered to have been thrown from the skies by celestial beings and to have unimaginable powers.

Another representation of the Internet extracted from the students' statements is that of *a mask which protects one's true identity.* This was alluded to by 58% of youths, while among those from lower income classes the number goes up to 77%. One can notice here that the so-called protection the Internet confers upon its user is being taken for real by the youths, who are actually unaware of the possible traps the Internet, like Theseus' labyrinth, can pose. Such an idea that the Internet has a great power to hide also appears, albeit in another form, among the representations of several teachers, however with a negative connotation, when it is regarded as an unreliable learning tool, since it can conceal the source of information or the true identity of the purported author.

Young people are not aware of the navigation plan and the difficulties of the journey. To them, what is attractive is the ability to open new windows, always "discovering" new territories, "strange lands," as fascinating as a labyrinth. The labyrinth is appealing for what it hides; it incites an incessant search for the "infinitely lost object" which is chased after but never actually found, but which, while searched, reveals a myriad of other paths where other objects can be found, thus sustaining the illusion of conquest. The magic of the Internet, as a labyrinth with several paths, allowing crossroads and impasse which is sometimes hard to solve, is defended by youths. To them, the representations of the Internet have a positive connotation, as some of their statements reveal: *limitless communication; connects the world; access to the world; best tool ever invented; an invention that changed the world; widening of territories; reaching several places without leaving home; how did I manage to live without it; infinite possibilities… infinite!!*

Actually, these representations by the youths contain not only the metaphor of the labyrinth, but also the symbol of the spiral. The spiral stands for the appearance of a circular movement starting at an original point, maintaining and extending this movement infinitely, and, therefore, is related to the labyrinth in that it represents both evolution and involution. It symbolizes extension, development, cyclical, albeit forward continuity, creational rotation. It denotes permanence of being within the fugacity of movement. It should be noted that young people's enchantment by the Internet also lies on these qualities.

Nevertheless, that which is attractive to youths—the search for what's new—is experienced as scary by many teachers, since it reflects the typically human sensation of being lost and of not knowing how to or not being able to return. Such is the representation that quite a big group of teachers make of the Internet, in this sense represented by a tress labyrinth.

In opposition to a spiral, an open and optimistic symbol, a tress is a closed symbol, a prison, without any chances of escaping, symbolizing, therefore, involution.[6]

The Internet, in order to be seen simultaneously as a spiral and a tress, requires that those browsing it define their identity very clearly, for otherwise they will get lost in it. This is what many teachers fear, as well as some of the youths from our research, as evidenced by these statements: *depending on its use, great; useful if well utilized; necessary but alienating; must be used with moderation and care; use it but avoid becoming addicted; sometimes stressful; a source of control of our lives by others; ingenious, though not being used constructively.*

Attractive or dangerous? What should really move the one who enters the labyrinth? Find the path that leads to the center and to what is to be revealed. How about the danger? It lies in not knowing how to return. The labyrinth only accepts those who set out to discover the plans it contains, those who can bravely forge ahead without fear of getting lost. Because of the threat of getting lost, the labyrinth can be rejected, but, with Ariadne's Thread given to Theseus, assuring the return and the possibility of, upon returning, going back in, it is desired and traversed. Ariadne is the figure that stays outside but is also inside, represented by the conducting thread given to Theseus.

On the Internet, we are inside, while also being outside; we are all Theseus with Ariadne's Thread, a synthesis of both, when we use the search tools on the Internet, when we get the answers to our queries, "solve" our riddles, just like Theseus who killed the Minotaur hidden in the labyrinth of Crete built by Dedalus. Herein lays the importance of those who patiently lay out their strategies and, once in the labyrinth, move form node to node, confident in their navigational charts and in the marks of their identities.[7]

If both teachers and learners adopt this pondering posture, if they become aware of the true value of this invention, it seems certain that the learning environment can only gain, for teachers can make use of it without losing their main role of guiding their students' construction of knowledge.

The analysis of the data showed that there is no significant difference between university students from different social classes as regards the importance and the use of the computer. A more detailed analysis of the representations of the computer and the Internet reveals the interdependence and the articulation of values and problems while building a judgement of the media, a space for the production and reproduction of a moral culture which, in the end, defines human experience.

The Book, Television, and the Internet: Conflicting Mythical Representations?

We regard "myth" as something which is, or until recently has been, "alive," in the sense that it provides elements for building human conduct, conferring, by itself, meaning and value on existence (Eliade, 1989). Thus, understanding the structure and the function of young people's mythical representations of the book, television, and the Internet not only means clarifying the thinking behind the statements they give us, but also better understanding a category of those contemporaneous with us. Understanding them means acknowledging them as human phenomena, cultural phenomena, creations of the spirit. Such was the path we followed while analyzing the responses collected during our investigation.

The book is the symbol of the universe, the supreme wisdom made available to the mortal man, associated with the symbol of the lion, a representation of power and wisdom. Perhaps that explains the responses provided by the youths concerning the book: *fundamental; all should develop a reading habit; the most classic way of obtaining knowledge; one of the best ways of obtaining knowledge.*

The book has an aura of truth, of reliability par excellence; thus the representation given by the youths as *safer communication.*

The book also has the symbology of synthesis, of unity, which offers to those who own it the possibility of infinite unfoldings. Some of the affirmations of the youths are delicious: *knowledge and entertainment in one word; a synthesis of information and knowledge; a voyage through a box full of other people's ideas which, when they are good, become ours.*

Well, if the book is the icon of culture and of knowledge, having them confers status on their owners and, merely by contiguity, makes them educated, which, in the common sense, might refer to a person's educational level.[8] Manguel (1997, pp. 182-183) clarifies this richly meaningful supposition by saying that:

In the first years of Christian Europe and until the twelfth century, common beds were simple objects [...]. Since only the rich possessed more sophisticated beds and few besides them had ornamented beds and books, these became symbols of a family's wealth.[9]

As concerns television, in Machado's (2000) view, which we agree with, communication theoreticians would have us believe that it is a medium for the masses, in the worst sense of the word. However, research shows that television has accumulated, over the last 50 years, a repertoire of creative works greater than commonly supposed. Such a repertoire is dense enough to be legitimized as one of the most important cultural phenomena of our time. On the other hand, Pierre Bourdieu (1997) points out that television is considered, in the common sense, an authority figure which legitimizes facts and renders credibility to that which it presents.

It is interesting to note that, in our research, the representation of television by most youths does not corroborate the above-mentioned line of thinking. Rather, it is seen as a symbol of frivolity and vulgarity whose main purpose is uncommitted entertainment. To quote them: *too overwhelming and appealing; a source of entertainment; lacks creativity; alienation ; I only watch it when I am resting or when there is nothing better to do; a distraction and mostly a waste of time.*

However, some youths noted the role television plays in broadcasting news in an almost instantaneous way, even though they are wary of its reliability. In their words: *easiest way to access knowledge whether it is useful or not; facilitates the fast dissemination of news; a source of information which should be used with critical sense; one should be cautious with the medium; manipulated by political influences.*

Finally, the Internet, our main object of investigation, has as its commonest social representation, besides those described above about new media, its usefulness, the fact that it is a *tool* which helps us in our accomplishments.

In relation to the Internet, to a great number of the youths participating in the research, we also encountered adjectives such as *fast* and *infinite,* which highlight two valuable attributes of this communicational space and signal the dimension of this access mode to information in the view of our interviewees. This can be confirmed by data obtained on services utilized by youths on the Internet: ranked first are search engines (Google, Yahoo, etc.). To all them is also the great facilitator of communication. This is seen as its main use, along with research and access to information.

These considerations make us regard the Internet as a mythical representation of a web, since the web symbolizes all of humankind's capabilities and virtualities, our searching and bringing to consciousness our most far-fetched memories. The web symbolizes a supernatural power given to an angel (Gabriel, in the Christian tradition) who then passionately searches for divinity. We therefore think that, by following this way of thinking, we can understand why the Internet exerts such fascination over those who browse through it. Its social representation is connected with the absolute power of reaching knowledge! On the other hand, we also believe that the strong connection made by the youths between the Internet and *information/research* is a reminder of Ted Nelson's 1960 fantasy of creating Project Xanadu, which was supposed to bring to life the Decouverse, a global online library containing all of the world's literature in hypertext (Sousa, 2006).

Finally, some other representations of the Internet by the youths were quite interesting in that they associated it with *life in* motion, which reminds us of the liquid and navigable dimension of this medium, as well as with communication: *a good way to communicate with people; limitless communication; reaching several places without leaving home.* In fact, several studies, such as Pierre Lévy's (1999), have portrayed infoways as travel and sailing pathways. On the Internet, one can travel on one's fingertips, digitally... and in record time!

Conclusion

After careful analysis of the data provided by the research, one can notice that youths establish representations of new media which are sometimes, but not always, predictable. This allows us to infer that the representations are forged based on everyday contact with patterns, values, attitudes, and socially established conventions which are built, torn down, and rebuilt all the time from socially constructed experience grounded in sociability and interaction.

Thus, we can conclude that the Internet is much closer to young university students because it can adequately match their everyday language, their knowledge, and their local experience. It is attuned to their time, which the university can no longer ignore.

On the other hand, one can also note that, at least in our research, analysis of data showed no significant difference among conceptions and opinions of university students from different social classes as regards how they use new media. Whatever their social class, and even those who belong to a generation not born under the spell of the Internet, university students are well aware of its positive and negative aspects, not only being affected passively. They possess critical judgement as well as a conscience of limits, advantages, and disadvantages.

Analysis of data from the *Youths Online* research allows us to assert that, in the world of representations, youths have a lot to tell us about how they ponder and understand the transformations they have participated in as subjects who live and operate with the reality of their times, our times.

References

Ardizzone, P., & Rivoltella, P.C. (2003). *Didattiche per l'e-learning*. Roma: Carocci.

Bourdieu, P. (1997). *Sobre a televisão*. Rio de Janeiro: Zahar.

Chartier, R. (1999). *A ordem dos livros: leitores, autores e bibliotecas na Europa entre os séculos XIV e XVIII*. Brasília: Editora Universidade de Brasília.

Chartier, R. (2001a). *A aventura do livro: do leitor ao navegador*. São Paulo: Editora UNESP.

Chartier, R. (org.) (2001b). *Práticas de leitura*. São Paulo: Estação Liberdade.

Chevalier, J., & Gheerbrant, A. (1995). *Dicionário de símbolos* (9th edição). Rio de Janeiro: José Olímpio.

Civin, M. (2000). *Psychanalyse du net*. Paris: Hachette.

Eliade, M. (1989). *Mito e realidade*. SãoPaulo: Perspectiva.

Elias, N. (1994). *O processo civilizador*. 2v. Rio de Janeiro: Jorge Zahar.

Lévy, P. (1999). *Cibercultura*. São Paulo: Ed. 34.

Lombard, G. (2004). Psychanalyse et technologie. Role of reference elements In Favez-

Machado, A. (2000). *A televisão levada a sério*. São Paulo: Senac.

Mamede-Neves, M.A.C. (2005). *Jovens em Rede: representação e significação da Internet pelo olhar de jovens universitários*. Rio de Janeiro: Departamento de Educação—PUC-Rio/CNPq.

Mamede-Neves, M.A.C. (2006). O Jovem no centro da dimensão oculta da Internet. In A. M. Nicolaci-da-Costa (Ed.), *Cabeças digitais*. Rio de Janeiro: Loyola, 2006

Mc Luhan, M. (2000). Visão, som e fúria. In: L. Costa Lima (org.) *Teoria da cultura de massa* (pp. 160-161). São Paulo: Paz e Terra.

Mc Luhan, M. (2006). *Os meios de comunicação como extensão do homem (understanding media)* São Paulo: Cultrix.

Moran, J.M. (2000). *Novas tecnologias e mediação pedagógica*. Campinas: Papirus.

Rivoltella, P.C. (2003). *Costruttivismo e pragmatica della comunicazione on line: Socialitá e didattica in Internet*. Trento: Erickson.

Santos, A. (2003). *Leitura de nós: Ciberespaço e literatura*. São Paulo: Itaú Cultural.

Sousa, C.R.P. (2006a). Hipertexto. Espaço Virtual—Mundo Real. In: *Homepages. Centro de Investigação para Tecnologias Interactivas*. Retrieved October 15, 2006, from http://www.citi.pt/

Sousa, C.R.P., and Nelson, T. (2006b). Espaço Virtual—Mundo Real. In: *Homepages. Centro de Investigação para Tecnologias Interactivas*. Retrieved October 15, 2006, from http://www.citi.pt/homepages/espaco/html/ted_nelson.html

Sousa, C.R.P., and Bush, V. (2006c) Espaço Virtual—Mundo Real. In: *Homepages. Centro de Investigação para Tecnologias Interactivas*. Retrieved October 15, 2006, from http://www.citi.pt/homepages/espaco/html/vannevar_bush

Vanderdorpe, C. (1999). *Du Papyrus à l'hipertexte: Essais sur les mutations du texte et de la lecture*. Paris: La Découverte.

Endnotes

[1]   This is a not-for-profit private institution which stands out by producing and transmitting knowledge based on respect for human values and Christian ethics, aiming above all at the benefit of society. Fur further information, access http://www.puc-rio.br.

[2]   This population was considered statistically significant, even when sorted by the students' majors.

[3]   ProUni (University for All Program) was created by the Brazilian government in 2005 granting full and part-time scholarships for undergraduate courses to low-income students at private universities in exchange for some types of tax exemption. The implementation of ProUni, which added to the creation of 10 new federal universities and 48 new campuses, significantly increases the number of enrollments in higher education in Brazil, brings public education to the countryside and fights regional inequalities. All of these actions meet the goals established by Brazil's National Educational Plan, which foresees that, by 2010, at least 30% of the population between the ages of 18 and 24 will be enrolled in higher education, as opposed to 10.4% currently.

[4]   According to a census carried out by the Brazilian Institute of Geography and Statistics (IBGE) in 2002, 72% of the Brazilian population owned at least one television set per household. For further information, go to http://www.ibge.gov.br.

[5]   Every phrase in italics is a literal transcription of the youths' words.

[6]   Chevalier & Gheerbrant (1995), Rio de Janeiro: José Olímpio, 1995 9th edition.

[7]   This topic is also covered in Mamede-Neves, M.A C. O Jovem no centro da dimensão oculta da Internet In: Nicolaci-da-Costa, A. M. Cabeças digitais Rio de Janeiro: Loyola, 2006.

[8]   Commonly, a person who has had a better education is said to be "erudite," "very intelligent," "educated."

[9]   This topic is also covered in Figueiredo-da-Costa, A. V; Fernandez, M. A.; Pedrosa, S. M.; Mamede-Neves, M.A C. O livro e a Internet: representações do jovem universitário Rio de Janeiro: PUC-Rio, 2007 (in prelo).

Chapter X

Rethinking Cognition, Representations, and Processes in 3D Online Social Learning Environments

James G. Jones, University of North Texas, USA

Stephen C. Bronack, Appalachian State University, USA

Abstract

Three-dimensional (3D) online social environments have emerged as viable alternatives to traditional methods of creating spaces for teachers and learners to teach to and to learn from one another. Robust environments with a bias toward peer-based, network-driven learning allow learners in formal environments to make meaning in ways more similar to those used in informal and in-person settings. These new created environments do so by accounting for presence, immediacy, movement, artifacts, and multi-modal communications in ways that help learners create their own paths of knowing using peer-supported methods. In this chapter, we will review the basics of the technologies and the theoretical underpinnings that support the development of such environments, provide a framework for creating, sustaining, and considering the effectiveness of such environments, and will conclude by de-

scribing two examples of 3D virtual worlds used to support course instruction at the university level.

Introduction

Three-dimensional (3D) online social learning environments have emerged as viable alternatives to traditional methods of creating spaces for teachers and learners to teach to and to learn from one another. While games are the most prominent example of the use of a 3D graphics interface (Wikipedia, 2006), our experience and research suggests that the use of this technology in non-game settings can positively impact learning and communications among students and with their instructors (Aldrich, 2004; Jones, 2004, 2006; Jones, Morales, & Knezek, 2005; Jones & Overall, 2004). Well-designed 3D online learning environments that combine social constructivist principles with immersive gaming theory support deep cognitive learning in powerful new ways. Robust environments with a bias toward peer-based, network-driven learning allow learners in formal environments to make meaning in ways more similar to those used in informal and in-person settings. These new created environments do so by accounting for presence, immediacy, movement, artifacts, and multi-modal communications in ways that help learners create their own paths of knowing using peer-supported methods. These environments move beyond current Web and text-based methods for instructional delivery to create new Internet-based delivery methods that can facilitate new interactions, higher levels of engagement, and deeper learning.

In this chapter, we will review the basics of the technologies and the theoretical underpinnings that support the development of such environments. Then, we will provide a framework for creating, sustaining, and considering the effectiveness of such environments on the abilities of participants to use their experiences in virtual worlds to make better sense of their experiences in the real one. We will conclude by describing two examples of 3D virtual worlds used to support course instruction at the university level.

3D Online Learning Environments

3D online learning environments take elements of massively multi-player online entertainment technology and overlay selected tools to create an interface that allows students and instructors to interact and to communicate within a designed environment for the purpose of accomplishing informal or formal learning. Online

Figure 1. 3D online learning environment used at the University of North Texas

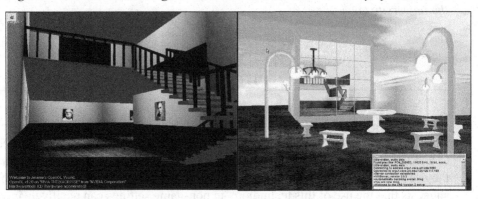

environments used in games are the "convergence of two technologies: video games and high-speed Internet" (Kushner, 2004, p. 98). When an environment is built and displayed correctly, the user understands intuitively the space as displayed. For example, in an environment representing a building, users feel as though they are walking the halls of the building, or are engaged with other users in discussions, or immersed in a training situation. The user moves through and interacts with the environment using the keyboard, a mouse, or other heptic devices. As users move, the computer generates new graphics in real time to give them feedback on their position in the environment. This gives the user the feel of movement through space. Placing objects in a contextual 3D framework provides users known reference points and creates a framework for communications and interactions. Students at remote sites assume control of a representation of themselves, also called an avatar, in a shared created environment such as a school building, a park, or any other space. These highly graphical 3D interfaces allow individuals, through their "avatar," to interact not only with the environment but also with other user "avatars" in the environment. The java-based 3D online learning environment used at the University of North Texas segments the environment into conversation areas based on physical spaces (i.e., a classroom, a meeting room, or a hallway) so that learners can move their avatars to areas for small group or private discussions. A screen-shot from the environment being used at the University of North Texas for distributed education is shown in Figure 1. These virtual worlds are persistent social worlds—spaces in which the artifacts of others help guide new learners and where users are free to move and interact as they please.

Immersive environments can range from simple instructional settings to environments created from any dataset. Created Realities Group (CRG) (2002) has created a 3D online multi-user environment that displays over 97% of the surface of Mars using NASA's Mars Orbiter Laser Altimeter (NASA, 2004). Figure 2 shows a screen shot of the summit of Olympus Mons captured from the CRG environment. Students in distributed locations are able to login, move over the virtual surface,

Figure 2. Mars 3D environment generated in real-time based on NASA MOLA data; Olympus Mons, Top Cone (MARS_19.0_227.0) (Created Realities Group, 2002)

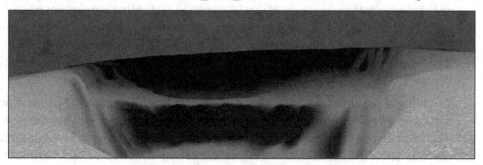

and perform math and science exercises using actual Mars topography data. The University of North Texas in the spring of 2005 developed curriculum materials aimed at middle-school students in after school programs interested in learning math and science problems using this mars online environment (Jones & Kalinowski, in press). The materials were aligned with the Montana Educational Standards for students' knowledge, skills, and abilities. Testing with students in Montana using the materials and software has not yet taken place at the time of this writing.

3D online learning environments are benefiting from advances in technology that earlier approaches to online learning lacked, thanks to the explosive growth of the computer entertainment industry. The combination of affordable consumer technologies such as personal computers and gaming consoles, widespread Internet access, and scalable server technology makes it possible for 3D online learning environments to emerge as the next generation of distributed learning technology. Multi-user online games are ubiquitous within contemporary pop culture (Steinkuehler, 2004), and emerging research suggests these games provide a complex and nuanced environment in which multi-modal social and communicative practices may be developed (Gee, 2003). What is at first limited to the online environment soon moves into other forums of communications. For example, a 3D online learning environment when used to enhance a Web-based course can improve a student's interaction and discourse. Students using a 3D online learning environment showed increased daily text-based communications, peaking earlier in the semester, and sustaining this increase in communications longer over the semester as compared to students who only used the Web-based environment (Jones, 2006). This research will be discussed in greater detail later in the chapter.

But learning is more than downloading, and courses are more than chats. The emergence of 3D environments as viable spaces for learning is also based on the social nature of learning and the affordances such environments supply. As Palloff and Pratt (1999) note, "people and the interaction among them in the distance education environment is essential to the development of a high functioning distance education class." The key is that 3D online learning environments bring students and instructors to the front of the interaction. They share the roles of creators and consumers of knowledge and learning, thus breaking the isolated roles commonly seen in Web-based methods where instructors are subject matter experts that create and students are the consumers of that information. 3D online learning environments make this possible, because the environment promotes equality of communications and interaction. In a fully interactive world that allows users to contribute content, there is no limit to what students can add to the learning environment and the learning itself.

The thing about interactive learning, however, is that you cannot just sit and ponder. At some point, learners are compelled to do something. But what can you do when you do not know what to do? How an individual behaves in an environment depends upon his/her understanding of the causal structure of that environment (Tenenbaum & Griffiths, 2001). A 3D online learning environment has the potential to generate structures that a user is already familiar with and can then more easily infer causation from the observation of the 3D environment as a metaphor. However, computational model structures and processes in the mind cannot adequately account for cognition in interactive learning environments alone. Lave (1988) contends that we must look at activity systems in which individuals participate in large systems. Within such systems, cognition is a complex social phenomenon that is distributed. Lave and Wenger (1991) state that the gradual transformation of an individual participant to a central member of a community through apprenticeship and increased participation is a key factor in learning. While there are numerous learning effects happening when a user is "in" the world interacting with others and the environment, the tenets of social constructivism, especially the role of the expert group in providing cognitive scaffolding, play critical roles in the success of the 3D online environments.

Social Constructivism and Online Learning Environments

Knowledge, according to social constructivists, is the artifact of decisions made by people in groups, based on their on-going interactions. In a sense, knowledge is a public record of transactions between like-minded people. It is grounded in the inquiring activities and commingled tasks through which people relate. What we each, individually, know is uncovered through the process of interacting with the world around us, and the others we find in it. And there is plenty "out there" to know, it seems. Constantly, people act based on a broad collection of assumptions—things they all seem to know to be true—that are tacit to some and mysterious to others. What differentiates those who "know" from those who do not is the process of learning that happens when one participates in a community of practice under the guidance of both more and less experienced peers.

Learning involves change brought about by experience and interaction between people and their environment. These changes manifest themselves in intellectual aptitude, cognitive strategies, motor skills, and dispositions. Some believe learning is a directly observable change in behavior—the result of conditioning by reinforcement. Others believe learning is an indirectly observable internal process where learners compare new information to existing knowledge and either build new or modify existing schemata. Social constructivists view learning as the result of neither solely intrinsic schema nor purely extrinsic motivations but, rather, as a contiguous process that exists each time people willfully interact with each other in the world around them. Any effort to develop an effective online learning environment must consider the ways in which the participants become part of a community of practice and are able to construct knowledge in a social context.

As will be discussed in the case studies presented at the end of the chapter, principles of social constructivist learning provide the foundation for the conceptual framework of the Reich College of Education at Appalachian State University. This framework provides the foundation for the students thinking about online learning environments. The conceptual framework is an evolving construct, but the underlying basis remains firmly girded in the following assumptions about learning:

- Knowledge is created and maintained through social interactions;
- Learning is participatory where students take an active role;
- Development proceeds through stages and among more- and less-experienced peers within a community of practice;
- A specific and general knowledge base emerges from learning through meaningful activity with others;
- Learners develop dispositions relative to the community of practice.

Knowledge is Social

What we know, we know together. Knowledge is situated within the communities and social interactions where it is crafted. Dewey (1897) suggests that education is both psychological and sociological, and that one cannot be considered without the other. Cognition is distributed; that is, individual thinking and problem solving are revealed through socially contextualized practices. Social constructivist learning environments provide ample opportunity for learners to interact with experts, peers, content, and activities in formal, informal, and serendipitous ways.

Learning is Participatory

Vygotsky (1978) suggests that deep learning occurs in a predictable cycle: first, on a social level and second on an individual one. Learning occurs through participation in communities of practice—loose collections of individuals with shared goals, both implicit and explicit, engaged in continuous collaborative activity. Communities of practice are generally not spontaneous, but rather develop around activity toward accomplishing tasks that matter to those involved. Communities of practice provide an important backdrop for learning because of their social nature. Social environments support the reflective thinking and complex problem solving required for learners to develop from less- to more-experienced members of the community.

Learning Leads Development

Learners develop in predictable stages and as a result of the social learning activities in which they engage. Guided by meaningful interactions with more accomplished peers and driven by the explicit expectation to engage in something useful, learners move from novice to expert over time. Learners develop from primarily externally driven reactors—appropriating the behaviors and strategies of those they believe are more knowledgeable—to more expert participants, able to organize knowledge and call upon theoretical constructs to solve contemporary problems.

Knowledge Emerges from Meaningful Activity with Others

As each community of practice evolves, their ways of thinking and the heuristics for action that emerge produce an identifiable knowledge base that is both general to the greater community and also specific to the domains that define the community. This knowledge base encompasses the shared beliefs, assumptions, and values that play a significant role in defining the communities in which learning occurs for those participating. The knowledge base frames both the public and tacit principles that guide interactivity within the environment, and also document the development of the community of practice over time.

Learning Dispositions

Each community of practice is defined by more than simply what they know or what they do. Communities of practice are defined in part by their dispositions toward that which they know and do. Dispositions serve an important role in communities of practice and, therefore, are an important component of the learning process of their members. Dispositions provide both subtle and glaring hints about what attitudes, beliefs, and values are shared by each member of a community. Dispositions shape the general nature or *ethos* of the community and, as such, form the backdrop for learning by all members within a community. Effective social constructivist learning environments accurately reflect the nature of the community in which they occur, thereby allowing new members to develop dispositions that allow each to engage in increasingly productive and useful ways.

As virtual worlds evolve into increasingly sophisticated social environments, it is important to both developers and members to recognize that as people interact within them, they are learning. Understanding the social nature of learning—and recognizing the environmental factors that impact the efficiency and effectiveness of that learning—is a critical skill. Virtual worlds are uniquely situated to serve as rich environments for engaging in communities of practice. The process of learning and the knowledge that results from the activity of these communities can provide useful insight for designers and users, alike. Environments that account for the principles of social constructivism offer users the opportunity to learn and to develop together in natural, effective ways.

Cognitive Scaffolding and Online Learning Environments

Cognition is central to learning because it describes what we do when we think we know what we are doing. This question highlights the important role cognitive scaffolding plays in helping learners move from novice to expert thinking. Kameenue and Simmons (1999) define cognitive scaffolding as a temporary framework that allows the learner to understand the first steps in the learning process. Cognitive scaffolding has also been defined as a form of incentive or help, adapted to the student's ability level, intentionally provided to help a student perform some task (Jonassen, Mayes, & McAleese, 1993). This broader definition of cognitive scaffolding holds that learners are supported during initial, as well as later learning stages, and that initial cognitive scaffolding is not discarded, but rather integrated into the learner's primary framework of cognition. Online learning environments that incorporate 3D elements provide a valuable opportunity to promote cognitive scaffolding. Cognitive scaffolding can play an important role in improving student satisfaction and accelerating discourse within the online learning environment. The 3D environment provides a temporary framework (scaffolding) for the user to integrate into existing cognitive strategies. As learners move into new areas of learning, the environment continues to support new cognitive scaffolding for more advanced learners at a decreased level than is required by more novice learners.

The concept of cognitive scaffolding links existing theories of situated learning (Lave & Wenger, 1991), sociocultural theory (Vygotsky, 1978), Piagetian constructivism (J.S. Bruner, 1961), and cognitive apprenticeship (Brown, Collins, & Duguid, 1989) and describes the mechanisms through which such theories may be put to practice via strategies that support thinking. According to Gagne, cognitive strategies are the specific means by which people guide their intellectual functioning. They are the tools that people use for learning, synthesizing, creating, and accessing other cognitive functions required to make sense of the world and to communicate that sense to others. As we think our way through the real world each day, we develop rules and other mechanisms to help us utilize our cognitive strategies efficiently and effectively. The motif of the real-world context presented by the 3D environment combined with existing real-life rules helps virtual world learners to transfer the rules and skills learned from real-life into the 3D learning environment and then to build within that existing scaffold more quickly and easily.

In 3D online learning environments, learners and their activities are *situated*—that is, they find themselves within and as part of the constructed environment, rather than existing separately from the environment (Bredo, 1994). A learner in a 3D environment moves and interacts with the environment as an active participant, not as a viewer of a static scene. As an active participant, learners complete tasks that are helpful and useful, not forced and external. The tasks in which learners engage via situated activities are authentic—that is, they emerge from naturally occurring interactions within the environment, rather than from neatly packaged and predictably embedded external prompts. Authentic tasks engage students in their zone of proximal development (Vygotsky, 1978) through activities that may be more difficult than students can handle alone, but not so difficult that they cannot be resolved with support from peers or teachers who model the appropriate strategies.

Situated learning is a naturally occurring phenomenon when people are compelled to learn together, because it is a natural way of learning. Premack (1984) suggests, "If the adult does not take the child in tow, making him the object of pedagogy, then child will never become an adult (in competence)" (p. 33). In a 3D learning environment, the new and inexperienced typically are mentored by more experienced learners and both gain from the social interaction between the two. In more advanced online settings, groups of users work in teams to solve problems or overcome obstacles. In cognitive apprenticeship, learners work together to acquire, develop, and refine new skills in an authentic domain of activity. 3D environments can be constructed to provide authentic domain activities in a wide range of situations, many of which are inaccessible in the traditional classroom. Authentic tasks and active building of knowledge are characteristics of constructivist learning environments (Bruner, 1961, 1997; Piaget, 1972). When a learner encounters something in the 3D environment that is new or different, then the learner constructs or adds new framework to his or her understanding.

These characteristics may explain why some students feel more comfortable communicating with each other over e-mail after having used the 3D online learning environment (Jones, 2006). Even meeting only as avatars in a created reality, some students report feeling more satisfied with their communications, because they feel they have actually met with other students and the instructor via a graphical interface (Jones, 2003). Today, many massively multi-player online games (MMOG) use segments of these theories to promote game play and interaction both explicitly and implicitly among and between users and the game. The educational environments discussed within this chapter are providing basic research into the use of such environments in education and insight into the effectiveness of cognitive scaffolding as a strategy for supporting learners within.

Creating and Sustaining Effective Learning Environments

An effective learning environment, one that the users could say fosters learning and community and the providers could say supports required learning outcomes, is only possible when the users and providers are both successful in fulfilling certain critical roles within the system as a whole. The role of the provider (schools, trainers, educational authority, instructors, etc.) is to design, develop, support, promote, and eventually migrate the learning environment. The role of the users (students, instructors, facilitators, etc.) is to communicate and interact, facilitate learning, and create community within the learning environment. The roles we discuss in this section are initial starting points for the relationships that participants might play in creating and sustaining effective learning environments. It is important to note that participants in the process might be part of one or both groups. Additionally there is no barrier to participants taking on more than one role.

For Providers

The "provider" is the group that begins the process. This could be any number of interested parties that have some stake in the development and eventual use of the learning environment. The eventual users of the environment might even be the group that begins this process. The specific roles that the provider group plays include development and implementation, production, and later migration. These areas should look familiar to anyone in software or project development, since they are based on the theories and concepts of project life-cycle management (Marchewka, 2002; Netsite, n.d.; WIPO, n.d.).

Development/Implementation

The concept of the 3D learning environment project drives both its vision and mission. The goals and desires for outcomes of the vision and mission provide the framework for the processes that follow. These fundamentals drive all the following development of requirement and design documents for the environment. During these stages the issues of who the environment is for (target audience), purpose, technological requirements for both the system and end user, and other important aspects of the system are determined. The decisions made early in the project need to be carefully considered since they will impact the final implementation of the system to be used. These decisions will then impact the users of the system and can make the difference between a successful and unsuccessful learning environment. As an example, selecting a technology that would require the users to have the most modern of computers and graphics card and broadband Internet connection might limit the initial group of users and could then jeopardize the potential of creating critical mass for the user community. How a group goes about this process will vary depending on the demands of the group and those involved. At the end of this initial stage, the learning environment is launched into production and users begin to use it for its desired purpose.

Production

After development occurs and the learning environment is launched (users are first allowed to use it outside testing), the production stage begins. Being "in production" means that users expect the system to be dependable and available on a daily basis to support their learning. The requirements and roles of the provider group in this stage are much less focused on development and much more focused on support and maintenance. The providers of the system must be able to provide support functions such as training, technical support, account management, administration, mainte-nance, and other like functions. These are all "mission" critical functions and roles that must be provided. Without a strong production support process in place, many issues occur that may seriously impact the potential effectiveness of the learning environment. Research suggests that new users to educational telecommunication systems can be negatively impacted by technology and training issues (Harris & Jones, 1995; Valauskas & Ertel, 1996), which, in turn, foster decreased satisfaction and reduced use of the system. Much of the success of a new learning environment hinges on the creation of a critical mass of users and over time a continual growth in use that maintains the critical mass. Ensuring users have a stable and produc-tive experience within the learning environment is critical. Depending on the type of learning environment being developed, users of the system itself might take on significant roles related to daily operations and administration.

Migration

Migration is an important topic because any learning environment that is successful over time will be faced with the issue that technology will change and the investment of time, money, content, and community will need to be moved into a new infrastructure. While migration would seem not to impact the creation of an initially successful learning environment, it has been seen as a barrier for some to fully invest in development of content and materials for the fear that the investments could not be recovered and as a result might have caused those projects to not be as successful as they might have been. While the cost of tools and expertise to build and maintain 3D environments and related scripting/interactions is decreasing each year, the issue of updating or moving existing content between platforms is still very much in flux.

The 3D content, which we will define as those objects and resources that make up the physical 3D environment, include geometry, textures, lighting, and other information (i.e., avatars, buildings, benches, lampposts, etc.). Exchanging 3D content has the easiest path for migration at the object level. The more complicated issue to be resolved is the migration of interactions and scripting. Creating a 3D online environment consists of modeling the environment (objects, textures, relationships) and then specifying interactions and behaviors of elements within the environment. These programmed interactions take a static 3D environment and make it a dynamic system that can support situated learning and simulations. The programming also represents an additional investment in development that takes the 3D content and makes it into something much more than atmosphere that helps with immersion. The difficulty with migration of this programming between platforms is due in most part to the custom nature of the current generation of 3D online environments. Most 3D online environments have developed procedures that control these interactions, and often these procedures are tied closely to the concept and technology implementation of the application. As a result, many of the core procedures that generate a unique environment are not as portable, because they are based on libraries or other routines that are proprietary.

Migration of the programmed interactions will become less of a problem as commercial engines and middleware approaches gradually replace custom development. With more standardized tools will come the emergence of agreed upon authoring tools that will allow novices the same ability as experts to specify interaction in these 3D online environments (Hendricks, Marsden, & Blake, 2003). The emergence of future authoring tools may help resolve the issue of migrating interactions and at the same time reduce the cost of 3D environment content development and maintenance. Migration will become less of an issue in the future for providers of these new systems.

For Users

Primarily the critical roles and functions that users provide to help create a successful learning environment take place during the production (live) phase of the system. Roles and tools can be broken into the areas of discourse and interaction, course and learning facilitation, and learning community. For this discussion, we will break user functions into roles and the tools within the system that would support those roles. As noted previously, users of the environment can play more than one role. The important issue is that someone fills the role in order to have a highest probability of success.

Discourse and Interaction

Discourse and interaction is the most basic building block in the environment. Users will be using chat interfaces (text and audio) to communicate in real-time and working together to provide interactions. Discourse and interaction is happening one-to-one, one-to-many, and many-to-many. Riel (1990a) identifies several structures that lend themselves to the electronic communications medium that focus on participant roles and their needs. Based on these structures, Riel (1990b) developed an analytic framework of participant structures to compare interaction within and across computer network communities. The basic roles, based off Dr. Jones' (2001) research at UT Austin, can be broken into the basic roles of the question-asking person, the information person, and the support person, seen as follows. When these roles are provided for, meaningful discourse has the best opportunity to occur.

- **The question-asking person:** If no one asks questions, then there can be no discourse. In online real-time communication, discourse can be fragmented in open areas. One role of the learning environment is to help focus discourse onto content topics when appropriate. Questions open the flow of communications. From a simple query like, "Is anyone here?" a dialog begins. In healthy environments, all participants become question askers and are involved with the discourse.

- **The information person:** Another important role is that of information provider. This role is not necessarily assigned to the subject matter expert or instructor exclusively, but can be filled by any one or more of the participants. Information sharing can be focused, specialized, expert help, or it can be a more general forum of advice and/or consultation. In new systems that lack a critical mass of expert users, facilitators or guides can be recruited to provide this role until the general user population is more educated. In more advanced learning environments, this facilitation is provided via scripted interaction that trains new users how the environment works.

- **The support person:** As the name suggests, the support person is someone who supports the environment. In a game, this might be the game master. In an online learning environment, always having someone on-call to handle problems and issues is an important role. Many times, users will ask for help from an information person. When that fails, having a support person to contact directly can be an important factor in whether or not the environment is functioning effectively. The support person cannot be seen as a crutch, since part of the purpose of the environment is for the users to build a community of support between and among themselves. However, there will be administration and technical issues that the user popular will not be in a position to solve.

These roles might seem trivial or self-apparent, but without them, a community of active users is difficult—if not impossible—to create. Discourse and interaction are essential elements of effective learning environments. Providing simple, compelling tools users can employ to assume their social roles is a critical design factor

Figure 3. The AET Zone Interface (3ʳᵈ Person View)

Figure 4. An overhead view of the entry area for AET Zone

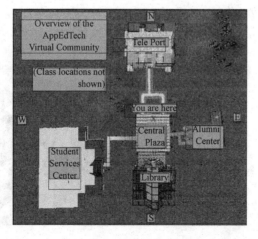

for effective 3D learning environments. The decisions regarding communications technologies are not the only applicable ones, however. Deciding upon a model of how folks learn is also essential to creating effective learning environments.

Learning

Some believe learning is a change in behavior brought about by some external stimulus. Others believe learning is a change in the way one thinks, instigated by considered interaction with both external prompts and internal rules. Still others view learning as a social act, a continual process in which people interact with others and appropriate one another's behaviors, beliefs, and dispositions. Regardless of how one believes learning occurs, it is important for users to consider the interplay between tool and technique when creating an effective online learning environment. Later, we will describe the use of both synchronous and asynchronous learning tools to support discourse, as well as collaboration and other interactions, in several univer-

Figure 5. The "Forum" in the issues class

Figure 6. Getting the perspective of a group of teachers in the issues class

Figure 7. University of North Texas Online Learning Environment

sity courses. The tools facilitate sharing and conveying thoughts and concepts, and include whiteboards, overheads, group management systems, and others. The type of use and organization of the environment, however, depends on the philosophy of learning that drives the course. While much research discusses the use of 3D environments within a constructivist framework, 3D environments can support other methodologies, as well. However, it is important for designers of online learning environments to think deeply and critically about the interplay between the technology in use and the pedagogy in mind. Underlying beliefs about how people learn drives all pedagogy; and all technologies, at some level, suggest their own use. Our experience suggests that 3D learning environments are most effective when they instantiate socially-oriented, actively situated learning methods.

Whereas 3D learning environments can support any type of methodology, no environment will be effective if essential questions about learning are not carefully considered and addressed. For example, how do we define learning? Is it knowledge or skill acquired by instruction or study, alone? Also, who is involved in the process of learning? Traditionally, we think of learning as a process that requires both a teacher and a student, but perhaps this is too limited. And how does the process of learning work, exactly? It is impossible—or, at best, impractical—to observe directly the process of learning, so when we assume learning is happening, what behaviors are important to observe and to verify? Often, these include goal setting, feedback, behavior modeling, and transfer, to name a few. Finally, why does learning occur, what conditions maximize the potential for learning?

Too often, online learning is reduced to focusing on implementing a particular "learning technology" into an environment, with little regard for how the content and the message are related to the manner in which they are presented. An effective learning environment is one that supports the transmission of information by providing a context for people to communicate. The structure of an environment helps give meaning to the interactions and information constructed within it. But simply accepting structures as-is, within the environment as it is experienced, results in "surface" learning. Creating collaborative structures is deeper and requires that users go beyond just that which is present on the surface of the online environment. Fostering more mindful engagement within the learning environment is key. Learning is most likely when the users within the environment foster the appropriate motivation, activity, and interaction with peers, experts, and others necessary to offer a reasonably full and complex knowledge base upon which each learner may draw.

Community

The type of community to be built depends greatly on the type of learning environment being developed. In this section we will talk about the types of learning environments we are using to support courses at the university level. Within these systems there are two types of users that visit the system. The first is the student that is taking a course and has assigned usage as part of a course. This usage might be in the form of interaction with the system or with other students in the system. The second are users that return to the system as part of the community. While students taking courses are a constant, one of the real benefits of the technology is when an active learning community can be built. A key to this is to build in mechanisms that attract new users or retain students that have used the environment in a course. These mechanisms vary according to the available interfaces from the technology. Promotion of the environment is necessary to keep new users inflowing into the system to replace those users that leave (Butler, Sproull, Kiesler, & Kraut, 2005). At the University of North Texas, we promote the free use of the system to support student gatherings and communications. Students use the system for weekly gathering in the virtual environment and for study groups for other courses. While students do log in, we have yet to achieve enough use on campus to have a group of regulars logged in. Students normally use e-mail to arrange times to meet in the environment. At Appalachian State, users report both planned and serendipitous meetings with classmates and instructors and utilize the communication and content resources for both course and non-course interactions. Although user citizenships remain available even after a particular course has ended, it is unclear how many users remain active within the virtual world after completing their course or degree program.

User contributed content is a very attractive mechanism to gain and maintain users in the environment. As was mentioned earlier, involving users in the management and mentoring of new users to the system is valuable. People also benefit from participating in social relationships (Baym, 1999). Building a system that helps students maintain social ties with people already known off-line, as well as those first met online, is very powerful (Butler et al., 2005).

Figure 8. Average number of messages sent by students by week shown averaged by type of course delivery

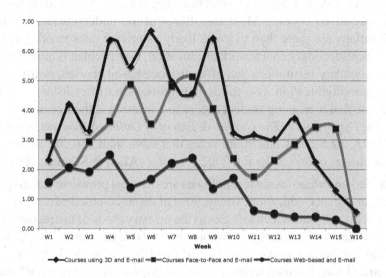

Creating the initial critical mass of users is essential to building a long-term online community. When a critical mass of users gather, the system becomes much more self-sustaining with less effort in promotion. This is because users recruit friends and other students to use the system. The more users using the system, the more opportunity there is to create new activities and interactions.

Going to College in 3D: Two Case Studies

Nearly all college students are online, and most use e-mail and IM/chat regularly. As the digital generation enters college and the workforce, the educational institutions that serve them are changing. Postsecondary enrollments are skyrocketing—and the growth is online. The U.S. Department of Education predicts new college enrollment records will be set every year during the first decade of the 21st century—reaching 17.7 million students by 2011. According to the National Center for Educational Statistics report, *Distance Education at Postsecondary Education Institutions: 1997-98*, half of all post-secondary institutions in the U.S. offered nearly 60,000 distance-based courses to nearly 2 million college students in 1997-1998 (Lewis, Snow, Farris, & Levin, 1999). More recently, the Pew Internet and American Life project reports that in their March-May 2002 survey, 7% of Internet users had taken a course online for college credit, and 6% had taken some other type of online course

(Madden, 2003). Today, most colleges and universities offer some form of distance education (Jones, 2005). One in five institutions offers at least one completely distance-based degree and/or certification program, and two-thirds offer at least some distance-based courses. Most are offered at the undergraduate level, and public institutions are more than twice as likely as private ones to offer distance education. Postsecondary coursework in education, in particular, is moving online. Of the postsecondary institutions that offer distance-based courses, nearly one-third offer programs in education. Two-thirds of institutions that offer distance-based education indicate that increasing student access to education is their primary goal. In *Sizing Up the Opportunity: The Quality & Extent of Online Education in the U.S. in 2002 & 2003*, the Sloan Consortium notes that more than 550,000 students took *all* of their classes online in the fall 2002 semester (Allen & Seaman, 2003).

Internet- and video-based technologies are the most prevalent teaching and learning tools in distance education. Today, 90% of distance-based education uses Internet-based, asynchronous technologies as the primary mode of instruction (Jones, 2005). Fewer than half utilize synchronous methods. Interestingly, while the usage rate of video-based technologies remained steady between 1995-1996 and 1997-1998, Internet-based learning technology usage *tripled*. By the fall 2002 semester, 11% of all higher education students in the U.S. were taking online courses. Next, we describe two universities' approaches to using virtual worlds as environments for learning.

AET Zone: Creating a Social World for Learning

The instructional technology (IT) program at Appalachian State University in Boone, North Carolina has developed the program into a three-dimensional multi-user virtual world, named AET Zone. AET Zone is an innovative online medium for supporting a community of practice among distance-based students, faculty, graduates, and support staff. AET Zone adds elements of space, movement, and physical presence, along with conversational tools, artifacts, and metaphors not usually found in more traditional Web-based counterparts. Users—referred to as "citizens"—are represented by avatars and move throughout course scenes interacting with other avatars and the objects that comprise the virtual world, itself. Objects may be linked to Web pages, conversation tools, or other resources. While text-based chat is available for avatars to communicate on a large group as well as individual basis, additional chat rooms are provided for multiple small group audio discussions.

The typical student is a K-12 classroom teacher who wants to integrate technology into her curriculum or who wants to become an instructional technology specialists or chief technology officer at the district level. Most are teaching within a 100-mile radius of the university. In fact, most students do not come to campus for any classes. All required courses are offered to off-campus cohorts based in locations near their homes and/or their workplace. While the virtual world is an integral component of the program, faculty and students do meet face-to-face regularly in courses at the beginning of the program with reduced numbers and frequency of meetings as the members of a cohort gain understanding of what is expected and how to proceed during the latter stages of the program. Most courses schedule a final class session during which students present term projects and articulate their understandings; however, a handful of courses are conducted entirely online within the virtual world.

AET Zone was constructed using Activeworlds, Inc. technology (Mauz, 2001). The world is one of several within the Appalachian State University virtual "universe." The universe server is hosted by the Appalachian State University technology services team on a fully redundant server system. Citizens download a customized browser—about 3 Mb in size—that connects each directly to AET Zone. The browser has four distinct areas (Figure 3):

1.   A 3D view of the world, either in first person or a third person view

2.   A text-based chat that allows users to interact individually or with all who are logged on

3.   A Web-based content browser that connects interactions of the user with objects in the world

4.   A utilities space with access to help files, telegrams sent by other users, tele-ports (similar to bookmarks), and contacts (similar to buddies)

Students can install the AET Zone browser on any Windows computer connected to the Internet. All students in the instructional technology program are provided with access to the browser and a username and password. Broadband access is useful, but not necessary, due to the caching technique employed by the Activeworlds server. Once logged on, students can see and interact with each other as well as with students in other courses, graduates of the program, and the instructors of the various courses.

AET Zone is comprised of many spaces (Figure 4). Behind the user, upon entry, is the library building. This AET Library is a 3D interface to the distance-based services of the physical library on campus. Students may read full-text articles from the university databases or order a book from the stacks. Students may chat directly with university research librarians. On the right side of the entry plaza is the Alumni Center building, with links to Appalachian State Alumni resources designed specifically for graduates of the instructional technology program. Straight ahead is a park. On the other side of the park is the Tele Port. Each gate within the teleport leads to a different course.

Each course within AET Zone is unique in appearance and operation according to the nature of the content and the form of interaction that is desired to meet course goals. For instance, a course on hypermedia presents students with "hypermazes," which allow students to experience hypermedia by choosing their own path through information and resources. A telecommunications course provides an opportunity to explore components of a network by walking through it, either from the Internet to the computer or vice versa. A course on Web design is organized that has physical levels through which students progress. Each level represents a set of skills encompassed by the course. Each set of skills is dependant on the skills of the previous level. A course on the integration of computer technology into instruction begins with a path around a lake. On this path, students are asked to address key questions and issues associated with the integration process. Later, a new path is opened that goes into a forest. In the forest, students are asked to build their own area (in glades set aside for the purpose) that demonstrates what they have learned in the earlier parts of the class. Also, a case-based seminar on the various issues of educational technology and organizations is set in a Roman forum (Figure 5), with teleports to a fictitious school building in which various characters present their points of view on a particular situation (Figure 6).

The organization of these areas allows students to move to them and between them in a non-linear fashion according to their needs and interests with timelines for projects, sharing (discussion, brainstorming entries, etc.), and establishing the flow of the class. All classes have discussion boards, forms for entering information to be shared with classmates for discussion, links to resources and readings, and audio chat areas where small groups can meet to discuss their projects.

The faculty in the ASU IT program has experimented with teaching multiple sections of the same class in the same virtual world environment during the same semester. Individual sections meet on different days, at different times, and are led by different instructors. Yet, all explore the same content in the same world and use the same threaded discussion board to discuss the same issues together. As each faculty member guides one or more sections of each course, each is engaged in the discussions, projects, and efforts of the entire group. Small groups form within these larger groups for various projects, assignments, discussions, and other needs. Some groups form between sections and even between classes. Occasionally, former students return to explore resources or add to the discussions. In AET Zone, participants are afforded many and frequent opportunities to interact with others who are in the same course, even if they are not in the same section of the course, with instructors from other sections of the course they are in, and with students who are at different stages of their program of study, creating a more natural and richer community in which to participate.

University of North Texas

The research at the University of North Texas (UNT) is focused on using 3D online learning environment to foster the creation of new forms of online course interaction and feedback that accelerate and increase discourse both among students and with the instructor. These online environments are showing that they also raise the satisfaction level of the students using the delivery method (Jones et al., 2004). The research has been focused on the impact that the technology provides through (a) using immersive environments that create a context for interaction, (b) cognitive scaffolding provided by the avatars and interactions, and (c) high-order communications supported by integrated voice and other collaborative tools. Unlike Appalachian State, UNT has not yet started to put content into the environment, but is examining the environment as it relates to community and interaction.

The University of North Texas uses a client/server portal-based 3D online learning environment developed by Dr. Jones' research group prior to joining the faculty at UNT (see Figure 7). Both the server and client software are written in java and allow students on Linux, Windows, or Macintosh computers to access the system for courses. The entry-level cluster system requires two servers. The first server supports database, system management, and other user applications. The second server supports user access to the cluster. Additional user servers can be added to the cluster depending on the number of simultaneous users the environment needs to support course delivery. In addition to supporting the display of the 3D environment and associated graphics and avatars, the client supports a simple set of tools that are presented within the environment to support course interaction and discourse. These tools include text, audio, overheads, whiteboard, and so forth. Additional tools can be added as needed. Students and instructors use different modes depending on their needs. Students who are uncomfortable speaking can use the text-based chat for voicing their questions in a course. The instructor can use the audio chat mode in order to provide more information than they could easily type in. Multi-modal interactions allow the system to utilize more than one mode over time to ensure that students with different learning styles are effectively reached.

In 2003, Dr. Jones began to use his 3D online learning environment with selected courses within the program of Computer Education and Cognitive Systems at UNT. He began to track message flow and later to analyze discourse in courses he taught that used both the 3D online learning environment and text-based communications. He then compared this to courses he taught that were Web-based only and those for hybrid courses that were some face-to-face and some online. For the research being presented here, no automated interaction was designed into the system. The participants in the learning environment create the discourse, interaction, and feedback. The system provides no feedback or direction to the user other than collision detection. This approach is similar to player-versus-player interaction in games, where the environment is static and the users interact with each other.

Student Satisfaction

The initial research at the University of North Texas focused on student satisfaction comparing face-to-face, Web-based, and 3D online learning environments for course delivery. Initially the attitudes toward information technology of students situated within a 3D online learning environment and students located in a traditional face-to-face classroom were compared (Jones et al., 2005). During a later semester a Web-based course and the 3D online learning environment were examined. The primary instrument used was a collection of measures gathered in the publication "Instruments for Assessing Attitudes Toward Information Technology," made available by the Institute for Integration of Technology into Teaching and Learning (Knezek & Christensen, 1997). What was of interest is that the 3D online learning environment (treatment) tracked the face-to-face course delivery (control). Students felt that the 3D online learning environment provided the same level of satisfaction and interaction as the face-to-face course. Student outcomes, based on grades, between the treatment and control were in the expected ranges and comparable to previous semesters. When the 3D online learning environment was compared to the Web-based course delivery, students felt that the 3D online learning environment provided a much richer and satisfying learning experience. A majority of students that participated in follow-up interviews indicated that this was because of the higher quality and higher fidelity of interaction they felt they had with the other students and instructor that the text-based communications did not seem to provide in their Web-based courses. The 3D online learning environment, using a similar amount of bandwidths as the Web-based course, performed at a higher level with regard to satisfaction and attitudes toward the materials and instruction for the students participating during both semesters of research.

Accelerated and Increased Text-Based Discourse

While video conferencing and other forms of high-bandwidth technology have widened the palette of communications options for distributed learning, text-based tools remain the lowest common denominator for a student population with varying levels of Internet connectivity. Web-based courses have received widespread acceptance and use for creating and supporting learning activities across disciplines within education (Hill, 2001). This is seen in the fact that more than 90% of postsecondary institutions that participated in a research study between 2002 and 2004 reported that e-mail was their primary course communications method, followed closely behind with Web pages and Web-based message boards at over 80% (Jones, 2005). The University of North Texas has been very progressive with the development of Web-based courses and now offers more Web-based courses than any other university in the region.

Dr. Jones' graduate research at the University of Texas Austin was focused on the factors involved with building high-levels of discourse and synthesis between students and mentors using text-based communications (Jones, 2001). The one pattern of interest that has emerged from the various studies is that the more message exchanges that can happen over a prolonged period of time by the participants, the better chance the participants have of attaining meaningful discourse. In his dissertation research, Dr. Jones found that participants in a facilitated message process focused on a curricula topic took between 10 and 18 weeks to reach a sustained, high-level discourse when using text-based e-mail. The participants only communicated via e-mail and never used alternate communications, like telephone, face-to-face meetings, and so forth. Even with facilitation and structuring of the initial discussion to help form successful discourse, only teams that maintained prolonged communication over 10 weeks reached meaningful discourse (Jones, 2001). Ten weeks is the better part of a long semester for most universities. This is one reason why cohorts are used, so that groups of students stay together for longer periods of time and are able to create and sustain high levels of discourse between semesters.

Courses taught at the University of North Texas take place in three modes: in-person face-to-face courses (traditional), Internet Only (no face-to-face meetings), and blended where there is a varying degree of face-to-face and Internet communications. In 2003, Dr. Jones began to track message flow and later to analyze discourse in courses taught that used each of these delivery modes. Figure 8 compares the average weekly e-mail flow per student between nine Computer Education and Cognitive Systems courses taught between 2003 and 2005 using each of the modes. Three courses were blended using an initial face-to-face class meeting, followed by 3D learning environment and e-mail exchanges to support course delivery and discourse. Three courses were blended with face-to-face meeting every two or three weeks using e-mail between class meetings. Three courses were Internet only using the university's Web-based course delivery system and tools. CECS 5100, a master's course in educational programming, used the 3D environment and e-mail. CECS 6210, a doctoral course covering theories of interactive multimedia, and CECS 5420, a Web-authoring course for educators, were taught using the face-to-face meeting every other week with e-mail. CECS 5400, a master's course in educational telecommunications, was taught using only the Web-based course delivery system. Each course was designed and taught by Dr. Jones and used the same methods and requirements for student discourse. The course sizes were between 8 and 15 students in each course. These factors allows for the comparison between the courses shown in Figure 8.

As was discussed earlier, text only communications used by the Web-based courses had student exchanges, but nothing prolonged or frequent. Initial looks at discourse revealed that students tended to answer the readings, but not move past the facilitated prompts as set in the course curriculum. The students using the 3D online learning environment showed accelerated discourse, a greater number of exchanges on average by week, and prolonged interaction via e-mail over the semester. The courses that met every other week had improved discourse, but we believe it was not as increased as the courses using the 3D online software because of the more frequent face-to-face meetings being used for high-level discussion. Blended courses are providing more feedback and structure that then allows discourse to grow in a faster manner.

The patterns of accelerated exchanges among students using a 3D online learning system are very promising. We believe that similar systems capable of providing the same types of interactive fidelity to the 3D online learning system (i.e., video conference) would produce similar results. These are at least two reasons for using the 3D online learning environment over other approaches. One is an Internet bandwidth consideration, since the technology is capable of supporting users on dialup connections. The second is, that like the Web, it can be provided into every home that has an Internet connection, a computer, and a 2000 or newer graphics adapter.

What we are surmising from this data is that students have more meaningful online discourse when involved with a blended course because of discourse/cognitive scaffolding. When students and their instructor have a visual or perceived environment or structure for communication, trust is more easily accomplished that results in more frequent exchanges earlier in the semester and that then generates higher-order discourse. We are looking at doing further discourse analysis (Harris & Jones, 1995; , 1999) on this data to determine the depth and message flow of the discourse in order to build a clearer understanding of the communications.

Conclusion

Whereas virtual worlds have opened new opportunities for effective online learning, they present unique challenges, as well. For example, learners are often outside their comfort zone as they begin working within this world. Many are not comfortable in taking responsibility for their learning, in being guided rather than being told, in learning for themselves rather than attempting to please the instructor. Often, we must help our students unlearn "the ways they have learned" in the past as they explore a different paradigm of what it means to learn. Students often need encouragement to converse and to collaborate with each other and in small groups, while also fostering serendipitous meetings that serve student needs. This requires constant modeling and guidance from more experienced users. One important lesson is the freedom—and challenge—of considering student learning experiences from multiple dimensions. Many times course organization is determined by a schedule that sequences all activities. Building in a 3D world challenges us to break out of that straight-line thinking

Teaching in virtual worlds also presents several new challenges to instructors. These new types of environments require the instructor to think differently about the role of teaching, learning, content, and interaction. Such environments may be built to represent real or imagined learning spaces that may differ greatly from the traditional four-walled school classroom. No longer bound by bricks and mortar, nor time and place, instructors may create a new paradigm for instruction, for guiding and learning, and for sharing and communicating content and experiences among students who possess all levels of expertise. Instructors must think about ways students will move through a 3D space and interact with various artifacts, tools, content, and other students. They must also seek to develop learning communities in which opportunities to communicate with other students, whether with their peers or others, are a central part of the experience.

Our experiences designing 3D learning environments remind us that learning activities may not necessarily be linear and prescribed by the course designer or instructor. The process of building classes, providing services, and interacting with students in our created worlds has left us ruminating key questions about the development of virtual environments—and how they differ in ways from those we consider when designing purely Web-based courses. Designing a class in 3D causes one to think differently about class structure, representation, and processes. The 3D character of the environment, the manner in which participants interact, and the very nature of the learning activities we are attempting to foster are all impacted by the environment, the interaction, feedback, and the engagements available.

In a 3D environment, courses may be linear or more exploratory (non-linear), with activities and assignments constructed to encourage investigation and with communication tools for students and instructors to share and to learn from the results of their exploration. Courses and online interactions may also be freeform, allowing students and instructors to simply meet and dialog. Planning for user interaction and participation takes on a different character from either face-to-face classes or Web-based classes. Participants are presented with innumerable ways to experience the environment. They are not restricted to pre-determined navigation. The environment facilitates learning activities that depend on participants "meeting," planned and unplanned, in real-time.

In these courses, we are attempting to have students take on the responsibility for learning, building upon their own background and experiences, as well as developing "scaffolding" that works for them. We have learned that as each student finds his or her "voice," powerful conversations emerge that share information, resources, and creative efforts. We find that we as instructors participate in the many discussions taking place collectively and in small groups, both synchronously as well as asynchronously, throughout the environment. It is this sharing, distributing, and building of knowledge that leads to new knowledge and ultimately a different kind of learning and understanding than that often found in more traditional learning settings. Understanding how the principles of social constructivism and practical applications of cognitive scaffolding impacts online learning, will allow for the creation of richer more fulfilling educational experiences for all involved.

References

Aldrich, C. (2004). *Simulations and the future of learning: An innovative (and perhaps revolutionary) approach to e-learning.* San Francisco: Jossey-Bass/Pfeiffer.

Allen, I. E., & Seaman, J. (2003). *Sizing the opportunity: The quality and extent of online education in the United States, 2002 and 2003.* Retrieved October 10, 2005, from http://www.sloan-c.org/resources/sizing_opportunity.pdf

Baym, N. (1999). *Tune in, log on: Soaps, fandom, and online community.* Thousand Oaks, CA: Sage Publications.

Bredo, E. (1994). *Cognitivism, situated cognition, and deweyian pragmatism.* Retrieved September 15, 2005, from http://www.ed.uiuc.edu/eps/pes-year-book/94_docs/bredo.htm

Brown, J. S., Collins, A., & Duguid, S. (1989). Situated cognition and the culture of learning. *Educational Researcher, 18*(1), 32-42.

Bruner, J. S. (1961). The act of discovery. *Harvard Educational Review, 31*(1), 21-32.

Bruner, J. S. (1997). *The process of education.* Cambridge, MA: Harvard University Press.

Butler, B., Sproull, L., Kiesler, S., & Kraut, R. (2005). Community effort in online groups: Who does the work and why? In S. Weisband & L. Atwater (Eds.), *Leadership at a distance: Interdiscplinary perspectives* (pp. 1-32). Mahwah, NJ: Lawrence Erlbaum Associates.

Created Realities Group. (2002). Retrieved January 5, 2003, from http://created-realities.com/marsonline.htm

Dewey, J. (1897). My pedagogic creed. *School Journal, 54*(3), 80.

Gee, J. P. (2003). *What videogames have to teach us about learning and literacy.* New York: Palgrave MacMillan.

Harris, J., & Jones, J. G. (1995, April). *A study of online communications among subject matter experts, teachers, and students: Message flow and functions.* Paper presented at the American Educational Research Association, San Francisco.

Harris, J. B., & Jones, J. G. (1999). A descriptive study of telementoring among students, subject matter experts, and teachers: Message flow and function patterns. *Journal of Research on Computing in Education, 32*(1), 36-53.

Hendricks, Z., Marsden, G., & Blake, E. (2003). A meta-authoring tool for specifying interactions in virtual reality environments. In J. Gain & A. Chalmers (Eds.), *Proceedings of the 2nd international conference on computer graphics, virtual reality, visualisation and interaction in Africa* (pp. 171-180). Cape Town, South Africa: ACM.

Hill, J. R. (2001). *Building community in Web-based learning environments: Strategies and techniques.* Retrieved September 20, 2002, from http://ausweb.scu.edu.au/aw01/papers/refereed/hill/paper.html

Jonassen, D. H., Mayes, T., & McAleese, R. (1993). A manifesto for a constructivist approach to technology in higher education. In T. Duffy, J. Lowyck, & D. Jonassen (Eds.), *Design environments for constructivist learning.* Heidelburg, FRG: Springer Verlag.

Jones, J. G. (2001). *A study of communications between subject matter experts and individual students in electronic mail contexts.* Unpublished doctoral dissertation, University of Texas, Austin.

Jones, J. G. (2003). Internet-based 3D graphical MOO software that supports distributed learning for both sides of the digital divide. In P. Kommers & G. Richards (Eds.), *World Conference on Educational Multimedia, Hypermedia & Telecommunications* (Vol. 2003, pp. 246-248). Honolulu, HI: Association for the Advancement of Computing in Education.

Jones, J. G. (2004). Hot topics panel: Advances in 3D image applications: Interactive and collaborative 3D online environments. In L. Schamber & C. L. Barry (Eds.), *American Society for Information Science and Technology: Managing and enhancing information: Cultures and conflicts* (Vol. 41, p. 590). Providence, RI: Information Today.

Jones, J. G. (2005). *Issues and concerns of directors of post-secondary distributed learning programs concerning online methods and technologies.* Paper presented at the American Educational Research Association, Montreal, Canada.

Jones, J. G. (2006). *Accelerating online text-based discourse via 3D online learning environments.* Paper presented at the Society for Information Technology and Teacher Education International Conference, Orlando, FL.

Jones, J. G., & Kalinowski, K. (in press). *Mars explorer! An immersive 3D expedition on the surface of the red planet.* University of North Texas.

Jones, J. G., Morales, C., & Knezek, G. (2004). Student attitudes towards an integrated 3D learning environment. In L. Cantoni & C. McLoughlin (Eds.), *World conference on educational multimedia, hypermedia & telecommunications* (Vol. 2004, pp. 1378-1382). Lugano, Switzerland: Association for the Advancement of Computing in Education.

Jones, J. G., Morales, C., & Knezek, G. A. (2005). 3D online learning environments: Examining attitudes toward information technology between students in Internet-based 3D and face-to-face classroom instruction. *Educational Media International, 42*(3), 219-236.

Jones, J. G., & Overall, T. (2004, February). *Changing logo from a single student system to a 3D online student collaboratory/participatory shared learning experience.* Paper presented at the Texas Computer Educators Association, Austin, TX.

Kameenui, E. J., & Simmons, D. (1999). *Toward successful inclusion of students with disabilities: The architecture of instruction.* Reston, VA: The Council for Exceptional Children.

Knezek, G. A., & Christensen, R. (1997). *Teacher and student attitude towards information technology questionnaire.* Retrieved July 20, 2004, from http://www.tcet.unt.edu/research/index.htm

Kushner, D. (2004, June). The wrinkled future of online gaming. *Wired, 12*(6), 98-110.

Lave, J. (1988). *Cognition in practice.* Cambridge UK: Cambridge University Press.

Lave, J., & Wenger, E. (1991). *Situated learning: Legitimate peripheral participation.* Cambridge UK: Cambridge University Press.

Lewis, L., Snow, K., Farris, E., & Levin, D. (1999). *Distance education at post-secondary education institutions: 1997-98* (No. Statistical Analysis Report NCES 2000-013): National Center for Education Statistics, U.S. Department of Education, Office of Educational Research and Improvement.

Madden, M. (2003). *America's online pursuits.* Retrieved October 10, 2005, from http://www.pewinternet.org/pdfs/PIP_Online_Pursuits_Final.PDF

Marchewka, J. T. (2002). *Information technology project management.* Hoboken, NJ: Wiley, John & Sons, Incorporated.

Mauz. (2001). *Mauz's active worlds pages.* Retrieved March 10, 2004, from http://mauz.info/awhistory.html

NASA. (2004). *Mars Orbiter Laser Altimeter (MOLA).* Retrieved January 14, 2004, from http://nssdc.gsfc.nasa.gov/database/MasterCatalog?sc=1996-062A&ex=3

Netsite. (n.d.). *Project life cycle.* Retrieved October 10, 2005, from http://www.netsite.co.uk/content-21

Palloff, R. M., & Pratt, K. (1999). *Building learning communities in cyberspace: Effective strategies for the online classroom.* San Francisco: Jossey-Bass Publishers.

Piaget, J. (1972). *The psychology of intelligence.* Totowa, NJ: Littlefield, Adams.

Premack, D. (1984). Pedagogy and aesthetics as sources of culture. In M. Gazzaniga (Ed.), *Handbook of cognitive neuroscience* (pp. 15-35). New York: Plenum.

Riel, M. (1990a). Cooperative learning across classroom in electronic learning circles. *Instructional Science, 19*(6), 445-465.

Riel, M. (1990b). Four models of educational telecommunications: Connections to the future. *Education and Computing, 5*(1989), 261-274.

Steinkuehler, C. A. (2004). *Learning in massively multiplayer online games.* Paper presented at the Sixth International Conference of the Learning Sciences, Mahwah, NJ.

Tenenbaum, J. B., & Griffiths, T. L. (2001). Structure learning in human causal induction. In T. Leen, T. Dietterich, & V. Tresp (Eds.), *Advances in neural information processing systems* (Vol. 13, pp. 59-65). Cambridge, MA: MIT Press.

Valauskas, E. J., & Ertel, M. (1996). *The Internet for teachers and school library media specialists.* New York: Neal-Schuman.

Vygotsky, L. S. (1978). *Mind in society: The development of higher psychological processes.* Cambridge, MA: Harvard University Press.

Wikipedia. (2006). *Game programmer.* Retrieved January 30, 2006, from http://en.wikipedia.org/wiki/Game_programmer

WIPO. (n.d.). *Project life cycle methodology.* Retrieved October 10, 2005, from http://www.wipo.int/it/en/projects/plc.htm

This work was previously published in Games and Simulations in Online Learning: Research and Development Frameworks, edited by D. Gibson, pp. 89-114, copyright 2007 by Information Science Publishing (an imprint of IGI Global).

Section III

Digital Literacy:
Definition and Perspectives

Chapter XI

Investigating Information in the Multiscreen Society:
An Ecologic Perspective

Manuel Joaquim Silva Pinto, Universidade do Minho, Portugal

Abstract

This chapter presents some new aspects to think about public service broadcasting, emphasizing the role of emotion and entertainment to the understanding of the television experience. Television is discussed in the context of the multiscreen society and technological devices, from an ecological point of view. This means to consider it in the context of the transformations produced by new media and their social distribution. These changes deeply impact on the consumption activity forcing it to assume new characters and modalities. According to this point, it becomes possible to discuss some aspects dealing with digital literacy.

Introduction

Let me start with a short personal story. More than 10 years ago, when I was about to discuss my PhD work on television in children's everyday life, I discovered the Internet. Using the popular browser Netscape, and the software Eudora for e-mails, I rapidly understood the radical innovation which was starting to happen in our world. And suddenly I discovered an enormous amount of new sources, the rapidness of contacts and the deleting of every kind of boundary, considering that since that moment my investigation had been based on a bibliography framed within the context of where I was working. A sort of order of time and space was fading, transforming into virtual space and time, with all its potentials made on nets and the multiplication of spots that, with relative simplicity, turned to be producers and receivers of information.

I easily remember that, overwhelmed by the multiplicity of doors that appeared to me as open, I experienced a sort of uneasiness that in some moments transformed into anxiety that can be described as follows: have I spent three years of my life studying a medium which in a short time was destined to disappear, sinking for the effect of Internet?

Ten years after the explosion of the phenomenon of Internet, this episode can be used to underline the meaning of a congress, organized by one of the most active international groups implied in communication and education, which has chosen television and the question of quality as study and debate topics. Television, despite the changes we have seen, seems to maintain an evident central position, especially as an institution and social medium of entertainment.

The history of ICT teaches us that a new medium do not displace previous existing media, but conquers its own place causing a recomposition of the main roles related to the previous media. As happening with the Web and the Internet, we are not simply in front of the emergency of a new communication medium, but also of an environment embracing and linking different logics.

It is clear, then, that my past anxiety had no reasons to exist. But, on the other hand, it was justified as it was based on the intuition that something new was going to happen.

Ten years later, we can affirm that everything has changed. At the same time, if we take a look beyond the foam of the day and we search for the answers to the main questions of existence, we can equally say that essentially we have not moved a lot. In the best hypothesis, we can count on a very wide variety of technologies that do not assure the fulfilling of all the promises normally advanced. It is not strange that this text, starting from the central topic of this congress, intends to focus on questions appearing not so in fashion, that in my personal opinion will be more vital and important. Within the frame of this discussion, I start with the definition of quality in television as the main attention of public service. Then I will reflect on the need to requalify the topic of entertainment and to evaluate the emotional dimension in order to understand the complexity and the central role played by the medium and television experience. I will conclude with a contribution to the ecological definition of communication and media, identifying some ideas that will support and deepen media education experiences in Spanish and Portuguese contexts.

Television, Quality, Entertainment

The quality in television—a concept that deeply depends on the system of values and specific interests—has to be read less as the result of a given and concluded definition and more as a naturally open process involving media protagonists, the creators of television products and TV viewers (Charo, 2000). Anyway, quality seems to be inseparable from offers' variety (vertical and horizontal), from professionalism, from editorial and programming freedom, and from the effectiveness of accountability processes and public evaluation.

As a process which is relatively independent from media logics but based on needs and interests of actors and social groups, quality concerns the social function of television and consequently the dimension of public service that cannot be handled only by public operators. Despite the crisis affecting the concept of television, I think that we can, with difficulty, deal with the problem of quality without including this dimension.

In actual circumstances, it has made sense to keep protecting the existence of an autonomous public service of television, not dependent on political power and not based on a merchant logic. Despite the evolution of offers' plan and the changes in the contexts of uses and sociocultural practices, its own existence represents a factor to support quality. Immediately because it creates an offer based on variety, even not sufficiently practiced; because it calls for the coresponsibility of citizens, asking for more, and because it is possible in this way to think and practice new forms of participation.

But we observe that public service television differs itself as specific reality, when and if it is considered as an institution in our society, acting in strict relation with remaining institutions, voted to give them voice without depending on the need for success. It is in this horizontal connection, creating a more interactive action project that we see the emergency of the existence of a new television broadcaster, acting for the community and to its service.

In this sense, the public title of a broadcaster, its action independence, and the definition of specific contents are not sufficient in order to differ the channel or the channels from private broadcaster. What is important is to consider media, and in particular television, as places where participation and evaluation can be practiced.

It deals with the idea that, in order to enrich and deepen democracy, the public entity of television defines and applies a new concept of presence in society, exploring communication forms that open to institutions, groups and organizations belonging to civil society, to their initiatives, worries, and situations. This makes public television a real citizens' television (Pinto, 2005).

In this context, I feel allowed to underline a topic not frequently analysed and investigated, which is central for the understanding of the role of television in our society. I refer to the function of entertainment and to its connection of the problem of quality.

The cultural project associated with television since its first appearance referred to the well known trilogy of information-culture-entertainment. Even today, national legislation and transnational norms keep on emphasizing this triple concept. But since its origin, a lot of misunderstandings appeared, to the extent that cultural and political agents supported the dream of a parallel school, complementary and extending formal scholarization with a more interesting shape, contributing in this way to the cultural promotion of people.

The difficult copermanence of intellect, educational institution, and television lies in the incomprehension and not acceptance of the main paths of the medium, far away from the paradigms of school and education. This disappointment with the banalization of TV, with its inscription in everyday life routines, combines now and then with a syndrome of loss (Pinto, 2000) marked by a nostalgia of a past and mythological time associated to properties (cohabitation, dialogue, relationship) deleted by television.

The truth is that entertainment turned to be the brand image and the identity factor of television. For the nostalgias of television as big educator of the masses and as promise of cultural promotion and development, the final bill cannot be more disappointing.

The actual situation we are living is not so satisfactory, especially because of the misunderstanding on the nature and function of television—and this is the main topic I would like to underline—but also on the impossibility of giving value to entertainment. Conceived as mere distraction, entertainment easily turns into a topic which does not appear interesting, into an agent of alienation of individuals, an element of collective sleeping, summing up, into a sort of contemporary version of the old people's opium underlined by Karl Marx.

Now the association of entertainment to a degrading cultural subproduct or even to social and political alienation disqualifies and illegitimates a complex and vital reality, which is part of human experience, a field that needs to be analysed in order to understand its relationship to the public of television (Blakley, 2001). The analysis and definition of operative criteria linked to the promotion of quality in television is problematic if we do not take into account this topic.

Something similar can be said on emotions. As underlined by Joan Ferrés (2003), a catalan researcher who deepened this issue, television is the reign of emotion. Quite everything in it works, massages, and calls the emotional dimension: visual signs, forms, colours, and movements. The vicarious participation, the processes and mechanisms of identification and the projection that bring viewers into the immersion in a given story, that result from what Samuel Coleridge defined as "voluntary suspension of incredulity," frequently work at the subconscious or unconscious level.

With theoretical models which give value to the logical and rational dimensions and which translate themselves in the analytical and critical perspective, it is not strange that we finish to miss some essential dimensions of television phenomenon and of television experience.

In relation to what I'm going to discuss, concerning the (dis)evaluation of entertainment and the inclusion of the emotional dimension, the emerging question is related to the evaluation of the effects on the topic of quality.

We enter in a vast field which needs more attention and more investments on the research level. The changes encountered by television makes this topic even more relevant. The digitalization supports the multiplication of channels and the enlargement of the variety of contents, without implicating at the moment a significant reduction of the generalist channels. But with the combination of different tools, the medium has been adapted to the role of cinema screen, first, to the role of games screen, later, and now in recent times to DVD platform.

At the same time personal computer, beyond its basic and common functions, is transforming into a terminal spot of a global net, allowing the access to traditional and new media, to music, games, database, and so forth.

With these new possibilities that will reach a new dimension with the wifi, also the concept of the use of our spaces is going to change radically. Concerning domestic or work places, the scene is going back to game room and above all cyber cafés, meeting places, and spots to connect to the net.

Besides this phenomenon, and inseparable from it, we cannot forget to look at other media and other devices where screen represents the entering door to access the world. The example of digital cameras is explicative. And more than this, the reference to mobile phones, which represent for telecommunication what the transistor represented in the second half of the past century for the radio, even though with a multifunctionality which does not stop to grow, tending to affect the television emission.

Media Culture and Education:
An Ecological Approach

In a context based on the multiplication of offers and possibilities, on the exponential growth of information, it is fundamental not to forget what is essential and what is secondary, what refers to tools and instruments and what is connected to aims and contents.

It is frequent to encounter the investigation on technological development and cyberculture in association with technophobic attitudes and resistance to change as if we were fatally condemned to the contraposition between technophiles and technophobia, between future paradise and the Orwellian nightmare, between the mermaid's song and the owl's screech.

On the contrary, I consider vital to conquer and enlarge a way in which we can recognize and give value to new forms of culture and new ways to live and act, but without scarifying the search for quality and sense in the name of compulsive innovation. We need to look for a "third way" based on culture in order to increase the horizons to a new comprehension of world and life able to act locally with a global vision.

And the search for meaning means to include in the agenda questions as the followings:

1. How ICT can turn to be more friendly and solidal?
2. Which opportunities and changes bring ICT to individual life, to groups, and to society in general? In which way is this change interfered or promoted?
3. What possibilities can ICT open for people to meet each other?
4. In which way can ICT be used to build a symbolic environment for quality and difference?

Basic questions, somehow ingenuous, but it is necessary to consider that technologies do not lose their instrumental nature. Their influence plays in a complex social context full of paradoxes and contradictions. Some of them can be discussed: the febrile agitation of passing time, fed by a consumerism already far from real needs, creates a space for silence and distance, or the need to cut with everyday life routine; the noise and the enchanting celebration of lights of external paths cannot cover the search for tranquillity and interior light as advent of contemplation and joy; the total communication that is in front of the experience of noncommunication and solitude, as passed by mythological discourses on technologies and media with the illusion of transparency; the global village in which the multitude of nets and technological devices is apparently transforming our world meets the growing gap of information, not only concerning access but also uses.

We are not opposing a determined social and cultural "order" to a different order. It is necessary to support the multipolarity of the path linked to the search of meaning and to defend the inscription of tension between two poles as the vital safeguards of the ecology of communication. A tension is the opposite of the mainstream. It is critical because it results from (or it creates) a crisis. It is asking. It takes what passes not as a fatality, but as provocation and convocation.

According to what we have discussed, the multiplicity and the multiplication of screen and, above all, of worlds to which these screens access or of which they are the terminal points, need to be compared and contraposed to the globality of human and social existence. They need to be considered as instruments and agents of a wider global ecosystem.

This perspective or ecological frame of communication and media seems to be actually a path worthy of an exploration. This is because media, creating a deep instance in the production and construction of a symbolic environment on a planetary level, has been studied in a disintegrated way. On the other hand, media has been considered marginal in relation to the environmental preoccupation, as if the symbolic field was not as fundamental for the quality of planet life and for societies as natural and human ecosystems. To adopt this ecological paradigm supposes to consider communication not only in its informative and transmissive level, but also its relational, dialogical and connecting meaning.

This discourse has many implications. I would like to discuss in particular the aspects which are more closed to media education considered as education to citizenship. We have to start first with paying attention to the fact that the concepts of education and learning are associated, even if every time less strongly, to an institutional and specific place (school) and to a specific time (childhood and youth). We are assisting what Joel de Rosnay (2002) called "hybridation" of access ways to knowledge and diversification of teaching actors. Both the hybridation and the diversification can be full of potentials. But never will we be allowed to forget that «education is fundamentally the interaction between people. This point is capital, especially when the effect of devices do not stop to announce sceneries where learners seems the inhabitants of Plato's cave.

In a digital culture, it is important that learning does not turn into a stupid jump from here and there, into an apparent choice of elements without a global perspective, in a collection of information more or less without meaning, in a sacrifice of the meaning of form and design.

In a culture signed by the acceleration and speed, by the profusion of stimuli and the multiplication of possible directions, it is necessary to work, now and permanently, on dimensions as: the meaning (aims, effects) of learning, considering project and common destiny; the memory (the path already done before) creating a solid temporal perspective; the "maps and compass" that help to position and to orient paths (Delors, 1996).

What we have to prevent is that education turns into an erratic path, into a wondering with no destination and sense or into a preformatted divagation into predefined paths. The interior (or interiorization) dimension, which now lacks of active silence and of the implicit change of seeing and speaking, cannot stop to accompany this process.

Conclusion

Finally, we need to analyze refers to the new possibilities created by digital media, in particular those which are defined as "empowerment tools" of citizens. Seen from the perspective of the promotion of autonomous individuals, solidal and critical, media as Weblogs, forum, wikis, RSS1, ipod, VoIP2, and for sure mobile phones, every time more polivalent and multifunctional, can represent—and actually are already representing—tools and opportunities for initiatives, projects for creation, discovery, and participation.

But, again, just as innovation does not happen by having computers and wide band Internet access, it is not in using the tools that innovation happens. Even if the logic of these media is, from case to case, P2P (peer-to-peer, or in other word, person to person) or the one of social networks, to implement what tools allow to make, it is necessary to act and to raise social actors' initiatives.

Weblogs affirmed not only as chance of conception, production, and "planetary" diffusion of media to citizen's reach, but also as instances of critical pursuing, contributing in this way to the deepening of democracy and citizenship.

It is, therefore, with this background of ecological orientation in relation to communication and technology, with this working in the field of maps and compasses orienting the path in a universe made of chaotic and magmatic profusion of offers, and with the intentional and creative conception of new tools supporting people's initiatives that I think it is possible to go on deepening theory and practical issues, from what starts to be conceived as digital literacy4.

A consequence of this orientation is represented by the fact that the universe of technologies, new or old, has to be converted into an object of analysis and study, in order to oppose the effects of the naturalization or neutrality that are polluting the discourses and the concrete uses of technologies. The origin, the emergency context and the diffusion of these technologies, their sociocultural impact, social appropriation modes, the political and mercantile logics associated to them, the inequalities in access and practices, the way and contexts in which they are used, and the social discourses on technologies, here we have some aspects that need to be examined, considering the instrumental nature of technologies for a human and social existence.

References

Blakley, J. (2001). *Entertainment goes global: Mass culture in a transforming world.* Lear Center Entertainment Goes Global Project/USC Annenberg School for Communication. Retrieved October 7, 2007, from http://learcenter.org/pdf/EntGlobal.pdf, consultado em 10.8.2005

Delors, J. (coord.). (1996). L'Éducation: Un Trésor Est Caché Dedans. Paris, UNESCO e Éd. Odile Jacob, p. 91

De Rosnay, J. (2002). Les risques de l'infopollution». Transversales, Science Culture, Nouvelle série n° 1, Mai. Retrieved October 7, 2007, from http://csiweb2.cite-sciences.fr/derosnay/articles/Tranversales_infopollution.html, consultado em 2.8.2005

Ferres, J. (2003). Educación en Medios y Competencia Emocional». Revista Iberoamericana de Educación, n° 32

Gutierrez Gomez, C. (2000). Televisión y calidad: Perspectivas de investigación y criterios de evaluación», enZER – Revista de Estudios de Comunicación, n° 9.

Gutierrez Martin, A., & Hotmann, A. (2002). *Democracy, multimedia literacy and classroom practice.* Berlin, Germany: Mondial Verlag.

Pérez-Tornero, J.M. (2004). Digital literacy and media education: An emerging need. Forum on

Digital Literacy. Portal eLearningeuropa. Retrieved October 7, 2007, from http://www.elearningeuropa.info/index.php?page=doc&doc_id=4935&doclng=16&menuzone=1>, consultado em 15.5.2005

Pinto, M. (2000). A Televisão no Quotidiano das Crianças. Porto, Edições Afrontamento

Pinto, M. (2005): Televisão e Cidadania – Contributos para o Debate sobre o Serviço Público. Porto, Campo das Letras.

Endnotes

1   Real simple syndication.

2   Voice over internet protocol or the possibility to talk and communicate with Internet.

3   The case of Weblogs, used as an example of teaching and learning environment and tool in universities, is from this point of view evident and explicit, allowing the access to words and expression, individual and in groups, and the creation of networks of different nature.

4   To discuss this concept, see Alfonso Gutiérrez Martín (2002) and Jose Manuel Perez-Tornero (2004).

Chapter XII

From Media Education to Digital Literacy:
A Paradigm Change?

Pier Cesare Rivoltella, Università Cattolica del Sacro Cuore (UCSC), Italy

Abstract

This chapter focuses on the cultural and educational shift from mass media to digital technologies. It is described with the category of the multiscreen society: its main element is the multiplication of the screens in social environment and, with it, the transformation of the modalities and significance of our sight on the things. Watch the reality with other eyes, means also to build knowledge in a different way and, finally, to accept to live in this new environment whose main character is the integration of virtual dimension into real life. This is the reason why a part of the chapter is devoted to defining the new technological devices as social objects able to become subjects of social acts. The conclusion is that traditional forms of media education must upgrade to digital literacy. In doing so, it becomes possible to prepare youngsters to become citizens of this new social environment. In this case, may be that digital literacy will be really the education of our next future.

Introduction

The idea of a "multiscreen society" is borrowed from Manoel Pinto (2005), a colleague working at the University of Minho (Portugal), who, during a recent meeting, suggested with this term a way to explain the changes occurring in reality marked by the presence of mass media. Pinto's idea— developed by him in the chapter XI of this book—is interesting and functional as it allows grasping three dimensions of this society. First of all, the multiplicity of screens indicates the multiplication of the spaces connected to the act of seeing. Cinema and television screens—by now classical—are accompanied by computer and portable consoles screens (such as Nintendo or PS Mobile videogames), public installations (in airports and railway stations), artistic and business installation as well (projecting images on a multiplicity of side by side plasma screens), DVD portable players, palmtops, and third generation mobile phones.

The multiplication of all these screens involves a clear redefinition of the forms and meanings of the glance. As suggested by Jacques Aumont (1989), the cinema device (and partly the television one), created an audience geometry connoted by a glance which is durable (in the dark room, a movie is followed from the beginning to the end), variable (from a temporal perspective, as the flow of images symbolizes also a temporal course of the events), isolable (what I see at cinema is what the movie allows me to see). This glance drastically changes with the introduction of the new technological screens. It becomes intermittent (the duration of movies is replaced by a mosaic of decontextualized visual stimuli), mobile (as it no longer refers to the representation of time within the work, but to the temporality of sight, moving from screen to screen), interactive (what I see is also what I want to see, through an active relation to different screens).

The new glance, with its qualities, redefines also the forms through which people access to knowledge. Screens multiplication, under this perspective, involves both an exponential increase of accessible information and the fall of central references. We can easily grasp the ambivalence of these aspects.

Figure 1. A multiscreen installation

Disposing more information on more screens means to have more access points to knowledge (the computer screen is different from the television or mobile ones): these accesses are more consistent with personal cognitive styles, powering learning (Gardner, 1999). Even information discovery improves through the inversion of traditional searching forms. Knowledge, in fact, is no longer stored in deposits (libraries, archives) where it is necessary to go to keep it, but is accessible through those same screens which are increasing its diffusion. Finally, following a law affirmed by the information theory, to recode information according to different modes means to make it redundant, supporting in this way the process which allows the acquisitiveness of its meaning.

If we deepen these aspects we can, on other hand, underline an oscillation of their meaningfulness. As a matter of fact, the multiplication of knowledge accesses creates a continuous dislocation of the addressee, compromising the integrity of what is represented. At the same time, physical availability of information (its presence on the screen) does not necessarily coincide with its cognitive availability. Indeed, its exponential growth makes it difficult to collect information that can be relevant to our needs. Finally, also the redundancy hides the risk of a state of entropy, as the remodulation creates new information, rather than closing the meaning, supporting an endless opening process.

The acts of seeing and knowing, the logics of vision and appropriation of meaning, have always represented two modes through which we decline our social life, especially in the current social context. To multiply screens means not only to multiply the possibilities to see and know, but also the spaces of our living, of our social frames. From this point of view, it is definitely revelatory what Sherry Turkle reveals about her experience of therapist, quoting the testimony of a young patient of hers. This boy speaks about his life on the screen like a chance for divide his mind in many parts; he tries to experience many selves in each one of the windows he opened on the desktop. Sherry Turkle (1996, p. 14) writes:

Windows has become a powerful metaphor for thinking about the self as a multiple, distributed system. (...) The self is no longer simply playing different roles in different settings at different times. The life practice of windows is that of a decentred self that exists in many worlds, that plays many roles at the same time.

As the young man says: Now real life itself may be just one more window. It is an interesting perspective, which we need to deliver from the temptation to banish it within the frame of pathologic experiences. As a matter of fact, affirming that real life is just an open window on our desktop is one of the deepest aspects (and then constitutive) of the multiscreen society, that is the substitution of physical place with a new social one. This means that, while in pre-electronic (predigital) societies the possibility to communicate structurally depended on physical place (so that walls

Table 1. The dimensions of the multiscreen society

Dimensions	Traditional societies	Multiscreen societies
See	Durable	Intermittent
	Variable	Mobile
	Isolable	Interactive
Know	Stored	Distributed
	Mono-visual	Multi-access
Live	Physical place	Social place

and doors represented the access limit or the exclusion from communication), in the multiscreen society made of mobile phones and Internet communication (but basically already with television) communication occurs within a new space which allows the sharing of meanings and the relationship among people (that is why it is social) apart from their location in the same place (Meyrowitz, 1985). When watching a football match, chatting in *Messenger* with audio-visual mode, (video) phoning with our mobile, we are sharing with other peoples a social place without sharing a physical place. And, even without this physical cohabitation, we cannot say that our communication is not real, not only because it is occurring, but mainly for the concreteness of the experiences that we are passing by through it.

Right in this statement we understand the weakness of the contraposition between real and virtual, not only theoretically as Pierre Levy (1995) already had shown reading Aristotle under Deleuze's perspective (Deleuze, 1968), but also according to very experiential point of view. We need to understand how it can be possible to get over it in order to define, later, according to this overcoming, the exact meaning of citizenship and education in an innovative context such as the current one.

Social Objects: Besides the Distinction of Real and Virtual

Let's start from the essential notes of Levy's analysis. It moved from the reconfiguration of the relationship between real and virtual through the discussion of their common meaning. This connotation appears clear in the lexicon developed in the 1990s with the diffusion of digital technologies: we talk about "virtual communities" referring to the people's communicating in chat and MUDs environments[1] and we use the term "virtual worlds" to allude to videogames spaces (just think about the virtual cities which different users can collaboratively build with games such as *Sim City*, or, more recently, to *Second Life*). Once again, we talk about "virtual

Table 2. Levy's states of being

State of being	Latent	Manifested
Substance	Possible	Real
Event	Virtual	Actual

Table 3. Categories of objects (Source: Ferraris, 2005, p. 69)

Physical objects	They exist within soace and time
Ideal objects	They exist out of space and time
Social objects	They require small portions of space and start witin time tempo

reality" to indicate a world populated by synthetic objects (as they are generated by computer) where it is possible to immerse getting in touch with these objects, thanks to devices such as *data glov*es or a *retinal Virtual Display* (thanks to which the 3D image—and the immersive effect—is magically built into our own eyes).

So, when we refer to the concept of virtuality in these different meanings, the implicit idea is connected to the fact that, having no corporal existence, no material shape, it has to be defined as opposite to the concept of real, which on the contrary is seen as concrete, material, corporal.

Levy's (1995) analysis is appointed on this focus, observing that, thanks to this conceptual popularity, the word "virtual" is used for indicating the absence of existence, the lack of a material presence. So, when we commonly talk about the "today's egg" we are talking about reality, meanwhile the "tomorrow's hen" is for us simply a virtual reality (Levy, 1995).

We can clearly note that there is an enormous difference between the virtual world of a videogame and the hen we where talking about: the first, in fact, even having a specific existence not in the flesh still exists, as, on the contrary, I could not play within it; the hen, then, does not exist currently and could never come to an existence. It means that opposing real and virtual, considered as what materially is and what on the contrary does not concretely exist, is not correct because virtual materially exists too. It evidently consists of a particular form of concreteness, made out of bits and generated by an algorithm, but in any case it consists of concreteness.

The consequence is that the opposition we started from does not stand: it has to be corrected. Levy (1995) does it, as suggested, coming back to Aristotle, in particular to the *pollachòs* doctrine, according to which being can be said in different ways (*pollachòs*, precisely, in Greek means "many ways"). In relation to substance and accidents, to true and false, to matter and shape, to actual and potential. We should underline this last famous categorical couple, as it offers us the starting point to define the difference between real and virtual. Let's start with a simple example.

Under the Aristotelian perspective, the seed itself is not the fruit and nevertheless there is not an absolute difference between them, such as the one occurring between black and white. As a matter of fact, there is a specific relation between seed and fruit, as the seed is already the fruit, but only "potentially," that means in a hidden and not yet spread way. What is needed is the activation of a process translating this potential state into act, that is the manifested existence. What is potential is not anything: it simply exists according to an existential state different from the actual one.

The substance of virtual would have been defined, following Levy, starting from this remark. "Virtual" (*virtus*, in latin, stands for the idea of potentiality) is not the opposite of "real" but of "actual." While the possible is static and already made, the virtual is a problematical complex, that means the necessity of anything for developing itself in any way (Levy, 1995).

For the French philosopher, we assist with the virtual to a double level of being in which what is potential (tomorrow's hen) is opposed to the real (today's egg); the virtual (the seed as system of forces able to transform it into a fruit) is opposed to the actual (the effective accomplishment of those forces). Possible and real define a static level of existence; virtual and actual define a dynamic one, so it is better to talk about them in terms of virtualization and actualization, processes better than statuses.

Levy's argumentation undoubtedly participated to correct a perspective on the digital world that affirms that it would not exist as virtual. But his analysis needs to be completed for at least two reasons.

First of all, we do not understand why virtual objects cannot be inscribed within the level of substances. The magnetic track of an audiovisual material on a tape, as a file in my computer, or the optic memory stored in a CD-ROM or in a DVD, really exists; they can all be somehow considered as substances.

Second, if virtualization consists in a process of problematization, then we do not understand why this process should only be part of digital world and not also of the simulation, as it happens with a role play or a mental experiment.

That concretely means that digital objects somehow exist, also in an actualized form, and it is necessary to explain what the difference is in relation to other phenomena marked by virtualization processes.

The possibility to go beyond Levy (1995) comes from the adoption of the concept of social object as defined by Maurizio Ferraris (2005) and, before him, by John Searle (1955). This term refers to a system of objects which is in the middle course between the system of physical objects (a house, a glass, a tree) and the other one represented by ideal objects (the square root of a number, the area of a circle). It refers to all those objects, such as a deed of sale or the representation of a commercial transaction on the computer screen, which do not exist in the same way of physical objects, but have a sort of existence, unlike ideal objects, within the physical space.

There are two essential elements of these objects: the presupposition of a social act and its inscription. For example, for a deed of sale, the fact that it is a social object depends on the presupposition of an agreement between two individuals concretely represented by the entry of what has been agreed, that is the recording (and for this reason it is considered as binding).

Extending this argument not only to mobile phones (as Ferraris, 2005) but to the entire digital communication, it is easy to verify the possibility to consider it effectively as a system of social objects: an SMS, an e-mail, a message posted in a discussion board or in a chat, imply a social act (communication is always a social act) recorded as informatic track. And this recording (as for a deed of sale) is useful to create a state of things. In this way, if I use a discussion board to reach a shared solution for a common problem, the track of my message which demonstrates the definition of this solution represents and indicates the agreement we have reached.

To be more precise, the digital world appears wider than the extension denoted by the definition of social object: first of all, because its inscriptions do not necessarily translate a social act intervened between two or more subjects (when I publish a Web site, it does not represent the track of an agreement I signed with other Internet users); second, because frequently, thanks to the interactivity typical of digital world, the space of sociality does not precede the inscription, but it is its own nature (the case of a discussion board or of a blog properly explains it). The social dimension, far from being the act at the basis of a social object, represents its own frame (a blog, as a wiki, is not the result of a social act but the space starting from which social acts can occur) or the same substance (every forms of telematic interaction are systems of social acts). So, in case of the digital world, we can for sure refer to it as a world of social objects, on condition that we think the system of inscriptions and social acts that define it in a wider sense, where social acts not only produce inscriptions, but they are their products. We are in front of that kind of pragmatic understanding of Internet communication we deeply referred to in other contexts (Rivoltella, 2003) and which symbolize the digital world as an action scenario where, after all, objects are acts.

From Citizenship to Digital Citizenship: A New Idea of Public Space

The two premises previously supported can be completed in the current paragraph. If the multiscreen society extends our experience of facts from the physical world to the digital dimension, and if this last world has to bee seen as a scenario of action within which occurs the definition of systems of social acts, then we can talk about this multiscreen society as a new form of public space where the idea and the forms of citizenship need to be redefined.

Why should the multiscreen society represent a new form of public space?

First, as suggested by the term itself, it is the scenario of a *new form of pluralism*. Following Roger Silverstone (1999), we are living in a plural world we share with the others. Their names are George W. Bush and Osama Bin Laden, the Taliban and so on: they are our life neighbours and at the same time people without a name living on the other side of the planet. Nowadays it is impossible to ignore this pluralism in media politics, and so it is impossible to ignore the media for any national or international politics.

Second, the multiscreen society represents the arena of a shift and a *reconfiguration of the limit between external and internal*, both considering the shape of the relation between public and private, both in the case of the connection between local and global dimensions. It is the case of politics, an area where the constant presence of mass media reshapes the image of power, making it more familiar and close to people, but right for this reason it also determines a reformulation of its symbolic effect (because politicians, always on the stage and always scanned by television cameras every second of their life, give also images of weakness, showing their limits). Or just reflect on how the application of new technologies on education are supporting a continuous erosion of free time in favor of a work time which is becoming more and more preponderant, in the name of flexibility. Finally, we have to underline that data sensibility, the problem of privacy, the protection of reserved information are now central topics of the agenda within a social system where our movements in the digital world are tracked, or phone calls are recorded, our files in our computer are mapped by search engines until becoming a precious data-bank to be used for a possible control of our choices and convictions.[2]

Again, the multiscreen society is the space of another shift between *human and nonhuman*, as indicated by Giuseppe Longo (2001) when he talks about the *homo tecnologicus* as homo sapiens transformed by technology; in the perspective of the Italian philosopher, this man is a new evolutive being, following a new form of evolution in a new environment. Even if immersed in a natural world, depending on its rules, this new form of life lives also in an artificial environment which is highly marked by information, symbols, communication and even more by virtuality.

Last, we need to mention the fact that the multiscreen society is also the place of the erosion of the difference—typical of modern experience of the world—between vision order and action order. The interactivity of digital technologies, in fact, transforms the act of seeing in an immediate action. It is the same logic of the computer desktop, where every icon is clickable. What we see (the icon) is at the same time what we can intervene on: the click implies some effects we are not completely conscious of, as behind it there are very complicated instructions on technical level. This is the logic that makes the destruction of aircrafts on a videogame console similar to the one acted on a flight-deck simulator or on the screen of a combat aircraft during a real war action. If the vision order resolves the order of action, everything becomes clean and aseptic, as in the "surgical war," but this fact does not necessary imply inquiring, especially on the ethical level.

Moving from this last remark on the ethical implications of the dissolution of the limit between seeing and acting, it is possible to observe how each aspect of this new public space supported by digital technologies can be referred to the four dimensions traditionally recognized within citizenship:

- **Civil rights:** Here lay the issues related to freedom and control, to the protection of personal data, to the respect and the violation of privacy;
- **Political citizenship:** The multimedia environment of the multiscreen society can weigh on the representation of politics and politicians (as previously noted), and also on the main forms of participation (from polls to televoting);
- **Social citizenship:** In this area we can recognize the problem of the reconfiguration of free time in our digital society, market by telejob and e-learning;
- **Cultural citizenship:** Here lay the themes related to citizens' cultural belonging, as the problem of the shift from human to nonhuman or the redefinition of the connection between seeing and acting.

So, while changing the public space, the digital environment also produces a clear redefinition of the idea and of the spaces of this citizenship. Evidently this implies the specification of new values and rules, the definition of a new concept of participation, the training of new competences, a particular attention to youth, and the accomplishment of new forms of social integration. This is a task which launches a new topic of reflection and intervention.

Conclusion and Future Trends: A Change in Media Education Paradigm

Education in a multiscreen society, if our argumentation stands, cannot be anything else except a media education. Or better: in a multiscreen society, what in a predigital society appeared as a specific task referred to a specific field of education (as media were not so pervasively present) turns out to be a task that cannot be omitted from education *tout court*. Media education, in the multiscreen society, becomes digital literacy and this, in an Informational Society, probably is simply education!

This kind of education, in this society, thanks to its mediatic characterization, connotes itself as the construction of citizenship. It represents a need which has been recently underlined in different occasions. We refer to two international congresses: the Spanish and Portuguese speaking countries congress on communication "Hacia una television de qualidad" held in Huelva, Spain, in October 2005, and the congress "La sapienza del comunicare," held in Rome in March 2006.

Different interventions in these two contexts have insisted on the need to reconceptualize the idea of media education itself, starting from the new challenges coming from digital media and the multiscreen society.

Vitor Reia Batista,[3] reflecting on how mass media today becomes a factor of civilization and on the measures that we have to adopt to live in symphony with them, underlines the problem of the development of new media ecology as a priority for education. Media education practices mean to educate people to live free and to be conscious of the new media-environment. This implies, evidently, the need to think about a new pedagogy.

Manoel Perez-Tornero[4] indicates the limit of many media education programs, that is the tendency of touching only "noble" topics (authorial cinema, quality television): the iconosphere today is not only made of movies and television series, but of young people living in Paris banlieux who film with their mobile phones the cars they burned. The result should be the inclusion of media education within cultural studies.

A similar perspective has been developed by Génevieve Jacquinot[5] who, quoting Pasquier (2005), stretches out the need to go beyond media education, bringing to the main stage the media-cultures which feed youth and within which they live. In this way, within a public space which is more and more fluid, "media cease to be alienating industries and they turn to be real media cultures" (Pasquier, 2005, p. 115) that means places where we can meet worlds more or less marked by the defense and the renunciation of identities (Jacquinot, 2007, p.139).

Also David Buckingham[6] seems to agree with this perspective, recalling the need to rethink the conceptual frame of media education starting from new media and their position within the digital world. This does not mean that the "performative square" on which the "old" media education built its identity (representation, language, production, audience) has to be abandoned; we rather need to begin a new path starting from that consciousness and that lesson in order to adapt new strategies and a new conceptual apparatus:

For example, the conventional notions of narrative and genre, often used in film and television analysis, do not easily adapt to videogames; and the concept of audience appears as an old-fashioned and strangely limited way to refer to what happens when we play with videogames. (Buckingham, 2007, p.119)

Finally we can synthesize all these argumentations: we need a new pedagogy (to study the media in a multiscreen society) and it probably points to the direction of a conceptual redefinition of media education represented by media cultures and cultural studies.

This change, this shift, can probably be represented through Foucault's categories (Martin, Gutman, & Hutton, 1988), considering the current phase as a transition from the old to the new paradigm.

The old paradigm was defined by "production technologies" and by the "technologies of signs." Media education practices consisted in making things with media (production technologies) and in reading media under a critical perspective (technologies of signs). The new paradigm, on the contrary, seems to be defined by the "technologies of the self."

These technologies of the self, according to Foucault, are represented by those techniques, such as self care for Greek philosophy or meditation for the monastic tradition, through which the ego acquires consciousness and self control. On these techniques we can (have to) build citizenship education when, as previously underlined, citizenship determines itself within the new media-environment. It consists in the overcoming of those approaches used until now to frame technologies under the perspective of education: the functionalist approach, today largely diffused, focused on how to use technologies; the critical approach, typical of traditional media education, focused on the construction of individual's autonomy through analysis and deconstruction practices. To educate a new digital citizenship means to maintain this critical approach integrating it within a new culturalist approach (Jacquinot's media cultures) which recognizes in the media a structural connection to the political dimension (in the Greek sense of the polis). First of all, because media for their own nature "imply a struggle for meaning and control: in the designing, in the development, in the distribution and in uses" (Silverstone, 2002, p. 226). Second, because media, as cultural forces, are also political elements: they depend on conflicts for access and participation; they are linked to struggles for the right of property and representation; they are always influenced by the uncertain and unpredictable consequences of every communication act. Media connect and at the same time separate, include and contemporarily exclude, give freedom of expression and claim the right of surveillance and control, allow and prevent, create new inequalities and try to fight against the old ones. (Silverstone, 2002, p. 227)

This tight connection among media, citizenship, and education had clearly emerged in 1991 with Ferguson (1991), a south African media educator, who noted that media education is the continuous way in which we are interpreting the world and the others are interpreting it for us. After all, this seems to be the meaning of the real democracy—as Jacquinot (2007, p. 141) observes—a democracy which is both cognitive and political and which does not only consist in "giving technologies to our students."

References

Aumont, J. (1989). *L'Oeil interminable*. Paris: Librairie Séguier.

Buckingham, D. (2007). La media education nell'era della tecnologia digitale. In M. Morcellini & P.C. Rivoltella (Eds.), *La sapienza del comunicare* (pp. 111-122). Trento: Erickson.

Deleuze, G. (1968). *Différence et répetition*. Paris: Presses Universitaires de France.

Ferguson, R. (1991). What is media education? In J. Prinsloo & K. Criticos (Eds.), *Media matters in South Africa* (pp. 19-24). Duban: Media Resources Centre.

Ferraris, M. (2005). *Dove sei? Ontologia del telefonino*. Milano: Bompiani.

Gardner, H. (1999). *The disciplined mind. What Alla students should understand*. New York: Simon & Schuster.

Jacquinot Delaunay, G. (2007). Dall'educazione ai media alle "mediaculture": Ci vogliono sempre degli inventori! In M. Morcellini & P.C. Rivoltella (Eds.), *La sapienza del comunicare* (pp. 131-141). Trento: Erickson.

Levy, P. (1995). *Qu'est-ce que le virtuel?* Paris: La Découvèrte.

Longo, G. (2001). *Homo tecnologicus*. Roma: Meltemi.

Martin, L.H., Gutman, H., & Hutton, P.H. (1988). *Technologies of the self: A seminar with Michel Foucault*. Amherst: University of Massachussets Press.

Meyrowitz, J. (1985). *No sense of place*. New York: Oxford University Press.

Pasquier, D. (2005). *Cultures lyceennes, la tirannie de la majorité*. Paris: Autrement.

Pinto, M. (2005). A busca da comunicação na sociedade multi-ecrãs: Perspectiva ecologica. *Comunicar, 25*, 259-264.

Rivoltella, P.C. (2003). *Comunicazione e pragmatica della comunicazione on line*. Trento: Erickson.

Searle, J. (1995). *The construction of social reality*. New York: Simon & Schuster.

Silverstone, R. (1999). *Why study the media?* Thousand Oaks, CA, New Deli, India: Sage, tr.it., *Perché studiare i media?*, Il Mulino, Bologna 2002, p. 227.

Turkle, S. (1996). *Life on the screen*. New York: Simon & Schuster.

Endnotes

1   A chat is a space on the Internet where people can meet and communicate in real time, with written or vocal interaction processes. A Multi User Domain (MUD) is a similar interaction system where this interaction is linked to a narration topic and to users' assumption of different roles (also through the construction of a self synthetic double called *avatar*).

2   Recently, the choice of some American search engines (e.g., *Yahoo!*) to make available for the government the tracking of the users search activities has been seriously critized.

3   Universidade do Algarve, Faro, Portugal.

4   Universidad Autonoma de Catalunya, Barcelona, Spain.

5   Université de Paris VIII Saint Denis, France.

6   Institute of Education, University of London.

Chapter XIII

Creative Remixing and Digital Learning:
Developing an Online Media Literacy Learning Tool for Girls

Renee Hobbs, Temple University, USA

Jonelle Rowe, Department of Health and Human Services, USA

Abstract

This chapter explores how media literacy education may continue to be responsive and relevant to the continually changing nature of popular culture through the development of innovative online multimedia educational programs. Because pre-adolescent and adolescent girls are actively involved in the consumption of popular music, competitive performance television programs like American Idol as well as online social networks, it is important to examine the constructed nature of these new types of messages and experiences. My Pop Studio (www.mypopstudio.com), a creative play experience for girls ages 9 to 14, was developed by the authors to address the need for media literacy skills among this group. We present a model for assessing the impact of the program on learning that incorporates the dimensions of pleasure, a sense of mastery, participation in an online community, media literacy skills, and other outcomes. Online games that use creative remixing techniques may promote metacognition, reflection, and critical analysis skills. Girls need opportunities to strengthen critical thinking skills about mass media and popular culture and the use of online learning environments may support the development of adolescents' media literacy skills.

Introduction

An important challenge facing educators today is the need to keep education relevant to the continually changing media environment of the 21st Century. Media literacy education, while still at the margins of mainstream educational practice, has made some significant inroads in a number of nations, as educators develop approaches to strengthen students' critical thinking and communication skills through activities involving critical inquiry, media production, discussion about media and society, and close analysis of media texts (Dickson, 1994; Felini, 2004; Hart, 1998; Hobbs, 2004). Of course, in some schools, teachers hesitate to explore topics related to popular culture, a phenomenon which may diminish one of the major strengths of media literacy: its perceived relevance in bridging the gap between the classroom and the culture. This problem is challenging to address, because teachers who have fears about the perceived value of popular culture may not want to continually adapt their curricula to match the changing media environment. With the intense schedule of teaching as many as 150 students per day, most teachers do not have the luxury of modifying their curriculum extensively. In some schools, teachers use video and print artifacts that are nearly 10 years old (Hobbs, 2007). There is a need for curriculum resources that can help educators incorporate media literacy into the curriculum with materials that represent the rapidly-changing world of technology, media, and popular culture.

Recently, there have been some explorations as to how to help educators introduce media literacy through the use of online media. This chapter explains one example of this new work: the development, implementation, and assessment of My Pop Studio (www.mypopstudio.com), an online creative play experience developed by the author under a contract from the U.S. Federal Government, Office on Women's Health. This chapter examines how online games can introduce key ideas of media literacy by taking advantage of the unique characteristics of the online environment's capacity to blend play and learning in a creative play environment where users can experiment with the processes of creating media, remixing existing content, and analyzing messages. This chapter examines how creative play, combined with meta-cognitive modeling, may promote learning of key media literacy concepts through activities that include media analysis and media production.

Targeting Adolescent Girls

Adolescence is a challenging time of life. Between age 10 and age 15, many girls in both developed and developing nations lose confidence and diminish their health outcomes as they move through puberty. At age 10, girls are confident, spunky, outspoken, and see themselves as healthy, capable, and strong. By age 15, 30% of American teen girls are smokers (Gidwani, Sobol, DeJong, Perrin, & Gortmaker, 2002). Many have chosen to avoid more rigorous courses in math and science, even when they have the capability to perform well in these classes. In the United States, teen pregnancy rates, while declining since the 1990s, are still high, especially among young women living in poverty. Tween and teen girls experience psychological depression. More than 4 million teen girls shoplift. Nutrition and body image create problems for the health of teen girls (Jones, Bennett, Olmsted, Lawson, & Rodin, 2004; Kilbourne, 1999; Lazarus et al., 2000).

For girls, life during adolescence can be especially stressful in the intense peer culture of adolescence. Expectations from peers and family, the pressure for material possessions, and social relationships take center stage. An online survey commissioned by Girls Incorporated and Harris Interactive between March 14, 2006, and March 30, 2006, examined opinions of more than 2,000 U.S. youth to focus on the ways gender stereotypes and expectations shape the lives of girls and boys (Girls Inc., 2006). The survey data reveal that there are persistent gender expectations being compounded by a growing emphasis on perfection, resulting in mounting pressure on girls to be supergirls. Three-quarters of girls (74%) in the study agree that girls are under a lot of pressure to please everyone. More than half of girls in grades 6 to 8 say they are under a great deal of stress. The online world of social networking, IM/chat, and cell phones, can be overwhelming, exhausting, and hard on the ego (Mazzarella, 2005). Many adolescents live in homes with parents who have slender knowledge about the complexities of online communication; as a result, many girls navigate the ever-changing waters of online media and mass media and popular culture with little meaningful guidance from teachers or parents.

Health communication theory suggests that media messages impact health-related behaviors by fostering knowledge, beliefs, and attitudes that are conducive to behaviors, either desirable or undesirable (Finnegan & Viswamath, 2002). The media-behavior link is well established in the areas of adolescent sexual behavior, aggression, body image, eating disorders, alcohol use, and tobacco use (Brown & Walsh-Childers, 1994). Many researchers attribute these ill effects to the ability of the mass media to act as a powerful agent of social influence—modeling, normalizing, and glamorizing unhealthy behaviors for impressionable young people (Bryant & Zillmann, 1986). Media literacy education can be a means to counter these influences by increasing awareness of media influence, helping young people recognize that media messages are often explicitly designed to make people, products, attitudes, and behaviors (frequently unhealthy ones) appear attractive.

A sense of competence is also important for adolescents. Girls can acquire a sense of competence in mastering different challenges of online media. The public health literature informs us that media literacy education can increase a sense of competence among adolescents, which is considered to be a *protective factor* (Bergsma, 2004). During a time when feelings of confidence diminish, high-interest technology activities that appeal to girls' interest in critiquing media and popular culture may help them to continue to see themselves as capable, competent, and part of a creative and critical community, able to make good choices about their lifestyle and health (Hamilton & Hamilton, 2004).

An Online Creative Play Experience for Media Literacy

In 2006, we created My Pop Studio in collaboration with Sherri Hope Culver of Temple University and Dave Shaller of Eduweb, a multimedia production firm in St. Paul, Minnesota. Fifteen different online play activities of My Pop Studio are designed to strengthen media literacy skills, promote positive youth development, and increase awareness of the role of media in health. Highly interactive creative play activities guide users through the process of deconstructing, analyzing, and creating media. Video segments, flash animation, media deconstruction games and quizzes, and moderated blogs make the Web site lively, fun, and educational. Users select from four behind-the-scenes opportunities to learn more about mass media: In the **Magazine Studio**, users compose a magazine layout featuring themselves as celebrities, exploring the differences between celebrities and heroes. They write an advice column to discover the formulas used in magazines. Girls can also explore the power of digital retouching and reflect on the role of body image in today's culture. In the **TV Studio**, users edit a TV show where they can experiment with juxtaposition of images to create multiple storylines. They reflect upon their TV viewing choices and screen use, comment on teen celebrities, and compare their daily screen time with others. In the **Music Studio**, users create a pop star and compose her image and song to learn about how values messages are communicated through image and language. Girls can explore the power of music in selling a product and search for truth in media gossip. In the **Digital Studio**, users test their multitasking abilities. They share the challenges of digital life online. They consider the "what if's" of social networking sites and reflect on the power of media and technology in their social relationships.

Iterative prototypes and playtesting are critical to the design of educational multimedia. Playtesting can "help resolve conflicts among pedagogy, content, and gameplay by moving disagreements from theoretical stances to demonstrated success or failure of design concepts" (Winn & Heeter, 2006, p. 1). In developing My Pop Studio, we used formative evaluation with 60 girls ages 9 to 14 from six different geographic regions of the United States to ensure that the learning environment was responsive to the lived experience of this age group. At key periods during the year-long development process, girls participated in a series of meetings where they could offer ideas, suggestions, and feedback about the development of the site. Girls reviewed prototypes and contributed ideas to all aspects of the content and design process; as a result, they developed an intense sense of ownership about the Web site.

Balancing Play and Learning Through Creative Remixing

Popular music takes center stage in My Pop Studio because the scholarly literature suggests that adolescent girls are making active use of music and celebrities in their own identity formation (Cashmore, 2006; Marshall, 2005). Among media literacy educators who specialize in skills related to critical analysis of news and advertising, this topic is just beginning to be explored. For example, British researchers have conducted case studies of girls' use of online media to explore topics of fashion, beauty, and identity, finding that girls' interactions with online fashion media can be a site of learning for girls to explore critical perspectives through fantasy play (Willett, 2005). Because girls this age are beginning to read fashion magazines, we wanted to address issues of body image and digital image manipulation. Girls are also actively participating in watching competitive performance television programs like *American Idol* and *So You Think You Can Dance*, so we wanted to build upon this interest in introducing media literacy concepts.

My Pop Studio uses an approach to creative composition that takes advantage of remixing as a creative aesthetic. Remixing is now an important part of contemporary media production that involves the appropriation of existing cultural products for the development of new creative works (Lessig, 2004). In remixing, media texts get re-interpreted by other creative people through techniques of collage, editing, and juxtaposition (Jenkins, 2006). Remixing can be a vehicle for people to comment upon the role of media and technology in society. From the point of view of media literacy educators, remixing can strengthen media literacy skills because it can deepen people's awareness of an author's purpose and context. Through strategic juxtaposition and shifts in context, messages change their meanings. Remixing can also illustrate the function of *context* in the meaning-making process. For example, in several activities on My Pop Studio, users can select small samples of existing media texts and juxtapose them to create new meanings to experiment with the relationship between meaning and context. In the TV Studio, users can select pre-

Figure 1. A model of program impact for My Pop Studio

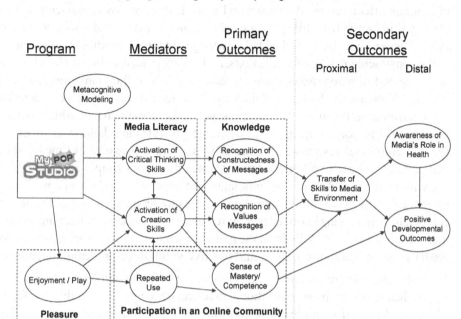

existing segments of video and edit them together to create original sequences. In the Music Studio, users can select small segments of audio and experiment with how popular music reshapes the symbolic function of various products targeted at girls and young women. With the rise of user-generated content online, remixing needs to be seen as a pedagogy that enables users to fully participate in contemporary culture (Jenkins, 2006).

As with much educational multimedia, the balance of play and learning is a complex and delicate one that calls upon and exploits certain expectations about personal and social identity (Hayes, 2005). Because My Pop Studio is designed to be used by girls, with or without a teacher or other gatekeeper, the experience must be inherently entertaining, or users won't play with it. In the online play environment, play and learning are related, so the format of My Pop Studio exploits the "behind-the-scenes" perspective to offer information about issues in media industries—minus the didacticism or preachiness that can be found on a number of media literacy Web sites that adopt a protectionist stance towards the dangers of mass media. Unlike traditional curricula, My Pop Studio is self-implemented. Users may choose which activities to engage in, to what extent, and how many times to play. These decisions result in program implementation or "dosage" levels that are likely to vary greatly among users.

In evaluating the potential of My Pop Studio to strengthen media literacy skills, we observed users playing with the program in order to develop a model that conceptualizes key elements to guide our current and ongoing research in the assessment of program effectiveness. As shown on Figure 1, there are two cross-cutting media literacy skills activated while playing: *critical analysis skills* and *media composition skills*. These two skills are linked to knowledge outcomes, including: (1) awareness of the constructed nature of media texts, and (2) awareness of how values messages are presented in media texts. Constructedness refers to the many choices that are involved in media production and the ways in which message design characteristics can contribute to meaning. Values messages refer to the ways in which messages are designed to convey ideas about desirable lifestyles and behaviors by evoking specific emotional responses. We are now piloting a measure of "media savvy" that addresses these two knowledge outcomes through a simple scale suitable for use with children and teens. We anticipate that users who find the site intrinsically pleasurable will play with the site enough times to develop a sense of mastery and competence, increasing knowledge. Figure 1 also shows secondary learning outcomes that include transfer of skills from the game environment to the home, awareness of media's role in health promotion, and positive youth developmental outcomes.

Youth development researchers, taking advantage of interdisciplinary studies of adolescent health research and educational practice, have identified additional features of various kinds of youth learning environments that contribute to success. These include age appropriate monitoring, opportunities to belong to a group, positive social norms with clear identification of values, and opportunities for skill building (Hamilton & Hamilton, 2004). These perspectives inform the work of the online learning environment we have created and future research will examine how users perceive and respond to these elements in the context of program usage.

Metacognition and Immersion in Online Learning

A sense of competence and mastery are believed to be intricately related to the pleasurable aspects of game environments. Compared to traditional, teacher-centered classrooms, online learning can simulate the processes of meaningful inquiry, presenting the user with increasing levels of challenge. According to James Gee (2003), users begin by mastering the mechanics of game play (what Gee calls the *internal design grammars*) then learn how to negotiate the context of play, coming gradually to recognize the design choices of its developers, a process referred to as the *external design grammars*. Video games allow users to simulate, learn, and manage design grammars, learning how to learn in unfamiliar environments. Users develop strategies for managing complexity and ambiguity. In doing so, they gradually acquire increasing levels of awareness about the constructed nature of the game environment. Our observations of girls using My Pop Studio supports this theory, as girls seem to enjoy the challenge associated with mastering the mechanics of play and gradually gain a sense of the values and critical perspectives embedded in the game.

Media literacy depends on the ability to actively control and reflect upon the process of thinking used in various encounters with media messages. Monitoring comprehension, reflection on the learning process, and evaluating the progress towards the completion of a task are examples of metacognition (Solomon, 1998). However, it is not always easy to create a learning environment where children and young people apply metacognitive skills. When presented with a media message about alcohol or tobacco, for example, researchers have found that children ages 10 to 14 are able to critically analyze it, but *activation* of this ability does not occur spontaneously (Brucks, Armstrong, & Goldberg, 1988). Young people often can demonstrate media literacy skills but often these skills are not evident without explicit prompting.

As a result, some types of metacognitive prompting are incorporated into My Pop Studio. For example, when users select music to accompany various types of advertising, a girl guide explains the impact of that choice on the interpretation of a message by a specific target audience. There has been some debate among the development team regarding the extent to which explicit metacognitive prompting should be incorporated into the program, with a solid argument that users should be allowed to come to these realizations on their own in their own time. The developers are considering adding a scaffolding element in the form of a character that "pops up" periodically to simply encourage users to critically reflect on their decisions. Additional elements that increase the variety and depth of the metacognitive prompting are also in development. External prompting may be necessary because of the powerful immersive pull exerted by the "play" component of the online learning environment, which may discourage distancing and critical analysis (Squire, 2005).

Of particular importance is the transfer or application of media literacy skills to the real-world media environment outside of the online game. Such transfer of learning is among the challenging of issues in the design and measurement of educational multimedia (Perkins & Salomon, 1988). Participating in an online community provides a means to cultivate transfer of learning. To examine this, we have begun to analyze the comments made by users on the eight different message boards of My Pop Studio. Future research will determine the extent to which users are making connections between the game and their real-life experiences. It will be important to assess the ability to transfer knowledge and skills from an online game environment to other settings, including home, family, and other media consumption experiences.

Conclusion

Classroom teachers find themselves on a steep learning curve in understanding the students of the 21st Century, whose level of online engagement is unlike that of previous generations. Rather than adopt the stance of the ostrich and ignore how children's culture has been changed by technology, or simply accede to the problem of young people's vulnerability to the world of mass media and popular culture, educators are beginning to adapt their own instructional practices to meet the needs of the multitasking, networked young people in their classrooms. It takes a confident teacher to incorporate play into a learning environment. It can be unnerving for some educators to experience the loss of control that comes from genuine student engagement. And some critics fear that appealing to the media proficiencies of children and young people can "yield the short-term advantages of increased student engagement….[while] catering to those students who seek to complete work with a minimum of effort" (Barnes, Marateo, & Ferris, 2007, p. 1). Certainly there is much we don't know about the appropriate uses of online creative play experiences as tools for learning in classroom settings. But these fears shouldn't blind us to the very real educational potential inherent in well-designed online learning environments. For years, educators have been accommodating children's learning styles by moving from the traditional lecture to discussion-based classes that allow for more individual expression. They have begun to incorporate mass media and popular culture into the curriculum in order to tap into student expertise and engagement. The use of online games as a means to promote critical thinking and metacognition is just another step forward in developing new approaches that enable girls and young women to thrive in a complex and rapidly changing cultural environment.

References

Barnes, K., Marateo, R., & Ferris, S. (2007). Teaching and learning with the net generation. *Innovate, 3*(4). Retrieved October 9, 2007, from http://www.in-novateonline.info/index.php?view=article&id=382

Bergsma, L.J. (2004). Empowerment education: The link between media literacy and health promotion. *American Behavioral Scientist, 48*, 152-164.

Brown, J., & Walsh-Childers, K. (1994). Effects of media on personal and public health. In J. Bryant & D. Zillman (Eds.), *Media effects: Advances in theory and research.* Mahwah, NJ: Erlbaum Associates.

Brucks, M., Armstrong, G., & Goldberg, M. (1988). Children's use of cognitive defenses against television advertising: A cognitive response approach. *Journal of Consumer Research, 14*, 471-482.

Bryant, J., & Zillmann, D. (1986). *Perspectives on media effects*. Hillsdale, NJ: L. Erlbaum Associates.

Cashmore, E. (2006). *Celebrity/culture*: Taylor & Francis Inc.

Dickson, P. (1994). *A survey of media education in schools and colleges*. British Film Institute & National Foundation for Educational Research in England and Wales.

Felini, D. (2004). *Pedagogia dei media: Questioni, percorsi e sviluppi*. Brescia: La Scuola.

Finnegan, J., & Viswamath, K. (2002). Communication theory and health behavior change: The media studies framework. In K. Glantz, B. Rimer & F. Lewis (Eds.), *Health behavior and health education: Theory, research and practice* (pp. 361-388). San Francisco: Jossey-Bass.

Gee, J.P. (2003). *What video games have to teach us about learning and literacy* (1st ed.). New York, Houndmills, England: Palgrave Macmillan.

Gidwani, P.P., Sobol, A., DeJong, W., Perrin, J.M., & Gortmaker, S.L. (2002). Television viewing and initiation of smoking among youth. *Pediatrics, 110*(3), 505-508.

Girls Inc. (2006, October). *The supergirl dilemma*. New York: Girls Inc.

Hamilton, S.F., & Hamilton, M.A. (2004). *The youth development handbook: Coming of age in American communities*. Thousand Oaks, CA, London: Sage Publications.

Hart, A. (1998). *Teaching the media:International perspectives*. Mahwah, NJ: Erlbaum.

Hayes, E. (2005). *Women and video gaming: Gendered identities at play.* Paper presented at the Games, Learning and Society conference, Madison, WI. Retrieved October 9, 2007, from http://www.academiccolab.org/resources/documents/gender_and_morrowind.pdf

Hobbs, R. (2004). A review of school-based initiatives in media literacy. *American Behavioral Scientist, 48*(1), 48-59.

Hobbs, R. (2007). *Reading the media: Media literacy in high school English*. New York: Teachers College Press.

Jenkins, H. (2006). *Convergence culture*. New York: New York University Press.

Jones, J.M., Bennett, S., Olmsted, M.P., Lawson, M.L., & Rodin, G. (2004). Disordered eating attitudes and behaviors in teenaged girls: A school-based study. *Canadian Medical Association Journal, 165*(5), 547-552.

Kilbourne, J. (1999). *Deadly persuasion: Why women and girls must fight the addictive power of advertising*. New York, NY: Free Press.

Lazarus, M., Wunderlich, R., Gilligan, C., Steiner-Adair, C., Dines, G., Steinem, G., et al. (2000). *The strength to resist: Beyond killing us softly*. United States: Cambridge Documentary Films.

Lessig, L. (2004). *Free culture: How big media uses technology and the law to lock down culture and control creativity*. New York: Penguin Press.

Marshall, P.D. (2005). *The celebrity culture reader*. Taylor & Francis Inc.

Mazzarella, S.R. (2005). *Girl wide Web: Girls, the Internet, and the negotiation of identity*. New York: Peter Lang.

Perkins, D., & Salomon, G. (1988). Teaching for transfer. *Educational Leadership, 46*(1), 22-32.

Solomon, P.G. (1998). *The curriculum bridge: From standards to actual classroom practice*. Thousand Oaks, CA: Corwin Press.

Squire, K.D. (2005). Toward a media literacy for games. *Journal of Media Literacy, 52*(1-2), 9-15.

Willett, R. (2005). *What you wear tells a lot about you: Girls dress up online*. Centre for the Study of Children Youth and Media, Institute of Education University of London.

Winn, B., & Heeter, C. (2006). Resolving conflicts in educational game design through playtesting. *Innovate, 3*(2). Retrieved October 9, 2007, from http://www.innovateonline.info/index.php?view=article&id=392

Section IV

Digital Literacy:
Educational Outlines

Chapter XIV

Educating in the Information Society

Kathleen Tyner, The University of Texas at Austin, USA

Abstract

As educational institutions struggle to accommodate the widespread social uses of digital media, tensions emerge between traditional and innovative school practices, resulting in unforeseen opportunities to rethink the design of physical spaces, curriculum resources, and pedagogical approaches. This chapter investigates digital literacy in pervasive computing environments as a driver for designing contemporary learning environments. Combined with open pedagogies, innovative resources, and well-designed virtual and physical learning spaces, technological advances have the potential to transform education. In the process, policymakers must reflect on the supports and challenges related to the social uses of pervasive, ubiquitous computing in the built world.

Introduction

Digital literacy tools and multimedia texts are increasingly ubiquitous in the world outside the classroom. Integrated into the environment in a seamless way, these resources are construed as a normal and unremarkable part of the landscape for contemporary students. Dramatic changes in the social uses of digital tools require schools to rethink—not simply to retool— the systemic design of learning spaces with new literacy tools as the pivotal, operational concept. These changes are architectural in nature, requiring different environments for the conceptual design of both physical and virtual spaces.

Learning is accomplished through the mastery of cognitive or skill-based tasks, designed for (more or less) specific outcomes. Some of these outcomes are less transparent than others. Values-based assumptions about the role and priorities of schooling tend to cloud the assessment of outcomes related to skill and knowledge acquisition across disciplines. But design is the central premise at both the micro and macro level of implementation.

Traditionally, a combination of three design elements provides the foundation for task mastery: pedagogy (how we accomplish tasks), intellectual resources (tools, texts, and people needed to complete tasks) and sensory aspects of the learning environment (how the environment supports or inhibits the tasks at hand). Environmental supports combine contextual elements related to the way that people interact with the world, for example, gathering, creating, working, socializing, documenting, watching, and so forth. These drive design features such as lighting, scale, modularity, seating, and traffic patterns. For centuries, alphabetic literacy and orality were crosscutting features in the curriculum that signaled entry into the learning context, thus creating some semblance of continuity and interdisciplinary coherence between various pedagogies, resources, and environments.

As digital media are used to apprentice learners into multimedia literacy practices, alphabetic literacy is now only one of a constellation of useful communication practices. When learning spaces are designed in a piecemeal way, instead of systemically, it is akin to stepping on a balloon. As one problem is addressed, pressure and tensions arise in other areas of the learning environment. Without a coherent design, built on some community consensus about the mission of schooling, experiments with the uses of new literacies in schools can result in a hodge-podge of old and new design elements.

At best, it can be said that an ad hoc approach to educational design is flexible, incremental, and rewards practitioners' creativity and strengths. At worst, the approach reveals redundancy, gaps, and incongruities in a curriculum that is increasingly divorced from real world literacy practices. As communities grapple with the design of socially responsive educational environments, it quickly becomes apparent that tweaking the system is no longer an option.

The Access Threshold

One example of incremental planning can be seen in strategies to address the digital divide. Studies indicate that students who have the opportunity to use a computer at school are more likely to also use a computer outside of school, especially with adult mentorship and encouragement (Morgan & VanLengen, 2005). As a result, schools struggle to bridge the digital divide, usually by supporting access to networked, personal computers in designated spaces. In late 2002, The National Center for Education Statistics reported that 99% of public schools had Internet access and the vast majority of these schools (92%) offered classroom access (NCES, 2003).

Unfortunately, statistics about digital access do not tell the whole access story. In spite of remarkable efforts to bridge the digital divide in a short time frame, access to digital tools and texts is far from universal, varying widely along gender, class, and racial lines (Jackson, Ervin, Gardner, & Schmitt, 2001; NTIA, 2000). And although student to computer ratio is getting better, district-by-district, the public school median is still likely close to one computer for every six students (Anderson & Ronnkvist, 1998, p. 4). The raw numbers often include computers that are dedicated for administrative or other restricted purposes (Gootman, 2004).

Fnding and planning still proceed as if the purchase of digital literacy tools will lead to the holistic integration of new literacy practices. Instead, it seems that the trajectory between access, critical literacy, and learning takes a far more circuitous route. Instead of retrofitting for technology as an extension of alphabetic literacy practices, planning for digital literacy is centered on the learner. It begins by capitalizing on the way that students authentically use multiple types of media and then leveraging their skill and knowledge via learning tasks in supportive environments. New literacy practices are aligned with an "open pedagogy" that embraces collaborative knowledge creation, participatory education models, experiential practices, mentoring, and apprenticeships, and a host of relevant educational design concepts.

How young people actually use media is central to a user-centered design sequence and apparently the way that young people use media is changing. A recent follow-up study of 2,032 young people aged 8 to 18 from the Kaiser Family Foundation indicates that students are more likely to prefer a multitasking style of information management, defined as using two or more media at the same time. Over one-quarter of the respondents reported that they were multitaskers "most of the time." Unsurprisingly, given the predominance of alphabetic literacy in schooling, data related to respondents' uses of print correlates with good grades in school (Rideout, Roberts, & Foehr, 2005, p. 56).

The report builds on older paradigms of media effects research that primarily position children's media use as problematic and other-directed. For example, discussion of the study's results frames contemporary media use as one of "exposure." However, the researchers acknowledge that causality between media use and factors such as "contentedness" cannot yet be inferred and that in spite of the studies' impressive findings, more research about media multitasking in the new media landscape is needed.

The pace of change in almost all communication media continues to call "old" information into question, and to raise new issues. For a generation now documented as devoting more than a quarter of each day to media, it is vitally important to update our information and address the new questions. (Roberts, Foehr, Rideout, & Brodie, 1999)

The study's discussion of students' multitasking echoes concerns of the "continuous partial attention mode" first raised by former Microsoft VP Linda Stone in 1998 (Maxwell, 2002; Tang, 2005, p. 2). In her 2006 keynote address at the O'Reilly Emerging Technology Conference in San Diego, Stone remarked that like technology, continuous partial attention is neither necessarily bad nor good, but instead "it's an adaptive behavior and we are actually on the way to adapting our way beyond it."

Continuous partial attention has been a way of life for many of us. It is a post multitasking behavior. The two are differentiated by the impulse that motivates them. When we multitask, we are motivated by a desire to be more productive and more efficient. In the case of continuous partial attention, we are motivated by a desire to be a live node on the network. We want to connect, we want to effectively scan for opportunity and optimize for the best opportunities—activities or people—in any given moment. This always on, anywhere, anytime, any place era has created an artificial sense of constant crisis. Continuous partial attention, anytime, anywhere, any place technologies, the era of connect, connect, connect, is contributing to a feeling of overwhelm, over-stimulation, and a sense of being unfulfilled.

The new mantra, the new differentiator, the new opportunity for all of us is: improves quality of life. Does this product, service, feature, message—enhance and improve our quality of life? Does it help us protect, filter, create a meaningful connection? Discern? Use our attention as well and as wisely as we possibly can? Seems to me, our opportunity is to move from being knowledge workers to becoming understanding and wisdom workers. (Stone, 2006)

History has shown that the uses of literacy, intertwined with schooling, can have both positive and negative aims. And so the hypothesis that students are tethered to an "e-leash" in continuous partial attention mode is certainly a legitimate research priority. Nonetheless, research evidence cannot be expected to resolve age-old debates about the competing missions of literacy and schooling: vocational, civic, or personal. The trick is to design relevant learning environments that can reconcile and celebrate all of these missions over time. In the meantime, a more positive and optimistic perspective on multitasking users might provide insights into forward-thinking user-centered designs for schooling.

Looking Beyond the Desktop

This is especially true as society moves from situated, networked desktop computers into the uses of smaller, dedicated digital tools, known as mobile autonomous devices (MADs). Anyone who has experienced the frustration of navigating overly complex and user-unfriendly software on a personal computer understands that computers command an inordinate amount of user attention for the simplest of tasks. In contrast, highly specialized computing devices, embedded seamlessly into the environment are designed to perform specialized tasks efficiently as needed. In this way, the MAD concept is less like a software tool kit and more like an extension of the human mind and body. Because they are integrated into the design of buildings and public spaces, these "minicomputers" blend into the environment in a ubiquitous way, giving rise to the term *pervasive computing*.

Former Xerox PARC executive John Seely Brown spotted the trend toward pervasive computing early on. He and co-researcher Mark Weiser position it as a counterbalance to concerns about continual partial attention concept and information overload:

What matters is not technology itself, but its relationship to us. In the past fifty years of computation there have been two great trends in this relationship: the mainframe relationship, and the PC relationship. Today the Internet is carrying us through an era of widespread distributed computing towards the relationship of ubiquitous computing, characterized by deeply imbedding computation in the world. Ubiquitous computing will require a new approach to fitting technology to our lives, an approach we call "calm technology." (Brown & Weiser, 1996)

Pervasive computing already allows people to interact with computer chips embedded into everything from clothing to cars. In educational spaces, pervasive computing means that teachers and learners can interact with content in a ways that seem like a scene from *Harry Potter*. Lights flicker on and users talk with computing devices, which greet them as they approach. Teachers lecture as a whiteboard records, prioritizes, and disseminates key points to students across the globe. Avatars coach, correct, and suggest as students access and reorder digital, multimedia source documents. With a wave of the hand, learners engage with simulated environments to perfect skill in dissection, art or mechanics. A student's online robot searches and retrieves artifacts from vast archives of multimedia source documents. Students distribute and receive feedback about their own, learner-created content from a worldwide audience in real time and virtual space.

Pervasive computing also makes it possible to use the human body as an interface by injecting a chip under the skin. Pet owners use chips of this type to track their pets. Although the uses of avatars in virtual environments has been conceptualized as second "skins," pervasive computing bridges the virtual with the actual environment through the real human body. Like cyborgs, humans can augment their own memories, senses, and intellect with chips inserted under the skin.

As filmed by the BBC in 1998, Kevin Warwick, a professor of cybernetics at the University of Reading MAD Lab, embedded a tiny silicon microchip under his own skin to study the relationship between man and machine. Since then, Professor Warwick continues to experiment on his own body with a device that links his central nervous system to a computerized robot arm via the Internet. By simply moving his hand, he can send neural signals over the Internet to open and close the robot hand. In the future, he plans to embed a chip into his brain to study the uses of mobile autonomous devices to improve his memory, analysis ability, and sensory perception. It is hoped that research of this type can provide important medical benefits such as limb movement to people with severe motor disabilities and tracking devices for Alzheimer patients (Melvin, 2006).

In some cases, people request a syringe-injectable radio frequency identification microchip (RFID) for less serious reasons. In a highly publicized case, patrons of the Baja Beach Clubs in Barcelona, Spain, and Rotterdam, Netherlands, have a Verichip embedded in their arm that will allow them access to a VIP lounge without standing in line and to pay for drinks with a wave of the hand. The VeriChip is offered by Florida-based Applied Digital Solutions (Purohit, 2004).

The Downside of Pervasive Computing

Some of these devices echo the wearable computers described by science fiction writer Vernor Vinge (2006) in *Rainbows End*. In this prescient novel, "wearables" extend the human intellect. The idea that humans will embed or adorn themselves with computer chips is a growing and amusing trend with an alarming downside. Governments, corporations, and other economic and political forces already have the ability to track individuals through GPS systems such as cell phones, as well as to collect, store, and retrieve personal data for all manner of criminal, political, economic, and social reasons. In institutional settings, MADs are more likely to be used as an instrument of surveillance. For example, a school in California abandoned the use of a wearable tracking device for students after community uproar (ACLU,

2005). Similarly, schools across the country have also purchased eye-scanning equipment to keep track of children by scanning unique features of their irises. The equipment was originally developed for prisoners and is now being marketed to track missing children and seniors (Prokop, 2005).

Of related concern, young people are increasingly accustomed to surveillance from cameras, telephones, and GPS systems in a way that 20th Century generations cannot fathom. Surveillance and personal data collection is one aspect of pervasive computing that is considered a normal part of life for people who have known no other system. As a result, it is feared that the trend can accelerate with waning public resistance. For its critics, this aspect of pervasive computing sets up the conditions for Orwellian surveillance never before seen in history. Groups such as the European Union and the Electronic Privacy Information Center in Washington, D.C., are working on policies to manage these technologies (Article 29, 2005; EPIC; EPIC, 2005).

At this juncture, it appears that even though governments can store data about individuals, it is highly possible that most bureaucracies are not yet sophisticated enough to effectively retrieve, manage, analyze, and use the avalanche of information they collect. Nonetheless, data management improves exponentially and the surveillance potential of pervasive computing is a troubling development for those who want to use these technologies for prosocial and educational purposes. Most researchers and policymakers acknowledge that pervasive computing is the wave of the future. As such, it is considered an explosive variable in planning for the design of contemporary learning environments.

Pervasive Computing in Learning Environments

As the move away from situated personal computer labs accelerates, it is inevitable that pervasive computing of this type increasingly permeates learning environments. Cell phones are one familiar example, used during school hours for text messaging, Web surfing, e-mailing, and also as location devices for worried parents.

The uses of digital technologies in academic settings commonly lag behind the models of early adopters in other sectors of society. The problem is that the move to integrate digital literacy tools in schools still depends largely on traditional uses of existing, shared physical spaces, for example, buildings and classrooms. Even contemporary factories are designed in a more modular way. As currently configured, it is difficult for school systems to accommodate and fund a more holistic view of pervasive computing based on the needs, preferences, and prior knowledge of the users. Even as students are moving in the direction of MADs and pervasive computing with wireless computers, GPS systems, and other mobile devices, schools are still installing situated, personal computer labs based on the desktop model.

Although many are beginning to offer laptop programs, handhelds and facilitate other forms of classroom access to a variety of digital tools, it is just as likely that access is available in a lab setting, with managed content and direct instruction. In 1998, about half of the computer access in high schools was available in a computer lab (Anderson & Ronnkvist, 1998, p. 8).

This situated and centralized computing model demonstrates a high degree of intertextuality in that it builds on and parallels the concept of a designated educator at the center of the room. If the design of learning spaces is to be forward-looking and authentic, it is also important that media research studies go beyond quantifying data based on the concept that media use is visible and at the center of the user's attention, for example, the personal computing model. Instead, as literacy tools move to the periphery, concepts and metaphors about the *invisible* and the *peripheral* inform the hypothesis and research variables for ubiquitous computing environments. Just as a camera lens can zoom in and out, through various depths of field, contemporary pervasive computing environments allow learners to strategically shift and prioritize their focus from background (periphery) to foreground information as needed. This skill builds on multitasking abilities while allowing a far greater degree of autonomy and flexibility.

It may even be that when the user's attention is focused on the task at hand and (ideally) not on wrangling with the tool box, time spent with multimedia, virtual environments, and gaming may actually represent a productive, authentic, and engaging activity set that aligns with traditional learning goals. In this regard, pedagogical designs modeled on dedicated peer communities of users in virtual and physical contexts would be useful. In addition, issues of information credibility and relevance, as well as the blend of formal and informal school practices, are areas in need of more research, modeling, testbeds, and discussion.

Emerging research indicates that a combination of humanities and social science research, with a focus on ethnography, is invaluable to studying cognitive processes, multitasking, play, and learning with new media literacies in pervasive computing environments (Weiser, 1993). Collaborative, field-building research of this type is beginning to emerge from groups such as the London Knowledge Lab (London Knowledge Lab, 2007), the Tangible Media Group (Tangible Media Group, 2007), and grantees of the MacArthur Foundation's Digital Media and Learning Initiative (MacArthur, 2007).

As promising practices for ubiquitous computing emerge in school settings, it is also imperative to consider the pressure on schools that have not yet moved far from the textbook. Old conversations about inequities in access to information technologies is moving from issues of tools, texts, and tech support to topics related to literacy practices, intellectual capital, and the wider social uses of IT. The gap between those who can easily navigate "always on, everywhere" technology and those who are hard pressed to tap into these new communication practices is shaping up to be the Digital Divide 3.0.

Bricks, Mortar and Pixels

The average school building in the United States is 42 years old and communities are struggling to design new architectural spaces for learning (Boss, 2001). With the vagaries of funding, political pressures, and the need for more research evidence about the learning potential for small schools, multiliteracies, and open pedagogies, most schools have taken a conservative approach to change. As a result, the integration of new literacies, when it happens, is still based on a "retrofitted access" model.

A more expansive vision, based on interdisciplinary work, would start planning based on the way environments support learning within the context of human interaction. In particular, the interplay between the arts and sciences, central to the uses and creation of digital media, have a long history in the discourse of architecture.

Architecture focuses on the "built world" with an emphasis on design that reconciles the art (aesthetics/form) with science (engineering/functionality). Successful architecture also focuses on the contexts of the built world, thus providing important insights into the intelligent design of human and civic spaces. In effect, architects rely on quantitative and qualitative data about human interaction to customize spaces that "work" in the world. Architecture's balance of form and function with situational contexts helps to reconcile disparate interdisciplinary concepts needed to design learning spaces that accommodate both physical and virtual spaces. Similar research questions, models, and testbeds are essential for rethinking schools around the social contexts for the uses of new literacies.

Building on this insight in his book, *Digital Ground*, architect Malcolm McCullough (2004) develops a human-centered theory of place for interaction design. He notes that the design of architectural space develops from a consideration of the body within time and space (McCullough, 2004). As such, understanding of the built world is successful only when it functions as a conduit for authentic human interaction and expectations. Personal computing is giving way to pervasive computing primarily because the PC model violates the comfort zone of human users. It provides both too much and not enough: too many features, not enough power; too much mental focus needed for too small a task. In this way, the last 20 years of personal computing is akin to the TV-Stereo-Radio-Clock units of decades past. Although smaller and smaller, computers cram feature after feature in one box, whether or not users need them, want them, or can use them efficiently. Pervasive computing breaks up the feature-accumulation cycle and attempts to customize human need with simpler, more precise functionality in the natural world. Increasingly, this can be done through "ambient, haptic and environmentally embedded interface elements" (McCullough, 2004, p. 67).

The architectural metaphor extends beyond the design of physical spaces to the design of virtual spaces, in particular the information architecture of user interfaces. As McCullough (2004) notes, virtual communities on the Internet are not actual places that people visit, since users' bodies are firmly, geographically situated in the physical realm, using an interface on a desktop computer. Instead, information architecture creates an artificial environment that mimics the metaphors of place; with all of the contextual cues that tell the user what kind of environment they are inhabiting and therefore inform and influence social behavior within the space. McCullough argues that especially in pervasive computing, "location still matters," He goes on to observe, "...If architecture and interaction design are to benefit one another as disciplines, they must work together on location models" (McCullough, 2004, p. 97). "Interaction design must serve the basic human need for getting into place. Like architecture, and increasingly as a part of architecture, interaction design affects how each of us inhabits the physical world" (McCullough, 2004, p. 172).

The Competing Contexts of Learning

The move toward pervasive computing presents the usual crossroad of challenges and opportunities for traditional educational institutions. Conversations about the design of "smart" learning environments come at a timely juncture as information access reaches a tipping point, new institutions replace aging public school structures, and as a new digitally savvy generation of teachers prepares to replace a retiring teacher work force. Although a customer satisfaction model is not the norm in educational bureaucracies, in many cases students and their parents have demanded institutional change, especially at the elementary and secondary level.

Nonetheless, from the over-reliance on print journals in the university tenure track to costly purchases of textbooks at the K-12 level, institutions have yet to fully embrace efforts to expand alphabetic traditions. Traditional academic institutions learned the hard way that bold and well-intentioned efforts can backfire. In the main, as they juggle competing missions and visions and until the dust settles on the digital revolution, their efforts remain tentative and ad hoc.

In the 1970s, architects designed open classrooms to accommodate assumptions about the benefits of child-centered, hands-on, interdisciplinary, and collaborative learning strategies. In spite of the modernist beauty of these buildings, open class-rooms proved to be outside the comfort zone of many educators who worked in them (Cuban, 2004). Because pedagogy, intellectual resources, and cultural values were not aligned, the physical spaces simply did not meet the needs of the human beings who worked and learned in these environments. In a personal example from the late 1990s:

I visited a school in Flagstaff, Arizona whose design was based on the pedagogy of the open classroom. The design was spacious, clean, and beautifully lit. The building featured a circular concourse, designed with minimalist interior walls. As I walk the concourse looking for the principal (who is walking far ahead looking futilely for me), crude sheets of plywood or moveable chalkboards create ugly, makeshift walls to disrupt the architectural beauty and define designated classroom spaces. In short, the school is a prime example of form over function. Because the architectural design did not reflect the needs and values of the school's inhabitants, it obviously became an expensive source of frustrations for teachers and learners. As a result, educators and administrators in this school came up with numerous, aesthetically questionable "workarounds" to return their classrooms to teacher-directed group instruction with quiet students sitting in rows before blackboards and focused on textbooks. (Tyner, 1995)

In another example, the Miami Museum of Science created a multi-year program for middle school girls to create virtual reality environments with VR software. Collaborative learning and peer instruction were central to the project's pedagogical design. As such, architectural contexts became a related and unforeseen variable in the project's implementation. The intensive weekend and summer program took place in a state-of-the-art computer lab designed with connectivity, personal computers, relevant software, and large octagonal tables complete with individual workstations. When users were seated at the table, it was believed that the monitors would inhibit interaction. And so, the monitors and keypads were embedded into the tables below eye level, thus making a clean line of sight across the table. In spite of attention to the design of the computer lab and the overwhelming success of the girls' VR projects, subtle lessons were learned about the need for rigorous front-end analysis and testing before integrating digital tools in the learning space. For example, scale was important. The tables proved to be too large for cross-conversation, inhibiting peer instruction, teamwork, and collaboration beyond the users' immediate seatmates. Although well intentioned and beautiful, they inadvertently proved to be counter-productive to the pedagogy (Tyner, 2003).

New Visions for Learning

In contrast, San Antonio Communication Arts High School in San Antonio, Texas, was designed around the central concept of multiliteracies. Founded in 1995, Communications Arts High School is a magnet school housed on the campus of William Howard Taft High School that specializes in multimedia, communications, and creative writing. Staff and administrators are committed to immersion in both analyzing and producing a wide range of media that adhere to Texas Essential Knowledge and Skills academic standards for "reading, writing, listening, speaking, viewing, and representing" in English, Language Arts, and Reading (TEKS, 2007). Designed as a "small school," the high school strives to customize the curriculum for students. A new school building was designed to provide easy access for collaborative work, contains both labs and mobile equipment throughout, and provides tables, lighting, and wide corridors to support project-based work. The school strives to accommodate "viewing and doing," as well as reading and writing. It integrates traditional with innovative design features and, as a result, was built with wide community consensus. In 2006, Communication Arts High School was ranked 64th on *Newsweek Magazine's* Top 1200 High Schools.

Other schools based on the small school concept are leading the way. Although still heavily influenced by traditional design elements, these schools have the potential to take the next step as pervasive computing accelerates. Northwest Regional Educational Laboratory devoted an entire issue to the way that school architecture builds successful learning environments (NWREL, 2001). Since the design of schools is a community project, researchers acknowledge the tensions that must be resolved as many interests come into play:

Teachers want flexible spaces that will accommodate more active classrooms, weave in the latest technology, allow them to collaborate with their colleagues, but also give them workplace basics such as storage cabinets and nearby restrooms. Parents often ask for attention to safety and smaller class sizes. School boards worry about escalating costs for buildings and the land to build them on. And community members, looking at the investment they're asked to shoulder, clamor for buildings that can be used around the clock by people of all ages. (Boss, 2001)

The influx of user-created content on the Internet plays up the need for spaces that accommodate student production, as well as viewing of digital materials. Flexible, modular spaces are the key. For example, students need workspaces with plugs, controlled lighting, controlled audio, and recording equipment need for collaborative and creative work, akin to a television studio. Conversely, they also need darkened, collective screening spaces to view, exhibit, and discuss media, for example, an auditorium. They also need well-lighted and private spaces for reading, writing, and producing print and artwork, like an artists' studio. They need spaces to exercise and rejuvenate. They also need spaces to network, play, and socialize. And, given climate change and the expense of utilities, it would be nice if new school buildings were efficient, sustainable, and "green." Architecture of this type is designed for human need, but it need not be inefficient or more costly to build and maintain than traditional school buildings. It does, however, begin with some community consensus about the guiding principles for the school's educational mission.

Until this type of architecture becomes the norm, other important innovations are in progress in schools across the United States. Examples of schools that position multiliteracies for teaching and learning at the center of their curriculum include Rowland Heights (CA) Animation Program, Educational Video Center in New York City, and Dayton Technology Design High School in Dayton, Ohio. Unfortunately, it is difficult to generalize about the extent of digital literacy practices in schools since state departments of education would be hard pressed to present a coherent database of sites and practices that explicitly support digital literacy practices. Until bureaucracies track data about new literacy practices, school design will be based on anecdotal information about what "works." In the interim, nonprofit organizations such as the National Alliance of Media Arts and Culture (Tyner & Mokund, 2004)), the Animation World Network (AWN, 2007), and Cable in the Classroom (Gallagher, 2007) are doing their best to collect information about new media production and analysis in formal and informal educational environments in the United States.

Youth media programs that operate from informal education spaces have fewer political mandates and therefore more flexibility for experimentation. As a result, networks for media practitioners have evolved to share information over time (e.g., Listen Up! at www.listenup.org). In a poll conducted for the National Alliance for Media Arts and Culture (Tyner & Mokund, 2004), youth media organizations identified supports and barriers to their organizational sustainability and spread. One of the supports identified was the need for strategic partnerships between nonprofit youth media organizations and public schools. Cases that bridge informal and formal uses of digital media represent fertile territory to evaluate best practices that contribute to the spread of multiliteracies across different kinds of learning environments.

Established programs in K-12, as well as university programs such as the Carnegie-Mellon M.A. in video gaming (Pausch, 2004), provide rich opportunities for research about the nature and design of relevant digital literacy practices. Emerging programs of this type are also interesting to observe for information about institutional and structural reform and the viability of change agents on the new media horizon.

In particular, recent efforts by the Los Angeles Unified School District Arts Education Branch to require a host of graduation requirements related to digital media environments is of great interest to educators. In addition to pre-, post-, and production skills and knowledge, the requirements detail learning about digital media analysis, the contexts of media production, and immersion in virtual environments (LAUSD, 2004). This 10-year plan is still in process, shaped by a national study group of experts and scholars. Nonetheless, educators who are in the process of designing their own digital learning spaces can immediately use its detailed curriculum guidance.

The Future of Teaching

As baby boomers retire from the teaching profession, the repercussions have yet to be seen. In spite of hype around the media savvy digital natives, it is unclear if the next generation of teachers has the ability or support to redesign learning environments around multiliteracy concepts. It is likely that a new generation of teachers will demand "every day" literacy tools both inside and outside the traditional classroom. However, required courses in preservice programs in informatics and digital literacy are still rare in teacher credentialing programs.

Moreover, questions still remain about both the specific and interdisciplinary skills needed to teach and learn with digital literacy tools. Existing and emerging research related to digital authorship and reception is beginning to shape a vision for critical literacy practices of the future. These include theory and practice around educational uses for digital poetics, remix genre, vast archives of open source materials, gaming, programming, and the restructuring of information through database applications.

Educational institutions that ignore the prevalence of new literacy practices will undoubtedly survive on a hollow half-life of tradition. In the meantime, schools that reflect students' preference for a wider range of contemporary literacy tools are working to redefine the mission of modern schooling. The architect McCullough (2004) posits that "rejecting technology outright is not an option...Even the most left-bank anti-technologists regrets it when the electric power goes out," (p. 213). The mission is to shape socially and ethically relevant learning environments that serve the common good. Literacy, in all its forms, is the crosscutting feature that reconciles pedagogy, intellectual resources, and the built world. As such, literacy in the context of pervasive computing is central to the design of schools—at least for as long as the power keeps flowing.

References

American Civil Liberties Union (ACLU). (2005, February 16). *Victory for students, parents and civil liberties groups - company announces it will end tracking pilot program.* Retrieved October 10, 2007, from http://www.aclunc.org/news/press_releases/victory_for_students,_parents_and_civil_liberties_groups_-_company_announces_it_will_end_tracking_pilot_program.shtml

Anderson, R.E., & Ronnkvist, A. (1998). The presence of computers in American schools. In Henry J. Becker (Ed.), *Teaching, learning and computing: 1998 national survey #1.* Irvine, CA: Center for Research on Information Technology and Organizations, University of California, Irvine and the University of

Minnesota. Retrieved October 10, 2007, from http://www.crito.uci.edu/tlc/find-ings/Computers_in_American_Schools/report2_text_tables.pdf

Animation World Network (AWN). (2007). Animation school database. Retrieved October 10, 2007, from http://schools.awn.com

Article 29 Data Protection Working Party, European Parliament and the Council of Europe. (2005, January 19). Working document on data protection issues related to rfid technology. Retrieved October 10, 2007, from http://ec.europa.eu/justice_home/fsj/privacy/docs/wpdocs/2005/wp105_en.pdf

Boss, S. (2001). Breaking out of the box. *Northwest Education Magazine, 6,* 4. Portland, OR: Northwest Regional Educational Laboratory. Retrieved October 10, 2007, from http://www.nwrel.org/nwedu/summer01/breakingout.html

Brown, J.S., & Weiser, M. (1996, October 5). *The coming of age of calm technology.* Retrieved October 10, 2007, from http://www.ubiq.com/hypertext/weiser/ac-mfuture2endnote.htm

Cuban, L. (2004, Spring). The open classroom. *Education Next,* 68-71. Palo Alto, CA: Stanford University, the Hoover Institution.

Electronic Privacy Information Center (EPIC). *Radio frequency identification (RFID) systems.* Retrieved October 10, 2007, from http://www.epic.org/privacy/rfid/

Electronic Privacy Information Center (EPIC). (2005). *Verichip.* Retrieved December 30, 2006, from http://www.epic.org/privacy/rfid/verichip.html

Gallagher, F. (2007, June 23). *The status of media literacy: Insights from a survey of state departments of education.* Report presented at the Association for a Media Literate America Conference, St. Louis, MO: Cable in the Classroom.

Gootman, E. (2004, April 3). Inventory shows an uneven distribution of school computers. *New York Times.* Retrieved October 10, 2007, from http://www.nytimes.com/2004/04/03/education/03school.html?ex=1082088000&en=f53fe6c3653cf0c2&ei=5070

Jackson, L.A., Ervin, K.S., Gardner, P.D., & Schmitt, N. (2001). The racial digital divide: Motivational, affective, and cognitive correlates of Internet use. *Journal of Applied Social Psychology, 31*(10), 2019-2046.

LAUSD. (2004, January). Interim report: Results of study group workshops January 13-14, 2004. Los Angeles, CA: Los Angeles Unified School District, Arts Education Branch.

London Knowledge Lab. London: Institute of Education & Birbeck, University of London. Retrieved October 10, 2007, from http://www.lkl.ac.uk/research/index.html

MacArthur Foundation's Digital Media and Learning Initiative. Chicago, IL: MacArthur Foundation. Retrieved October 10, 2007, from http://www.digitallearning.macfound.org/site/c.enJLKQNlFiG/b.2029199/k.BFC9/Home.htm

Maxwell, J.H. (2002, January). Stop the net I want to get off. *Inc Magazine*. Retrieved October 10, 2007, from http://www.inc.com/magazine/20020101/23805. html

McCullough, M. (2004). *Digital ground: Architecture, pervasive computing, and environmental knowing*. Cambridge, MA: MIT Press.

Melvin, D. (2006, December 23). Age of the cyborg crawling closer, chip by chip. *Austin American Statesman*, A5.

Morgan, J.N., & VanLengen, C.A. (2005). The digital divide and k-12 student. *The Journal of Issues in Informing Science and Information Technology, 2*, 705-722.

NCES. (2003). *Internet access in U.S. public schools and classrooms: 1994-2002*. Washington, DC: National Center for Education Statistics. Retrieved October 10, 2007, from http://nces.ed.gov/pubs2004/2004011.pdf

NTIA. (2000). *Falling through the net: Towards digital inclusion*. Washington, DC: National Telecommunications and Information Administration. Retrieved October 10, 2007, from http://search.ntia.doc.gov/pdf/fttn00.pdf

NWREL. (2001, Spring). Designs for learning: School architecture. *Northwest Education Magazine*, 6, 4. Portland, OR: Northwest Regional Educational Laboratory. Retrieved October 10, 2007, from http://www.nwrel.org/nwedu/summer01/index.html

Pausch, R. (2004). *An academic's field guide to electronic arts*. Carnegie Mellon University. Retrieved October 10, 2007, from www.etc.cmu.edu/about/press_articles/EAFieldGuide.pdf

Prokop, M. (2005, June 14). Biometrics and kids. *Computer World Blogs*. Retrieved October 10, 2007, from http://www.computerworld.com/blogs/node/356

Purohit, C. (2004, June 9). Technology gets under clubbers' skin. *CNN International. com*. Retrieved October 10, 2007, from http://edition.cnn.com/2004/WORLD/europe/06/09/spain.club/

Rideout, V.R., Roberts, D.F., & Foehr, U.G. (2005, March). *Generation M: Media in the lives of 8-18 year-olds*. Menlo Park, CA: Kaiser Family Foundation. Retrieved October 10, 2007, from http://www.kff.org/entmedia/7251.cfm

Roberts, D.F., Foehr, U.G., Rideout, V.J., & Brodie, M. (1999). *Kids and media @ the new millennium*. Menlo Park, CA: Kaiser Family Foundation.

Stone, L. (2006, March 7). *Attention: The *real* aphrodisiac*. Keynote presented at the O'Reilly Emerging Technology Conference, San Diego, CA. Retrieved October 10, 2007, from http://radar.oreilly.com/archives/2006/03/etech_linda_stone_1.html

Tang, J.C. (2005). *Ubiquitous computing: Productivity at the expense of social good*. San Jose, CA: IBM. Retrieved October 10, 2007, from http://www.

vs.inf.ethz.ch/events/ubisoc2005/UbiSoc%202005%20submissions/04-Tang-John-NEW.pdf

Tangible Media Group. Cambridge, MA: Massachusetts Institute of Technology. Retrieved October 10, 2007, from http://tangible.media.mit.edu/projects/ambientroom

Texas Essential Knowledge and Skills (TEKS). (2007). Retrieved October 10, 2007, from http://www.tea.state.tx.us/rules/tac/chapter110/index.html

Tyner, K. (1995). *Notes from the Arizona initiatives for children.* San Francisco, CA: Far West Labs.

Tyner, K. (2003). NSF evaluation report for GREAT! Miami, FL: The Miami Museum of Science. Retrieved October 10, 2007, from http://www.miamisci.org/great/reports.html

Tyner, K., & Mokund, R. (2004). Mapping the field: A study of youth media organizations. In K.Tyner (Ed.), *A closer look 2003: Focus on youth media.* San Francisco, CA: NAMAC.

Vinge, V. (2006). *Rainbows End.* NY: Tor Books.

Weiser, M. (1993, January). The world is not a desktop. *Interactions, 1,* 7-8. Retrieved October 10, 2007, from http://doi.acm.org/10.1145/174800.174801

Chapter XV

Media Education, Digital Production, and New Media:
What Do Teachers Need to Know?

Andrew Burn, University of London, UK

Abstract

The aim of this chapter is to reflect about the teachers' training in media education. This training in England is quite insufficient and almost based on the transfer of reading competencies: this means that is does not prepare the teacher to work with digital media, normally characterized by authoring activities. Starting from the experience of a master degree developed in the London Institute of Education, the chapter tries to show how many of the problems involved in this training were discussed and solved with the teachers enrolled in the master. The hypotesis presented is based on the mix between theory and practice, the creative activity of the participants, and the centrality of the role of the learner.

Introduction

Like most countries in Europe, the UK has no formal provision for the training of media teachers as subject specialists. Media education, along with drama, is provided for in the national curriculum within English; so in principle, English teachers are trained to teach English, Media, and Drama. However, provision here largely depends on the expertise and enthusiasm of specific training providers in universities. While some centres provide substantial elements of media training within their courses, others may provide a bare minimum. In all cases, the emphasis is on media as an element of English, especially at key stage 4 (11 to 14 years old). Here, the focus is on the analysis of media texts, since media is represented within the reading section of the English national curriculum.

This leaves many gaps. There is no training for primary teachers, and the media element within English does not exist in the primary curriculum. There is no training for the specialist examination courses in media studies at GCSE and A-Level (the public exams for 16, 17 and 18 year-olds). And there is no real provision to train teachers in approaches to media production, which is, as many have pointed out, the "writing" side of the media literacy coin (Buckingham, 2003; Burn & Durran, 2007).

With the advent of digital authoring tools for the production of media texts, it is this last omission which has become most pressing in recent years in the UK. Most English teachers are happy to include an aspect of media analysis in their courses; and these are frequently analyses of advertising, newspapers, or film (Hart & Hicks, 2002). Far fewer are equipped to embark on complex forms of media production, and may feel daunted by the prospect of using digital video cameras, editing softwares, or animation softwares.

More generally, there is a need for teachers to acquire what in the UK is called "subject knowledge," as well as a sense of the pedagogies of the subject. Here, then, they need to learn about traditions of media education and media literacy. The model provided by Buckingham (2003) in *Media Education* gives a good overview of what this might mean. It includes notions of critical literacy, creative practice, the use of digital media, and the importance of popular culture. It spells out the conceptual framework around which there is a good degree of international consensus, and which includes concepts of representation, institution, and audience. While these are foundational concepts, and Buckingham's model has a valuable stabilising effect on a subject which has never become fully realised through the apparatus of the mandatory curriculum and its training regimes, it is also important to recognise difference. Legitimate variations of approach and emphasis exist in current media education practice; and to some degree, these reflect both the background of particular teachers and the curricular location of media education in particular schools.

In this chapter, then, I will describe ways in which I and colleagues at the Institute of Education in London have worked with teachers on our Masters' programme to address some of these questions, looking first at a general overview of relevant courses teachers can follow, then considering in more detail a course in digital video production, and finally reflecting on what the future might hold.

A Masters' Experience of Media Education: Plugging the Gaps

Currently, then, there is a need for professional development courses which "plug the gaps" left by initial teacher training. There are a number of high-quality courses offered by well-known providers in the field of media education, notably the English and Media Centre, the British Film Institute, and Film Education. At the Institute of Education, we have developed a range of courses at Master's level, within the MA in media, culture and communication. This chapter will draw on the experience of some of these courses, and the work of teachers who are students on our programme.

The MA includes a module taught by the British Film Institute which aims to introduce teachers to these ideas if they are approaching media education with little or no experience. It takes them through the conceptual framework, and models how appropriate pedagogies might be developed around the key concepts, around different media, and around processes of both analysis and production.

This kind of course helps to fill in the gaps left by the brief experience of media education work on English teacher training courses. However, it is still a relatively short experience, which cannot fully replace a dedicated training in media education. Our hope is that teachers who complete our whole MA programme will have experienced more deeply some of the key areas relevant to how media education is developing today. Some of these areas are problematic, either rehearsing old questions which remain unresolved, or provoking new questions about an uncertain future. Some of these will be raised in the final section of the chapter. In the meantime, I will sketch out what an imaginary student on our MA might encounter, through a series of optional courses.

First, then, they might follow our core module in cultural theory. Here, they will engage with classical Marxist ideology theory, classical semiotic approaches to textuality, the birth and development of cultural studies and the audience research tradition, post-structuralist and postmodernist theory, and neo-Marxist theories of discourse. Teachers on the course are encouraged to think how thinkers such as Raymond Williams, Walter Benjamin, Louis Althusser, or Jean Baudrillard are relevant to the work of the media classroom. Among important theoretical questions they explore is the structure-agency dilemma, which stretches from classical Marxism to current cultural studies and sociology (Tudor, 1999). This question reveals a constant uncertainty for the media teacher. While in the UK, the emphasis recently has been very much on the cultural agency of young people, particularly in relation to their expressive use of digital authoring technologies and the Internet, it is impossible to teach a topic like advertising without considering the effects on consumers of such concentrations of representational resources in the hands of powerful multinational interests. Also, teachers who have drifted into media education from other disciplines (by definition most of them), may have inherited hazily-conceived residues of older protectionist approaches, still often dominant in popular discourses and in certain research traditions. A theoretical course like this, then, gives them the opportunity to reconsider how young people engage with the media, and whether they really need protecting.

Second, they might go on to do a module in Film Theory and educational practice, co-taught with the British Film Institute. Here, they can choose from theories of film semiotics, genre, narrative, and audience, read the work of theorists and researchers in these fields, and interpret their work in the context of their plans for classroom projects, usually for more advanced courses such as A-Level media studies or film studies. While some teachers may have undertaken course on semiotics, or structuralism, or narratology, as part of their undergraduate degrees, very few have a detailed idea of how these theories are developed by film theorists. This course looks at examples of theory and research in film, such as Barthes' (1978) work on film narrative, Metz's (1974) approach to film semiotics, or Steve Neale's (2000) work on genre. However, it also looks at pedagogic research in media studies classrooms, exploring how teachers mediate difficult theory for older students.

Third, they might follow a course on computer games and education. This does not pursue current dominant arguments for games in the curriculum as remediators of curriculum content—as enjoyable learning devices. Rather, it explores how games can be studied within a media education paradigm: as cultural objects like film, television, or comicstrips. On the one hand, the course asks students to consider how their familiar notions of narrative are both extended and challenged by computer games, especially adventure and role-playing games. On the other hand, it introduces them to the domain of "ludology," the study of games and play, and central concepts which govern the rule-bound systems of game sequences.

The course also asks them to consider how the analysis of games might grow into the production of games. While access to the production of video, music, Web page, and graphic design has been relatively easy with the advent of editing, authoring, and composition softwares, this has never been really true for games, which have always required some degree of programming skills, beyond the reach of media classrooms, teachers, and students. However, during a recent research project our research centre has developed, with a software company, Immersive Education, an authoring tool for computer games for use in schools. We are able, then, to give teachers this course a taste of the benefits of such software, and the ways in which game design of this kind allows students to gain a conceptual grasp of game systems, rules, and economies. One teacher was able to take the software back to his school. His essay indicates how production work with games enabled creative forms of identity play for students whose self-images are always related to disability:

Another key concept that we examined was the creation of new identities. This was by far the most enjoyable aspect of the making games process. The students attempted to select and create different characters, incorporate their own media texts. At a very basic level, this action allowed the students to create a character, which was not how they perceived themselves, therefore creating a new identity and representation of themselves. ... Students commented that normally they would never have the opportunity to display images of themselves in a computer game as their image (disability) is not normally an aspect that is published eagerly in computer games.

Finally, as well as choosing further experiences of digital design (in a multimedia design module, and a digital video module, described below), students might continue with modules which explore the media cultures of young children or teenagers.

The conclusion of the course, like all Masters' degrees, involves a dissertation. For many teachers, this is an opportunity to conduct an action research project in their own school. Examples have been a study of a group of disaffected boys working on an animation project (Henson, 2005); a multimodal analysis of horror film sequences made by 13-year-old girls within ICT (Doyle, 2005); and a study of the cultural experience of film among a group of A-level Film Studies students (Plowright, in progress). These studies give a clear idea of how teachers use such research to reflect on their current practice, but also take on board new ideas which change what they do or how they perceive it. For example, one teacher found that her school's current approach to creativity, dominated by psychological accounts, could be complemented by the more cultural emphasis typical of media studies. Another found that semiotic analysis of student videos allowed a systematic emphasis on meaning which technology-dominated ICT pedagogies had no way of addressing. Another found that it was important to recognise students' own cultural experience of the media more, rather than displacing it by the choice of texts prescribed by the exam board.

The next section will look in more detail at the course in digital video production.

Making Digital Videos

Seven years ago, I began planning, with Mark Reid of the British Film Institute, a modular course at Master's level in response to a need expressed by teachers for help with the use of digital video, then a very new technology in most secondary schools. The module became part of the Institute of Education's MA in Media, Culture, and Communication, though it has continued to be delivered by the BFI as an independent course for teachers who wish only to gain expertise in this specific field, rather than completing a whole MA.

It was evident that the need existed. The course recruited approximately 50 teachers in its first year, and has continued to be the biggest module in our MA. There were three distinct constituencies among our students. The largest, as we had anticipated, was teachers of English and Media who realised the importance of digital video production work with their students, but had never used editing software before, and wanted an introduction. The second group was teachers of specialist media courses in Further Education (16-19), who often had expertise in the use of editing softwares, and wanted to develop this further, and to explore the theoretical aspects of such work. The third (a very small group) were technicians supporting such courses in Further Education, and in some cases Higher Education). Typically, this group had advanced expertise in editing softwares, and in some cases professional experience, but had never had the chance to gain accreditation of their expertise, or to study theoretical aspects of moving image production.

The module is made up of two successive courses. The first introduces teachers to classical theories of editing, in particular montage theory on the one hand, and the so-called continuity system on the other. Students are provided with readings which explore these models, such as extracts from the standard Film Studies textbook, Bordwell and Thompson's *Film Art* (2001). There is a focus on the editing of short forms of film, since these are the most popular genres for production in schools for the obvious practical reasons of time constraint. Much media production work in UK schools, then, consists of the making of TV adverts, film trailers, introductory or title sequences for films, and music videos (see Fraser & Oram, 2003, for a detailed practical account of how such work can be undertaken in schools). The course contains, then, an article by Carol Vernallis from the British journal *Screen* (Vernallis, 2001), looking at the form of the music video, and theorising it in terms of montage and continuity editing theory.

The first section of the course leads up to a practical assignment: the editing of a trailer for the Orson Welles (1959) film *Touch of Evil*. Again, the rationale here is that this kind of short form is typical of the projects undertaken in school media courses. Also, however, this film has its own interesting history in terms of editing. The original release of the film was edited by the studio, which had sacked Welles, who responded with a 50-page memo complaining about the studio cut, and detailing the changes he would wish to see. In recent years, a restoration project has been undertaken, in which a team (including the eminent editor Walter Murch) revised the film as much as possible in accordance with Welles' wishes. During the course, then, students are shown both the restored version of the film, and a documentary about the restoration process, including detailed accounts of editing work involved.

The second section of the course looks at both filming and editing. It includes classic theories of editing, such as Pudovkin on the use of asynchronous sound in film. The practical assignment at the end requires students in groups to develop a plan for a title sequence for an imaginary film noir. They plan, storyboard, script, shoot, and edit their sequences.

In terms of editing software, two considerations are made. First, which editing softwares teachers already have in their schools. Second, what level of sophistication they require, depending on their prior experience. Complete beginners are introduced to editing on Apple's i-movie; more experienced participants are offered either Adobe Premiere or Final Cut Pro.

Finally, in the last part of the course, students read research articles in the use of digital video in the classroom and other relevant topics, such as the nature of group work in media production, and the nature of creativity in relation to practical media work. They interpret and evaluate these accounts, considering them in the light of their own practical work on the course, and their work in the classroom.

What, then, can we say they have gained from this kind of course? I propose three broad headings under which the benefits of such work for media teachers can be considered: connecting theory and practice, creative digital work, and the learner experience.

Connecting Theory and Practice

There are two kinds of theory in this course. One is pedagogic theory, covering areas such as the social nature of group production (Buckingham, Grahame, & Sefton-Green, 1995), the semiotic use of digital video by Media Studies students in schools (Burn & Reed, 1999), and the nature of creativity in digital video work (Reid, Burn, & Parker, 2002). The second is classical editing theory, as referred to earlier in the chapter. For many teachers, a rudimentary grasp of the "grammar of film," in effect, the basic conventions of filming and editing in the continuity style, is all they have been able to pick up. Others have already encountered more theoretical accounts. Whatever the case, this is an opportunity to match complex theories of editing practice, such as Bordwell and Thompson's (2001) typology of relations in editing, or Eisenstein's theory of montage, with their own creative work. As is the case with their own students in school, the exploration of such concepts through the construction of a piece of edited film allows a complex and profound grasp of the concepts in a way no textbook or process of film analysis can provide. This extract from one student's essay, for example, shows the detailed way in which he has understood the concept of montage by relating Eisensteinian theory to the juxtapositions of shots in his own trailer:

We then returned back to implying narrative by placing shots in conflict. Welles looks down and chews on his candy bar, which establishes something significant has been said or realised and the cut implies this has some connection with the narrative in the proceeding shots. His downward movement is echoed in the next shot by Leigh lying back into her bed, and in a contrasting relaxed manner in a change of setting (and clothes) with obvious connotations. Whilst her motion marks a progression to the next 'episode', it also helps to imply a temporal connection to the previous action and the link is suggested between his appetite for food and sex. This is also reinforced by the introduction and duration of the new chord in the music.

Our methods echo Vernallis' assessment of Eisenstein:

Eisenstein gave the word montage a special sense, to signify the way in which two shots edited together could create a new meaning that could not inhere in either shot alone. Eisensteinian montage, like the Kuleshov experiment, is predicated on the absence or incompleteness of meaning, but it establishes connections based on conceptual relationships. (Vernallis, 2001, p. 36)

Two points are important here. First, while this teacher had a basic grasp of what continuity and montage styles of editing were, he had the opportunity to extend and deepen his reading and conceptual grasp of the complexities of these notions. The article he cites by Carol Vernallis (2001), for example, is a sophisticated application of these theories of editing to the compressed, intense form of the music video. Second, the concepts have been worked through in practice, and applied to new meanings created through montage in the equally compressed form of the trailer. The relation between theory and practice, and its justification in terms of Vygostkyan models of learning and creativity, is something we routinely argue for school students—teachers experience it much more rarely (Vygotsky, 1931/1998, 1978).

Digital Creative Work

Many of these teachers, even those with some prior experience of editing softwares, had never actually made their own piece of creative moving image work. In the UK, this is a common feature of media and English teaching: media teachers do not see themselves as practising film-makers, any more than English teachers see themselves as practising poets or novelists. Both subject areas have in the past been constructed as analytical disciplines; and both have their origins, in the UK, in literary studies. However, we also have a smaller number of primary teachers as students, who are even less likely to have actually experienced practical editing work themselves, as this student notes:

Being a novice at media making (editing in particular) and apprehensive about using the technology, I found myself in a similar situation to that of my primary aged pupils when they are asked to complete a task which requires them to move in to unfamiliar territory: I felt vulnerable.

The advent of digital authoring softwares has begun to move the emphasis from analysis to production in recent years, though the motivations to shift media education into a more creative mode are of course social. Just as in society the boundary between media production and consumption has been blurred, with consumers and audiences beginning to make their own products and display them through social networks such as YouTube, so schools have become increasingly interested in what their students can produce, as much as how they can analyse media texts. In addition, in the UK, there has been a policy emphasis on the importance of the creative industries. The creation by the government of media specialist schools was notable for its choice of terminology: the schools (now about 40 in number) are called "media arts colleges," not media studies or media education schools. The emphasis on the arts relates to policy perceptions of the importance of preparing future workers in the media industries. Similarly, the launch of the new media regulator, OFCOM, which has a responsibility for the development of media literacy in the UK, led to their own definition which constructed media literacy as the ability to access, understand, and *create* media texts. Here, the value of creating is as much to do with expressive opportunities as part of fulfilling lives for citizens as with possible professional roles.

For all these reasons, media education in the UK has begun to move a little away from its origins in English, and a little more towards the Arts subjects. But while Art teachers have always seen themselves, in some sense, as artists, and music teachers as musicians, no such tradition exists for media teachers, as we have seen. In a small way, this course has offered at least the beginnings of that opportunity for some of the teachers.

In one sense, this is to do with professional identity. For media teachers to see themselves as media-makers is a change in how they perceive their professional roles and their professional selves. It is the equivalent of courses for English and Drama teachers which encourage them to write poetry or develop group-devised drama. It is an attempt to overcome the sense of lack in teaching about the creative arts without practising them.

In another sense, however, it is an opportunity to reflect on what it means to be creative in the context of media production. Media education has an uneasy relationship with the idea of creativity. Buckingham has pointed out how early pioneers of media education in the UK viewed the idea of creativity with suspicion, as something which might obscure what was perceived as the main function of the subject, to unmask ideological meanings (Buckingham, 2003). The debate about creativity in media education is part of a wider debate in the UK about creativity in education, which seeks to move away from elitist post-Romantic notions of artistic genius towards more inclusive, democratic notions of everyday creativity, or "little-c" creativity (Craft, 2002). In a recent study by my own research centre, we have proposed that understandings of creativity in education can be seen as "rhetorics," which make claims about how creativity relates to educational achievement and to broader social values (Banaji & Burn, 2007). Within these rhetorics can be seen wide contradictions: between cognitivist and culturalist views of creativity; between views of creativity as a special artistic function and views of creativity as part of everyday life; between views of creativity as pro-social and collaborative and views of more subversive, individualistic, even antisocial creative enterprise.

Caught up in these conflicting rhetorics, teachers are in danger of confusion. In the arts (including, for our purposes, the media arts), they might be caught between popular views of the film-maker—or even game-designer—as creative artist and policy-inspired views of creativity as a form of collaborative problem-solving, or as a kind of cognitive booster. In this digital video course, then, we provided students with readings about creativity, encouraging them to reflect in a more informed way on their own work and on their classroom teaching.

This teacher, for instance, considers what kinds of process her group has undergone during the filming and editing of their film introduction:

Skills which are realised during production include generating ideas, making connections, using the imagination, evaluating, reflecting, reasoning, decision making, analysing, problem-solving, problem-identification, communicating, self-expression, metacognition. All of these skills are necessary for creativity to take place (Craft, 2002; DfES/DCMS, 1999; Fontana, 1995; Sharples, 1999). For example during the continuity project myself and my colleagues where continuously evaluating our project as we edited shots as well as reasoning about the order of shots, effects and transitions. I think that during my experience, theory and production work enjoyed a reciprocal relationship with one mode informing the other, this reflects the recursive learning which can take place where DVP is used. This mirrors Tyner's (1998) theory that in order for learning to be enhanced and creativity to take place, acquisition, dependent on apprenticeship must occur.

The positive aspect of this account, perhaps, is that it moves away from the vague perceptions of creativity as a mysterious liberating force which we found in earlier research into teacher's views of creativity and digital video production (Reid et al., 2002). This teacher is conceiving of her creative work in terms of skills, and, importantly, is perceiving creativity as a rational process involving evaluation and collaboration. She is also relating it to learning, arguing that creativity develops through recursive processes, and, citing Kathleen Tyner (1998), involves certain kinds of cognitive apprenticeship.

She goes on to consider how her new perceptions of creativity might impact on her classroom practice:

In terms of my own practice in school I need to work towards achieving a balance between the two, as rather than not having enough practical work I had too much with very little theory; this was however prior to our continuity project. This resulted in pupils not understanding exactly how they could achieve their intended outcomes. It also meant that the metalanguage which "gives pupils access to expression through DV" (Reid et al., 2002) was not being developed. Developing a metalanguage is a vital part of the creative process as it enhances understanding. Here the "intellectually undemanding" work which Ferguson (1981) cited in Buckingham et al. (1995) suggested took place in production, was definitely prevalent as well as the first model of creativity as described in paragraph two of this assignment. Here my own understanding of DVP and indeed its relationship with creativity was insufficient. This was because I had not been through the entire process of production myself at this stage and was unable to see how each stage from readings which were provided, planning, storyboarding, filming right through to editing informed one another. Because of my inexperience I was also unable to effectively reflect on the process in such a way that would inform my teaching and result in pupils going through a creative process.

Her argument here is, again, that creativity needs to be related to theoretical understanding of the medium, in this case digital video. Her courses have embarked on production work without equipping students with critical understandings of the medium. Arguably, there is a danger here of confusion between creative aspects of media production and the dimension of media work or media literacy usually described as critical understanding. However, while such distinctions need to be made, it is also important to relate creative work and critical understanding. Vygotsky's (1931/1998) essay on creativity in adolescence makes it clear that only the alliance of imagination and thinking in concepts leads to mature creativity—creativity is a rational as well as an imaginative process.

Other members of the course reflected on how creativity, counter-intuitively, can thrive on constraint, an argument elaborated in the course reading in the work of Sharples (1999). She gives an idea of how her group production on the course was constrained in various ways, relating this to Sharples' account:

The first activity to be completed on this project was creative in the traditional sense of thinking originally and artistically, here to design a concept for a film opening. From the outset, the group project had constraints applied to the creative process, in that the project brief gave a series of constraining factors to help focus group discussion. The idea of fostering creativity within set parameters echoes Sharples' assertion that: constraints allow us to control the multitude of possibilities that thought and language offer. There are so many ideas that we might have, and so many possible ways of expressing them, that we have to impose constraints to avoid thinking and writing gibberish. (Sharples, 1999, p. 42)

The initial creative activity would have been almost impossible without the guidelines of the brief as there would simply be too much choice and scope for the project to be effectively completed in a short, controlled time frame. Here the constraints applied to the task were: the genre; the possible locations; length; shot types to be used; key props and the group itself.

The same teacher recognised also, however, that creativity was informed by cultural experience, in this case of film:

Being educated, adult media consumers, our experience of creating a media text would be significantly different to the experience of a student as we have a greater level of knowledge of the theoretical aspects of film production and genre requirements. In some ways, however, this constrained our creativity as we were conscious of emulating other successful thriller films. This was particularly explicit in the shower sequence which we were aware of as being heavily influenced by Alfred Hitchcock's Psycho.

Interestingly, she conceives of this as a constraint, suggesting that the references to the Psycho shower scene inhibited the creativity of their piece. This reflects, arguably, naïve perceptions of creative originality common in education: that originality must be completely new. By contrast, Vygotsky's view was that creativity always draws on and transforms cultural resources—the originality lies in the transformation, the operation of imagination and rational thought to recombine semiotic raw material into something new. In this case, the group did not simply replicate *Psycho*, but referred wittily to it through the inventive use of shower images. Transformation here included the signalling of genre in a new narrative, and humorous indications of pastiche.

The Learning Experience

This teacher's account also makes it clear that her approach to creativity will be different because she has, for the first time, gone through the same production process that she takes her children through. Our informal understanding of this is that most of the teachers on our courses have been in the same position. The point made here is both simple and profound. On the one hand, it seems obvious that teachers need to have experienced the processes they are taking their students through; and it is worth emphasising this. On the other hand, this experience is complex. It changes the learner's view of themselves, seeing themselves as creative editors for the first time, but also as apprentice-learners, like their students, and again, this teacher invoked Tyner's (1998) model of cognitive apprenticeship to understand the learning process she has undergone:

The editing process was the aspect of the project which I found most difficult. Having had little experience of editing outside of the previous DVP workshop, it was difficult to view the film as a coherent whole. It made me appreciate the tough task asked of GCSE students in creating a two minute film as their first encounter with digital video production. This formed a strong link in my mind to Tyner's master/apprentice style of teaching where students create shorter pieces of media prior to their final project and the opportunities that could be available within the syllabus to allow for these activities to take place.

Finally, one student, whose background is in Art teaching, related the nature of the creative process to the way in which creativity is represented in different course syllabi she is familiar with. Her argument is developed from one of the course readings, and suggests that creativity is under-represented in media studies syllabus documents. She contrasts this unfavourably with the Art syllabus she is familiar with:

I realise that creativity comes in many forms, but as an Art teacher I have the luxury of being able to award students marks for "a sense of discovery and a willingness to take risks" *with their work. No such freedom is allowed in the Media syllabus. Instead the only mention of creativity is in a very dry context, insomuch as the candidate needs to employ* "…a range of media skills that demonstrates flair, creativity and imagination in working with available resources," *which means that the only available marks for creativity in its own right, is if a student uses the equipment well. For an Arts subject, this is appalling. The Art syllabus on the other hand goes to great lengths to try to break down the creative process by allowing marks to be awarded for a variety of attributes; descriptions such as* "the full appreciation and understanding of the characteristics of media and the functional constrains of materials," *or the ability to show* "sequential thinking, but also imaginative leaps at appropriate times" *or that the* "work is intuitive, imaginative, exciting and original" *are all legitimate definitions of a confident and creative student. This comparison provides some evidence that Media Studies is not as prepared for "creative work" as it should be. Creativity should be an opportunity for all to excel in and the taxonomy in the Art syllabus allows for this in a way that the Media syllabus does not.*

Here, then, the reflective work required by the course, as well as the readings provided, have encouraged a critical reading of how media production is constituted by the syllabus, and how teachers and students need to exceed these technical requirements if they are to approach production work creatively.

However, as many teachers on the course have remarked, the opportunity to go through the same kind of learning experience as their students go through can be an eye-opening experience. While the teacher cited above made sense of this in terms of creativity and the differences between Media and Art courses, others focused on different aspects of the learning experience. Some reflected, for instance, on the nature of group production work. As with school students, this often led to tensions, such as disagreements about how a piece might be edited, or, more commonly, about how to plan and film the film sequence in the second part of the course. Teachers almost always managed to see in such tensions the same kind of complexities they have to manage in their own classrooms, and to use the experience to see group production from the point of view of the student. At the same time, they could locate such experience within the theoretical frameworks offered by accounts such as that offered by Buckingham et al. (1995), who explore in detail the group roles of media production an the social processes involved.

Conclusion: Where Next?

As I indicated earlier, the current lack of provision for the training of teachers of media education in Europe suggests that it may be best to adopt a consensus model of what media education is, and focus on the key elements of such a model. This chapter has, then, demonstrated ways in which teachers might learn about the conceptual apparatus of media education, about appropriate pedagogies, about the analysis of different kinds of media text, about forms of practical production, about newer digital media, and about the popular cultural experience of children and young people.

Nevertheless, it seems also important to recognise variation and difference, as well as the rapidly-changing landscape of media texts and practices in the digital era. I will conclude, then, by speculating on the implications of these issues for the training of future teachers of media education.

First of all, I address the question of variations in the experience of teachers. Most media teachers in the UK begin as English teachers (Hart & Hicks, 2002). A much smaller number move across from Art, as in the example given in the previous section. Some of our students have been specialist ICT teachers, incorporating elements of media education into their ICT work. A very small number may really be media specialists by background, either because their first degree was in Media or Film Studies, or because they attended one of the few English teacher training courses with a significant media element, such as the course provided by the Central School of Speech and Drama in London.

These different backgrounds have always coloured the work of different media teachers, lending emphases on literacy, or on the media arts, or on digital technologies. One the one hand, here is always a danger that these emphases correlate to distortions or omissions—an over-emphasis on analysis, or too strong a stress on technologies, or on artistic canons, or a failure to recognise the popular cultural experience of young people, or lack of familiarity with the "languages" or semiotic systems of media texts.

However, on the other hand, we should be courageous enough to embrace different versions of media education. A research study of the first two media specialist schools in the UK found, for instance, that one emphasised the media arts, while the other had developed more of a media literacy model. This was a legitimate difference of emphasis, rather than a problem. In the future, we might hope for a more productive dialogue between media teachers and ICT teachers, in which the latter recognise the value of cultural and critical approaches to media texts and technologies, while the former learn how to conceive of media texts as computable (Manovich, 1998). Rather differently, but equally importantly, we might hope that teachers across the arts can collaborate with media specialists, so that aspects of visual design, the role of music in film and games, or the dramatic functions of film, television drama, and games, can all be considered in a multidisciplinary way which realises the complex nature of multimodal texts and cultural practices. Such meeting of different pedagogic traditions cannot, of course, be taken for granted; and often the rigid compartments of curriculum design, whether at national or local level, restricts what is possible, and may well continue to do so. It is in the interests of media educators to creatively subvert such restrictions.

Finally, the pace of change in social uses of the media, in the technologies, and in the commercial contexts in which the media are produced and consumed, is such that already the old securities of familiar genres, texts, and modes of production and consumption must be reassessed. At the same time, the teacher's relation to this changing landscape also should be explored.

Our MA, for example, has raised the question of what media teachers might do about computer games. The problems here for teachers lie in their possible lack of experience (though increasingly our students have grown up with games in their own media cultures), school disapproval of games, a matter of local cultural politics, the need for new ways to conceive of textuality and audience, which our course addresses, and the difficulty of embarking on creative production work, which we have also addressed.

However, in many ways games are easy to conceive of in terms of conventional models of media education. More difficult are the array of communicative and representational practices made possible by the Internet in general and by social softwares in particular. While these practices require more detailed attention than is possible here, I will make two general remarks. First, we might distinguish between practices whose function is predominantly communicative and those whose function is predominantly representational. Instant messaging, chatrooms, blogging (to some extent), and mobile phone calling and SMS messaging seem to me to fall into the first category. They are clearly of interest to scholars of communication studies, sociology, and Cultural Studies. However, it is not immediately obvious that they are so relevant to media studies, whose focus has traditionally been more emphatically on representation. The second category, then, including the making of digital video and the exhibition of it on YouTube, or the taking of photographs and displaying them on MySpace or Flickr, or the use of cameras on mobile phones for functions of "citizen journalism," seem to be closer to the interst of media education in representation: in the production, circulation, and reception of texts which aspire to represent the world in some way which exceeds the banal and the ephemeral, and to address a wider audience than friend and family.

It is hard to predict how these practices will change and develop, even in the near future. What new textual forms will emerge? Will the porous barriers between the professional realm of media production and the committed production practices of amateur groups and even casual creativity hold their own or dissolve still further? Will the powerful corporate interests of the media industries ever really let the audience in? Will the new democratic spaces of cyberspace continue to evade regulation and conventional economies; or will they be incorporated by multinational muscle as rapidly as MySpace and YouTube were snapped up by Rupert Murdoch and Google?

Whatever transpires, media teachers will have to keep up and try to recognise what their students are doing with new media. However, while they keep a finger on the pulse of the contemporary, it will always be part of their role to introduce students to experiences of the media which are new to them. While this will include forms, genres, texts, and contexts outside the preferred realm of their cultural experience, it will also include the media of the past, the cultural histories of their parents' and even grandparents' experience. Media teachers ride the wave of the new, but must also be instruments of time travel.

References

Banaji, S., & Burn, A. (2007). *The rhetorics of creativity: A review of the literature.* London: The Arts Council of England.

Barthes, R. (1978). The third meaning. In S. Heath (Trans.), *Image-music-text.* New York: Hill and Wang.

Bordwell, D. & Thompson, K. (2001). *Film art: An introduction* (6th ed.). New York: McGraw-Hill.

Buckingham, D. (2003). *Media education; literacy, learning and contemporary culture.* Cambridge: Polity Press.

Buckingham, D., Grahame, J., & Sefton-Green, J. (1995). *Making media.* London: English and Media Centre.

Burn, A., & Durran, J. (2007). *Media literacy in schools: Practice, production and progression.* London: Paul Chapman.

Burn, A., & Reed, K. (1999, Autumn). Digiteens: Media literacies and digital technologies in the secondary classroom. *English in Education, 33*(3), 5-20.

Craft, A. (2002). *Creativity and early years education a lifewide foundation.* London: Continuum.

DfES/DCMS. (1999). *All our futures, creativity, culture and education.* London: Department for Education and Skills; National Advisory Committee on Creative and Cultural Education.

Doyle, E. (2004). Unpublished MA dissertation, London, Institute of Education, University of London.

Fontana, D. (3rd ed.). (1995). *Psychology for teachers.* London: Macmillan Press Ltd.

Fraser, P., & Oram, B. (2003). *Teaching digital video production.* London: bfi.

Hart, A., & Hicks, A. (2002). *Teaching media in the English classroom.* London: Trentham.

Henson, D. (2005). Unpublished MA dissertation, London, Institute of Education, University of London.

Manovich, L. (1998). *The language of new media.* Cambridge, MA: MIT Press.

Metz, C. (1974). *Film language.* Chicago IL: Chicago University Press.

Neale, S. (2000). *Genre and Hollywood.* London: Routledge.

Plowright, M. (in progress). Unpublished MA dissertation, London, Institute of Education, University of London.

Reid, M., Burn, A., & Parker, D. (2002). Evaluation Report of the BECTa Digital Video Pilot Project, BECTa. Retrieved October 10, 2007, from http://www.becta.org.uk/research/reports/digitalvideo/index.html

Sharples, M. (1999). *How we write: Writing as creative design.* London: Routledge.

Tudor, A. (1999). *Decoding culture.* London: Sage.

Tyner. (1998). *Literacy in the digital world: Teaching and learning in the age of information.* London: Lawrence Erlbaum Associates.

Vernallis, C. (2001, Spring). The kindest cut: Functions and meanings of music video editing. *Screen, 42(1).*

Vygotsky, L.S. (1931/1998). Imagination and creativity in the adolescent (1931), *The collected works of L.S. Vygotsky, vol. 5* (pp. 151-166). R.W.

Vygotsky, L.S. (1978). *Mind in society.* Cambridge, MA: Harvard University Press.

Chapter XVI

Globalisation and New Technology[1]:
The Challenge for Teachers to Become "Translators" and Children, Knowledge Seekers

André H. Caron, Université de Montréal, Canada

Abstract

Whether globalisation results in a "métissage" of cultures or the hegemony of one culture will depend on the analytical and social skills of those who make up our communities. The introduction of new technologies in education such as laptops, MP3s, and Ipods and the new concept of mobile learning require an examination of the teacher's role in facilitating innovation, conveying culture, and acting as a conceptual translator. By modeling and teaching students critical and social skills, teachers can help tomorrow's citizens to use the new flow of information to meet the challenges of globalisation.

Introduction

Is new technology the magic bullet for education? In many places, policy makers have embraced new technologies as the answer to most of education's ills. They have persuaded the public that spending money on computers and high-speed Internet connections is a concrete, easy-to-understand, quantifiable way to improve education. New technology has been said to reduce dropout rates, increase innovation, and spark student enthusiasm. However, examination of discourse on these issues reveals that new information and communication technologies (NICT) might not be the whole solution.

As we get caught up in the mythical information society ideology, NICT's real usefulness and potential for education often gets overlooked. As its short history shows, NICT's role in education has to be analyzed in accordance with the dynamics of learning and teaching, as well as the aims of education.

The issues that arise in using new technologies in education are much the same as those raised by globalisation. New technologies give us rapid access to incredible quantities of information and vast new markets, but we should ask ourselves: do they always provide us with the tools for assessing and analyzing the information and how reliable is that information? Having the data is useless if we do not have the skills to make links and draw justifiable conclusions. Likewise, globalisation, which could indeed be facilitated by the use of new technologies, presupposes getting different cultures and subcultures to work together, not merely in parallel. Whether globalisation results in a *métissage* of cultures or the hegemony of one culture will depend on the analytical and social skills of those who make up our communities.

In this chapter,[2] we will look at the discourse in specific cases where educators have used new technologies in their classes, or government and administrators have implemented programs to promote the use of new technologies in education. The experiences in these cases may shed some light on the challenges we face in education with respect to new technologies as globalisation increasingly becomes a reality.

Attitudes to Globalisation, New Technologies, and Education

Some depict globalisation as a kind of crusade, an *épopée*, a grand tale of actors. It is linked with the technological evolution of history, in which archaic resistance to opening up markets, states, and cultures has been overcome, and the right way of doing things has been revealed (Lessard, 1998). Others adopt a more critical discourse, and denounce the cult of adapting to the dominant trend (Petrella, 1997). They take a somber view of capitalism, seeing it as a source of social confrontation. For them, the discussion on globalisation requires that we reconsider old questions of equality, links between local and global forces, and frontiers between nations.

In *Le Bien commun*, Petrella (1997) argues that the past few decades have produced six new commandments. The new commandments are (1) globalisation, (2) technological innovation, (3) liberalization, (4) deregulation, (5) privatization, and (6) competitiveness. These terms are very familiar to us. They are increasingly present in governmental and educational discourse today. Indeed, the second commandment, technological innovation, is at the heart of many newly announced social changes. On this view, new information and communication technologies are to be integrated and resistance is not only futile but wrong, for they are the keys to achieving an information society.

According to Petrella (1997), obeying the commandments means seeing the world as a series of new markets to conquer, with education obviously one of them. He draws a parallel between the conquests 500 years ago and a renewed culture of conquest of the global village. We speak of new areas to be exploited, new electronic highways to be built, and so forth. However, while the main actors in the 15th Century were political, such as the Kingdoms of Portugal and Spain and the Republic of Venice, today they are multinationals, private financial groups, and private industries. This vision could appear somewhat radical to some, but should not appear more so than the opposite view, which celebrates the mythical virtues of new technologies. Also we should remember that the anticipated role of new technologies in a global village is not new. Some 35 years ago, a certain Marshall McLuhan (1965), and even before him his mentor, Harold Innis (1951), described the coming of a new society and era of communication in which universal networks of information transmission would bring humankind closer together. McLuhan wrote, "Time has ceased, space has vanished, we now live in a global village, a simultaneous happening" (McLuhan, 1967). In his poetic way, he was proposing that if the networks and channels exist, then people will connect as intensely and quickly with people across the planet as with people in their own community.

In a review of McLuhan's work, Benjamin Symes notes:

It is easy to see why McLuhan was popular in the counter culture of the 60s, and is again today, with the computer revolution, for his ideas encompass an ideal that has perhaps in some ways always been with us...Is there not a possibility that if we place too much importance in achieving an idealistic, unified global village, we perhaps risk losing a sense of our physical humanity and our identity and thus forgetting why we are communicating at all. (Symes, 1995)

This brings us back to a basic question about what communication is in education, that of what education's role should be in this brave new world.

In his report to UNESCO, Jacques Delors (1998) says that education has to be viewed first and foremost as an ongoing process for both the individual and society and as something that extends beyond the classical physical and geographical boundaries of school and university. It is an ongoing process of enrichment of knowledge. In particular, it is the process of construction of the person and his or her relationship with other individuals, groups, and nations. Delors warns, "often we want quick answers and instantaneous solutions when the problems encountered require strategic patience, co-operation and negotiation" (Delors, 1998, p. 15). Strangely, these last three concepts are seldom associated with new technologies in government discourses.

Today, some children come into class with more information than their teachers. However, this does not mean that they have more knowledge. As Delors (1998) points out, "education has to enable each individual to access, gather, select, order, manage and use information." New technologies might improve access, but they cannot do the rest. They do not teach us judgment.

How will students learn in the 21st Century? Surprisingly today, they will learn in much the same way that they learned when formal schooling was first introduced. This might seem impossible, with all the changes in society, all the information available, and the technologies today, but the basics remain the same. Children learn by interacting with each other and teachers on a personal basis. They learn ways of coping in society, critical skills, problem-solving strategies, and so on.

Children as Seekers of Knowledge

If they are taught properly, children become seekers of knowledge. This is where new technologies, such as the Internet, can be really useful. However, we must first invest in people, discovery, and innovation so that they can use the technologies properly. We need to think less in terms of information-rich societies and more in terms of knowledge-rich societies.

Our children have much the same stance with respect to NICT as we adults now have with respect to television. As a sociotechnological object, the television set is somewhat of a black box for us. In other words, we do not have to know anything about its internal components or even wonder about how it works or how the actors and technologies bring us our favorite evening program in the comfort of our homes. Immersed in an ultratechnological universe since their birth, our children are much more at ease with the new black boxes than are their parents and teachers. The new technology is not, however, merely various objects that unexpectedly emerge in our world as tools or instruments for work. As some have noted (Tardif & Mukamurera, 1999), they are much more than that. The technical objects are built and "boxed" by human beings, and they embody tangible mediations and practices and, especially, represent symbolic systems. They carry *praxis*.

Each piece of technology is a cultural artifact, created for specific purposes. Moreover, it is used by people in well-defined social contexts for their own aims and brings about new forms of "moving cultures" (Caron & Caronia, 2005, 2007). Inserted into a school setting, new technology conveys certain aspects of the culture of its creators. However, it is also used by teachers and students for their own purposes and in accordance with their own culture or cultures. The technology becomes adjunct to the social interaction in the classroom.

Central to the interaction is communication between the teacher and pupils, which has to go far beyond the linear transmitter-message-receiver model to become instead a model of intersubjectivity. A teacher is neither an educating machine programmed to simply process data nor a means of filling a brain with information as if it were a hard disk. In the classroom, the teacher is present with the students and interacts with them, which often leads to unexpected and innovative situations. A classroom is a place where there is sharing of meanings and symbols, mutual understanding and cooperation. If the number of instances of communication is multiplied by the number of years that a child spends in school, we soon see that communication is an enduring and powerful force. School strongly socializes students, integrating them into a specific culture. At school, students learn to live and survive in society.

From Global to Local:
A Few Observations from Canada

As the interconnections become more tangible and globalisation is felt at various levels in Canadian social institutions, we have had no option but to adapt those institutions, particularly in education. Moreover, in the early 1990s, many Canadian children began demonstrating information acquisition and mastery of new technologies resulting from contact with new information and communications technologies (NICT) elsewhere than at school (at home or their parents' workplaces). They therefore often came to class with skills and knowledge that their teachers did not have. In order to adapt to such new social changes, school had to reassess its way of doing things, particularly with respect to school use of NICT.

In Canada, education is under provincial jurisdiction. Each province is therefore responsible for developing an educational system that meets the needs of its population. In Québec, the Ministry of Education is responsible for creating educational programs. However, another independent government organisation assesses the

Ministry's programs in view of the current situation in Québec: the *Conseil supérieur de l'éducation*. Its mandate is to reflect on major needs in education and it publishes an annual report on its findings.

In 1994, the *Conseil supérieur de l'éducation* issued its first report on action to be taken to ensure that school adapts to the knowledge society into which we were being swept by major developments in NICT (Conseil supérieur de l'éducation, 1994). The Council members recommended that Québec schools pursue three main objectives with respect to use of NICT: (1) Schools needed to enable students to develop the cognitive and social abilities required to participate fully as citizens and workers in a society where NICT play a major role; (2) Students also had to develop critical thinking skills with respect to the role of NICT in society and media; (3) Teaching practices had to be changed to integrate NICT, which was considered to have a net positive effect, particularly with respect to student interest and motivation. These broad principles could probably be seen in one form or another at the time, and even today, in most institutional discourse on education in many countries.

In 2000, the results of this action were assessed. The amounts promised had been invested, and the objectives seemed to have been met. Within 5 years, the number of children per computer had gone from 21:1 to 7:1, and Internet connection from 56:1 to 10:1 (Ministère de l'Éducation du Québec, 2001). Young people now had access to the Internet at school, thanks to investments from the Ministry of Education, and also in other public institutions, such as libraries, through a high-speed telecommunications network. The Connecting Families to the Internet Program also made it easier for families in Québec with modest incomes to buy a computer and get access to the Internet at home. In short, a few years after the wave of computerisation in schools, democratisation of access was relatively advanced. However, the need for effort of another order was becoming increasingly clear.

The *Conseil supérieur de l'éducation* issued another report in 2000 on the integration of NICT in schools (Conseil supérieur de l'éducation, 2000). While it recognized the importance of having adequate equipment in sufficient quantity, it noted that a key component seemed to have been left out of the Ministry's action plans: pedagogical use of NICT and the results of such use. The Council expressed its disappointment in the lack of assessment of how classroom use of NICT affected school results. At the same time, there seemed to be less enthusiasm for NICT than before. Whereas the previous report had sung the praises of NICT's effects on student motivation and interest, the 2000 report was more realistic. It said that NICT had to be used in all areas of learning in order to acquire, produce, and transmit knowledge in line with the program of studies. NICT had to be a catalyst for the development of new skills and knowledge and it was no longer seen as a miracle solution.

School officials seemed to have come to this conclusion when they saw that, despite several years of use of NICT, there had been little progress in student motivation and success. Use of NICT had not significantly reduced school dropout rates, which were 20% among those aged 19 in the year 2000 (Ministère de l'Éducation du

Québec, 2002). The real solution seemed to lie in deep changes to how things are done in school. It had become clear that new technologies, that is, hardware, alone would not bring about innovation. Instead, a way had to be found to improve school culture and student motivation as the real engines of success.

Thus, whereas the second half of the 1990s was marked by the integration of NICT into the Québec school system, the early 2000s focused on success in school for all students, as set out in the Québec Ministry of Education's 2000-2003 strategic plan. Various measures were planned, but in particular the Ministry hoped to increase school success by promoting the value of education to all of Québec's population through major media campaigns (Ministère de l'Éducation du Québec, 2000).

The first campaign, *L'éducation: pour qu'éclatent les passions*, was launched in fall 2000. It lasted 3 years and was intended to promote education and success using traditional media such as television, film, radio and print. Another campaign was pursuing the same objectives with respect to students from underprivileged communities. The New Approaches, New Solutions strategy specifically targeted 200 secondary schools in underprivileged areas where the drop out rate was abnormally high. The strategy primarily involved local action and therefore did not involve the media.

Also, the Ministry of Education contributed to a campaign launched by the Québec Department of Health and Social Services in 2000. Its purpose was to prevent depression among young people aged 13 to 17. *Parler... c'est grandir* encouraged communication on various topics. In this case, a broad media campaign on television, film, and radio was accompanied by a competition. Interestingly enough, after these first initiatives, the ministry published research in 2004 that reported how teachers were using new technologies in their classroom. A little more than half (58%) said they often or very often used new technologies in their formal teaching and approximately the same number of teachers (56%) mentioned also using them for seeking information on the Web (Bertrand, 2003, p. 87). This did indicate, however, that close to half the teachers did very little use of ICTs. Profuse to say that the overall strategy of the Ministère de l'Éducation in these times of new technological mutations still require important new initiatives.

A few recent observations in the field, at this point, should be made. The first observation concerns a policy adopted by a major business school in Montreal. A few years ago, the administrators decided that all students should be wired to the information highway, so they required every student to purchase a laptop. All students were required to buy the same model so that, hopefully, all information in the school could flow electronically, with no boundaries. A few years later, it was discovered informally that many of the idealistic illusions had disappeared, at least from the students' perspective. Substantial numbers of teachers did not want to provide information on their courses electronically, or did not have the time to do so. When students began coming to class with their laptops on, many teachers found it distracting to see the fronts of 150 laptops instead of their students' faces. The noise of incessant typing sometimes made it difficult to hear. Then it became clear that students were not necessarily taking notes, but sending each other jokes, chatting, and so forth. Attempts were made to use filters and to adopt certain codes of conduct, but to little avail. The end result is that today PC use is even discouraged in some classes. There are still thousands of students walking around the school with laptop cases over their shoulders, but actual classroom use is much more limited than anticipated. Yet this year the school is offering students an even more expensive model with a high-speed connection. The question is whether this decision is technology-driven, pedagogically well-thought through, or simply an advantageous business deal, not perhaps for the students but for the school.

In the last few years, there has been some interesting explorations in new pedagogical uses of technologies in the classroom such as the use of Weblogs for more interaction between students and teachers and the new concept of mobile learning (Corbeil & Valdes-Corbeil, 2007; Naismith, 2004; Quinn, 2000). This latter concept has most recently focused on "podcasting": the new word of the year appearing in the New Oxford American Dictionary, as the newest form of e-learning.

As in the past, this has created, in the educational world, an infatuation by universities and school administration for the technology itself and not necessarily for its content, its optimum pedagogical use or the way it should be introduced in the educational system. This, of course, raises many questions. Beyond access and interest, students need to acquire their skills through a dialogical approach with their teachers; a clear-cut differentiation must be made between information obtained and knowledge acquisition.

The introduction of MP3 and Ipod technologies in universities is a good example. Indeed, some universities have rushed into "Ipoding" their classes, which could seem at the onset as a good idea, allowing students to complete their curriculum with mobile learning. Although one can find a number of recent articles making useful observations on this technology (Corbeil & Valdes-Corbeil, 2007; Whindham, 2007), few if any have invested in systematically sound research in defining what would be the best possible conditions before introducing such technologies. One study that is now being completed at the University of Montréal, in Canada, attempted to look at this question more rigorously. Some 125 students were provided for a full semester with Zen Creative and Ipod technologies. Teachers in English and Italian languages, Communication, Pharmacy, and Urban Design volunteered to include podcasts in their curriculum. It ranged from some teachers providing full length two and a half hour podcasts of their course to others offering short "meet the authors" capsules or simple interview podcasts. Students filled in diaries, Weblogs, questionnaires, and participated in interviews. Although it is still at the preliminary stage of analysis, first indications are that we often overestimate student's facility to appropriate the technology. In fact, only half the students owned a MP3 or Ipod technology before this trial and few knew what podcasts were. Their real mobile use most often went towards music, radio reception (Zen Creative), using it as a USB stick, and recording classes. Rarely did it include the podcasts provided by their teachers. Why? Lack of common cultural references and mostly expectations of a much more down to basic approach to educational content (such as summaries, exam drills, etc.) partially explained their low interest. As for the teachers, they found they needed a whole new way of preparing and finding content for their courses. Interestingly, although one of the participating teachers had been honored as the best teacher in his faculty the previous year when it came to his podcast material, they were rarely consulted.

It could be thought that this is another example of a technological fiasco, given that among other MP3 technologies, Ipods remain a one way media (Corbeil & Valdes-Corbeil, 2007). But on the contrary, what it raises is the possibility that we are on the verge of a cultural transformation where teachers could solicit their students for finding relevant contents that can be shared as podcasts, and that this material could become an integral part of the curriculum if properly validated. This would lead to a mutual construction of credible knowledge for a given course and the students would truly become active knowledge seekers. The technology then becomes a facilitator and the teacher the "translator" of knowledge and provider of cultural skills.

Innovation, Information, and the Role of Culture in Education

Some major universities are rethinking their approaches to the use of new technologies. For example, the importance of the teacher's role is illustrated and affirmed by MIT (Massachusetts Institute of Technology in USA)'s Open Courseware project, as is the difference between having access to information and getting an education. MIT has been publishing the lecture notes, reading lists, exams, and answers of some of its professors' courses online, with the goal of eventually making the content of all of its courses available free of charge. However, MIT will not be actually offering any courses online. In order to get a degree from MIT, people will still have to attend classes in person. As quoted on the MSNBC Web site, the MIT spokeperson argued, "We are fighting the commercialization of knowledge, much in the same way that open-source people are fighting the commercialization of software." (Festa, 2002)

New technologies, however, are still seen by many politicians and school administrators as a way to achieve a more profitable educational system. But the MIT initiative is forcing some to re-evaluate their objectives. Tony Masi, Vice Dean, Information Systems and Technology, at McGill University says:

All the major universities—Stanford, Colombia, Harvard and, alas, McGill—are trying to make money with the Internet, to commercialize teaching. At MIT, they are going back to a university's primary role: educating people, in a universal way. In universities, we are starting to lose sight of the fact that students are not consumer products. (Leduc, 2002, p. A1)

Financial investment and the electronic highway linking all schools and homes to an ever-abundant flow of information are therefore for many still considered the key to innovation. In Canada and many other countries, this has been the official political position for a decade. Yet should we maybe reassess what really is innovation?

In a series of articles published in the *Harvard Business Review* (2002), a number of very successful business entrepreneurs were asked about how they encourage innovation in their companies. Surprisingly, when describing how they brought about innovation, Dells (of Dell Computer), Bushnell (the creator of Atari), and Wynett (of Proctor and Gamble) failed to mention the two concepts we have just been discussing above: new technologies and money. The top people in a wide range of businesses instead mentioned people and the organisational culture they fostered. For many of these people, being innovative is a question of culture or, in a sense, to solve problems.

Michael Dell, CEO, Dell Computer reported that:

At Dell, innovation is about taking risks and learning from failure. To tap into this kind of innovation, we do our best to make sure the people aren't afraid of the possibility of failure. And we do a lot of experiments. (Harvard Business Review, 2002, p. 41)

Nolan Bushnell, the creator of Atari, said, "I think it's essential to build a culture where there's no such thing as a bad idea" (Harvard Business Review, 2002, p. 46). Finally, according to Esther Dyson, chairman of EDventure Holdings:

So how do you encourage useful innovations? By doing two things. One, you have to promote risk taking, be open to experimentation, and philosophical about things that go wrong. My motto is "Always make new mistakes." There's no shame in making a mistake, but then learn from it and don't make the same one again. Everything I've learned, I've learned by making mistakes. (Harvard Business Review, 2002, p. 49)

What we see in these remarks is that the most fruitful activities are those in which people explore ideas together. In other words, the attitudes of the captains of innovation mentioned above are inspired by an underlying constructivist approach according to which learners build knowledge themselves. As they try to integrate their experiences, they classify or structure new material in accordance with past knowledge so as to make sense of it.

Applied to new technologies, the constructivist approach redefines our views about the pedagogical styles to be used in classrooms in the future. However, we must be careful to avoid thinking of information technologies purely as information providers. They are, in fact, tools that can be used flexibly while offering learners opportunities to construct their own models of learning. Technology should not be seen as the way to change the teaching environment in a class; instead, teachers should know how to use the technology in innovative ways.

We often believe that the most significant aspect of technology is its speed and effectiveness, which is rooted directly in the cybernetic paradigm. However, communication is a transaction between active participants, not an operation in which information is transferred from one hard disk to another.

The key to using communications networks to their full potential is culture. A struggle over any issue is possible only if those involved have judgment, knowledge, control of the language, and a clear purpose. Without these components, we immediately find ourselves in a primitive, instinctive situation that can be resolved only through inarticulate brute force. Just as it is useless to give NICT to someone who is technologically illiterate, it is useless to give it to a cultural illiterate. Education with NICT therefore has to be carried out on two fronts: cultural and technical.

Teachers as "Translators"

On the cultural front, we need teachers to help pupils find ways of understanding new information in their own terms. Just as a translator ideally bridges the gap between cultures and languages, a teacher restates new concepts in various ways so that they become notions that students can use in their own contexts. In translation terms, this is known as "localisation," which is a growing business with globalisation, and involves adapting text to a specific culture or subculture so that it has the same impact as in the original or source culture. In the classroom, this involves negotiation, as the teacher and students ask each other questions and test each others' meaning. Not only does this allow students to broaden their horizons, but the teacher serves as a model so that students can learn similar skills and ways of conveying information to others.

One of the major problems now arising with respect to NICT and culture is the risk of losing certain essential experiences and knowledge. People are increasingly called upon to research information in various databases in different formats. This can create beings who are informed, but completely ignorant of the whole social, political, and economic world in which they live. This means the death of communication in the intersubjective sense. In other words, learning online without a teacher could make people look knowledgeable, but they would not really be so because they would not have developed their critical skills.

As previously mentioned, teachers have to become translators for students because content delivered by NICT cannot become stable without real interaction. Does this mean that only interpersonal teaching will succeed and that the media and new technologies are of no use? Not necessarily. However, we have to be careful when they are promoted as solutions to economic and political problems, and proposed and packaged in political discourse, to look good.

Undeniably, the role of teachers is important in a world of increased circulation of information allowed by ICTs. It is even more imperative nowadays because of the impact of the global market on the education sector that follows the trend toward neo-liberalism, deregulation, privatization of services, and withdrawal of state intervention. For these reasons, the Québec *Conseil Supérieur de l'éducation* did look at this question in its Annual Report titled *The Governance of Education: Market Logic or Political Process?* The Council saw the problem in terms of equity and justice pitted against efficiency and competitiveness. Obviously, the former do not exclude the latter, and vice versa, but the Council recommended state intervention as a means of promoting these values. The Council warned against returning to an educational system not governed by a democratic political process because equitable educational infrastructure is so expensive that it can be delivered only by society as a whole. Similarly, the way that education is provided and the tools that are used will have to be negotiated with a view to the community's basic values.

There is no doubt that globalisation will continue to transform education, but what remains undetermined is the capacity of education to keep a critical distance, its capacity to be something other than the echo of an economic imperialism. If some distance cannot be maintained, public educational services will inevitably be seen as a form of merchandise and not as something that is for the common good.

As Hargreaves (1994) points out, we must reflect on the following questions: Will there be a culture of uncertainty, with knowledge developing at an ever quicker pace, but also becoming more and more temporary? Will universal, scientific certainties be replaced by contextualised certainties constructed by stakeholders in a community of meaning?

Educational institutions no longer hold or control a monopoly over information. A significant portion is now produced outside such institutions. Their role is now not so much to produce more information, but to analyze the implications and uses of information, thereby selecting and converting it into knowledge. The history of our efforts to bring electronic technology into schools has, in many instances up until now, been one of missed opportunities. This is not because innovations did not work, but because we did not understand that successful technological change in education is always linked to events, attitudes, and values in the society at large.

Acknowledgment

I would like to express my gratitude to a number of people who played an active role in the research and the preparation of this presentation. These people are Marie-France Vermette, Laurent Lux, Mary Baker, and Nicoletta Dolce. I would also want to express my appreciation to the Ministère de l'Éducation du Québec.

References

Bertrand, D. (2003). *Diversité, continuité et transformation du travail professoral dans les universités québécoises (1991-2003)*. Québec: Conseil supérieur de l'éducation. Retrieved October 11, 2007, from http://www.cse.gouv.qc.ca/fichiers/documents/publications/EtudesRecherches/Renou2.pdf

Caron, A.H., & Caronia, L. (2005). *Culture mobile: Les nouvelles pratiques de communication*. Montréal, Canada: Les Presses de l'Université de Montréal.

Caron, A.H., & Caronia, L. (2007a). *Moving cultures: Mobile communication in everyday life*. Montreal, Canada: McGill-Queen's University Press.

Caron, A.H., & Caronia, L. (2007b). *MP3, zen et Ipod: La culture mobile dans le monde de l'éducation*. Rapport de recherche. Montréal, Canada: CITÉ, département de communication.

Charland, J.-P. (2002). *Le rapport à l'histoire et à la citoyenneté des élèves des régions métropolitaines de Montréal et de Toronto*. Ph.D. Québec, Canada: Université Laval.

Conseil supérieur de l'éducation du Québec. (1994). *Les nouvelles technologies de l'information et de la communication: Des engagements pressants. Rapport annuel 1993-1994 sur l'état et les besoins de l'éducation*. Québec, Canada: Les publications du Québec.

Conseil supérieur de l'éducation du Québec. (2001). *La gouvernance de l'éducation. Logique marchande ou processus politique. Rapport annuel 2000-2001 sur l'état et les besoins de l'éducation*. Québec, Canada: Conseil supérieur de l'éducation.

Conseil supérieur de l'éducation du Québec. (2000). *Éducation et nouvelles technologies. Pour une intégration réussie dans l'enseignement et l'apprentissage. Rapport annuel 1999-2000 sur l'état et les besoins de l'éducation*. Québec, Canada: Conseil supérieur de l'éducation.

Corbeil, J.R., & Valdes-Corbeil, M.E. (2007). Are you ready for mobile learning? *Educause Quarterly, 2*. Retrieved October 11, 2007, from http://www.educause.edu/apps/eq/eqm07/eqm0726.asp?bhcp=1

Delors, J. (1998). *Education: The treasure within*. Paris, France: Task Force on Education for the Twenty-First Century, UNESCO.

Festa, P. (2002). *MIT offers all its courses free online*. Retrieved October 11, 2007, from http://www.msnbc.com/news/819892.asp?0si=-&cp1=1

Hargreaves, A. (1994). *Changing teachers, changing times: Teachers' work and culture in the postmodern age*. New York: Teachers College Press.

Harvard Business Review. (2002, August). Inspiring Innovation. *Harvard Business Review, The Innovative Entreprise*.

Innis, H.A. (1951). *The bias of communication*. Toronto, Canada: University of Toronto Press.

Julien, M. (2005). *La mobilité internationale des étudiants au sein des universités québécoises*. Québec, Canada: Conseil supérieur de l'éducation. Retrieved October 11, 2007, from http://www.cse.gouv.qc.ca/fichiers/documents/publications/EtudesRecherches/50-2098.pdf

Leduc, L. (2002, September 30). Le MIT virtuellement gratuit. *La Presse*, p. A1.

Lessard, C. (1998, March 26-27). *Globalisation et éducation*. Conférence d'ouverture du forum Éducation et Développement, ayant pour thème: éducation, développement, coopération et recherche dans le contexte de la mondialisation. Faculté des sciences de l'Éducation, Université de Montréal. Retrieved October 11, 2007, from http://www.unige.ch/fapse/SSE/groups/life/textes/Lessard_A1998_01.html

McLuhan, M. (1965). *Understanding media: The extension of man*. Toronto, Canada: McGraw-Hill.

McLuhan, M., & Fiore, Q. (1967). *The medium is the massage*. New York, Toronto: Bantam Books.

Ministère de l'Éducation. (1996). *Les technologies de l'information et de la communication en éducation.Plan d'intervention*. Québec, Canada: Ministère de l'Éducation. Retrieved October 11, 2007, from http://www.mels.gouv.qc.ca/nti_plan/plan_nti.htm

Ministère de l'Éducation. (2000). *Plan Stratégique 2000-2003 du Ministère de l'Éducation.Mise à jour 2001*. Québec, Canada: Ministère de l'Éducation. Retrieved October 11, 2007, from http://www.meq.gouv.qc.ca/ADMINIST/plan_strategique/PlanStrat0003/abrege_f_miseajour.pdf

Ministère de l'Éducation du Québec. (2001). *L'introduction des technologies de l'information et des communications (TIC) à la formation des jeunes et des adultes. Bilan de l'an IV du plan ministériel d'intervention. Année scolaire*

1999-2000. Québec, Canada: Ministère de l'Éducation, du Loisir et du Sport, direction des ressources didactiques. Retrieved October 11, 2007, from http://www.meq.gouv.qc.ca/drd/tic/pim.html

Ministère de l'Éducation du Québec. (2002*). Indicateurs de l'éducation*. Québec, Canada: Ministère de l'Éducation, direction générale des ressources informationnelles.

Petrella, R. (1997). *Le bien commun: éloge de la solidarité*. Lausanne: Éditions Page deux.

Symes, B. (1995). *Marshall McLuhan's global village*. Retrieved October 11, 2007, from http://www.aber.ac.uk/media/Students/bas9401.html

Tardif, M., & Mukamurera, J. (1999). La pédagogie scolaire et les TIC: l'enseignement comme interactions, communication et pouvoirs. *Éducation et francophonie, 27*(2). Retrieved October 11, 2007, from http://www.acelf.ca/c/revue/revuehtml/27-2/Tardif.html

Whyndam, C. (2007). Confessions: Podcast junkie. *Educause Review, 42*(3). Retrieved October 11, 2007, from http://www.educause.edu/apps/er/erm07/erm0732.asp

Endnote

[1]   The present chapter is a revised and updated version of a text that was originally published in Italian under the title *Le nuove tecnologie è la riposta...Ma a quale domanda?* in "Senso della politica e fatica di pensare" (pp.260-274) a cura di Antonio Erbetta con la collaborazione di Piero Bertolini Clueb 2003

Chapter XVII

The Future of Digital Society and the New Values of Media

José Manuel Perez Tornero, Universitat Autonoma de Barcelona (UAB),
Spain

Abstract

This chapter concerns the conceptualization of information society and its social impact. From this point of view it worked like a myth, emphasizing the role of technology and producing some effects on social behaviours. This idea is develop in three main ways. First of all the chapter explains how the myth was born and how it is producing effects. Second, it investigates how it is changing the anthropology of how we are thinking about technology and its development. Finally, it imagines how media education is affected by this process, pointing out some ideas for re-designing its epistemological profile.

Introduction: Ways of Considering the Future

The sudden appearance of an information or knowledge society has strongly focused the attention, in the last few years, on the future. In this way such a discourse has turned into a force to shape actions and social strategies. Nevertheless, there are different versions and modalities of interpreting future. Some are "prophetic" and assume the form of predictions and wishes used as moral stimulus and reflection; others are "catastrophic" and apocalyptic. According to this perspective the end is always tragic and pernicious and people should always be ready for the next cataclysm. The first versions are enthusiastic and optimistic and they promise a kind of informative and well-being paradise, which would develop itself as an inevitable consequence of the determinant processes of technology. The second versions calculate what might happen and depict future descriptions through market and statistical models (Breton, 1993).

Nevertheless, in my opinion, none of these forms of future perspectives is completely adequate to know what is about to come. They are not adequate to free and improve our capacity of imagination in the present to face the future. In fact you cannot say they are either completely wrong, or completely wise: each one contains a certain degree of valid knowledge, but none represents by itself the absolute truth.

This is why an undisputed original axiom is latent within these approaches. The majority of these perspectives consider the future as inescapable, written in the present and shaping inevitable destiny.

Nevertheless, these are fundamental discourses. Although they can only be considered as intuitions; without them they cannot understand either the human or the social action. Such discourses support human freedom of conscience and human capacity to drive its life. These elements are essential in the process of acquiring consciousness of humanity, but are also fundamental in educational process, and so in media education.

This principle, applied to the development of information society, is based on two main ideas:

- First, future is designed and depends on decisions and alternatives adopted in the present. This means that nothing is specific beforehand and that, therefore, nothing or nobody can present or imagine the future as an inevitable setting.
- Second, our intuition or knowledge of the alternatives that is coded in the future depends, above all, on deep understanding of past and present. The deeper our knowledge of past and present is, the more they will be able to imagine the possibilities that the future encloses.

If they want to know which is the future of digital society, they must acknowledge the need of a deep consciousness of their present and the acceptance of the freedom to face any speculation on future. Consciousness and freedom are two aspects that, in my opinion, characterize a fundamental part of the essence of human dignity. These aspects are also essential in Media Education.

Digital Society as Myth for Social Action

Digital society, or its related terms, information society, knowledge society, post-modern society, refers much more to the future than to the present. The terms are projects, more than realities.

But they are also confused and vague projects. They cannot precisely define both what digital society is and in which areas of the world it has developed. It is not possible to identify its characteristics and its physical reality. This impossibility depends on the fact that the term digital society is, above all, a slogan. They can say, without doubt, that it worked and works more as a kind of myth, an object of desire than as an empirical reality. But the influence of this myth is and has been so important that it has caused deep transformations almost all over the world. These transformations concern traditional ways of living, economic and industrial changes, education and job government forms, and even personality and individuals' ways of being.

It is necessary, therefore, to acknowledge that digital society has been an idea of a value, trying to direct and to arrange the action of many sectors. It is and has been a sociological and political leitmotiv that has tried to justify the action of econo-mists, sociologists, political scientists, technicians, and so forth. It has been and is a discourse oriented to a deep social re-engineering.

Why is the concept of digital society a myth in itself? Because a myth is an attractive, dazzling, symbolic reality that awakes reverence and respect, although its reality is only conventional. And this is the idea of digital society.

In this sense, it is important to investigate how this mythical sense of digital society worked in order to know which consequences it has had on our ways of thinking and acting and which anthropological changes it is producing nowadays. As our ways of thinking and acting are fundamental for a renovation of Media Education and since the possibility of future alternatives depends on them, we have to focus our attention on this issue.

I will refer to three aspects I consider very important:

- The role that the myth of digital society plays within the most extensive dis-course on social change.

- The anthropological transformation that this myth is activating in our society and in humanity. I will speak of new media anthropology.

- Finally, the possibility of defending, through the Media Education, the autonomy of consciousness and the promotion of human dignity, creating a kind of counter-myth that would create an up-to-date and renewed Media Education.

The Myth of Digital Society as Focus of the Discourse on Changes

When the terms information society and digital society began to be used, almost 20 years ago, the world was rapidly changing. The cold war was ended and the east countries' control by the USSR was dissolved. The U.S. was expanding its hegemony in the world because of the success of its economy and the power of its army. The principles of new-liberalism and of the world markets opening was guaranteed by the agreements of the World Commerce Organization. The privatization of public services and of financial systems, but also the improvement of some economies, above all that of poor countries, seemed infallible.

The development of mass communication and of communication and information technologies seemed essential in that project of new-liberalization and world economic globalization (Mattelart, 2001).

The concept of digital society seemed adequate to justify markets' globalization. Which were the reasons for this fact?

First, there was a real reason. Progress of computerization reinforced both the possibilities of control of production and the capacity to improve the process of production and of work rationalization. In this way, the hope of an improvement of productivity without any further load on human work seemed reasonable.

Second, digital technologies—characterized by flexibility, userfriendliness, and interactivity—created a less centralized and despotic communicative horizon than that of traditional mass communication. They also raised a certain hope of democratization of communication linked to democratizing ideas exhibited by old east countries and to the new demands of democracy in western countries.

Third, the total opening to international flow of messages and communication, old liberal American ideal, could be considered inevitable with new technologies, and was a suitable, parallel support to the process of liberalization of world trade.

Fourth, digital promises could be presented to less developed countries, those which required a strong economic improvement, as a kind of miraculous panacea that would be able to increase their productivity and wealth.

Finally, the omnipresence of the digital discourse, that affected all the processes of life, work, culture, and society, could be the starting point for a social re-engineering of institutions and ways of living of a predigital society.

In this way, the slogan of information society became a kind of technological ideology that tried to redesign social life and could inspire any action programme. Furthermore, it had the character of technological inevitability that technocrats and the supporters of scientific thought so much liked. In this sense, during the 1980s these two concepts coincided: neoliberalism, increase in globalization, doctrinal justification of information society, and technological development oriented to society re-engineering.

The result of that decade was manifold, although analysts do not completely disagree. The rich areas of the planet underwent economic growth, through important social and work changes; collapse and crisis characterised the poor areas. They assisted to an increase in misery and unknown sufferings, and crystallization of a consumerist environment all over the world so that they can affirm that consumerism has become a kind of doctrine of great significance everywhere.

Other consequences of those changes were: the massive exodus of the population from some countries to others, open military risky conflicts of indeterminate duration, and a latent and worldwide war against terrorism which certainly stimulated, paradoxically, terrorist actions.

In the meantime, the doctrine of information society, or digital society, has been a justification of many government and international actions. It has inspired agreements on government programmes and, in general, it has been a process of redesigning or re-engineering of social institutions.

The Media Citizenship, Fruit of an Anthropological Transformation

We try now to focus our attention on the changes produced in human life by the discourse on digital society and social forces. Media, digital or not, represent the environment in which our life develops. This is a relatively recent, decisive, and new fact in the history of humankind.

In the first half of the 20th Century, nature and fields were the habitat of the majority of the population. Very few people lived in towns or cities, and most of them lived in the spaces imposed by nature and according to its rhythms. Tools and houses technologies were still so little developed that they barely supported human actions and protected, and, anyway, at a distance, people against inclemency of nature.

With the massive and irreversible process of urbanization produced during the 19th and 20th Centuries, cities began to convert themselves gradually in a new human environment. Perceived as different and separated from fields, progressively far away from natural time and rhythms, cities introduced artificiousness in everyday life and a new form of socialization, mainly characterized by proximity, on the one hand, and a growing technological complexity, on the another hand.

From an historical point of view, humankind went through a change, from being a peasant to being a citizen, in a relatively abrupt and at the same time very intense way.

In few decades, the phenomenon of urbanization affected everyone and almost all the areas of everyday life. But, almost without transition, and of a more intense and so abrupt way, we have assisted in the last decades to the conversion of urban citizen to media citizen to inhabitant of cities to inhabitant of mass media.

This phenomenon caused innovations and historical changes. Mediation has become an indisputable fact (Thompson, 1995). From an historical point of view, cities were at the beginning only new areas of dwelling and contact. Then they have been built and now they are being built everywhere, not without excess, and have become new media metropolises. They are characterised by such engaging social relationships that living there is a much deeper experience than in traditional cities. Thus, progressively, media metropolises built on digital technologies have been embedded within traditional cities, in particular from the 1960s on. They are metropolises within others, a kind of symbolic bubbles imprisoned in greater bubbles. They are subcities located inside traditional cities.

Television, as the hegemonic media, and the Internet as the great one recently arrived, are the main representatives of this human migration towards media environments.

The apparition of new media metropolises inside traditional metropolises has introduced in people's life a new space and time, both different from natural space and time.

The new space and time are characterized by a semiotic and especially symbolic nature, and they have a strong virtual and imaginary character, completely different from the material character typical of traditional metropolises.

If the life of media citizens takes physically place in cities much more populated, characterized by streets full of cars, and tiny houses—it is certain that, from a cognitive and semiotic point of view, that same existence develops simultaneously in a new space and time created by mass media: television, the Internet, radio, telephone, press, and so on. This new media city creates a mediated, digital citizenship, that is to say, supported, driven by, and centred on mass media.

Of what does that new media citizenship consist? Which is its nature and which consequences have its apparition for the future of the humankind?

The Bio-Space of the Media City

When peasants massively migrated to cities, they found a habitat very different from the previous one: crowed spaces they weren't accustomed to, mostly, ephemeral, more abstract and less deep personal relationships. Those spaces were plenty of objects to contemplate, use or admire, innovations and constant changes, smaller and less independent houses and a different way of working, compared to that of fields.

In this new physical context, both perceptions and psychology of people changed radically, as authors such as Simmel or Ortega y Gasset pointed out. But the media development has transformed many of these factors. The evolution of media, as Meyrowitz (1985) underlines, has reduced the importance of physical presence in the experience of people and events. Nowadays, a person can be part of the audience of a social event without being physically present; one can communicate directly with others without being in the same place. As a consequence of that, physical structures that once divided our society in many different spatial situations for the interaction have come to a drastic reduction in their social meaning.

Walls of family homes, for example, are no longer effective barriers that can isolate the family from society or a more extensive community.

The house is no longer the only environment where the members of the family can access other places and other people. This is linked to the introduction of radio, television, and telephone. And this is more true with the media evolution of the last years of the 20th Century since digitization has favoured the growth of a media "skin" that wraps individuals and communities.

This is not only related to family but also to school. McLuhan (1964) also speaks of "the classroom without walls"referring to the idea that walls of schools no longer provide a limitation to the acquisition of knowledge and know-how by children and that mass media are parallel to school.

Through mass media people experience extensive spaces and expand their. Many restrictions and previous limitations do not exist any longer. This produces what Giddens (2000) identified as a characteristic of modernity, although without attributing it directly to mediation: the arrival of modernity gradually separates space from place and promotes relationships among "absents" located at a distance.

The result is a full dislocation of society, which causes not only a loss of real space but also the loss of its social meaning and its re-situation in the interior of another type of space: the media space.

With current mass media, the distinctions Goffman did to describe the territories of the "I" began to be out-of -date, or, at least, to lose importance.

Thanks to the Internet, mobile phones, and television, an individual can be called, questioned, and seen by others located thousands of kilometres away and without the traditional barriers.

The "discourse order" regulated by the control of spaces and languages of mediation—and, therefore, of the access to other people—has been switched off abruptly. This has brought about social and psychological consequences we are recently experiencing in depth and that will be more extensive in the immediate future.

Spaces and their limits have changes. House walls, like we have already said, become windows open to the outside thanks to television and new screens. But, at the same time, they turn out to be accessible with facility, by the Internet. They are two parallel movements, one of projection or of exteriorization, another of penetration from the outside or internalization. Education centres have also been opened to the media. On the one hand they are involved in a movement of internalization, because of the influence media have on the education of children and teenagers. Education can no longer be controlled and administered by educational institutions (and less by families). On the other hand schools, in a movement of exteriorization, are projected and open to the outside. Thanks to new mass media they become actors and observers of the social and natural world.

At the same time institution walls, of any kind of power—walls of palace, city, or department—have become, thanks to media, more permeable. Politicians tend to represent their actions in front of the television cameras—it is a more theatrical than transparent exteriorization—and, at the same time, they are scrupulously observed by citizens through the investigations and registrations of all media systems.

Nations and borders of countries too yield the media. Nowadays the debate activated by the United Nations and the UNESCO in relation to the possibility (or impossibility) that, in the name of national sovereignty, countries could regulate (or had the right to do it) what was called the "free flow of information" seems out-of-date and dismissed to us.

Nowadays, with satellites and digital television, with the Internet and the new media, the possibility of political regulation, or even restriction, of this flow seems impossible. But this has not prevented regulations and restrictions based on other instances to be produced, such as those which determine wealth or economy, nor hidden regulations, like those produced in terms of what is called "gap or digital fracture."

This helps us in understanding the meaning of the phenomenon of dislocation within the new communicational context, that is to say, the loss of value of space and at the same time the explosion of the barriers that marked and delimited space in the past.

The phenomenon is very clear: the increase in nomadism that characterizes new communications. Humanity has been nomadic for thousands of years. The search for hunts and their pursuit obliged men, grouped in hordes and tribes, to move constantly from a place to another in search of food and refuge. This determined their life: thrifty, without too many objects to transport, passing and ephemeral, without stable dwellings and with little identification with the place in which they were used to staying from one migration to another. But, gradually, the discovery of the mining industry, stockbreeding, and agriculture facilitated the establishment of hordes and tribes in fixed places. They began, then, to build the first stable refugees and the first houses. Men started progressively to take possession of place and to conquer it from a semiotic point of view, that is to say, to recognize it, to mark and possess it: it was no longer a transit place, but a habitat in which they could identify themselves.

This appropriation of space, place, and nation was followed by the transformation of beliefs and religions. If specific Gods for nomadic and wandering towns had existed, the settlement gave rise to new religions that affirmed the identity of inhabitants and of certain sacred places. The religion of Zarathustra, for example, one of the first historic monotheisms, was born, in good part, as a speech destined to give sense and to legitimize relationships of people to places they lived in, to their own seasonal cycles, to agriculture, as new source of life, and to stable stockbreeding. Also the religion of the Romans, (that was) originally a town of peasants, believed in the home Gods—those that sanctified and they enriched the fruits of land and the objects that configured what Goffman called the precinct. Beliefs were all organized in order to maintain a strict spatial order.

Those changes in beliefs created distances from the first nomadic stadium of the humanity. It was also useful to affirm doctrines that permitted to face towns that continued to be nomads and that periodically besieged legitimate places and nations. But, curiously, technological development obliges us to face a new kind of universal and planetarium nomadism, since mass media decentre, dislocate, and sow everywhere the chaos of the constant pilgrimage.

The New Media Time

Along with spatial changes, the media city has introduced many changes in the perception of time. Peasants and farmers were used to the seasonal nature of their work, to cycles that related climate with cultivations and their life were subjected to the rhythms of nature. In the same way, their ways of socialising, the rhythm of their meetings, their duration and opportunity had much to do with weather, the rhythms of daylight, and their limited mobility and slowness. Cities mark a breach with those subjections and restrictions.

On the one hand, work is no longer seasonal and is separated from natural rhythms. Industry, as opposed to agriculture, has no longer to wait in order to obtain fruits in specific moments of the year, but their production can be programmed and organized at will, and this has also consequences in the rhythms of satisfaction of the demand.

Table 1. The digital society: tensions and alternatives

Orientation of the digital society.	Weaknesses and tensions.	Alternatives.
Without space	A complete dislocation brings about rootlessness, loss of security, and loss of stability both for individuals as for communities. It causes tensions between local identities and communication identities.	Reinventing the local spaces. Removing their condition of closed precincts through communication but in the same time appreciating its potentialities of security, recognition, and environment of development.
Without time	It causes the loss of the sense of the history and of continuity, thus, as in last instance the capacity to project and to plan.	Using communication and memory as new tools useful for comprehension and meaning.
Immediacy	Converting the wait and the effort into a psychological suffering and driving to impulsiveness.	Balancing the direct access to the objects and realities with the value of the effort. Recovering the sense of patience.
Globalization	It can bring to the homogeneity and flattening of identities more than an authentic intercultural encounter.	Taking advantage of globalization to promote the open diversities and the pluralism with sense of the universal thing.
Total visibility	This visibility is above all appearance, because there are areas of darkness and occultation, but it introduces a false sense of transparency and, besides, it nullifies the discretion.	Expanding the areas of authentic visibility, but permitting the shyness and the limit that allows the intimacy and the autonomous personality.
Complete rationalization of life	It tends to hold the life to its measurable and calculable side leaving the qualitative part and the psychological depth of the actors that take part in them.	Recovering the sense of a personal life, overturned towards human and interior values, when it takes advantage of the efficacy that try the new rationalizations.
Consumerism	It is the consecration of the objects of consumption. It obliges a permanent tension that tends only to the maximization of the benefits of business.	Reorienting the use towards the concrete satisfaction of needs. Recovering a sense of austerity. Orienting the economy towards the authentic needs of humanity.
Permanent connection	Although it contributes to advantages and concrete benefits, such as the communicability and the fast aid, or updated information, it empowers the invasion of the private sphere through the media and a focus on the autonomous personality.	Balancing the connection and privacy, dialogue, and silences. Opening to the others and solitude and isolation.
Constant change	It leaves without sure backup to the person, although it improves the processes of adaptation to the changes of the environment.	Search of a new stability based on the continuity affirmed through the changes, the constancy, and the continuance.

continued on following page

Table 1. continued

Fragmentation and decontextualization	It empowers the superficial feeling to be reported, but it impedes the deep and complex knowledge of causes and effects.	Promoting the explanatory, deep information, and the recovery of the contexts that facilitates the intelligibility of the world.
Mimicry	It prompts the community sense but it empties the personal autonomy.	Balancing the imitation of models with autonomy person.
Focus on economics	It can save resources, but it tends to convert people into merchants.	Compensating the focus on economics with the new sense of humanisms and the significance of the human person.
Apathy and excitement	It facilitates time going by and entertainment, but it is accustomed to demanding prefabricated excitements and to confusing authentic emotions with those canned. Promoting the interest in the reality and in human actions.	Stimulating action instead of passiveness and participation instead of submission.
Sterilized virtuality	It facilitates the process of learning and catharsis, but the contact with the reality dissolves us and creates a feeling of de-responsibility.	Recovering the exercise of virtuality in a context of reality and intervention on the reality.

On the other hand, meetings in the city are more frequent, even only because of the concentration of population. Along with the enlargement of cities, also the use of means of transport and journeys increases. All these facts make the citizen have another consideration of the meaning and value of time. Mass media in particular have changed radically the situation. Practically, we can speak of temporary revolution. The rapidity in the circulation of information has changed every time humankind became accustomed to it. It has changed the rhythms of work, that of business. They both tend to follow the evolution of demand. Marketing and its strategies in particular can have an impact on the demand of citizens, on the notoriety of products, ideas, or inclinations. And all in increasingly shorter and giddier times. Innovations are diffused with haste and rapidity; people meetings themselves do not last more then a phone call or an e-mail. News is known in a few hours or even live. Services are produced online. And media citizens in general are available and accessible for communication most of the time.

The time of wait, therefore, has condensed and tends to zero. In the same way, the time of answer obliges us to answer immediately to a call to an e-mail or to an offer. The rapidity with which we transmit our expressions, reactions, and messages is also much more reduced in time. This let us be simultaneously connected with others and live our own time in a different way. Duration is no longer how it was. According to the rhythm of information, states of things, objects, and relations (with objects and people) have increasingly become more ephemeral and interchangeable. The term duration in itself has barely a meaning. It is no longer considered a value the fact that objects or our relationships with them nor personal relationships last; nor it has a lot of sense, to consider duration of an object or of a message (for example a film) as a value as, thanks to technology, we can control to our craving his duration (we can slow down, repeat, freeze, stop and resume...). Even the perception of time has changed. Mass media is more absorbent and increasingly more capable of abstracting us from our environment and erasing any reference or orientation to the passing of time. We could spend hours on the Internet or answering e-mail without barely realising. In the same way this happens to us with television or with movies. The hypnotic power of media is causing a constant attack and making it lose a firm support to our intuition on the time, our internal temporary sense. Also the globalization of communication and its capacity of penetration makes our contacts and our calls, as well as our television or any another media programming—in particular the Internet—be, day by day, more and more far away from the cycles of day and night or from the rhythms of dream and wake. They all seems always accessible; you have only to be in front of the screen.

Memory, that is, also, an essential element in the subjective and objective configuration of time, has changed so much that it alters our coordinates of reference. Memories have been more and more external; they do not depend on us neither on our brain and, furthermore, they are accessible to will. The perception of the sense of history, of past, and their value is then different nowadays. Everything can gravitate on the present because memories are part of it and, at the same time, only the present seems to have value. In this way, simultaneity, the present, the permanent accessibility, the tendency to zero of the time of wait and, finally, hurry, acceleration, and rapidity are essential elements of the new time launched by the mediation.

The New Anthropology of the Digital Society

The digital society is not a mix of instruments useful to humanity. It is the context for a new process of humanisation, an opportunity for the rise of a new anthropology (Castells, 1996). It is necessary to be conscious of it and to recognize in the present some of the directions towards the future. We are going to treat this issue from an individual perspective. Later on we will deal with the subject from a social and institutional point of view.

How are the Individuals, the Media People?

- **They are connected people:** they live a consistent part of their life connected to a screen, to some headphones, to a console, and so forth, three, four hours of their life. Through such connection, they weave their social relationships, their ways of life, and their way to react to the world.

- **Impulses and flavours for the rapid change:** They are accustomed to adopting styles subject to rapid changes, to pay attention to the esthetics of the environments,and to accept the importance of the style. Things that change fast attract them. They mythicize the velocity.

- **They are oriented towards the sterilized virtual environments:** they like to experience virtual sensations, battles, conquests, and so forth. But this is properly sterilized: without blood, neither deaths nor real risks. They live in an almost total simulation.

- **They are centred on the consumption:** They live to consume and they experience the maximum pleasure in waste. The consumerism is devotion and almost a religion.

- **They are apathetic and they look for excitement:** They do not fully participate in real life; they tend to be passive spectators. Therefore they seem to have no will. To compensate for this psychological state, they seek the constant excitement, above all in the form of shrill audiovisual discourse.

- **They are politically mild:** as they do not participate actively in social life, they are prone to drag for the mimicry and the manipulation of masses.

- **Adaptable:** They adapt to arrogance. They are not protected in stable and firm institutions and they can change easily in case the environmental changes require them to.

- **Community lovers:** they like to feel integrated in communities. Those who obtain models and psychological securities are not individualists, nor authentically part of the community. To those who belong to them, these communities are formal and they are based on appearances. We would be able to say that they are communities properly "sterilized."

- **Fragmentary:** The dispersion and saturation of the messages that they receive brings about a vision of life full of fragments, of remaining, of decontextualized speeches and with no memory.

- **Unstable:** their predisposition to the behaviour change, to the lack of security and to the psychological instability. They are vulnerable and they like that instability.

How are the Digital Institutions?

- **Dislocated and decentralized:** they have lost their place, their space, and they no longer constitute precincts. But they have to be projected through communication nets if they want to keep being efficient.

- **Adaptable and flexible:** They have to transform their forms and their behaviours to be adapted to the psychology of the new users. These new users do not accept fixed and immutable structures. They try to reach the main value of flexibility.

- **Checkers and automated institutions:** They are institutions that have to rationalize the processes, to control them through statistical algorithms, and to improve the effectiveness of the resources that they use. A certain economics sense has invaded the way of operating of any institution.

- **Unstable:** Their own sense of adaptability and flexibility makes them unstable, far away of firm principles and overturned from change.

- **Low emotional:** As they are separated from space and from real time, they promote a human contact which is virtual and lacking of emotions and of psychology.

- **Global:** the separation of space and resources caused by the communication technologies multiply their global reach.

- **Mild towards economic politics:** as consequence to its own internal rationality to the prices reduction politics and maximization of the benefits. This makes them sensitive to the overall economic system.

These are the individuals and harmonious institutions within the digital society; sensitive people to the mimicry of others, to the continuing change, to style, to consumerism, to the sterilized potentials; mild unstable institutions to the economy, overturned from the continuing change and from the adaptation, global, cold and little emotional, rationalizing. This can be our digital future.

The Alternative to the Myth

Can we aspire to another digital future? Can we avoid the negative aspects of the dominant digital future? How and with what strategies? We are going to the great promises of the digital future and we are seeking its effective and realistic counterpart.

If we think of alternatives and counterproposals, if we admit that the digital society is something escapable and evitable, then we will identify the discourse and the practices that inspire it the opportunity for an improvement of humanity and the occasion for a deep reflection on our future. This implies deep reflection and participation. A new sense of community that tries to bring back the media environment we live in towards the intrinsic values of the dignity and autonomy of people. Finally to distance us from the focus on economics that prompts the efficacy at any cost and the consumerism, to situate the human person with its sense of significance and of universality, in the centre of the social and communicative action. In this sense, the digital society, distant from a coercive and mythical prophecy, becomes a hope and an occasion for our improvement as human beings and moral people.

New Values of Media Education

Media Education should be considered an answer to the phantasmagorical myth of the digital society and it should build a sense of the reality focused on freedom and on human dignity.

It has to combine its traditional role of analysis and criticism with a renewed capacity of imagination and a search of future alternatives. It cannot be mere contemplation. It has to promote participation and production in the processes that are shaping the future. It has to be inspired and based on the new values and counter values deriving from the demythologizing of the concept of digital society: the access to the real thing, the austerity, the productive imagination, the reinvention of spaces and times, individual conscience, memory, freedom of thought, common and supportive sense, confidence in the human person and in its significant value, constancy, coherence, and so forth.

The new media education has to take advantage of the positive values that the same configuration of the digital society, with its dark and light sides, is representing for humanity. But this should be done taking a serious and deep critical conscience regarding myths and abuses introduced by a despotic and deterministic vision of the information society.

Media education has to rescue the values that help to constitute the audiovisual net—Internet and digital television—that is globalizing the planet. This Internet, that is not exempt of risks and traps, can represent the union and a certain sense of communication and of community. The Internet implies dialogue, exchange of points of view, search in agreement, and consensus. It also means aspiration to an egalitarian flow of information, abolition of the class and status' differences.

The Internet as a value is an aspiration to unite, to communion in which the media education has to be based. The Internet, beyond its possible perversions, has a peaceful sense and contributes to the construction of a cosmopolitan statute, of a universal and global citizenship in which all the citizens of the world can be considered compromised.

It is true and obvious that the acceptance of this audiovisual Internet by different cities of the world indicates that Internet and the digital television constitute good news, a happy announcement, that can be greeted with happiness. But it is certain that apart from this good news it is found what Kant called the "visit of the merchants": they frighten the injustices that commit when they visit foreign towns and lands. Visiting is for them is the same than conquering. Browsing the Internet may be, in this sense, a new version of old conquests.

Values' Destructions and Constructions

The Internet can open new horizons of know-how, of exchanges, and of relationships. It can help people in their work, in facilitating their tasks, in integrating them with others. Although they can be far away, they can share their objectives and desires. The Internet can promote the comprehension of the individual on his/her own world. It can prompt more conscience and autonomy. It can connect us to others and with what happens in the world. It enlarges our sense of compassion, of solidarity, and of what according to many religions is known as charity. These are the constructive aspects. But the Internet can be a trap for the independence and autonomy of the individuals and constitute a way of penetration and invasion for marketing strategies and commercialization, besides being able to be a vehicle of ideology and very powerful handling. The Internet can also trap us, oblige a permanent connection that move away us of interior our own world. The Internet could trap children and young people and carry them to an empty existence: it drives them continuously to chats empty of sense and to aggressive and violent play. The media education has to focus on this alternative of values, on these dilemmas. It has to propose a critical review of the processes and require meanwhile a transformation of the negative conditions.

On Education

The audiovisual Internet can build a universal school that approaches the resources of knowledge from different point of views. It can be a perfect vehicle to connect those who learn. E-learning can change the forms of learning. It can make it deeper, solid, and different. The use of e-learning in schools can promote new styles of learning, adapt the tasks and the didactic resources to the needs of each student or each apprentice, and simulate situations that would be impossible to acquire in different ways. The lecturers of the world can feel supported and helped in their work by the Web. All these aspects are constructive.

The Internet also brings about destructive elements. The indiscriminate use of the Internet may introduce in the interested learning sources, little severity, and obscurantist.

This can be produced in fields such as medicine, pharmacy, genetics and others; as far as social, civic, and political thought is concerned its effect is subtle. The Internet, and above all, television, can shift from the authentic pedagogical act to substitute the authentic teaching and the effort of the learning by broadcasting knowledge, by the saturation of the information and by a technicality empty of content. The Internet can also deprive the sense of originality and creativity, that has to characterize the authentic learning, through the use of massive copy and paste. The Internet can take us to the mirage of substituting information quantity by the wisdom of the life.

On Government and Institutions

The Internet, in its more constructive aspect, can promote what is called e-government.

That is:

1.   The growth in electronic administration;
2.   The advance towards electronic democracy.

The electronic administration is related to the utopia of an accessible and transparent bureaucracy; being able to solve all the administrative procedures through the Web: permissions, licenses, consultations, payments, and so forth. The electronic democracy connects with some of the current thoughts that require deeper public deliberation, an active citizenship and a greater participation of the citizens. Nevertheless, surfing the Internet can imply for our governments and our democratic institutions a backwards movement. The electronic administration can convert us in numbers. It can shift from the personal contact with the administrators and substitute the human choice with information systems that decide for the people. The electronic administration can, perhaps, establish an electronic identity which is the result of all the data administered, that is able to substitute us without any guarantee of respect for our private dignity.

On Reflections

We conclude focusing on the way of thinking, on the way we perceive the world and our beliefs. What does build and destroy the Internet?

I believe that the Internet can suppose a consolidation, an advance towards a better, universal ethics, better said, global ethics. With this I refer to the possibility of establishing a tribunal in which value judgments can be debated, shared, and treated in cooperation. This global ethics that will be a limited level, limited of the personal ethics conscience, because it will be the result of a consensus, can be woven by dialogue between cultures and forms to think and to be comprehensive and supportive. But also this ethics can be very superficial and respond only to a minimum common denominator, to a banalization of our moral conceptions and to a superficial equalization. We can think that the Internet can conduct towards a universal citizenship.

All these values, dilemmas, problems, and alternatives have to inspire the new media education. And this inspiration is the best answer to the values that the audiovisual Internet represents. In this sense, the media education would be revealed like a philosophy of the present that anticipates a conscious future with the tools and practices of the education and that assumes as an object the construction of the Internet and the emergency of the new digital society.

References

Breton, P. (1993). *L'utopie de la communication*. Paris: La Découverte.

Castells, M. (1996). *The rise of the network society*. Malden, MA: Blackwell.

Giddens, A. (2000). *The third way and its critics*. London: Polity Press with Blackwell.

Mattelart, A. (2001). *Histoire de la société de l'information*. Paris: La Découverte.

McLuhan, M. (1964). *Understanding media*. New York: McGraw-Hill.

Meyrowitz, J. (1985). *No sense of place*. New York: Oxford University Press

Thompson, J.B. (1995). *The media and the modernity. A social theory of the media*. Cambrdige: Polity Press.

Chapter XVIII

Digital Literacy and Cultural Mediations to the Digital Divide

Monica Fantin, Universidade Federal De Santa Catarina (UFSC), Brazil

Gilka Girardello, Universidade Federal De Santa Catarina (UFSC), Brazil

Abstract

This chapter discusses the digital divide from the perspective of education and culture and highlights the forms in which the problem is presented in Brazil, understanding that it is not exclusive to this context. Given the complex challenges to digital inclusion in the context of globalization, the chapter emphasizes that for children and young people to be able to appropriate new technologies and languages in a significant manner, the promotion of digital literacy should be realized with respect to the concept of multiliteracies. Digital inclusion means much more than access to technologies and is understood as one of the fronts in the struggle against poverty and inequality. The authors propose that the understanding of the digital divide be enriched with the valorization of cultural mediations in the construction of digital literacy. In this sense, a culturalist perspective of media education can promote digital inclusion that is an experience of citizenship, belonging, and critical and creative participation of children and young people in the culture.

Introduction

In the early days of the popularization of personal computers in the 1980s, many people spoke of the infinite potential of the information highway that promised egalitarian and multidirectional communication among all peoples, groups, and nations. But another metaphor, critical of the naive optimism of the early years, did not take long to appear: that of the digital divide. How can the abyss that separates the digitally literate from the digitally illiterate—commonly understood as those excluded from the technological promise—be gapped? What other image could represent this tension in an alternative form, not as an unpassable chasm but as a space to be traversed? A river, which both separates and unites? A sea of currents that at once flow together and apart? How can this river be crossed, this sea be navigated?

This chapter proposes to discuss this problem—the distance between those who have and those who do not have complete access to the archives of culture made available by the media and the possibilities of recreating them critically. We focus on the new configurations that the problem takes with the intensification of the presence of digital technologies in education and culture. Our discussion seeks to identify possible contributions to the dilemmas of media education and of digital literacy that emerge from the Brazilian scene—a country of continental dimensions, where the pulsation of globalized media culture co-exists with a strong and sometimes preliterate popular culture, often in the same city and just a few blocks away. Our anchor in the problems as they are presented in Brazil does not mean, however, that we see the Brazilian or Latin American context as exclusive.

The diversity of semiotic practices and dislocations resulting from the forms by which industrial culture was incorporated into local contexts has challenged Brazilian thinkers for a number of decades. Concepts such as syncretism and cultural anthropophagy marked sociological, anthropological, and literary thinking in the country during the past century, in the search to understand the tensions between the "local" and "global" images and narratives, tensions that are at times generative and at times paralyzing. Paulo Freire's (2000) proposal for a pedagogy of liberation, with its emphasis on a dialogical methodology that would be a space for a radical and micropolitical criticism of oppression, continues to inspire a large number of educational experiences, in and outside of schools. Nevertheless, although these conceptual proposals are on the horizon of an increasing number of media education practices, they are rarely explicit.

This chapter identifies a number of theoretical themes and concepts that have been instigating and challenging the field of media education in Brazil. The digital divide will be understood as the contradiction between digital exclusion and inclusion, recognizing however, that one is not always opposed to the other. We will focus on concepts associated with practices that strive to establish a digital inclusion that transcends a merely operational access to machines and programs, that is, inclusion that is also political, social, and cultural—and thus meets the broad needs of education.

It is first necessary to locate the place from where we write, both from a theoretical as well as a geographic perspective. Our reflection about this theme is based on the Brazilian condition, although we believe that many of the issues that we will discuss here are analogous to those found in other countries at the periphery of capitalism. We are both professors and researchers working at the interface between education and communication in a large federal, public university. For this reason we feel comfortable speaking about the issue of the digital divide, since it would be impossible to consider the relationship between the media and education in our country without recognizing the social inequality, made evident in statistical data presented below. It is also necessary to recognize that exclusion is far from the only theme discussed in Brazilian or Latin American academic spaces that work with media education. We will thus attempt to consider the material precariousness in our country and the challenges that it creates for digital education, while highlighting those ideas, themes, and processes that, being fruit of the cultural singularity of our context, can contribute in a positive way to considering digital literacy and the digital divide.

Considering Inclusion in Education and Culture

Digital exclusion is not to be without a computer or a cell phone. It is to remain incapable of thinking, or creating and organizing new more just and dynamic forms of production and distribution of symbolic and material wealth. (Schwartz, 2000)

When we speak of digital inclusion, one immediately tends to think in the expansion of access to computers. Another way of thinking of the issue, however, is to give importance precisely to that which resists being done with computers, which tends to remain outside technological rationality. For Latin Americans, by taking simulation to the extreme, the new communication technologies "make visible the non-digestible, non-simulative, *remains* that from cultural alterity resists generalized homogenization" (Martín-Barbero, 2004, p.183). These "remains,", which resist media dilution, are related to the existence of popular culture, an expression that on our continent designates not the pop universe or the museum, but a space for symbolic exchanges and tensions that are still very much alive in society.

In this context many authors in our field highlight the importance of resistance to the model of technological and economic acceleration that is dominant in contemporary Western society and "that appears to condemn all other societies to an integration to its paradigm or to disappearance," as Santos (2003) warns. He adds that resistance to this model includes the maintenance of the diversity of cultures and societies, particularly of the "diversity of temporalities and of rhythms that are not annihilated by the imperative of total acceleration" (Santos, 2003, p.28).

Thus, a first presumption of this chapter is the need to consider the access to digital culture dialectically, abandoning any naïve enlightenment ideas or welfare-type programs that merely distribute equipment. We also seek a distance from the logic of globalized integration and the dichotomy between backwardness and modernity, which impels entire populations to the quest for the latest electronic gadgets. To think of digital inclusion in countries considered peripheral, requires paying attention to the cultural manifestations that take place outside of cyberspace. The absence of the latest technology is not necessarily understood as backwardness, a form of symbolic poverty or incompetence, but perhaps as a situation that composes a valuable and eloquent difference—a possible space for creative and critical constitution. It also requires paying attention to public policies for teacher education, as well as special educational and cultural programs. We consider it to be important to have this cultural perspective as a horizon, to assure that the democratization of digital access signifies the broadening of the social and cultural participation of various sectors of the population and not only a new form of ceding to old modes of discrimination and domination.

To think dialectically of digital inclusion in Latin America thus requires a careful look at the relationship between education and communication. Once again, it is Martín-Barbero who indicates that schools push young people to social-cultural marginalization, by encouraging passivity, redundancy, uniformity, anachronism, and provinciality, which contrast so strongly with the activity, diversity, curiosity, currentness, and opening of frontiers that mark the world of communication (2004, p. 350). The most grave consequence of this contradiction, according to the author, is that schools deny the poorest portion of the population the strength of orality found in their original culture, at the same time in which the poor are not introduced to the grammars of the new media. For the author, the cultural specificity of Latin American modernity lies in the complicity and interpenetration between oral and visual cultures.

The productive co-existence, whether marked by tension or partnership, between different cultures and imaginaries in Latin America, has been the object of analysis of a long critical tradition, exactly because this co-existence highlights the most eloquent of artistic and literary expression on the continent. To cite only two examples, we can begin with the "antropophagy" movement of the Brazilian modernist vanguard of the 1920s: "Tupi, or not Tupi, that is the question. I am only interested in what is not mine," Oswald de Andrade declared in his celebrated manifesto of

1928, permeated by nationalist references to the joy and creative potential of cultural syncretism. A second reference that is equally important is the concept of "hybrid cultures" developed by the Argentine García Canclini, which had wide academic circulation in the 1990s throughout South America. Based on this concept, the author discusses the new and original uses that each local community makes of videogames, videocassettes, and copying machines, emphasizing the egalitarian vitality of the singular mixes between the academic, the popular and the mass culture that the technologies favor.

These interactions allow the relativization of fundamentalisms, whether "religious, political, national, ethnic or artistic, which hold as absolute certain patrimonies and discriminate against the others," said Canclini (1998, p. 307). In relation to education, a fragmentary relationship with texts, books and annotations can also, Canclini suggests, induce "more fluid ties among the texts, among the students and knowledge" (1998, p. 308). In addition to these interesting aspects, however, he also points to the inequality in cultural capital and therefore the differences among the meanings constructed by youths for technologies in various social contexts. Appropriation of technologies is not the same for "poor adolescents who go to video-game arcades and for middle and upper class youth who have them in their homes." (Canclini, 1998). In addition, large sectors of Brazilian society pass from the traditional oral culture directly to audiovisual culture, or to the media orality, without passing through written culture. This evidently interferes in the various types of relationships with the new media products—given that the meanings of the technologies depend on the way that they are inserted in daily life—and how culture appropriates and then transforms them.

To dialectically consider digital inclusion in Latin America also requires paying attention to the relations between education and popular cultures. In Brazil, a large variety of manifestations linked to different traditions are still very much alive. Dramas and ritual and or religious festivals, musical narratives, and poetic repertoires are relatively easy to access, even in urban centers. As Azevedo (2006) said,

If for students of the middle and upper classes, children and grandchildren of literate people, the discourse of the school appears to make sense, for students coming from an oral tradition – the large mass of the Brazilian population, it presents an authoritarian, prejudicial, discriminatory and exclusionary character.

The prejudice of the school against traditional oral culture, Azevedo (2006) adds, leaves many children without references, because of the institutional disdain for the knowledge and values of their parents and thus with a difficulty in identifying with the educational "truth." The result, we can say, deepens the sociocultural marginalization to which we referred earlier.

A reflection that clearly and critically locates the relationship between education and social exclusion in Brazil is conducted by Muniz Sodré. He begins by recalling that we educate not only for what is viable today, but for what is possible tomorrow.

To educate means establishing an (ethical) distance from the animal condition and preparing for complete citizenship, which presupposes knowledge by the subject, in addition to that of technical-operative instrumentation, of the political and administrative processes of its *Polis*, that is, of its Human City. (Sodré, 2002, p. 87)

The dominant change of paradigm and new forms of labor organization have provoked alterations in pedagogical relationships at various levels of schooling, in the forms of teaching and learning and in curricular content. Moreover, in the new social-cultural order, he explains, common knowledge, or knowledge about the self, is in crisis. The transmission of information in media space has become characterized by persuasion or fascination and this fascination with the media wonders can result in an ideological practice that attributes to technological innovation itself a "magic power to resolve problems (…) generating a *technical temptation*" (Sodré, 2002, p. 99-100). Muniz Sodré maintains that this ideology is instilled not on an ethical but on a corporate horizon, in the framework of a private-sector oriented educational matrix.

Many projects with this technocratic and private sector focus can have consequences that can misguide educational policy, because they are based on market interests, Brazilian, and foreign, often, but not always, imbedded in the guidelines of international agencies.[1] In many programs said to promote digital inclusion, "the real intention to promote business competition with support for the implantation of electronic commerce, new security policies and other government objectives was camouflaged by the official discourse as 'digital literacy' and public education" (Sodré, 2002, p.104). More than transforming the real conditions in which the old educational structures are placed, Sodré maintains that these programs intend to include the largest possible number of people, qualifying them for the labor market as "cybernetic simulacros for 'inclusion of everyone in the Web', in other words, there is no reflection of a collective desire, but only an adaptation to a techno-bureaucratic scenario" (idem).

By emphasizing technical instruction, education abandons the socialization of knowledge linked to human values and enters the market for goods and services. According to Sodré this perspective cannot understand that what is most important in terms of education "is not in the technical means and the disciplinary content (knowledge and information) but in the *cultural form* by which the knowledges are incorporated and the pertinent connections are promoted among them" (2002, p.106) Thus, when programs for inclusion said to be innovative emphasize only access to equipment, they understand the school merely as a physical place and not as a cultural form.

These ideas establish a reference horizon that allows us to consider the challenges of digital inclusion in the complex scenario in which we live. These include developing: a capacity to pay attention to cultural—and not merely technical—dimensions of the relationship of children and youth with the technologies; a dialectical understanding of the relationship between school, media, and popular cultures; a focus on the local uses of the medias and a recognition of the possibility that the critical and creative tensions of the repertoires and languages that occur there can point to routes for the mediation, even if circumstantial, of digital exclusion.

Globalizations and Contexts of Inequality

The fight against exclusion is part of the rhetoric of the "information society" in the context of the dream of a "second Renaissance" based on creativity, scientific discovery, cultural development, and community cohesion, as proposed by the European Forum for the Information Society. The concern for inclusion was also recommended in the 1990s by the G7, which sought a transition to the "information society" including: global interaction of broadband networks, transcultural education, support for libraries, museums, and electronic art galleries, environmental management, natural resources, and healthcare, interconnection of public administration and a global multimedia inventory of projects and studies for the development of the Global Information Society (Cadimo, 2004, p. 4).

Certain experiences have shown that the new communication and experiential paradigm present real opportunities for the democratization of media and messages and for citizens to overcome their condition as consumers and or spectators and transform themselves into reflexive and participative subjects. However, in general, what we find is not only a growing distance between the info-rich and the info-poor, but also the production of a new type of illiteracy, digital illiteracy.

There is considerable regional disparity in the reach of the Internet, given that the most highly developed countries, with nearly 15% of the world's population, in 1998, accounted for 88% of all Internet users. In Latin America, 90% of the users are in the highest income groups as Castells (2006, p. 433) notes. "The spatial inequality in the access to the Internet is one of the most impressive paradoxes of the information era, due to the characteristic supposedly independent from the space of the technology " he maintains (Castells, 2006, p. 434). "Globalization acts selectively, including and excluding segments of economies and societies from networks of information, wealth and power that characterize the new dominant system" and for Castells "the new information technologies are the instrument of this global storm of accumulation of wealth and diffusion of poverty", that relegates entire peoples and territories to irrelevance from the perspective of the dominant interests of global informational capitalism (Castells, 2002, p. 191-192).

In this light, the situation in Brazil is concerning: 54% of Brazilians have never used a computer and only 14% of all homes have Internet access.[2] Three percent of school age children (6 -14) are out of school, corresponding to 1.5 million children.[3] Of the

162,000 public schools in Brazil, 129,000 do not have Internet access, 40,000 do not have a library, 25,000 do not have electricity, and 1,000 do not have a bathroom.

This data reinforces the certainty that the digital divide truly cannot be understood only as a question of access to technologies, because it involves much broader questions of a cultural, political, and social order.

At the same time in which we seek the universalization of schooling, reading and writing, for the first time in the history of humanity enormous changes are taking place within a single generation and no longer from one generation to another. In a country of continental scope such as Brazil, problems also take on enormous proportions: the challenge of digital inclusion coexists with these social challenges that have been resolved in other locations. For these reasons, this is a time of searching for paths and alternatives given the complexity of the problems that are not only related to education.

Another question that we must keep in mind when we speak of digital exclusion is its dynamic character, requiring that countries that are not at the vanguard of technological production develop a critical capacity for analysis of technological trends. At the minimum, "it is necessary to discuss the technology politically and get to know the possible technological options to avoid that they are not presented as inexorable and that we swallow them whole" (Santos, 2003, p. 33). Although it is common for us to hear that poor countries can "skip certain phases" of development, absorbing more advanced technologies, this development is continuous and moved by competition. Thus, each "last generation" of devices is quickly surpassed and becomes obsolete and "the highly dynamic character of the new technologies is a constantly renewed barrier to the capacity to approximate the poorest countries to the wealthiest ones" (Sorj, 2003, p.61). Considering that a large portion of the Brazilian population does not have physical access to the new technologies, in order for the country to begin to participate more broadly in the cyber-culture, public policies are needed that guarantee access, software development, the work of educational-cultural mediation and the training for citizenship through these technologies.

Thus, the access to communication technologies and technical knowledge provided by digital inclusion programs is not sufficient to construct an experience of citizenship, since it can be oriented towards critical as well as passive uses. It is necessary to promote conditions for the development of autonomy in the interaction with the media, in order to favor the critical formation of citizens, not only of users. This includes an ability to develop search criteria, to encourage technological fluency means to critically use information and communication technologies, interact with words, graphics, images, and sounds, locate, select and critically evaluate information, and know and have command of the rules of the social practice of communication supported by the media, in a search for significant, autonomous, and continuous learning, as Almeida (2005) affirmed. This facilitates the production of knowledge that is needed to improve living conditions, thus creating and organizing social relationships, communicative interactions, and cultural participation. This perspective of digital literacy as a social practice goes beyond learning about codes or technology. It implies the attribution of meanings to information that comes from different texts, as Almeida (2005) proposed. That is, it is a perspective aimed at the production and representation of knowing oneself, the others and the world.

Digital Literacy and Multiliteracies

Demographic data also present disturbing statistics indicating low literacy rates[4] forcing us to think of a new form of *dual illiteracy*: the functional and the digital. Is the complete computerization of schools the solution to this problem? The question does not have a single response, but we can say that the distribution of computers in schools would not be sufficient if there is no teacher training policy aimed at cultural and artistic enrichment so that the use of the equipment can gain social meaning. Dual illiteracy creates a dual challenge—or perhaps a multiple one, if we consider the need for literacy in multiple languages—to promote digital inclusion and digital literacy as public policies that confront the inheritance of functional illiteracy and at the same time combat technological apartheid. To believe that it is first necessary to eradicate one and later confront the other would be a fundamental error, as Silveira (2001) emphasizes. Without a policy to invest in writing there would be a continuous production of inequality in digital literacy, since this requires a command of writing.

In the early 1960s, Paulo Freire recognized that the reading of the world preceded the reading of the word. In the 1980s, Emília Ferreiro and Ana Teberosky emphasized that children already have contact with written language before they enter school and highlight the importance of the social function of writing and learning to read and write as a form of representation, more than as a simple acquisition of an alphabetic code. Even so, in Brazil and in other countries, the word that designates learning to read and write "alfabetização" refers primarily to the process of acquisition of an alphabetic system. The word literacy "letramento" is used to emphasize the social function of writing.

In various countries such as Brazil, it is found that many children, although they know how to read and write, do not practice the social use of reading and writing. This is the other reason for the distinction in our context, between the terms "alfabetização" and "letramento," which, although they are interrelated, have specific meanings. Implicit in the concept of literacy, "is the idea that writing has social, cultural, political, economic, cognitive, and linguistic consequences, whether for the social group in which it is introduced, or for the individual that learns to use it," said Soares (2005, p. 17).

From this perspective, literacy can be understood as a condition that the individual acquires in virtue not only of knowing how to read and write, but of having appropriated the social dimension of writing, incorporating it into their life, and transforming oneself, as Soares (2002) emphasizes. The author uses the term in the plural, literacies, recognizing that different writing technologies create and require different literacies, above all since the introduction of cyberculture.

Some scholars even broaden this concept to that of multiliteracies, in order to include the audiovisual and digital grammars that involve a certain level of understanding of reading and production in all these dimensions. There is an interesting aspect in this notion of multiliteracies, which is the need that we have today to circulate in other types of representation of reality that transcend writing and involve the visual, musical, corporal, digital, and other forms of representation. It is important to work with these dimensions in a transdisciplinary manner, with an emphasis on circulation, transit, and interaction, involving scientific, literary, aesthetic, and cultural literacy.

The notion of digital literacy is related to print literacy in Buckingham's (2003) analogy:

As with print, children also need to be able to evaluate and use information critically if they are to transform it into knowledge. (...) As with older media, children need to be empowered to make informed choices on their own behalf, and to protect and regulate themselves. And just as print literacy involves writing as well as reading, digital literacy must involve creative production in new media as well as critical consumption. (Buckingham, 2003, p. 177)

In this perspective, digital literacy is associated to play, art and narrative, as languages that are essential for children to be able to express and communicate their feelings, ideas, and experiences. The specificities of each language should be considered, given that different abilities are required, for example, to write words, take photos, watch a film, or make a video-clip.[5] An articulation between the different languages and contents involves a collaborative work of experimentation, creation, and discovery. It also involves dialogue, negotiation, polyphony, openness, flexibility, criticism, and collaboration. In this process, the languages of different fields of knowledge can be understood based on different perspectives: as forms of expression of the subject and of the culture, as a means of communication, as a form of interaction and human development, and also as a social-cultural object of knowledge. This perspective requires that the initial and on-going education of teachers also considers their own experience with expression and creation, based not only on scientific knowledge, but also on the recovery of their experiences with languages that at times are dormant (artistic, performatic, literary).

It is through the different languages that children use, verbal and nonverbal, that they express their wealth of imagination and produce culture. In this perspective, speech, crying, gesture, observing, silence, play, sciences, arts, and experiences with media are part of a network of symbolic systems that is the context of a plural literacy. This leads us to reconsider what it means to be literate. For the teacher today it is not enough to have information from books, to dominate codes of writing and understand them as a form of representation of speech. To what degree is an individual literate if he or she is not capable of seeing, interpreting, and questioning TV images, watching and understanding films, critically analyzing advertising and news, using a computer, conducting research, navigating the Web or creating and inserting texts and images in the flow of social circulation? And to what degree are we as teachers literate in these languages and are we working in a suitable manner with the multiple literacies?

In sum, to be literate in the 21st Century involves multiple literacies, including digital literacy, which also concerns the construction of real and virtual citizenship and the possibility of effectively participating in society. For this reason, the media can no longer be excluded from the literacy process. Even if it seems obvious, this idea has still not been sufficiently adopted and converted into a transformative practice in many social-cultural contexts.

The concept of multiliteracies as a new understanding of the appropriation of the social practices of reading and writing, demands considering the theoretical bases that are its foundation and giving it legitimacy. In this sense, the multiliteracies can be understood as a repertoire of related capacities, some generic and others specifically related to the media and other areas, as Bazalgette (2005) emphasizes. This concept is related to media education, particularly to an ecological approach to media education (Rivoltella, 2002), understood as the interface between the various fields of knowledge, involving science, art, and literature.

Three elements have been identified that sustain this approach to media education: culture, as the expansion of and opportunities created by various cultural repertoires, criticism, as the capacity to analyze, reflect, and evaluate, and creation, as the creative capacity of expression, communication, and construction of knowledge. To these three words that begin with the letter C,[6] we propose adding the C of citizenship, thus establishing the "4 Cs" of media education: culture, criticism, creation, and citizenship, which must be present to make possible transformative work in the schools (Fantin, 2006).

Citizenship and Digital Inclusion of Children and Youth

Based on the conceptual fluidity of the concept of citizenship, Rivoltella (2005, p. 155) identifies some dimensions that qualify citizenship and the citizen: civil law, political citizenship, social citizenship, and cultural citizenship. Relating these dimensions of citizenship with media education, Rivoltella emphasizes what he calls the "dual exercise of citizenship" or the combination of *citizenship of belonging* with *instrumental citizenship*. On one hand media education can call the attention of civil society and political power to the values of citizenship, and on the other, through its specificity, media education contributes to building this citizenship. It involves "a dual exercise of citizenship, which is active and passive, composed of solicitation of rights and of a set of efforts to build them" (Rivoltella, 2005, p. 156).

For Rivoltella (2005), to educate for citizenship involves an inclusionary education based on the recognition of universal rights, the formal and legal factors of citizenship as well as social and cultural rights, school education that conducts transversal work among the disciplines, considering the implicit and explicit curriculum, and an education that seeks solidarity. It also implies favoring interaction with territory, developing multiple and complex identities, and promoting a sense of belonging to the local, national, and global context. This perspective of educating for citizenship strives to favor: *the acquisition of knowledges* (knowledge of the world and the cultural, social, and economic reality in which we live, as well as of the laws, institutions, and their functioning); the *acquisition of social competencies* (knowing how to perform the role of citizen, to cooperate, construct and realize common projects, to assume responsibilities, resolve conflicts and intervene in a political debate); and the *acquisition of ethical and interpersonal abilities* (knowing how to express solidarity, to be open to difference, etc.).[7]

By encouraging this type of education, schools would be taking on new responsibilities in society and could contribute to the construction of a new form of cultural mediation, integrating with the communication media in order to reduce the asymmetries on the plane of cognitive and participatory capacities of individuals, as Morcellini (2004) emphasizes. Upon transposing this idea to the concern for the digital divide, we note that the term "digital inclusion" cannot always be understood as the opposite of exclusion, given that it often only describes programs that propose alternatives to the problems presented by social inequality. In order to struggle against the forms of domination and control caused by the digital divide, the public calls for digital inclusion began to appear, with the impact of the Internet on the world in the 1990s. To be inserted digitally comes to be a condition for citizenship and a right of individuals for their existence in the world of information and communication.

The debate about the forms of insertion of Brazilian society in this scenario is even more important when we analyze the data from the "Map of Digital Exclusion" which indicates that 85% of the Brazilian population is excluded from the information society (Néri, 2003). Although the federal government has invested in various digital inclusion programs, data indicates unequal growth among the regions of the country. From 2000-2004, Brazil had a 286.2% growth in the number of Internet users, becoming the country with the tenth most users in the world, with nearly 19 million people navigating the Internet. This growth is incomparably greater than that of the other means of communication.[8] Nevertheless, the penetration of the Internet in the country is unequal, concentrated in the upper classes. According to the map of digital exclusion, 79% of Brazilians never touched a computer and 89% never accessed the Internet. According to a study conducted in Latin America, only 10% of the poorest 40% of the Brazilian population have Internet access. Among Argentina, Brazil, Chile, and Mexico, Brazilians pay the most to have a computer (IBOPE).[9] This reveals that Brazil still has much to do to gap the digital abyss.[10]

While from a simplistic perspective the recipe to transpose the digital divide would be to make technology available, we see that this is important but not sufficient, and we must consider the many complexities of the problem. We can ask what is the significance of including and what are the forms of inclusion, since the digital divide can be examined from its social, economic, cultural, technological, and/or intellectual dimensions, and based on its technical, subjective, or economic specificities. What does it mean to include? What rights does technological access to the use of the computer promote if this access is not accompanied by literacy in the multiple languages? Is to access a computer without being literate allowing its use without assuring the rights to citizenship it makes possible? Is digital inclusion a right of citizenship or a market necessity? While much of the international literature about the digital divide emphasizes the technical nature of inclusion, the questions above seek to point to the cultural and social aspects of inclusion, which seem fundamental from a Latin American perspective.

The term inclusion today, in some public debates, appears to have become a consensual politically correct label, immune to reflection and discussion. The principle that society must be included in the information era is accepted without questioning, and the question "who will be included and what will he or she do with this new tool?" appears to have little importance. Without guarantees of employability, without real opportunities to use digital tools to participate in decision making about their communities and schools and in formulating and accessing public policies and services for healthcare, education, housing and so forth, and given the speed of technological change, it appears that the discourse of digital inclusion is satisfying to only a few companies, NGOs, and technocrats who sell this ideology as one more technological novelty.[11] In this context, to include appears to mean in most cases to offer material conditions (skill and access to the Internet) to manipulate technologies. More than developing critical and questioning cognitive processes, it appears that in this vision, to include is to merely adapt pre-existing procedures to current technologies.

If to include is to give access to proprietary computers with primitive software and mechanically train people to use them efficiently at work, as is implicit in most of the inclusion projects,[12] Lemos (2003) asks why should society be included? For whom and for what does inclusion serve? In societies such as ours, where basic rights are still not assured, inclusion appears to be a goal and a utopia in some social fields such as healthcare, education, housing, and public safety. Is it possible to evaluate digital inclusion by the number of computers, people navigating, and other similar statistics, Lemos (2003) asks, highlighting that in this perspective, to include appears basically to adapt and mold. But to include is much more than to adapt to a technocratic logic. After all, it is by participating and acting in the world that we construct ourselves and "it is in the *insertion* in the world and not in the *adaptation* to it that we become historic and ethical beings, capable of choosing deciding and overcoming" said Freire (2000, p. 90).

Digital inclusion must include social, cultural, technological, and intellectual dimensions, in order to favor forms of belonging and assure the effective participation of people in the culture. Thus, the policies of digital inclusion should also encourage the deconcentration of power and local, regional, and national autonomy and not subordination to monopolies and imprisonment to private networks. This is the position taken by numerous authors, such as Silveira (2003), who see the open software movement as an important route to autonomy and a possibility for a creative mediation of the digital divide. In his analysis, "the open software movement is an authentic expression of this potential of the network and the great model for consolidation of shared solutions before complex questions, based on multiethnic, multinational and multicultural interaction" (Silveira, 2003, p. 38). He understands the open software model as an economically viable option, which is technologically innovative and stable, and explains that an extensive use of open software in Brazil would not only save money in royalties, but also establish the country as an important producer and distributor of solutions in open code. This use of open software can exemplify imaginative alternatives to the monopolistic tendencies of technological globalization. As Boaventura Souza Santos affirms, "it is through the imagination that citizens are disciplined and controlled by States, markets and other dominant interests, but it is also from the imagination that citizens develop collective systems of dissidence and new designs for collective life" (2002, p. 46).

Now we can examine some implications of these developments in the cultural lives of children and young people.

Childhood, Youth, and Contemporary Dialogues

How can we consider the possibilities of citizen participation of children and youth in contemporary society? If on one hand technological developments offer certain forms of interaction and participation, above all in networks, many authors indicate that on the other hand technological interactions with the most immediate local context become more difficult. The matter is still open to debate. Could it be that the exacerbation of individualism in the society of consumption also offers possibilities for overcoming this individualism through the contradictions that are revealed? Can children and young people, through educational mediation and by interacting with technologies, transcend the limits created by individualism and build other dimensions of participation? To think of forms of participation only as a reproduction of the usual form of conducting politics would be an insufficient contribution to democracy and to the questioning of cultural standards. It is necessary to think of social and digital inclusion as a form of participation in culture and as a possibility for change in the forms of seeing and relating to society. We will discuss some of the many challenges this poses.

Children and young people are increasingly present on the public scene. In addition to their recognition as consumers and citizens, it is recognized that they are particularly vulnerable to social changes. Although child labor is generally restricted to peripheral countries, children are targeted as consumers in borderless campaigns by globalized marketing. Cultural products aimed at children, video, television, cinema, cartoons, computer games, children's literature, and other products for children, fashion, candy, school supplies, recreational services, and so forth, constitute one of the most important segments in the consumer market. In this sense, the child is seen more as a consumer than as a citizen.

In this process, childhood comes to share the same media repertoires, often by developing a "single taste." We know that in each context there is an active reinterpretation of cultural products, in a process in which globalized cultures cross and recombine with local cultures.[13] But it is important to explore the possibilities for autonomy of childhood, in a context in which economic and cultural globalization operate in a complex and contradictory form on the status of childhood.[14] On one hand, hegemonic forces lead to the use of children's labor, to an increase in poverty, social inequality, and to the constitution of a global children's market, with effects on behavior, lifestyles, and the cultures of childhood. On the other hand, contra-hegemonic globalization promotes the rights of children and strives to establish a political agenda that focuses on childhood.

Tensions between *heterogenous living conditions* and *homogenizing pressures* contribute to the formation of fragmentary and changing identities, and the contemporary social space of (re)institutionalization of childhood can also imply a possibility for alternative paradigms. Given this situation, schools can be seen as one of the important faces of counter-hegemonic globalization.[15] While the school is the institution that has contributed most to the definition of the social status of children, Brazil's deep educational problems challenge the structure and symbolic order of school's as well as public educational policies, questioning the meaning of educational actions. Therefore, schools cannot remain divorced from the movement to construct rights for children, including the right to digital citizenship. As a public service, schools cannot be merely a preparatory space devoted to the aim that one day each individual can become a citizen. They must be places where citizenship is a reality even in childhood.

In order to accomplish this goal, education must consider the complexities of being a young person today, especially in its subjective aspects, which also depend on the sociocultural context. A recent study[16] revealed that Latin American children and youth say they are happier, more nationalist, and live closer to their families than boys and girls in developed countries. In contradiction, this same group occupies the worst position in well-being, due to their concerns for public safety. According to the study, these children and youth are concerned about losing their parents, with physical appearance, education, and in getting a job. This survey revealed two distinct worlds: "In the developed countries, young people are rich, but pessimistic about the future. In the developing world, children and adolescents are optimistic and hopeful, despite the fact that they confront large daily challenges."[17] The study also shows that more than 70% of youth and 80% of children in Argentina and Mexico said that they are happy, in contrast with the data obtained in the United States and England, where less than 30% of youth and less than 50% of the children say they are happy.[18]

This data confirms the degree to which subjective production is involved in the identity of young people and consequently in the perspectives that they have for the future. The data shows, once again, how important it is for digital inclusion to go beyond mere technical access and achieve towards cultural inclusion. This indicates the need to promote digital inclusion, while considering the specificity of memories, traditions, aims, values, fears, and hopes of youth in each culture. Projects designed from top to bottom (or from the "center" to the "periphery") in which there is no space for the emergence of different responses to these subjective and differing realities, will certainly have limited results from the perspective of participation and citizenship.

Another theme that is obviously part of the situation that we are examining is the relationship between adults and children in the scenario of digital culture. The emergence of a new type of subjectivity in the new generations, as a result of complex factors, has been identified by researchers in various fields. Others argue that the vision of a *deficiency* of new generations—that identifies their cognitive and cultural poverty—should be substituted by a vision based on *difference*. Based on theories that consider the combination of technological identity with human identity, Green and Bigum (1995), for example, have provocatively suggested that if a moralist panic tends to see children and youth today as aliens—a culture that is "designed, motivated and constructed differently," (Green & Bigum, 1995, p. 212)—on the other hand, it is adults who should be increasingly seen as aliens, given that it is "youth that inherit the earth" (Green & Bigum, 1995).

If we accept the provocation of these authors and admit that we as adults are increasingly *alien*, foreign, and—from the cultural perspective of children and young people, it is not for this reason that we are exempt from responsibility. We need to sharpen our tools for understanding, invest in the transformation of languages, contents, and contexts of reception, and on improving our capacity to understand the needs and desires of the young. In fact, we find ourselves today at the edge of various abysses—between generations, cultures, classes with unequal access to material and immaterial goods. At the same time, the new cultural forms are also means for bridging these gaps. Faced with the creation of this new culture, we need to adapt ourselves to new ways of seeing, reading, thinking, learning, interacting, and intervening in reality; but at the same time we need to continue to demand the presence of oral, written, and audiovisual culture in the school space. The various forms of production of knowledge that emerge among us can only dialog with each other if we give potential to the diversity of experiences in different social spaces.[19]

Thus, it is important to promote an *intergenerational dialogue*: children, young people, and adults of all ages need to hear one another. In addition, it is also necessary to have more *intragenerational dialogue* and promote forms of perceiving what exists in common between the challenges and rights of each generation. This is one more reason for an understanding of digital inclusion as more than a mere technical issue, or as a method to expand old forms of sociability and of teaching-learning. Digital inclusion should not be about using media in the schools to mitigate the tedium of education. Digital inclusion should involve a new form of insertion of children, young people, and adults in the complex processes of communication of society today.[20]

Education mediated by technology can favor the recovery of a playful dimension in the production of knowledge. We can say that in this game, one generation can contribute something to the other. On one hand, children and young people continue learning from adults that history, memory, and cultural inheritance are the foundations of current experience. On the other hand, there are many indications that adults have learned from youth the playful dimension of the use of digital technologies. It can be said that to play with or against these machines is a form of recovering liberty in a world programmed by technology, as Flusser (1998) suggests.

A sociocultural redefinition of the school can lead it to incorporate the new technologies, reaffirming the specific trait of education in modernity, which is that of basing the socialization of knowledge on technologies of intelligence. This is discussed by Sodré (2002), who suggests that the use of the computer in classrooms could be understood as a new form of arts and crafts, in a playful approach to software production. The *bricolage* offered by the culture of simulation allow the appearance of new forms of learning and of resolution of problems that emphasize concrete thinking in relation to the abstract and an exploratory approach to the conceptual, approximating the modes of production of knowledge of adults and children.

Culture and education can be "spaces of emancipation and not only of reproduction, domination and hegemony," observes Belloni (2006, p. 22). This author adds that this perspective for integration of technologies in educational practices in schools can be based on two elements: "the category of *generation*, [which] allows us to perceive the importance of the young, of the new generations, as actors in the construction of the future and of change" and *media education*, that "appears as an unescapable route for the basic education of all children to become complete citizens"(Belloni, 2006, p. 17).

Media education and a Cultural Perspective of Digital Inclusion

For digital inclusion to be implemented in a way that it provides more than simple access to a model of technical education in which students learn to use software and navigate the Internet, an ecological perspective of media education (Rivoltella, 2000) can contribute to another perspective of digital inclusion.

The ecological paradigm of media education presents an integrated concept, which calls for using all the media and technologies available: computers and the Internet in addition to photography, cinema, video, books, and CDs, and for articulating educational proposals with the demands of the communication environment based on each technological innovation in order to integrate them to each other.[21] As much as the computer, Internet, and the World Wide Web are important today, and can even be considered necessary conditions for social insertion and participation, media education is not limited to them. As we have suggested above, it is essential to analyze the needs of each group, project, and context. In this perspective, the objective of media educational work in school is not only the use of the computerized classroom or multimedia laboratory, but for children to act in these and other spaces to establish interactions and build relations and meanings. This mediation should be thought of as a form of affirming corporality—gesture, voice, movement, look—and relationships with nature as essential dimensions for the construction of meanings.

The different forms of citizenship—civil, political, social, and cultural—are challenged by new media in contemporary society, requiring new forms of thinking of education and social inequality. In relation to media education, new emphases are being thought of: one, on a *new media* education, another on a new *media educa-*

tion (Rivoltella, 2006). The first perspective accentuates that the new media create new educational demands, and that children and young people need other forms of education (medialiteracy, cyberliteracy). The second perspective highlights that with the change in the social role of the media in our society, the paradigm of media education must also change, based on an integrating and nonexclusionary perspective, which seeks responses to the challenges of a society in which the media play central, and not secondary, roles. A new media education aware of these challenges would have to go beyond functionalism and criticism towards, again, a culturalist perspective. For Rivoltella (2006), this hypothesis should depart from technologies of production and of signs to reach the *technologies of self*,[22] in a scenario in which every educator would have to be a media-educator and citizenship would be a central factor.

In the field of media education, the confrontation of the digital divide thus implies proposals for mediation that assure the possibility for a critical and creative appropriation of the technologies, oriented towards the development of authorship in children and young people, their insertion and participation in the culture.

Participation in the Culture as Mediation of the Digital Divide

When we emphasize the role of cultural participation in a media education concerned with inclusion we need to make clear what mean by *participation*, since it is a polysemous concept. We think of participation, here: as action of the individual in society, as autonomy and authorship in the political exercise of citizenship. Participation also connotes diversity, plurality, and liberty. It is a strong and politicized word, colored by various values and interests, and for this reason has been subject to different uses or simplifications.

Thinking of participation from the perspective of marginality—as we are doing—we cannot forget that in heteronomous societies such as ours, the excluded are symbolically included, because they are always an implicit or explicit reference, whether present or absent, *participating* in and integrating the same shared imaginary, or that is, the same culture. In this sense, the nonparticipant is paradoxically, a participant. The "outsider" is "inside."

The reconfiguration center-periphery is central to understanding the dynamics of cultural participation in Brazil today. The production of art and culture with the use of digital technologies in poor neighborhoods of large Brazilian cities has taken on increasing social, aesthetic, and economic importance in recent years. According to anthropologist Hermano Vianna, "the most important novelty of Brazilian culture in the past decade was the appearance of the voice straight from the periphery speaking up throughout the country" (2004, p.8-9). This voice is clearly related to the technological possibilities for its amplification and reproduction, which make it a bit more accessible to poor artist communities and collectives, and which are thus able to hear their own music, see their dance, film their stories and histories. A respected analyst of Brazilian culture, Vianna is an enthusiast of *telecentros*[23] (centers of free community Internet access): "the telecenters," he said, "can both produce community and citizen pride in the peripheries as well as connect all these peripheries to each other and to the world, not allowing these conquests to be coopted by political-cultural systems from "outside" or criminal organizations from "within" who only want to make the periphery more peripheral"(Vianna, 2004). He describes how more than 100 telecenters in the city of São Paulo are constantly full of young people, who lose their fear of the computer "treating it as a toy" and, as soon as they become intimate with the machines, come to program them. Since these telecenters work with open-source software, programming is encouraged. "The machines do not have secrets, their codes are open, and whoever wants to investigate the core of its operating system can do so" Vianna explains, reporting a representative example:

This opening led people like Cléber Santos, 18 (whose father is a recently unemployed construction worker –and mother a maid who earns the minimum wage), to frequent the telecenter in the city of Tiradentes (the first inaugurated by the municipal government in 2001), who made various open code programs with the programming resources that he learned totally on his own. Cléber, who is now a monitor at the telecenter in his "city" (and the fact that he participates in a pioneer project produced his pride of living there), speaks as if it is completely normal to know and have exchanged ideas with Richard Stallman, the father of the world's open-source software movement, the principal creator of this new concept of liberty. I never get tired of admiring this direct connection between the poorest periphery of São Paulo (the telecenters were installed in places with the lowest Human Development Indexes in the city) with the political, cultural, and economic movement that I consider to be the vanguard and most important taking place in the world today. Any other political movement, of antiglobalization or the landless movement, will prove to be inefficient in light of the conquests of free software. Any cultural movement, from punk to Luther Blissett, seems like a "childhood disease" in face of the free software ideology. (Vianna, 2004, p.8-9)

Vianna maintains that the movement has a revolutionary meaning, although it is taking place in near silence.

We can of course question the importance Vianna (2004) attributes to the free software movement, or, at least, await greater evidence of its results. Nevertheless, we cannot ignore that what the author calls "a revolution" is based in fact on a "collaborative and decentralized regime, with no political party in command, but with pieces of code in different computers spread across the planet, commanded by people who work not to get rich, but for the common good" (Vianna, 2004). This is certainly important from the perspective of inclusion. The effervescent production of youth at the Brazilian telecenters, is also highlighted by their public and visible character, an alternative to what is seen as one of the obstacles to the democratization of technologies, which is their invisible and individual use.[24]

Enthusiasm for the telecenters is not unanimous in Brazil, although they are part of most digital inclusion projects.[25] Lemos, for example, criticizes the idea of the telecenters, arguing that although they are seen as the "new panacea of inclusion" they are nothing more than a palliative to the problem of access and education, because the trend is toward generalized dissemination of the network to all areas (schools, squares, entire cities) "where each citizen, whether they want to or not, will have to deal with connected communication machines" (Lemos, 2003, p. 2). Whatever may be the political form of implantation of technologies in communities, however, the aspect that we want to highlight is the opportunity for artistic and cultural creation, and for participation in social life, that they make possible.[26]

It is in this sense that the digital culture can be understood as a new concept, because "it is based on the idea that the digital technology revolution, is in essence, cultural," according to Gil (2004). This is because the use of digital technology changes the ways people interact socially. Technology is no longer considered simply as a tool, it becomes part of a person's personality and identity. In this perspective, the complete use of the Internet and of free software, for example, creates great opportunities to democratize access to information and knowledge, broaden the potential of cultural goods and services, expand the values that form our common repertoire and therefore, our culture, and also give potential to cultural production, even create new forms of art, Gil (2004) adds. This occurs because the technology itself, as a means for social inclusion, takes on a new form, "not only as incorporation to the market, but as incorporation to citizenship and to the market" when it assures access to information and the reduction of costs of the multimedia means of production, which can broaden the creative potential of the citizen. Considering that this citizen is also a consumer, broadcaster, and receiver of knowledge and information, who has relative autonomy and who is connected in networks, which are a new form of collectivity, this process can redimension his or her participation in the culture.

In the field of education, participation is related to the need for decentralization and democratization of school management, to the social rights of children, adolescents, and youth and to certain concepts of teaching-learning, making it a central concept in recent years based on the perspective of education for citizenship. If the dimension of participation necessarily involves the "other," promoting participation in the school or outside of it implies working on the formation of groups; this brings us to the importance of the group and of situations of cooperative work from the perspective of digital inclusion within the framework of media education.

We can situate this perspective from the social rights of children and adolescents, both the "passive rights" linked to *protection* and *provision*, as well as the "active rights" of *participation*. In order to better elaborate on this theme, we can explore the possible tensions between these 3 Ps and their forms of mediation. How can we protect children's privacy and security while encouraging them to participate in open networks? Will the provision of access to sites, software, and new technologies be done in a restricted way that controls this access or that creates real opportunity to participation in these new media? Is it possible that encouraging the forms of participation of children in the culture involves anticipating certain responsibilities? What are the gains and losses of the different forms of participation of the children in the culture? Are there requirements and presumptions for promotion of participation of children at an active and visible level? How can the participation of children be guaranteed in such a way that there is personal action, self-expression and the establishment of another relationship with time that is less alienated and production-oriented than that which guides the daily life of contemporary urban societies?

A number of educational contexts have sought to support the playful-expressive *participation* of children through teaching-learning games and various opportunities found in daily activities. We are speaking here of other modes of participating in society: those in which children interact, communicate, plan, propose, share ideas, intervene, produce, create dialogue, and conduct experiences (Fantin, 2006a). A central objective of these actions is the promotion of agency and of the authorship of children. When we defend the participation of children from a perspective of digital inclusion, it is important to recognize that there are different realms of participation, whether in the space of the global society, social movements, communities, schools, and other cultural institutions or in the intimacy of domestic space. Each of these realms can be a space for critical and creative use of the digital media that promote inclusion.

The participation of children at school, our priority focus, gives new dimension to the paradigms of learning. A new paradigm has emerged in contemporary society: some authors affirm that while the production of knowledge had been principally defined either as acquisition from experience (empiricism) or as construction (constructivism), it can now be understood as participation. Although this thesis may be debatable from an epistemological point of view, since participation is not separated from acquisition and construction, it reconfigures some questions for educational mediation: to go beyond "knowing by doing" and "working cooperatively" a vision of "learning by participating" arises.[27]

Thus, for digital inclusion projects—thought of from their social, economic, technological, aesthetic, and cultural dimensions—be truly inclusive, they need to be linked to a perspective for cultural-educational mediation, based on interactivity, on citizenship, on access, and on critical and creative appropriation. Although this emphasis may be part of the rhetoric of many projects, most of the programs still appear to be too highly centered on the economic needs. From the concept of participation that we are discussing, and with a cultural understanding of technology access and digital inclusion, educational mediation can make viable some situations of participation, whether in classrooms, laboratories, workshops, or other cultural spaces that the relationship with technology encourages.

One precaution that should be taken in this sense is not to demean the cultural production of children and of young people through the media, qualifying it simply as "social inclusion" actions. It is common, for example, for videos and home pages produced in school and cultural projects in poor regions to be appreciated principally for what they represent in terms of the construction of "self-esteem" of their authors and not for their own merits as forms of art, communication and language. This paternalist posture contradicts the true sense of inclusion, according to which not only do young and poor children have the right to express their vision of the world, but that the entire society has the right to hear what these young people and children have to say. In the Brazilian case, many of the most interesting aesthetic innovations and the most vigorous analyses of the social situation come precisely from "alternative" uses of technological resources invented by groups in impoverished regions from the very lack of more advanced material resources.

The educational proposals that are made to overcome the digital divide will depend on what is understood by a digitally literate person. If only the technical capacity to use the computer is considered, access to computers would be enough. But if a broader concept is adopted, from the perspective of media education and of citizen participation in the culture, which also involves a development of multiple languages, we can propose a few fundamental objectives of the educational and cultural mediations:

1. Competence in reading and writing of various texts and images and their use as social practice.

2. The education of critical and creative subjects who are able to appropriate, read, and write in various media languages through public access to the multimedia and the Internet in schools and communities.

3. Initial and continued education of teachers for media education. This is essential so that digital inclusion projects are not only palliative measures and episodic campaigns, because without investment in the school perspective and teacher training, the digital divide will continue to be produced.

4. Integration between digital media and the traditional systems of access to cultural production (museums, libraries, film clubs , and artistic workshops) to approximate different generations and trajectories and stimulate the linking of different cultures, broadening the concept of inclusion, with emphasis on the perspective of participation in culture.

It is clear that all of these objectives require specific policies and financing, with an emphasis on the education of and respect for teachers.

Given these objectives, the proposals for digital inclusion from a cultural and educational perspective involve the production of art, knowledge, subjectivity, politics, information, research, and memory, which encourage different types of participation.

In the realm of the classroom they include:

- Various types of peer-interaction (those who know/with those who don't know; those who are eager/ with those who are resistant);
- Different forms of communication between groups (using the various languages and both traditional and new technologies);
- Various forms of organizations of work groups (spontaneous, casual and directed);
- Different spatial contexts, in the classroom and outside of it (to explore the spatial configuration of the classroom; to extend pedagogical encounters to other cultural spaces, such as workshops, museums, theaters, squares, communities; to explore possibilities for virtual spaces);
- Situations that involve different attitudes (active, passive, critical, collaborative, resistant, indifferent, concentrated, moved);
- Different types of interaction with knowledge and with culture (critical, instrumental, productive);
- Different theoretical-methodological tools for research (observation, interview, video-recording, photography, participant-observation);
- Possibilities for reflection and socialization of the observations made, reflecting on the representations observed;
- Different forms of navigation, interaction and audiovisual production(creation of sites, screenplays, blogs).

In broader realms of participation they include:

- Action in the school: student clubs, meetings for evaluation and class councils, parent, teacher and student associations, management of places for play in the schools;
- Action in the community: resident associations, community councils, cultural associations, youth, artistic, musical, theater, and religious groups;
- Action in the city: student movements, popular movements, NGOs and other forums;

- Interaction in cyberspace: collective action on the Internet, forums and chats, virtual communities.

Finally, the reflections and proposals that we have discussed seek to emphasize that while the economy of the information society is globalized, individuals continue to be local, and that there is an abyss between the global nature of wealth and power and the local significance of individual experiences. We propose the image of educational mediation from the cultural perspective as a possibility for navigation not in a river—which separates and unites—of which we spoke at the beginning, but in a large digital sea. As in the song *Pela internet*, by Gilberto Gil,[28] this kind of mediation involves discovering "with how many gigabytes one makes a *jangada*, a boat that can sail in this info-sea."

We hope to have provided some leads in this direction and an understanding of digital inclusion as construction of citizenship in which media education assures the real participation of children, young people, and adults in the culture. Even if we clearly did not exhaust all the issues involved, the complexity of which are renovated each day, we sought to contribute to the discussion in a tone which, although critical, is also hopeful.

References

Adorno, S. (2002). *As cidades brasileiras do século XXI*. São Paulo: Publicação do Centro de Gestão e Estudos Estratégicos.

Almeida, M.E. (2005). Letramento digital e hipertexto: contribuições à educação. In N. Pellanda, E. Schlünzen & K. Schlünzen (Eds.), *Inclusão digital: Tecendo redes afetivas/cognitivas* (pp. 171-192). Rio de Janeiro: DP&A.

Andrade, O. (1928). Manifesto antropofágico. *Revista de Antropofagia, 1*(1)

AZEVEDO, R. (2006). *Formação de leitores, cultura popular e contexto Brasileiro*. Retrieved November 18, 2006, from www.ricardoazevedo.com.br/artigo10.htm

Bazalgette, C. (2005). Media education in Inghilterra: incontro con Cary Bazalgette nel suo ufficio. In *Boletim InterMED*, anno 10, n.3, Roma.

Belloni, M.L. (2006). Infância, Técnica e Cidadania: Cenário de mudanças. Retrieved October 11, 2007, from www.comunic.ufsc.br

Buckingham, D. (2000). *After the death of childhood: Growing up in the age of electronic media*. Cambridge: Polity Press.

Buckingham, D. (2003). *Media education: Literacy, learning and contemporary culture*. Cambridge: Polity Press.

Cadimo, F. (2004). Miragens digitais. Retrieved October 11, 2007, from http:www. fcsh.unl.pt/cadeiras/httv/artigos/Miragens%Digitais.pdf

Castells, M. (1996/2006). *The rise of the network society [A sociedade em rede, vol. 1]*. São Paulo: Paz e Terra.

Castells, M (1996/2002). *End of millennium [Fim de milênio, vol. 3]*. São Paulo: Paz e Terra.

Fantin, M. (2006). *Mídia-educação: Conceitos, experiências, diálogos Brasil-Itália*. Florianópolis: Cidade Futura.

Fantin, M (2006a). *As crianças interagindo nos cenários contemporâneos: A "escola estação cultura."* Unpublished paper presented at Universidade Federal de Santa Catarina.

Flusser, V. (1998). *Ensaio sobre a fotografia: para uma filosofia da técnica*. Lisboa: Relógio d'Água.

Freire, P. (2000). *Pedagogia da indignação: Cartas pedagógicas e outros escritos*. São Paulo: Editora Unesp.

García Canclini, N. (1989/1998). *Culturas híbridas: estratégias para entrar e sair da modernidade [Culturas híbridas: Estratégias para entrar y salir de la modernidad]*. São Paulo: Editora da USP.

Gil, G. (2004). *Aula Magna* at Universidade de São Paulo. Retrieved October 11, 2007, from http://www.cultura.gov.br/noticias/discursos/index. php?p=833&more=1

Green, B., & Bigum, C. (1995). Alienígenas na sala de aula. In T.T. Silva (Ed.), *Alienígenas na Sala de Aula: Uma introdução aos estudos culturais em educação*. Petrópolis: Vozes.

Jobim e Souza, S., Gamba Jr. (2003). Novos suportes, antigos temores: tecnologia e confronto de gerações nas práticas de leitura e escrita In Jobim e Souza, S. (Ed.) *Educação@pós-modernidade: ficções científicas e ciências do cotidiano*. Rio de Janeiro: 7 Letras.

Lemos, A. (2003). Dogmas da inclusão digital. *Correio Braziliense*. Retrieved October 11, 2007, from http:www.facom.ufba.br/ciberpesquisa/andrelemos

Lemos, A., & Costa, L. (2005). Um modelo de inclusão digital: O caso da cidade de Salvador. In *Revista de Economia Política de las Tecnologias de la Información y Comunicación*. Vol. VIII, n.6. Retrieved October 11, 2007, from http:wwweptic.com.br/português/Revista%20EPTIC%20VIII%20-%20AndreLemos-LeonardoCosta.pdf

Martín-Barbero, J. (2002/2004). Ofício de cartógrafo: travessias latino-americanas da comunicação na cultura [*Ofício de cartógrafo: Travessias lationoamericanas de la comunicación en la cultura*]. São Paulo: Loyola.

Martin-Barbero, J.(1998). Herdando el futuro: Pensar la educación desde la comunicación. In *Cultura y Comunicación, 9.* Universidad de Salamanca, Salamanca.

Morcellini, M. (Ed.). (2004). *La Scuola della Modernità: Per un manifesto della media education.* Milano: Franco Angeli.

Neri, M. (2003). *Mapa da exclusão digital.* Rio de Janeiro: FGV/IBRE, CPS.

Pinto, M. (1997). A infância como construção social. In Pinto, M. e Sarmento, M. *As crianças, contextos e identidades.* Minho: Centro de Estudos da Criança.

Rivoltella, P.C. (2002). *Media education: Modelli, esperienze, profilo disciplinare.* Roma: Carocci.

Rivoltella, P. C. (2005). *Media education: Fondamenti didattici e prospettive di ricerca.* Brescia: Editrice La Scuola.

Rivoltella, P. C. (2006). *Screen Generation: Gli adolescenti e le prospettive dell'educazione nell'etá dei media digitalli.* Milano: Vita e Pensiero.

Rogoff, B. (2003/2005. *The culture nature of human development [A natureza cultural do desenvolvimento humano].* Porto Alegre: Artmed.

Santos, L.G. (2003). A informação após a virada cibernética. In L.G. Santos et al. (Eds.), *Revolução Tecnológica, Internet e Socialismo.* São Paulo: Fundação Perseu Abramo.

Schwartz, G. (2000). Exclusão digital entra na agenda econômica mundial. *Folha de São Paulo,* São Paulo, 18 de junho 2000.

Silveira, S. (2001). A. Exclusão digital: A miséria na era da informação. São Paulo: Editora Fundação Perseu Abramo.

Silveira, S. (2003). Inclusão digital, software livre e globalização contra-hegemônica. In S. Silveira & J. Cassino (Eds.), *Software livre e inclusão digital.* São Paulo: Conrad Editora do Brasil.

Soares, M. (2002). Novas práticas de leitura e escrita: letramento na cibercultura. In Dossiê *Letramento, Revista Educação e Sociedade,* n.81. Campinas: Cedes.

Soares, M. (2005). *Letramento: um tema em três gêneros.* Belo Horizonte: Autêntica.

Sodré, M.(2002). *Antropológica do espelho: uma teoria da comunicação linear em rede.* Petrópolis: Vozes.

Sorj, B. (2003). *brasil@povo.com: a luta contra a desigualdade na Sociedade da Informação.* Rio de Janeiro: Jorge Zahar; Brasília: Unesco.

Souza Santos, B. (2002). *A globalização e as ciências sociais.* São Paulo: Cortez.

Taylor, M., & Saarinen, E. (1994). *Imagologies: Media philosophy.* London: Routledge.

Thompson, J. (1995/1998). *The media and modernity: A social theory of the media [A midia e a modernidade: uma teoria social da mídia].* Cambridge: Polity Press. Brazilian translation, Petrópolis: Vozes.

Vianna, H. (2004). A disseminação silenciosa do software livre. Caderno Mais, *Folha de São Paulo*, 18/04/2004

Suggested Sites

Comitê para a Democratização da Informática: www.cdi.org.br

Comitê Gestor da Internet Brasil: www.cgi.org.br

Cúpula da Sociedade da informação: www.wsis.org

Digital Divide Networks: www.digitaldividenetwork.org

Free Software Foundation: www.fsf.org

From Acces to Outcomes: Digital Divide Report – Morino Institute: www.morino. org.divides

IBOPE - Instituto Brasileiro de Opinião Pública e Estatística: www.ibope.com.br

Internet World Stats: www.internetworldstats.com

Programas do Governo Federal para Inclusão Digital: www.idbrasil.gov.br

Somos@telecentros: www.tele-centros.org.br

UNESCO–Internet Rights Forum: www.foruminternet.org

Endnotes

[1] Sodré observes that there is often a buying and selling of technologically outdated equipment, making it clear that Brazilian and foreign commercial interests are stronger than the needs of civil society.

[2] Ministry of Communications and the Internet Management Committee of Brazil, 2006.

[3] INEP/MEC/Pro Brasil 2005.

[4] Brazil has 15 million illiterate people 15 years or older (IBGE).

[5] A dimension related to this issue is that of self-learning, which has an important role in the processes of development of multiliteracies.

6   Bazalgette (2005) proposed the "3 Cs," culture, criticism, and creation, as three essential aspects of media education.

7   Personal notes from the course "Tecnologia dell'istruzione e del aprendimento," given by Pier Cesare Rivoltella, at UCSC, Milano, 2005.

8   Internet World Stats, www.internetwordlstas.com

9   IBOPE: www.ibope.com.br

10   There has been a significant increase in the purchase and use of cell phones among Brazilians of a variety of classes and age groups. Considering that today a cell phone can be a multimedia center, becoming at the same time a camera and a video, a pocket computer with Internet access, and a television receiver and broadcaster, and that Brazil is a country open to new technological developments, this trend can bring new possibilities for digital inclusion. After all, mobile connections are changing the perception of cyberspace, and we are increasingly more "immersed in a nomadism that articulates the space of flow with the space of place." (Lemos, 2003, p.2). The relationship between the multiplication of cellular telephones and digital inclusion is beyond the scope of this study. We merely note this complexity, from a socio-economic as well as cultural perspective.

11   See Lemos and Costa (2005, p. 6).

12   Analyzing various projects of digital inclusion, Lemos and Costa (2005) maintain that the majority of them emphasize the technical dimension at the cost of the social, cultural, and intellectual.

13   See Canclini (1998) and Thompson (1998).

14   See Pinto (1997) and Buckingham (2000).

15   See, for example, Pinto and Sarmento (1997).

16   Reported by MTV Networks, the study was conducted over six months. Interviews were conducted with 5,200 children (ages 8 to 15) and young people from 16 to 34. The survey was conducted in the following countries: Argentina, Germany, Brazil, China, Denmark, the United States, France, India, Indonesia, Japan, Mexico, England, South Africa, and Sweden. Retrieved October 11, 2007, from http://www.multirio.rj.gov.br/portal/riomidia/rm_materia_conteudo.asp?idioma=1&v_nome_area=Materias&idMenu=3&label=Materias&v_id_conteudo=66749

17   Noel Gladstone, research of vice-president MTV Networks.

18   When the issue is concern for beauty and aesthetics, Brazilians take first place. Nearly 66% of Brazilian children, 50% of Indonesian, and 41% of Mexicans said they are concerned with their weight. For the children of Brazil (93%), Argentina (87%), and Mexico (84%) to take care of oneself is a sign of status. In relation to sex, Latin American youth from 6 to 34 believe they have better

sexual performance. Brazilians come in first place, (66%), then Argentines (48%), and Mexicans (46%). The Japanese were last (5%). Terrorism occupied the eighth place on the list of the main fears of youth today and in tenth place among the children. In general, children and young people said that they are afraid of losing their parents, of having cancer or AIDS, and of frequent crime in large cities. All of these issues are clearly influenced by the representation of these themes in the media, and are thus directly related to the role of media education.

[19]   See discussion by Jobim and Souza (2003, p. 38).

[20]   See Martin-Barbero (2000).

[21]   Various authors have considered the relationship of children with the media in the realm of "cultural ecology." In their philosophy of media, Taylor and Saarinem (1994) maintain that dealing with children means accepting the responsibility for "creating and sustaining structures and networks to support life." In the culture of the media ("simcult"), they add, "this means that we must act to shape and reshape the telecommunications environment that is the world in which our children are destined to dwell." (Taylor & Saarinem, 1994, p. 37).

[22]   In the Foucaultian sense, stressing here the reflexive practices around media use and consumption.

[23]   Telecenters are spaces with computers with broadband Internet connections, which offer free use of equipment, basic computer courses, and special work-shops. According to the federal government proposal, "each Telecenter has a Management Council, formed by members of the community elected by the community, who help the staff monitor and manage the space. It is a project for intensive use of information technology to broaden citizenship and combat poverty, seeking to guarantee digital privacy and security for the citizen, his insertion in the information society, and strengthen local development. One of the principal objectives of the project is to organize a network of units of multiple functions that allow people to acquire basic technological autonomy and privacy based on open source software." Retrieved October 11, 2007, from http://www.idbrasil.gov.br/docs_telecentro/docs_telecentro/o_que_e

[24]   See Graham (apud Lemos, 2005, p.3).

[25]   There are various examples and the experiences of projects that support the call for digital inclusion in Brazil. In the field of public policy, the Brazilian government sought the integration of existing digital inclusion programs at the federal state and municipal levels, and created the Brazilian Digital In-clusion Model, which was an attempt to improve the activities and avoid the duplication of projects. From the many projects of NGOs, we can highlight the pioneer work of the Committee for the Democratization of Computing. See http://www.idbrasil.gov.br and http://www.cdi.org.br

26   This is even more relevant considering the social reality of the favelas in Brazilian cities. According to Adorno "the thesis that sustains causal relations between poverty, delinquincy and violence, is now highly questioned by many studies. Nevertheless, relations between the persistance, in Brazilian society, of the concentration of wealth, the concentration of the precarious quality of collective life in so-called peripheral neighborhoods in large cities and the general explosion of violence, must be recognized. Maps of violence, created for some Brazilian cities such as Rio de Janeiro, Salvador, Curitiba, and São Paulo (…) indicate that homicide rates are much higher in these areas than in neighborhoods that compose the urban belt better served by urban infrastructure, a labor market and leisure and cultural services." Adorno (2002). "As cidades brasileiras no século XXI." Retrieved October 11, 2007, from http://www.nevusp.org/conteudo/index.php?conteudo_id=367

27   See Rogoff (2005).

28   Gilberto Gil is a prominent Brazilian singer-songwriter and the current Minister of Culture.

About the Contributors

Pier Cesare Rivoltella is full professor in education technology at the Catholic University of Milan. In the same university, he is president of the Center of Research about Education, Media, Information, and Technology (CREMIT). He is also president of the Postgraduate Program in media education and of the International Master in communication and education. He is vice president of the Italian Society for the Research about Media and Education (SIREM), he wrote and edited 26 books and more than 80 articles about media education and education technology.

*****

Giuseppe Ardrizzo is full professor of theory of knowledge and he is head of Scientific Research at the School of High Studies Majise (University of Calabria, Italy). He collaborates with several scientific reviews and is author of many books and articles including *Ragioni di confine. Percorsi dell'Innovazione* (2002), *Governare l'innovazione. La responsabilità etica* (2003), and *L'esilio del tempo* (2003).

Evelyne Bevort-Brumder is deputy director of Clemi (a center dedicated to media education for the French ministry of education). A member of Unesco and European Commission expert groups in this field, she is involved in numerous research projects, partnerships with different institutions and medias, and production of educative tools. She is the author of reports about media education for the Council of Europe and for UNESCO and co-author of research reports about Media Education Evaluation (1999), the Young People and the Internet (2001), and the Appropriation of New Media by Youth (2006).

Isabelle Bréda works in the Centre for Liaison between Teaching and Information Media (CLEMI), Ministry of Education—France, since 1989. She manages the sector "electronic medias" (piloting and follow-up of teacher trainings in France and abroad, creation and management of the Web site of the Centre, off-line and online pedagogical publications, and so forth). She is co-author of European programmes about Internet critical education (Educaunet, Mediappro) and a member of French scientific committees about these questions.

Andrew Burn, PhD, is a reader in education and new media at the Institute of Education of the London University. Here he is associate director of the Centre for the Study of Children, Youth, and Media, chief of the London University and course leader of the MA in media, art, and culture. Author of several books and articles, his research areas are: media literacy, film, games, the and relationship between computer and literacy.

Lorenzo Cantoni graduated in philosophy and holds a PhD in education and linguistics. He is a Professor at the University of Lugano (Switzerland), Faculty of Communication Sciences, where he is also deputy-director of the Institute of Institutional and Educational Communication. He is director of the laboratories webatelier.net: production and promotion over the Internet; NewMinE Lab: New Media in Education Lab. He is executive director of TEC-Lab (Technology Enhanced Communication Lab) and Scientific Director of eLab (e-Learning Lab). His research interests are where communication, education and new media overlap, ranging from computer mediated communication to eLearning and usability. He devotes special attention to quality in CMC, interpreting usability in a broad sense, and to communication in equips that work in CMC projects.

André Caron, a graduate of Harvard University (EdD, 1976), is presently full professor in the Communication Department of the Université de Montréal. He is the Bell Canada Chair in Interdisciplinary Research on Emerging Technologies, founding director of its Centre (CITÉ), and founding director of the Center for Youth and Media Studies .At the international level, Dr. Caron has been on the international scientific advisory board of a number of institutes and has been invited speaker at conferences in Asia, Australia, Europe, and North and South America.. As a specialist in mass media and new technologies. His research interests include broadcasting policy, educational, political, and cultural appropriations of media, and influences of new technologies on society. Some of his more recent publications include *Culture mobile: les nouvelles pratiques de communication* (Montreal: Presses de l'Université de Montréal, 2005) and *Moving Cultures: Mobile Communication In Everyday Life* (Montreal: McGill-Queens University Press, 2007).

Letizia Caronia, PhD, is professor at the Department of Education (University of Bologna, Italy) and visiting scholar at the Centre of Interdisciplinary Research on Emerging Technologies (CITÉ), University of Montreal, Montreal, Canada. Her domains of inquiry are methodology and epistemology of social sciences research and media education. She carries qualitative and ethnographic research on the role of everyday language, interactions, and culture in the process of domestication of information and communication technologies. Her r recent works include La socializzazione ai media, (Milano: Guerini, 2002); Television Culture and Media Socialization across Countries: Theoretical Issues and Methodological Approaches, (with André H. Caron, in S. Livingstone (Ed.), International Handbook of Children, Media and Culture, (London: Sage, 2007); and Moving Culture: Mobile Communication in Everyday Life, with André H. Caron (Montreal: McGill-Queen's University Press, 2007).

Monica Fantin, holds a PhD in education from the Federal University at Santa Catarina, Brazil (UFSC), where she is professor in the Department of Teaching Methodology. She is a researcher in the group Childhood, Communication, and Art (CNPq/UFSC). She participates in the management committee of the New Technologies Laboratory and of the Toy Museum of Santa Catarina. She is a consultant to educational projects and works with cultural productions for children. Her publications include various articles in the field of education and communication and the books *No mundo da brincadeira: jogo, brinquedo e cultura na educação infantil* (2000) and *Mídia-educação: conceitos, experiências diálogos Brasil-Itália* (2006).

Paolo Maria Ferri, PhD, is associate professor of educational technology at the University of Milan "Bicocca." Here he is member of the teaching staff of international and interdisciplinary PhD about "society of information" and of the Academic Board for E-Learning. Among his research areas are: e-learning and distance teaching, theories of hypertext and hypermedia, and children and computers. He is author of several articles and books among which include *E-Learning. Didattica e comunicazione e tecnolgie digitali* (2005), *Fine dei Mass Media. Le nuove tecnologie della comunicazione e le trasformazioni dell'industria culturale* (2004).

Flavia Nizia da Fonseca Ribeiro is an undergraduate in design—visual communication, and an MA in design at the Catholic University of Rio de Janeiro (PUC-Rio) and a PhD student in education at the Education Department of PUC-Rio. She is also a researcher of the Laboratory of the Design Pedagogy (LPD) and the *Youths online* research group (PUC-Rio), her interests are: pedagogical practices, didactic material, e-learning, and image and new media literacy. She is the author of several international and national articles about these subjects.

Gilka Girardello is a professor in the graduate program in Education at the Federal University at Santa Catarina, Brazil. With a PhD in communication sciences from the University of São Paulo, she coordinates the research group Childhood, Communication and Art at UFSC. Since the 1980s she has been studying the relations between children's imagination, media, art, and culture and has published a variety of articles, organized books, and coordinated cultural projects with children in low-income communities.

Renee Hobbs is a professor of communication at Temple University in Philadelphia, Pennsylvania, where she directs the Media Education Lab. She is the author of *Reading the Media: Media Literacy in High School English,* an empirical study of the impact of media literacy education on adolescent literacy. She has worked extensively with school districts across the United States and developed numerous award-winning multimedia curriculum materials, including *Assignment: Media Literacy*, developed in collaboration with the Discovery Channel and the Maryland State Department of Education.

Maria Apparecida Campos Mamede-Neves is a full professor at the Catholic University of Rio de Janeiro (PUC-Rio), where she is also pedagogical coordinator of Central Coordination for Distance Learning (CCEAD PUC-Rio). She holds a PhD in psychology, an MA in psychology, a MA in education, and also specialized in psychopedagogy. a researcher of Brazilian National Research Council (CNPq), her main interest is distance learning and the relationship between youth and the Web. She is the author of several books and international and national articles about these subjects.

Susanna Mantovani is a full professor of education at the University of Milano-Bicocca and, at present, the Dean of the Faculty of Educational Sciences. Her work in the past 30 years has dealt with early childhood and early childhood policies making her one of the leading figures in ECEC in Italy and a consultant for many international projects. She has been involved in the OECD ECEC projects both in the 1970s and in recent years (Starting Strong, 2001) and she has served in the National Committee for the Guidelines for Nursery Schools. The author of several books and articles, she is coordinator of the Italian entries for the Encyclopedia on Early Childhood Education (B. New & M. Cochran, Eds., Greenwood Publishing Group, 2007).

Mario Morcellini is a full professor of sociology of Communication, dean of the Communication Sciences Faculty, and council member of CUN (National University Council). Since 2002, he has been the president of the National Conference of Communication Sciences Deans and Deans Interconference National spokesman. He has been a member of the Board of the Italian Association of Sociology (AIS) from 1985 to 1987, and from 2000 to 2001 a member of the Commission for TV frequencies. He was also member of the technical-scientific committee in the project "Defence of Minors" of the Authority for Communications Guarantees. In the last few years his research work was focused on socialization and media in order to analyse media influence on identity, cultural industry, and television in Italy.

Josè Manuel Perez Tornero, PhD, is full professor at the Universidad Autónoma de Barcelona (Spain), where he directs the international master in communication and education program. A journalist for the press and television, he has produced more than one thousand hours of cultural and educational programs. He published various books about media education, information society and the impact of the media and new technologies. He is the current vice-president of the international media education Association MENTOR.

Manuel Joaquim Silva Pinto, PhD, journalist, is an associate professor and chief of the Research Group in Communication and Society Studies at the University of Minho, in Braga (Portugal), as well as the general secretary of the Media Education Association MENTOR, he is author of several books and articles about media education and the utilization of the press in the classroom.

Jonelle Rowe joined the Office on Women's Health in September of 1997 as senior medical advisor for Adolescent Women's Health. Dr. Rowe is responsible for the development and implementation of programs on adolescent and preadolescent women's health. Several of her projects include eating disorders, adolescent self esteem, and positive youth development. Most recently, Dr. Rowe has spearheaded "GirlsHealth.gov," an innovative online effort to increase awareness about health, nutrition, and positive health behavior among young women in America today. Rowe, a board certified pediatrician and neonatologist, is professor emeritus of Pediatrics and former chief of the Division of Neonatology at the University of Connecticut Health Center (UCHC).

Stefano Tardini is researcher at the University of Lugano (Switzerland), Faculty of Communication Sciences, where he is also the executive director of eLab: eLearning Lab. His research interests lie in the overlap between computer mediated communication, e-learning, (online) communities, cultural semiotics, and argumentation theory. In 2002 he discussed his PhD thesis about the linguistic and semiotic aspects of virtual communities. Since then, he has developed his research in three interrelated directions: in the field of CMC, focusing mainly on a socio-historical approach to CMC and on the pragmatic behavior of Internet search engines, in the field of e-learning, focusing on the introduction of e-learning activities and tools in given communities, and in the field of communities, elaborating a semiotic approach to online communities.

Kathleen Tyner is an assistant professor in the Department of Radio, Television, and Film at the University of Texas at Austin. She is author, co-author, and editor of numerous publications, including *Literacy in a Digital World: Teaching and Learning in the Age of Information*. Tyner also works with producers, researchers, and educators around the world to develop media and education projects.

Index